ADVANCED DUNGEONS & DRAGONS™

SPECIAL REFERENCE WORK
DEITIES & DEMIGODS™
CYCLOPEDIA

by James M. Ward with Robert J. Kuntz

Edited by Lawrence Schick

© 1980 — TSR Games
POB 756, Lake Geneva, WI 53147

Illustrations by

Jeff Dee	Erol Otus
Eymoth	Darlene Pekul
Paul Jaquays	Jim Roslof
David S. LaForce	David C. Sutherland III
Jeff Lanners	D. A. Trampier

Cover Painting by Erol Otus

ISBN 0-935696-22-9

FOREWORD

When work first commenced on **ADVANCED DUNGEONS & DRAGONS**™ Fantasy Adventure Game, one particular aspect of fantasy role playing was foremost in my mind: there was either a general neglect of deities or else an even worse use by abuse. That is, game masters tended to ignore deities which were supposedly served and worshiped by characters in the campaign, or else they had gods popping up at the slightest whim of player characters in order to rescue them from perilous situations, grant wishes, and generally step-and-fetch. Obviously, there is a broad ground between these two extremes, and that is squarely where I desired **AD&D** to go. As the various manuscripts were being written, I informed both James Ward and Rob Kuntz of the direction which the overall work was to take and then followed up with draft copies of the manuscripts. Thus, both authors were well-appraised of the form and content of **AD&D**. Their work, the **DEITIES & DEMIGODS**™ cyclopedia, reflects the fact that they not only were kept abreast of the game as it developed, but that they also adhered to the concepts which were instrumental in making **AD&D** what it is. **DEITIES & DEMIGODS** is an indispensable part of the whole of **AD&D**. Do not fall into the error of regarding it as a supplement. It is integral to Dungeon Mastering a true **AD&D** campaign. Experienced players will immediately concur with this evaluation, for they already know how important alignment is, how necessary the deity is to the cleric, and how interaction of the various alignments depends upon the entities which lead them. Those readers not well-grounded in ongoing campaigns must take my word for all this, although they will soon discover for themselves how crucial the deities of the campaign milieu are.

In general, deities are presented in pantheons. You can select which ones, combinations, or parts of pantheons best suit your campaign. Players knowing which gods are ''real'' in the campaign world are able to intelligently choose to serve one (or more) suitable to the character's alignment, profession, and even goals. Included are major, minor, and almost-gods (demigods). There are also a few ''divine'' monsters and magic items herein. These are creatures and devices so connected to mythology that this work was the only place to properly present them. Not included are those minions of Evil found in **MONSTER MANUAL** and the attendant volumes forthcoming. Diabolical and demoniac deities are important to the campaign milieu. Without Evil, what does Good have to strive against? It is no great matter to extract these beings from the other works and include them amongst the other deities, however.

The format used to present the beings in **DEITIES & DEMIGODS** was actually developed through close consultation with myself. It was chosen for clarity and completeness of information. The reader can extract basic information quickly, just by glancing at the statistics pertaining to the being in question. Greater detail is then presented in the explanatory paragraphs which follow the initial data. It is worth commenting that the strength and powers of the beings contained herein are appropriate to the overall work. Thus, addition of these deities and demigods does not imbalance the campaign. Furthermore, characters who become a match for them are obviously to be ranked amongst their number, no longer suitable for daily campaign interaction, but to be removed to another place and plane and treated accordingly.

The authors have prepared exactly what **AD&D** needed to make it a complete work. They deserve praise for the excellence of their effort. It is also necessary to acknowledge the contributions made by the TSR staff, developmentally and editorially alike. The writing of this work was a long and complex project which involved countless hours of research. Both authors were willing to step back from it and allow the team at TSR to emend and augment their creation to assure that the whole would meet each and every need of DM and player alike with respect to the deities and demigods of the campaign milieu.

DEITIES & DEMIGODS deserves to be a part of **AD&D**. It was designed to provide the much-needed information on how to include these ''divine'' beings in the campaign milieu, how to have the participants interact with them, and offers a broad selection from which to choose. It is with sincere pleasure that I welcome James Ward and Rob Kuntz into the **AD&D** fold. I trust that you will find their efforts most rewarding to your gaming enjoyment.

E. Gary Gygax
1 May 1980
Lake Geneva, Wisconsin

CONTENTS

PREFACE

This work, as all **AD&D** works, is an attempt to clarify and produce material for those referees who expect and demand high quality information for their campaigns. Within its pages, you will find details and facts that will be highly useful to you as the DM and to your player clerics.

It is not intended as a treatment of world religions and the rightness or wrongness of their philosophies. It is a simple statement of the historical or literary details man has recorded for all to see. Do not look for a favoring of good versus evil or neutrality versus everything else. When historians or authors wrote about a deity in a way that made them powerful or feared, that is the way we made them. In the same light, when a being was made too all-powerful (in **AD&D** terms) we scaled them down to make them compatible in game terms.

The creative processes of this book differ from the other **AD&D** works in that three-fourths of the information given within was drawn from knowledgeable sources rather than from the imagination of the authors. The names of the deities and heroes, the weapons and powers they used, and many of their personality traits are plain for everyone to discover for themselves. What had to be creatively done dealt with concepts that were purely **AD&D** in nature. All of the leaders of the pantheons were given 400 hit points and the rest were scaled down from there; the relative resistance of beings to blows and magic was derived from studies of their battles with natural and supernatural forces; while concepts like strength were easily assigned in the case of deities of strength or war, this concept is less easily applied to the more powerful deities who have no need for massive muscles. Alignments were perhaps the hardest **AD&D** concept to deal with, and the one that will have the most debate among the interested users of this work. Beings like Set, Loki and Arioch are easy to classify, but when working with the middle-of-the-road deities who were often chaotic but known for consistent kindness, or were rogues of the worst sort but very companionable, it became necessary to consider them as a whole to make a judgment. While it will be easy in any campaign to change the powers and alignments of those beings whom you differ with, remember that drastic changes can also influence the all-important game balance of any given campaign.

While **DEITIES & DEMIGODS** is ideally suited to the task of working deities into an **AD&D** campaign format, everything has not been covered in the book. In the 6,000-year plus span of this work mankind has spent a lot of that time adding to the myths dealt with herein. We did not try to encompass everything, and it is silly to assume that the five years or so of research that created **DEITIES & DEMIGODS** could suffice. There are areas that were stressed because they were useful to DMs, whereas others were left out for the very same reason. The book should be used as a beginning framework for the DM. Sample it, take what is wanted, and start the gods as well as the players in a universe. While **DEITIES & DEMIGODS** reveals a great many divine powers and a great many powerful devices, it is the duty of the DM to add to, change, and otherwise modify the information on these pages for use in a campaign.

There is a large list of people that helped in some way with this endeavor, and I want to take this opportunity to mention and thank them: my parents, my wife Janean, Brian Blume, Ernie Gygax, Will Niebling, Mike Carr, Kevin Blume, Dave Sutherland, and E. Gary Gygax, who created a game that will outlast us all.

James M. Ward

CREDITS AND ACKNOWLEDGEMENTS

The authors would like to thank the following people for their special assistance in the development and production of this work: Lawrence Schick, Dave Cook, Allen Hammack, J. Eric Holmes (especially for his help with the Cthulhu Mythos), and Harold Johnson. Thanks is also due to all the people who contributed in some way to the completion of this volume: Kevin Hendryx, Jeff R. Leason, Steve Marsh, Frank Mentzer, Tom Moldvay, Brian Pitzer, Paul Reiche III, Evan Robinson, and Jean Wells. The organization and completion of this book was an immense task, and the TSR Product Development staff deserves recognition and praise for their excellent work.

Special thanks are also given to Chaosium, Inc. for permission to use the material found in the Cthulhu Mythos and the Melnibonean Mythos.

EDITOR'S INTRODUCTION

Well, here it is, **DEITIES & DEMIGODS**, the latest addition to the series of **ADVANCED D&D** volumes. But what exactly is it? Let's see, it has a nice cover — open it up, inside there are lots of pictures next to sets of stacked statistics . . . it must be just like the **MONSTER MANUAL**! There, that was easy. Now that we know what it is, we know what to do with it, right?

Wrong.

DDG (for short) may resemble **MONSTER MANUAL**, and in fact does include some monsters. However, the purpose of this book is not to provide adversaries for players' characters. The information listed herein is primarily for the Dungeon Master's use in creating, intensifying or expanding his or her campaign. No fantasy world is complete without the gods, mighty deities who influence the fates of men and move mortals about like chesspieces in their obscure games of power. Such figures can be perfect embodiments of the DM's control of the game. They are one of the Dungeon Master's most important tools in his or her shaping of events.

The gods serve an important purpose for the players as well. Serving a deity is a significant part of **AD&D**, and all player characters should have a patron god. Alignment assumes its full importance when tied to the worship of a deity. The possibility of the invocation of divine wrath, should the player make a serious misstep, makes alignment conduct a much more vital concern.

Of course, serving a deity is of greatest importance to clerics. This book should help that sometimes-neglected class come into its own. Players whose characters are clerics will find much more range and many more possibilities in their roles when the information herein is used to flesh them out completely. Clerics can and should have a great influence on the course of an **AD&D** campaign. They are prominent members of society (much more so than the common fighters or the reclusive magic-users and thieves); they often have a close relationship with the populace, and are usually well-acquainted with local leaders. They are looked up to as masters of ritual and keepers of knowledge. In addition to this special relationship with men, a cleric has a special relationship with his or her deity, an affinity usually denied to other mortals. This makes clerics a special class indeed, a class with a lot of room for creative innovation on the part of experienced players.

At first glance, Dungeon Masters may well find the profusion of gods and goddesses in this work confusing. The DM will have to consider with care before choosing which pantheon or pantheons to use in his or her campaign. The DM should consider the *flavor* of the campaign: is it medieval, ancient, oriental, or different from all of these? Which pantheon(s) will be most appropriate to the milieu? (It is possible to imagine a campaign where all the gods in this book — and perhaps more — are co-existent. This would require a truly vast world, one large enough to contain all of the worshipers necessary to sustain such a multiplicity of gods! Perhaps, as in the ancient world, such different pantheons are worshiped in different regions.)

The most important thing to remember about this book is that, unlike the other **AD&D** volumes, everything contained within this book is *guidelines*, not rules. **DDG** is an *aid* for the DM, not instructions. We would not presume to tell a Dungeon Master how to set up his or her campaign's religious system. Probably no facet of **AD&D** varies more from campaign to campaign than this, and that's the way it should be. Many DMs will choose to use pantheons or systems other than the ones included herein, or will alter the information presented. Feel free.

In our research and compilation of this book, we ourselves have altered many facts, either for reasons of game balance and consistency or because sources conflict. **DEITIES & DEMIGODS** is not a scholarly work or reference — it is a game accessory. After choosing which pantheon(s) to use, the best thing you can do as Dungeon Master is to take a trip to the library or bookstore and read up on the background of the chosen mythos. There you will discover the fascinating stories behind these immortal characters, and get a really solid feel for how to play them.

The other half of Heroic Fantasy is Mythology. With **DEITIES & DEMIGODS** as an introduction, you can open up whole new realms of wonder. As someone else has said, the possibilities are limitless!

LJS

EXPLANATORY NOTES

FREQUENCY: This refers to the likelihood of a particular creature being encountered in a region or area where it might be an inhabitant. *Very rare* indicates a 4% chance of occurrence, *rare* indicates an 11% chance, *uncommon* indicates a 20% chance, and *common* indicates a 65% chance. *Unique* indicates that there is only one of the creature in existence.

NUMBER APPEARING: This indicates a good average spread. The RANGE is furnished as a guideline only, and it should be altered to suit the circumstances particular to any adventure as the need arises. It is not generally recommended for use in establishing the population of dungeon levels or similar encounter areas.

ARMOR CLASS: This is a measure of how difficult it is to hit a creature, and subsumes the general type of protection worn by humans or human-shaped beings, protection inherent to the creature due to its physical structure or magical nature, or the degree of difficulty in hitting a creature due to its speed, reflexes, etc. Occasionally, a god's or hero's armor class may not jibe with the being's stated armor and dexterity, but this is due to the magical nature of the being.

MOVE: This shows the relative speed of a creature on a constant basis. Higher speeds may be possible for short periods, but as this is generally applicable to all sorts of beings, a constant is shown. It can be scaled to whatever time period is desired by adjusting ground scale accordingly. A standard time scale is inches per turn. The number might be double, and this indicates that the creature can travel in two mediums or modes:

/ # ''	= flying speed
/ / # ''	= swimming speed
(# '')	= burrowing speed
* # ''	= speed in web

Infinite indicates that the entity can travel to any point desired with no time lapse, and this is the being's preferred mode of movement. Infinite movement is a sort of continuous no-error *teleport* ability.

HIT POINTS: This indicates the amount of damage a creature can withstand before being killed (or, in the case of deities, temporarily banished back to their plane of origin). It is not used as a measure of the attack ability of the being, as that is determined by using the entity's most advantageous character class ability.

HIT DICE: This indicates the parameters of the number of hit points a creature can withstand before being killed. Unless stated otherwise, hit dice are 8-sided (1-8 hit points). The indicated number of dice are rolled, and the numbers shown on each are added together to arrive at a total number of hit points. Some creatures have hit points which are less than a full 8-sided die, and this is shown by stating their hit dice as a point spread. Some creatures have additional points added to their hit dice; this is indicated by a plus sign followed by a number shown after the number of hit dice they have, i.e. **HIT DICE:** 4 + 4 (which equals 4-32 hit points + 4 points, or 8-36 hit points). Creatures without character classes use hit dice as a measure of their attack ability.

% IN LAIR: This indicates the chance of encountering the creature in question where it domiciles on the Prime Material Plane (if it ever does). If a creature encountered is not in its lair it will not have any treasure unless it carries "individual" treasure or some form of magic. Whether or not an encounter is occurring in the creature's lair might be totally unknown to the person or persons involved until after the outcome of the encounter is resolved.

TREASURE TYPE: This refers to the table of treasure types on page 105 of **ADVANCED DUNGEONS & DRAGONS, MONSTER MANUAL**. The description of the table's use is on page 5 of the aforementioned book.

NUMBER OF ATTACKS: This shows the number of physical attacks the being is able to make during a given melee round. This number can be modified by hits which sever members, spells such as *haste* or *slow*, and so forth. It does not usually consider unusual or special attack forms. Multiple attacks usually indicate the use of several members, such as multiple heads, or two claws and a bite, or multiple attacks due to a being's high-level fighter or monk ability. A listing such as "3/2" indicates 3 strikes per every 2 rounds.

DAMAGE PER ATTACK: This simply indicates the amount of damage a given attack will cause when it hits expressed as a spread of hit points. In the case of intelligent beings who can use weapons, the damage from the primary weapon(s) of employment is listed, but this may vary if other weapons are substituted. Magical weapon bonuses are *not* included.

SPECIAL ATTACKS: This notes such attack modes as breath weapons, poison, magic use, inherent abilities, special weapon powers, etc. A full explanation of the mode is detailed in the body of the description below. This listing only includes special abilities above and beyond character class abilities (if such are listed in the statistics).

SPECIAL DEFENSES: These are simply what the term implies and are detailed in the material describing the being.

MAGIC RESISTANCE: This indicates the percentage chance of any spell absolutely failing to affect the magic-resistant creature. It is based on the spell being cast by a spell-caster of 11th level, and it must be adjusted upwards 5% for each level below 11th or downwards 5% for each level above 11th of the spell-caster casting the spell. Thus a magic resistance of 95% means that a 10th level spell-caster has no chance of affecting the creature with a spell or spell-like effect, while a 12th level spell-caster has a 10% chance. Even if a spell does affect a magic-resistant creature, the creature is entitled to normal saving throws (if applicable). A creature's magic resistance extends only to its immediate possessions, i.e. anything carried or worn. Area-effect spells will still function if targeted with a magic-resistant creature within their area; the creature itself might not be affected, though all others in the spell area will be subject to spell effects. (A *fireball*, for example, may wipe out a cluster of orcs, and a devil standing in their midst might be totally unaffected due to its magic resistance). The magic resistance of a creature has an effect on certain existing spells such as *hold portal*, where it indicates the probability of the magic resistance shattering the existing spell.

Special Note: Certain deities have special abilities (of a magical origin) that "never fail", e.g. a weapon that never misses, or an ability against which there is no save. Creatures with magic resistance may still avoid the effects of these abilities if they make a successful magic resistance roll. To determine level of the deity with the magic ability, use the deity's highest level character class ability, unless it is less than 15th level for demigods, 20th level for lesser gods, or 25th level for greater gods, in which case the aforementioned levels should be used.

INTELLIGENCE: In monsters, this indicates the basic equivalent of human "IQ". Certain monsters are instinctively, or otherwise, cunning, and such is accordingly noted in the body of the descriptive material. The ratings correspond roughly to the following character intelligence scores:

0	Non-intelligent or not ratable
1	Animal intelligence
2-4	Semi-intelligent
5-7	Low intelligence
8-10	Average (human) intelligence
11-12	Very intelligent
13-14	Highly intelligent
15-16	Exceptionally intelligent
17-18	Genius
19-20	Supra-genius
21+	Godlike intelligence

SIZE: This is abbreviated as: "S", smaller than a typical human; "M", approximately man-sized (5' to 7' tall and of approximate human build); and "L", larger than man-sized in one way or another and generally having greater mass.

ALIGNMENT: This shows the characteristic bent of a monster or hero to law or chaos, good or evil or towards neutral behavior possibly modified by good or evil intent. It is important with regard to the general behavior of the being when encountered.

The above is also true as regards the alignment of divine beings, except that deities are not always constrained to follow their alignment to the letter. Their motives and purposes are far above the mortal, and though a deity will generally follow his or her alignment, the being's specific actions may sometimes seem to contradict this.

WORSHIPER'S ALIGN: This refers to the general alignment of those who worship, adore or propitiate the deity. This does not necessarily apply to the alignment of the deity's clerics, which must be identical with their patron's.

SYMBOL: Fairly self-explanatory, this is the symbol by which the deity and his or her faithful followers are known. It will be found engraved upon most holy items.

PLANE: This refers to the deity's plane of origin. Usually this will be an outer plane corresponding to the deity's alignment, but sometimes it varies due to the being's particular sphere of influence, as with those deities originating on the elemental planes or actually existing on the Prime Material Plane. Also, some deities may be located on a plane which seems to conflict with their alignment because other deities of the same pantheon with whom he or she is associated are also located there.

CLERIC/DRUID: This refers to the being's ability to function as a cleric and/or druid. Wisdom spell bonuses apply to the number of spells that being can have. Note that a divine being need not be of neutral alignment to have levels of druidical ability. Furthermore, nothing prevents deities from functioning in several different apparently-inconsistent classes at once.

FIGHTER: This refers to the being's ability to function as a fighter, paladin or ranger. Note that alignment does not necessarily preclude inconsistent classing here, either.

MAGIC-USER/ILLUSIONIST: This describes the level of the being's general magical spell ability, if any. Simultaneous classification in both areas is possible.

THIEF/ASSASSIN: This refers to the being's level of ability in regard to the thief and/or assassin classes. Once again, alignment does not preclude inconsistent classing.

MONK/BARD: This refers to the being's abilities as a monk or bard, if any. Note that alignment is not necessarily a consideration here for either of these classes, and that bardic ability indicates only that a being has the corresponding bardic powers, and does not necessarily imply abilities in the fighter and thief classes.

PSIONIC ABILITY: Where psionic abilities are indicated for heroes or monsters, they are listed as a strength point value, with attack and defense modes noted. However, the gods' psionic abilities are somewhat standardized, and fall into the following six classes:

Class	Psionic Strength	Disciplines	Attack Modes	Defense Modes
I	326-365	5 minor, 2 major	All	All
II	276-315	4 minor, 2 major	All	All
III	236-265	3 minor, 2 major	All	All
IV	181-210	3 minor, 1 major	All	All
V	91-110	2 minor, 1 major	A,B,C,E	F,G,H
VI*	Nil	Nil	Nil	Nil

* Beings listed as class VI cannot use psionics and are invulnerable to any type of psionic attack, including psionic blast.

Psionic disciplines function at a minimum level of 15th for demigods, 20th for lesser gods and 25th for greater gods.

S: I: W: D: C: CH: These are the abbreviations for the being's abilities. They are followed by the entity's scores. Ability scores that exceed 18 are explained below.

STRENGTH: This score is always followed in parentheses by the being's bonus "to hit" and damage, if any. These correspond to the following table, for those scores above 18:

Score	"To Hit" Bonus	Damage Bonus	Weight Allowance	Open Doors	Bend Bars/Lift Gates
19	+3	+7	4,500	7 in 8 (3)	50% (as hill giant)
20	+3	+8	5,000	7 in 8 (3)	60% (as stone giant)
21	+4	+9	6,000	9 in 10 (4)	70% (as frost giant)
22	+4	+10	7,500	11 in 12 (4)	80% (as fire giant)
23	+5	+11	9,000	11 in 12 (5)	90% (as cloud giant)
24	+6	+12	12,000	19 in 20 (7 in 8)	100% (as storm giant)
25	+7	+14	15,000	23 in 24 (9 in 10)	100% (as titan)

The numbers in parentheses under **Open Doors** indicate the chance of forcing open a locked, barred, magically *held* or *wizard locked* door, but only one attempt ever (per door) may be made, and if it fails no further attempts can succeed.

INTELLIGENCE: The following table applies to intelligence scores over 18:

Score	Chance to Know Each Listed Spell	Minimum Number of Spells/Level	Spell Immunities
19	95%	11	first level illusion/phantasm spells
20	96%	12	second level illusion/phantasm spells
21	97%	13	third level illusion/phantasm spells
22	98%	14	fourth level illusion/phantasm spells
23	99%	15	fifth level illusion/phantasm spells
24	100%	16	sixth level illusion/phantasm spells
25	100%	17	seventh level illusion/phantasm spells

Beings of very high intelligence will not be fooled by *illusion/phantasm* spells; they will note some inconsistency or inexactness which will prevent their belief in the illusion. A being with a 19 intelligence will never believe a 1st level *illusion/phantasm* spell, even if cast by a high-level spell-caster, and will thus avoid all effects. Beings with greater intelligence can also ignore higher level illusions, as indicated. All effects noted are cumulative (e.g. a 20 intelligence gives immunity to first and second level illusions).

DEXTERITY: The following table applies to dexterity scores over 18:

Score	Reaction/Attacking Adjustment	Defensive Adjustment	Picking Pockets	Open Locks	Locate/Remove Traps	Move Silently	Hiding in Shadows
19	+3	−4	+15%	+20%	+10%	+12%	+12%
20	+3	−4	20	25	15	15	15
21	+4	−5	25	30	20	18	18
22	+4	−5	30	35	25	20	20
23	+4	−5	35	40	30	23	23
24	+5	−6	40	45	35	25	25
25	+5	−6	45	50	40	30	30

Note: The last five columns (**Picking Pockets**, etc.) apply *only* to beings with thief, assassin or monk abilities.

CONSTITUTION: The following table applies to constitution scores over 18:

Score	Hit Point Adjustment*	Poison Save	Regeneration
19	+5 (no 1s rolled)	+1	Nil
20	+5 (no 1s rolled)	+1	1 point/6 turns
21	+6 (no 1s or 2s)	+2	1 point/5 turns
22	+6 (no 1s or 2s)	+2	1 point/4 turns
23	+6 (no 1s, 2s or 3s)	+3	1 point/3 turns
24	+7 (no 1s, 2s or 3s)	+3	1 point/2 turns
25	+7 (no 1s, 2s or 3s)	+4	1 point/1 turn

* The additions to each hit die are for fighter, paladins and rangers only; all beings without one of these classes can receive no more than 2 bonus points per die. The other modifications to the dice are applicable to any class. The notation "no 1s rolled" indicates that any 1s rolled when hit points are being figured should be counted as 2s. At 21 and 22 constitution, 1s and 2s are counted as 3s, and so on.

CHARISMA: The following table applies to charisma scores over 18:

Score	Maximum No. of Henchmen	Loyalty Base	Reaction Adjustment	Awe Power
19	20	+50%	+40%	Up to 1 HD/level
20	25	60	45	Up to 2 HD/levels
21	30	70	50	Up to 4 HD/levels
22	35	80	55	Up to 6 HD/levels
23	40	90	60	Up to 8 HD/levels
24	45	100	65	Up to 10 HD/levels
25	50	100	70	Up to 12 HD/levels

Awe Power is defined as the reverential fear or dread or overpowering desire to worship caused by the mere sight and presence of a divinity. In

WISDOM: The following table applies to wisdom scores over 18:

Score	Spell Bonus	Spell Immunities
19	One 4th & one 1st	Cause fear, charm person, command, friends, hypnotism
20	One 4th & one 2nd	Forget, hold person, ray of enfeeblement, scare
21	One 5th & one 3rd	Beguiling, domination, fear
22	One 5th & one 4th	Charm monster, confusion, emotion, fumble, suggestion, telempathic projection
23	Two 5th levels	Chaos, feeblemind, hold monster, magic jar, mass domination, quest
24	Two 6th levels	Geas, mass suggestion, rulership
25	One 6th & one 7th	Antipathy/sympathy, finger of death, mass charm, Otto's irresistable dance

Beings of very high wisdom are immune to the effects of certain charm-type spells, psionic abilities and spell-like effects. These immunities are cumulative with higher wisdom. Beings with high wisdom are simply able to automatically throw off the effects of these spells.

every case dealing with the levels listed, creatures that gaze upon a divine being will be stunned into inaction so that they will be aware of nothing but the presence of the deity until the deity disappears from sight (no saving throw). This works through *any* control up to and including a *magic jar* spell. Stunned creatures cannot initiate any other action than physical defense if attacked while under the influence of the *awe power*. Note that the *awe power* applies *only* to divine beings (gods and demigods). Mortal-born persons who somehow acquire godlike charisma will not radiate this aura.

In certain instances, some divinities are so loathsome and repellent as to actually have negative charisma. This applies only to the truly ghastly divine beings. The *horror* which their appearance and presence inspires causes creatures in the hit dice or level range noted below to be stunned with fear and detestation until the being is no longer in sight. While in this condition a creature can do nothing but defend itself physically against attacks. As with *awe power*, even if a person were to be given negative charisma through some terrible curse or change, he or she would not acquire the *horror* ability. The reaction of the average creature to a hypothetical non-divine being with a negative charisma would be a desire to kill it immediately.

Charisma Score	Reaction Adjustment	Horror
−1	−40%	Up to 1 HD/level
−2	45	Up to 2 HD/levels
−3	50	Up to 4 HD/levels
−4	55	Up to 6 HD/levels
−5	60	Up to 8 HD/levels
−6	65	Up to 10 HD/levels
−7	70	Up to 12 HD/levels

Beings with negative charisma will never have henchmen of a normal nature.

STANDARD DIVINE ABILITIES

Unless otherwise specified, all gods and demigods have the following special abilities, above and beyond whatever other abilities are listed:

Command: as the spell, but lasting 2 rounds for lesser gods and 3 rounds for greater gods. There is no saving throw vs. this divine ability.

Comprehend languages: as the spell, except the deity also gains the ability to speak or write the language in question.

Detect alignment: this ability enables the deity to detect the alignment of objects or creatures with no error.

Gate: the deity can only attempt to *gate* in other beings of the same mythos.

Geas: as the spell, but with a range of 9''.

Quest: as the spell, but with a range of 9'', and no saving throw.

Teleport: this is an inherent ability which allows the deity to teleport from place to place or from plane to plane with no error.

True seeing: as the spell.

The above abilities all function instantaneously and at will, but not continuously. The gods sometimes manifest surprising abilities that are not otherwise noted, such as the power to change characters' ability scores, grant *wishes* (or their opposites), or *teleport* others wherever they wish. Exercise of such bonus powers falls entirely within the realm of the DM's judgment.

Saving Throws: All gods and demigods have a saving throw in all categories of 2 (i.e., only on a 1 on a d20 will they miss their save). This is in addition to any other magic resistance, of course. All heroes delineated in this book have saves in all categories of 3. Gods' and heroes' saving throw numbers are irreducible regardless of magical aids and adjustments.

DUNGEON MASTERING DIVINE BEINGS

In **AD&D**, when the deities deign to notice or interfere with the lives of mortal men, it is the Dungeon Master who must assume their roles. DMing a divinity presents a far greater challenge than playing the role of a merchant, a sage, or an orc. Players will quite naturally pay special attention to the words and deeds of the gods, so the DM must make a special effort to understand how to present them.

First and foremost, deities and divine beings are *not* merely super-powerful humans. They have powers, abilities, and qualities totally unavailable to the mortal-born. (See **Explanatory Notes.**) Even if a human should, through some ultra-potent magic, have his or her abilities raised into the 20's (unlikely and inadvisable), that person would not gain those powers reserved for the gods. The source of a deity's godheads is in some way connected to his or her earthly worshipers, though in what manner the gods derive this power is a mystery totally beyond mortal (or immortal) comprehension. However, it is true that a god's power often increases or decreases as the number of his worshipers varies. Thus deities, and clerics as their agents, constantly try to increase the quantity and quality of their worshipers.

The statistics given in this book can be of great aid to DMs, but they do not tell *how* a deity should be played. The gods are not lists of armor classes, hit points and attack forms; treating them as such reduces them to the role of mere monsters. They are, rather, beings whose very *presence* profoundly affects the course of events. Many of them represent elemental or natural forces that man can barely influence, let alone conquer. Introduction of a deity into active play in a game is a step that cannot be taken lightly. Players must understand who they are dealing with, and that improper behavior toward a god can bring swift and dire consequences.

Gods generally have egos proportionate with their power and importance. Most deities simply will not stand for mere mortals behaving beyond their station, e.g., treating gods as equals, or not showing proper respect in other ways. Attempting to coerce or intimidate a god in some way will nearly always result in divine punishment. Mortals who meddle with the gods are usually dealt with harshly in order to provide examples for others who may contemplate such actions.

Most gods enjoy flattery, but any god with a wisdom score above 15 will know it for what it is, and will generally not allow his or her opinion of the flatterer to be altered by the flattery. Deities will usually be able to guess at the flatterer's motives.

In any encounter between characters and a divine being, there are several things that the DM must continually keep in mind. The first is the *divine awe* (or *horror*) inspired in mortals by most deities' extraordinary charisma. Even if characters are of sufficient level to avoid the direct results, the deity's pronouncements should carry great weight. The second thing to remember is that most gods' intelligence and wisdom far exceed that of mortals. They can rarely (if ever) be fooled or tricked by mere humans. Their great wisdom usually enables them to tell when a mortal is lying. In fact, as DM, you can usually assume that if you know why a character is saying or doing something, the deity would know it as well. This should help to simulate the deity's superior intellect and wisdom, and impress the characters. Gods with intelligence scores above 20 can often tell what kind of action a mortal is about to attempt just from a few preparatory motions, and knowing this, a god (with his or her superior dexterity) can often react to the action before it is completed!

If a god enters combat (willingly or unwillingly), he or she will always attempt to avoid any situation where the god can be physically defeated. A little reflection will show that the idea of a deity fighting mortals "to the death" is absurd. The easiest avoidance of combat is the god's innate *teleport* ability, which enables him or her to leave combat entirely, or "blink" away to a convenient distance and resume combat in a manner of the god's choosing (spells, special abilities, etc.). This *teleport* ability takes no time or concentration during battle — the divinity just wills it to happen.

If engaged in combat, deities will almost always call upon whatever aid they can. Some gods have specific aids or attendants listed in the text. Those who do not have creatures listed can still usually summon a retinue of appropriate beings from the Prime Material or the god's plane of origin. After summoning aid, many gods will depart the field, leaving their retinue to do the fighting for them. (That is, after all, their function — gods have better things to do than fight with mortals.) This summoning of aid takes no more time or effort than the *teleport* ability.

Unless they have a history of mutual antipathy, deities will always be unwilling to fight other deities. They will back off from confrontation situations whenever possible, preferring to work through underlings or chosen champions. For example, if a meddling party of characters accidentally summoned an evil god, they might wish to attempt to *gate* in a good god to protect them. They are almost sure to be disappointed. In all probability, the most aid they will receive through the *gate* is one (or more) of the god's servants, or a quick *teleport* to a safe location.

In fact, *gate* spells in general are more likely to result in the appearance of one of the god's followers, rather than the deity itself. A *gate* spell cannot compel a deity's appearance — a god will come only if he or she chooses.

The gods are not unwilling to aid their worshipers. The fact is, gods have so many worshipers that they prefer to give aid of a less specific and more general nature — subtle aid that will help their worshipers as a whole. This type of aid usually goes unnoticed in the short run (except by high level clerics, who know what to expect). Specific aid to individuals is extremely rare, despite the fact that this is the kind of aid deities are most frequently requested to supply. If the supernatural powers of the various Outer Planes could and would continually and constantly involve themselves in the affairs of the millions upon the Prime Material Plane, they would not only be so busy as to get neither rest nor relaxation, but these deities would be virtually handling all of their own affairs and confronting each other regularly and often. If an entreaty for aid were heard one time in 100, surely each and every deity would be as busy as a switchboard operator during some sort of natural disaster. Even if each deity had a nominal number of servants whose purpose is to supply aid to desperate adventurers, the situation would be frenzied at best. It is obvious that intervention by a deity is no trifling matter, and it is not to be allowed on a whim, even if characters are *in extremis*!

This is not to dictate that deities will never come to characters. The mighty evil gods, demons, and devils are prone to appear when their name is spoken — provided they stand the possibility of gaining converts to their cause. The forces of good might send some powerful creature of like alignment to aid characters on a mission in their behalf (e.g., a ki-rin, couatl, or good dragon). Certainly in the case of some contest between opposing deities all sorts of intervention will take place — but always so as not to cause the deities themselves to be forced into direct confrontation! Otherwise, the accumulation of hit points and the ever-greater abilities and better saving throws of characters represents the aid supplied by supernatural forces. This is particularly true when characters advance to high level and become prominent. Deities often regard such characters as important among their mortal worshipers, and the characters themselves may be asked to (or be given no choice but to) take part in the maneuverings of the gods' forces upon earth. Characters are usually totally without knowledge of the part they play. In these cases, rather than being requesters of divine intervention, characters may actually become part of the intervention itself!

As Dungeon Master, you will have to determine the amount of involvement of deities as you develop your campaign. Spur of the moment intervention can be handled as follows: If the character beseeching help has been exemplary in faithfulness, then allow a straight 10% chance that some creature will be sent to his or her aid if this is the first time the character has asked for (not received) help. If 00 is rolled, there is a percentage chance equal to the character's level of experience that the deity itself will come, and this chance is modified as follows:

Each previous intervention in behalf of the character	−5%
Alignment behavior only average	−5%
Alignment behavior borderline	−10%
Direct confrontation with another deity required by the situation	−10%
Character opposing forces of diametrically opposed alignment	+1%
Character serving deity proximately (through direct instructions or by means of some intermediary	+25%

The above applies only to activities on the Prime Material Plane. Deities will not intervene on the planes which are the habitations of other deities, i.e., the Outer Planes. They will neither venture to involve themselves in

the Positive or Negative Material Planes. Intervention in the Elemental Planes is subject to DM option, based upon the population he or she has placed there. (If there are elemental gods, the deities from the Outer Planes will NOT go there.) Intervention occurs only on the Prime Material Plane in most cases, with occasional intervention in the Astral and Ethereal Planes.

CLERICS AND DEITIES

When a DM is deciding which gods will be commonly worshiped in his or her campaign, he must be aware of the fact that not all gods are equally powerful, and that this affects their ability to grant spells to their clerics. As is explained in the **DUNGEON MASTERS GUIDE**, 1st and 2nd level spells are gained through the cleric's knowledge and faith. All other spells are gained through prayer. Third, fourth and fifth level spells are granted by the supernatural servants or minions of the cleric's deity. These servants range up to *demigod* level. Clerics whose patrons are *demigods* (and not *lesser* or *greater gods*) will receive their 3rd through 5th level spells directly from their deity. A *demigod* cannot grant spells above 5th level, so a cleric of a demigod could never receive 6th or 7th level spells.

Sixth and seventh level spells are granted to clerics directly from their deities. Only the *greater gods* may grant 7th level spells.

In each mythos included here, the deities have been divided into *demigods*, *lesser gods* and *greater gods*. The DM may carefully consider altering these designations if they do not suit his or her campaign or concept of the deity.

Deities of all types, from the highest to the lowest, expect a great deal of work from their clerics in return for the power to perform miracles. Clerics are expected to behave in a manner exemplary of the teachings of their faith. Even common everyday concerns must be viewed in the light of their beliefs. Clerics must stand out from the common fold as role models of correct behavior, exhibiting greater wisdom and thoughtfulness, and living out the precepts of their religions and alignments.

The DM must also make sure that the cleric is aware of his or her place in the community and the church hierarchy. Cleric "adventurers", which includes nearly all **AD&D** player character clerics, are often greatly respected and admired (or feared) by the populace. However, due to their somewhat unorthodox behavior, they rarely have any important place in their religion's hierarchy. They are required to maintain appearances and perform the proper rituals essential to their faith and alignment, regardless of their special mission in life.

A cleric, no matter where he or she is, acts as an agent and representative of his or her deity. The cleric should miss no opportunity to explain and show to others, through both word and deed, the truth and rightness of his or her religion. When clerics rise to high level, they are often expected to be judges, interpreters and arbitrators of the congregation's needs.

One of the more dangerous functions of any cleric is that of pawn of the god he or she serves. Clerics are sometimes required to attempt to block the plans of the servants of other deities, and they may even be sacrificed for the ultimate goals of the god they serve.

In addition to the above, there are other requirements which a cleric must fulfill if he or she is to remain in good standing with the patron god. Depending upon the religion (and the DM's decision), certain rituals and services must be performed, sometimes at precise and regular intervals. The cleric should also freely undertake the performance of exceptional duties in the form of quests, heroism, and even (if necessary) voluntary martyrdom.

One important and sometimes expensive duty of a cleric is the creation of places of worship for his or her deity. This could mean the building of simple roadside shrines at low level, while at a high level a cleric might finance the construction of an entire temple. These structures or areas must be put in places of relative security, for the desecration of a temple is a terrible blow to a religion's honor.

There may come a time in the campaign when a cleric may fall away from the path of the deity he or she serves and need to be corrected or punished in some way. Clerics using only first and second level spells usually need fear little direct retribution from their deity; the god expects higher level mortal servants to be aware of transgressions and to take the proper action.

In the case of higher level clerics, if the offense is minor, he or she will often receive a warning of some kind, typically an unmistakable omen of some sort. These are usually sent by one of the deity's servants. If a cleric once again commits a minor transgression or dereliction of duty, the servants of the deity (and the DM) may require that he or she appease them by engaging in one or more of several types of penances. If the questionable act was unknowing or unwilling, simple receipt of an *atonement* spell may be sufficient. If it was not, several days of fasting, prayer and meditation and/or minor sacrifices may be necessary. In certain religions, this may include some sort of scourging or physical punishment.

Greater and repeated transgressions require greater expiation to atone for them. The erring cleric may have to make a major sacrifice, probably including money and magic items, and he or she may be given a minor quest of some sort. Some religions may even require public degradation and humiliation for the cleric as recompense for his or her sins. Until the atonement period has been completed, use of certain spells or spell levels may be denied the cleric.

Grave transgressions require grim punishments. A cleric who commits a grievous sin against his or her god may have to sacrifice all of his or her possessions and then go on a major quest in order to restore good standing. During this period use of many or even all spells may be denied the errant cleric. Commission of irredeemable sins or terrible heresies, of course, will result in immediate and total excommunication of the cleric: that person may never again use clerical spells in the name of that deity or hope for aid or safety from his followers. The worst of these acts may also invoke direct divine wrath upon the head of the offending one. Divine vengeance upon one who has betrayed his god can take many forms, each one worse than the previous.

The above, of course, are rare cases. A faithful and true cleric does not balk at those tasks necessary for proper worship, and does not even consider committing actions which oppose those of his or her alignment and religion. The path of truth for most clerics is narrow but well-marked.

OMENS

Omens are signs or indications from deities that display the pleasure or displeasure of the gods or serve to foretell the future. This section deals with many of the common omens of historical reality, but omens can be useful in an **ADVANCED DUNGEONS & DRAGONS** campaign as well. Whenever players transgress their alignment, and especially when clerics violate the dictates of their sect, they will receive a bad omen. This can take several forms, but the most common one is a partial loss of power: a magic-user might find it impossible to remember some of the higher level spells, a fighter might suffer constant illness (and thus the loss of one-fourth or one-half of his or her hit points), or a cleric might be unable to renew even first or second level spells on a daily basis. Any of these happenings should be taken as a sign to the player that he or she has done some wrong that merits punishment. In short, omens are devices for judges to use in correcting players that constantly do improper things in the campaign. If a temporary loss of power does not deter a player from constantly violating his or her alignment or not following the ways of the deity, then more severe omens can be given or the effects of some can be made permanent.

Following this paragraph will be a list of omens and signs, along with their purported meanings. Some of these predicted happenings are quite specific, others are rather vague ("good luck"); whether specific or general, the DM is reminded that any or all powers or results are entirely optional. The same care must be taken with these omens and luck symbols as with the alleged mystical properties of gems (see **DUNGEON MASTERS GUIDE**, p. 27: "NOTE REGARDING THE MAGICAL PROPERTIES OF GEMS, HERBS, et al."). Under no circumstances should a player be allowed to badger a DM into, for example, giving the player a bonus on saving throws simply because he or she is carrying a pouch full of four-leaf clovers! In the **AD&D** universe, such an occurrence might foretell seven years of ill fortune to follow . . .

Certain omens are recognized as portending good luck. These include finding a four-leaf clover, seeing the crescent moon, and finding a toadstool. Symbols of good luck include dice, crossed fingers, a shoe, a fish, a dog, a wheel, and the three apes that see, hear, and speak no evil. The finding of mistletoe in the wild is good luck, and if boiled and combined with pure spring water is supposed to be a universal cure for poisons. The wearing of leather from top to bottom is said to repel demons and devils.

Dung is said to have both good and bad properties. Objects or persons that are covered in dung reputedly cannot be touched or hurt by the undead. On the other hand, if even a small bit of dung is cast upon an altar consecrated to good, the altar is defiled and only evil can be contacted there. The forces of good must go to great lengths to resanctify such a tainted object.

Far more omens and signs predict ill luck than good. Breaking a mirror and spilling salt are universally recognized as bad omens. The appearance of meteors, comets, and eclipses portend great changes or happenings, usually not good. Meeting an old woman as one sets out on a journey is ill fortune, as is a bat flying in the window, or tripping as one enters a doorway. If a bird perches on a holy symbol, it means horrible things are going to happen to that sect in the near future. If someone enters a room unasked and finds knives crossed in the room, it is considered a sure sign that that person will be cut the very next time they are attacked. Thirteen of anything in one group is the height of bad luck, and this should be avoided at all costs. Taking objects from a group of thirteen, or especially removing the whole group from whatever resting place it had, is said to invite a horrible death. The coming of a will-o'-the-wisp is interpreted to mean that some building is going to burn to the ground within seven days, while the wail of a banshee certainly means that someone is going to die that very night.

The appearance of a rainbow is a definite statement from a deity. Its appearance means either that the deity wants to converse with a mortal, or that the deity wants the mortal to undertake a quest. In Norse legend, men and women of power could travel to Asgard merely by touching a rainbow (part of the bridge Bifrost) and wishing to be there.

MORTALITY AND IMMORTALITY

AD&D assumes that the *anima*, that force which gives life and distinct existence to thinking beings, is one of two sorts: *soul* or *spirit*. Humans, dwarves, halflings, gnomes, and half-elves (those beings which can have a *raise dead* or *resurrection* spell cast upon them) all have souls; all other beings that worship deities have spirits. This latter group includes (but is not limited to) elves, orcs, half-orcs, and the other creatures specifically mentioned in the **NONHUMANS' DEITIES** section of this work. The DM may decide on a case-by-case basis whether other creatures have spirits and worship deities; the only parameter is that monsters with spirits must have at least an intelligence rating of Low. Please note that the following system is only a suggested one. Individual Dungeon Masters should use a different system if they find this one unsuitable.

When a being from the Prime Material Plane dies, its soul or spirit goes to one of the Outer Planes. (See **THE KNOWN PLANES OF EXISTENCE** section.) Selecting which plane the soul or spirit goes to is the province of the DM, based upon the alignment behavior of the creature during its mortal life. If a human cleric died professing to be lawful good, he or she might expect to go to one of the Seven Heavens. The DM might judge some of the cleric's acts as more neutral than lawful, and decide that a more appropriate plane would be Elysium. If a being has been faithful to the teachings and tenets of its deity, however, it is likely that the soul or spirit will pass into the plane where the deity resides. Moreover, the soul or spirit will go to that part of the plane most strongly influenced by that deity; for each plane is infinite, and most planes have more than one deity residing there (Olympus, Asgard, etc.).

Another difference between souls and spirits lies in what happens to them when they arrive at their destination. For souls, it is the beginning of eternity; it is on this plane that the soul will remain forever, enjoying the benefits or suffering the torments thereof. Spirits, on the other hand, may be but temporary residents of the plane. Their rewards and punishments are less than that received by souls. At some time in the future, at the will of the deity, the spirit can be returned to the Prime Material Plane — reincarnated. The new creature will not have any sort of overt memories of its former life, nor will its new form necessarily be the same as its old. If an elf becomes evil during his or her life, his or her spirit would go to one of the evil planes at death. The ruler of that plane might, a century later, decide to send the being back as a Drow, for example; this Drow would have the same sort of good-evil choices during life as the elf had (albeit from a different viewpoint), and conceivably could go to yet another plane upon death if he or she did not remain evil and loyal to the master of that place. The amount of time that a spirit must spend in a plane before returning to the Prime Material Plane is extremely variable. It could range from as little as ten years to a millenium or more — time is *not* important to a deity.

(*Note:* The above is only a suggested method for dealing with character life-after-death. The DM may, of course, use whatever system is most appropriate to his or her campaign.)

There is a time lag between death and arrival at the plane of destination. Although time is meaningless to the soul or spirit, the long journey to the proper plane can take 3-30 days of time relative to those in the Prime Material Plane. Thus the rationale for the progressive time limit on the *raise dead* spell becomes clear: the farther the soul has travelled on its way to its destination plane, the more powerful the cleric needed to summon the soul back to its mortal coil. The road through the Astral Plane to their destination is clearly marked for the dead, but it is not free of peril. Some monsters roam the ethereal and astral planes at will, which is why burial chambers often include weapons, treasure, and even bodyguards to protect the soul on its journey.

A *resurrection* spell functions in a different manner from a *raise dead:* the cleric literally recalls the soul *from the plane of its deity* back into its former body, where flesh and blood have been magically restored to the bones. As this involves the cooperation of the deity on the plane where the soul was, clerics must use extreme caution in employing this spell. If a cleric *resurrects* a being of radically different alignment, the cleric's deity (who gave the cleric this power) may be greatly offended. Similarly, if a cleric *resurrects* a being of different alignment simply to serve the purposes of the cleric or his or her deity (to extract information, for example), the deity on the plane where the soul was may be highly displeased and may take appropriate action.

The servants, functionaries, and minions of some deities (demons, devils, couatl, ki-rin, titans, and others) are actually spirits put into those forms for the purposes of the deity. It should be noted that the forms listed in the **MONSTER MANUAL** are by no means the only ones these servants can take — some chaotic deities rule planes where no two beings have the same form!

Immortality in **AD&D** does not confer or imply everlasting existence; in essence what the gods enjoy is eternal youth. Many of the gods can, of course, alter their forms at will and appear young or old; though this appearance is sometimes dictated by their followers (the ruler of a pantheon should appear older, wiser, and more mature than, for example, a god of mischief). Any description of gods as "young" or "old" is at best extremely relative and has no bearing on their powers. A character who obtains apparent immortality through many *potions of longevity* need not fear death through "natural causes" (until he or she finally drinks the potion that reverses the effects of all the previous ones), but can still be slain by normal means.

When deities or their minions travel to planes other than their own, they are mystically anchored to their home plane by a metaphysical "silver cord"; this is similar to the one described for *astral spell*, but cannot be broken by the Psychic Wind or any other means. This cord is what pulls a spirit back to its plane of origin when its material form is destroyed. The return occurs near-instantaneously, in contrast to the trek of a soul. The energy expenditure of this is enormous, and will weaken the returning being: servants, devils, demons, and even the deities themselves. Thus Type V and VI demons must rest a century before returning unaided to the plane where they were slain (see **MONSTER MANUAL**); demon princes and lords, and greater devils and arch-devils require 2-8 weeks to restore their energies to a point where they can plane travel or send a servitor to another plane; and even greater deities require 1-4 weeks of rest before dealing with activities outside their home plane. During this dormant period, it will be impossible for any clerics of the resting deity to acquire or recover any spells of third level or higher; this may be interpreted with dismay by the deity's earthly followers as a bad omen, but *no* information will be forthcoming until the dormancy is over (and even then it's unlikely that a deity would admit to its followers that it had been defeated!). It is important to remember that when a deity "dies" on the Prime Material Plane, the being's person and possessions fade away and disappear, though certain items might remain (at the DM's discretion).

If *any* servant or minion of a deity (*or even the deity itself*) is slain on its home plane, that being is absolutely and irrevocably dead. **No** power in the multiverse can restore that being, including action by other deities. In one's own plane a being is figuratively backed into a corner, with no-

where for the spirit to go upon death. All creatures are most powerful in their own territory, so it should be next to impossible for anything except another deity to slay a deity on its own plane — and direct confrontation between deities is *extremely* rare. Should mere characters be so brazen as to challenge a deity on its home plane, they should be dealt with severely, the god bringing to bear all the powers that the being has.

DIVINE ASCENSION

As study of the various mythologies will show, it is remotely possible for mortals to ascend into the ranks of the divine. However, there are certain requirements that must be fulfilled before such a thing could happen.

First, the character in question must have advanced to an experience level that is significantly above and beyond the average level of adventure-type characters in the general campaign. (This includes all such non-player types as military leaders, royal magic-users, etc.) For example, if the average level of characters in a campaign, both player and non-player, is around 5th level, then a candidate for ascension should be something like 9th or 10th level. If the average level is something like 15th, then a character would have to be in the realm of 25th-30th level!

Second, his or her ability scores must have been raised through some mighty world-shaking magic to be on par with the lesser demigods. (Should such an act be lightly considered, remember that a *wish* spell is the most powerful magic that mankind can control, and such an average increase in abilities would literally take the power of *dozens of wishes!* Each use of that spell weakens the caster and ages him 3 years into the bargain, so they are *not* easy to come by.)

Third, the personage must have a body of *sincere worshipers,* people convinced of his or her divinity due to their witnessing of and/or belief in the mighty deeds and miracles which he or she has performed (and continues to perform). These must be genuine worshipers, honest in their adoration or propitiation of the person.

Fourth, the person in question must be and have been a faithful and true follower of his or her alignment and patron deity. It is certain that any deviation will have been noted by the divine powers.

If all of the above conditions have been met, and the character has fulfilled a sufficient number of divine quests, then the character's deity may choose to invest the person with a certain amount of divine power, and bring the character into the ranks of the god's celestial (or infernal) servants. This process of *ascension* usually involves a great glowing beam of light and celestial fanfare, or (in the case of those transmigrating to the lower planes), a blotting of the sun, thunder and lightning, and the disappearance of the character in a great smoky explosion. Characters thus taken into the realms of the gods will serve their patron as minor functionaries and messengers. After several centuries of superior service and gradual advancement, exceptional servants may be awarded the status of demigod, which includes having an earthly priesthood and the ability to grant spells (of up to 5th level) to the demigod's clerics.

Naturally, ascension to divinity effectively removes the character from the general campaign, as the person will become a non-player member of the DM's pantheon. The section on **DUNGEON MASTERING DIVINE BEINGS** applies in general to the summoning of these characters as well, as their patron deity has more important jobs for his or her servants than to continually send them when called to interfere in worldly matters.

AMERICAN indian mythos

The gods of the Indians of North America were as close to nature as their worshipers could make them. The natural world is the most important aspect of the Indians' existence. The gods will always prefer to appear in the form of a creature of the land. They can, if necessary, appear in human form, but such appearances require great energy and may only last a short time.

In all Indian rituals where a cleric wants to control something, he or she must have part of it already. If the cleric is summoning rain he or she must sprinkle water on the ground in the process of the spell. If the cleric is casting a quest upon a being for whatever purpose, he or she must have a part of that being for the spell (a piece of hair, article of used clothing, etc.). The symbolism of a name is very important to the Indians, so important that no charm spell will work on an Indian priest without knowledge of that priest's name. All Indian rituals involving demons or devils require the use of a large fire for control of the creature.

Rituals revolve around the seasons. The ebbing of one season into another is a time of sacrificing important possessions of the tribe. Food, finely made jewelry, weapons used successfully in battle and the like are burned at these times for the good of the tribe in the upcoming season. Indian clerics are expected to be apart from the tribe daily in meditation with the village's patron deity. When great evil comes on the tribe, it is up to the cleric to protect the tribe, either by direct action or personal sacrifice.

All Indian clerics dress with a number of magical symbols and relics that they have fortified with holy power. These relics are buried with the cleric in the event of his death. The selection of these symbols is personal to the cleric, based on visions he will have received at the beginning of his or her career. One of these symbols will always reflect the patron deity's symbol.

Young Indian clerics enter battle alongside the rest of the warriors of the tribe, while the older clerics attempt to enlist the help of the tribal gods for the battle. It is the job of the tribal priest to make the warpaint of the warriors and bless the men and weapons before battle.

The tent or lodge of the cleric(s) is a place taboo to the rest of the tribe and supposedly guarded by strong spirits. Worship of most deities is held in the open.

SACRED BUNDLE

With the help of a tribal cleric and the advice of an Indian spirit that has been summoned for this purpose, a warrior can make a sacred bundle. This thing could be made out of anything that the summoned spirit indicates is sacred to that Indian. It gives the owner the following benefits: +2 on all saving throws; the warrior is surprised only on a roll of 1 in 6; he has an armor class of 2; and one point is subtracted from each die of damage done to the being in battle.

There are always from 5 to 10 items in a bundle, and the summoned spirit chooses several of the items so that they are very dangerous to secure (thus proving the worthiness of the supplicant). Things like a rattle from a cave of giant snakes, a feather from a high nesting giant eagle, or the hair of 13 enemies killed in battle are the type of items that go into a sacred bundle. When all of the items have been acquired, the priest of the tribe must be brought; he will demand that the last offering placed in the bag be of his choosing. This thing is always something that the priest can use a part of for his own purposes.

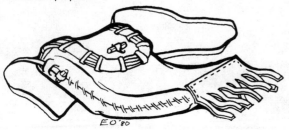

RAVEN

Greater god

ARMOR CLASS: 0
MOVE: 24''
HIT POINTS: 400
NO. OF ATTACKS: 3
DAMAGE/ATTACK: 3-18/3-18/3-30
SPECIAL ATTACKS: *Polymorph others (−3 to save)*
SPECIAL DEFENSES: *Polymorph self, shape change*
MAGICAL RESISTANCE: 75%
SIZE: M (6')
ALIGNMENT: *Chaotic good*
WORSHIPER'S ALIGN: *All alignments*
SYMBOL: *Large raven*
PLANE: *Elemental Plane of Air*
CLERIC/DRUID: *12th level in each*
FIGHTER: *10th level ranger*
MAGIC-USER/ILLUSIONIST: *16th level in each*
THIEF/ASSASSIN: *14th level thief*
MONK/BARD: *Nil*
PSIONIC ABILITY: VI
S: 19 (+3, +7) I: 24 W: 24 D: 25 C: 23 CH: 22

The Raven is the great transformer-trickster who is responsible for the creation/transformation of the world. Because of his great *polymorph/shape change* abilities he can appear in virtually any form he chooses. In addition to a raven, he may also appear as a fox, a jay or the moon. He will fight only as a last resort and then only as a giant raven. Although known as the great provider for mankind (including the giving of fire) the raven loves to play tricks, usually for the purpose of obtaining food to satisfy his ravenous appetite.

He is most likely to intervene on the behalf of his worshipers when they are in need of necessities. The most successful way to appeal to him is by offerings of food.

COYOTE

Lesser god

ARMOR CLASS: 2
MOVE: 24''
HIT POINTS: 330
NO. OF ATTACKS: 2
DAMAGE/ATTACK: 3-30
SPECIAL ATTACKS: *Nil*
SPECIAL DEFENSES: *Nil*
MAGIC RESISTANCE: 75%
SIZE: L (8')
ALIGNMENT: *Chaotic neutral*
WORSHIPER'S ALIGN: *Thieves and chaotic neutrals*
SYMBOL: *Coyote*
PLANE: *Prime Material Plane*
CLERIC/DRUID: *14th level in each*
FIGHTER: *15th level fighter*
MAGIC-USER/ILLUSIONIST: *14th level magic-user/17th level illusionist*
THIEF/ASSASSIN: *18th level thief*
MONK/BARD: *Nil*
PSIONIC ABILITY: III
S: 20 (+3, +8) I: 24 W: 19 D: 24 C: 21 CH: 16

Although Coyote is responsible for teaching arts, crafts and the use of light and fire, he is primarily a bullying, greedy trickster. This chaotic personality makes him difficult to understand. As a trickster he will usually be accompanied by a giant wolf or sometimes by a giant fox, wildcat, badger or porcupine. Often his tricks will backfire on him. His role is primarily that of a cowardly thief. His followers will most often appeal to him to improve their thieving abilities or to be granted tricks involving illusionist spells of fire, light or darkness.

Coyote can *polymorph* himself once per day but is limited to the animal kingdom. Coyote will flee combat whenever possible, but when cornered he will fight. He bites for 3-30 points of damage.

Whenever Coyote is involved in trickery, his two favorite spells are *invisibility* and *animate object*. With these two abilities he is able to make objects (including himself) disappear and move about.

HASTSELTSI *(god of racing)* "Red Lord"

Lesser god

ARMOR CLASS: 3
MOVE: 24"/48"
HIT POINTS: 320
NO. OF ATTACKS: 2
DAMAGE/ATTACK: 2-12 (+14) or 1-10 (+14)
SPECIAL ATTACKS: Nil
SPECIAL DEFENSES: See below
MAGIC RESISTANCE: 50%
SIZE: M (6')
ALIGNMENT: Neutral
WORSHIPER'S ALIGN: All alignments
SYMBOL: Running horse
PLANE: Prime Material Plane
CLERIC/DRUID: 10th level cleric
FIGHTER: 15th level ranger
MAGIC-USER/ILLUSIONIST: 12th level in each
THIEF/ASSASSIN: 12th level assassin
MONK/BARD: Nil
PSIONIC ABILITY: IV
S: 25 (+7, +14)   I: 19   W: 18   D: 25   C: 24   CH: 22

This god appears as a man, all of whose equipment is red. When he enters a tribal area it is because he desires to race, with any person and in any way. He never shows his godlike abilities (always running just a little faster than his opponent). His horse is a giant maroon animal (AC 5, HD 15, hp 70, #AT 3, D 2-20/2-20/1-12) and is enchanted so that it will run faster than anything it is competing against.

Hastseltsi cannot be hurt by any projectile or aerial attack. His hand axe inflicts 2-12 points of damage on a hit and is a +3 weapon; his throwing knife does 1-10 points of damage and is a +2 weapon.

This god is sometimes symbolized by a massively-muscled running horse, and his priests always have this image on their lodges and shields.

HASTSEZINI *(fire god)* "Black Lord"

Lesser god

ARMOR CLASS: –3
MOVE: 21"
HIT POINTS: 320
NO. OF ATTACKS: 2
DAMAGE/ATTACK: See below
SPECIAL ATTACKS: See below
SPECIAL DEFENSES: See below
MAGIC RESISTANCE: 45%
SIZE: M (6½')
ALIGNMENT: Lawful evil
WORSHIPER'S ALIGN: See below
SYMBOL: Torch
PLANE: Elemental Plane of Fire
CLERIC/DRUID: 12th level in each, offensive spells only
FIGHTER: 12th level ranger
MAGIC-USER/ILLUSIONIST: See below
THIEF/ASSASSIN: Nil
MONK/BARD: Nil
PSIONIC ABILITY: II
S: 24 (+6, +12)   I: 20   W: 19   D: 23   C: 24   CH: –1

This being is jet black and extremely ugly. He always appears wreathed in flames (the heat of which inflicts 2-20 points of damage to all that are within 10 yards of him). He is aware of anything that happens in any area that has a fire within 50 yards of it. The god is very fond of destroying villages by fire if they do not make sacrifices to him. All tribes fearing the god's wrath (especially in the dry season) will sacrifice food and fresh meat to him by burning these items at high noon.

He uses a +5 shield in battle, and this item cannot be wielded by any other being. In addition, he cannot be attacked from behind. While in battle he uses a bow that shoots a shaft of fire for 1-10 points of damage; its range is line of sight. His hand axe does 2-20 points of damage and he often throws it at the strongest enemy he faces. His lance of fire does 3-30 points of damage (he never throws this weapon).

When hard-pressed in battle by more than 5 enemies, he will use fire spells of any type as a 30th level spell caster.

HENG *(thunder spirit)*

Lesser god

ARMOR CLASS: 2
MOVE: 12"/24"
HIT POINTS: 250
NO. OF ATTACKS: 3/2
DAMAGE/ATTACK: 6-60 or 3-30 (+12)
SPECIAL ATTACKS: Nil
SPECIAL DEFENSES: Nil
MAGIC RESISTANCE: 20%
SIZE: L (20')
ALIGNMENT: Lawful good
WORSHIPER'S ALIGN: Good alignments
SYMBOL: Lightning bolt
PLANE: Elemental Plane of Air
CLERIC/DRUID: 10th level cleric
FIGHTER: 10th level ranger
MAGIC-USER/ILLUSIONIST: 12th level in each
THIEF/ASSASSIN: Nil
MONK/BARD: Nil
PSIONIC ABILITY: VI
S: 24 (+6, +12)   I: 23   W: 23   D: 22   C: 24   CH: 20

This god is favored among all the Indian tribes because he can sometimes be relied upon to bring rain to those that suffer, and give luck to those that hurt.

His bow shoots lightning bolts for 6-60 points of damage per strike, and it has a range of 30 miles. His lance does 3-30 points of damage, but the god never uses it unless closely pressed in battle.

Heng is made aware of the need for rain by his priests, who must sprinkle large qualtities of water on the ground to attract his attention. If he chooses to answer the summons, Heng will appear in a rolling thunder cloud as a braided warrior of the tribe that summoned him. The warrior that he chooses to copy for that summoning will have luck in battle for the whole year (in the form of a +2 to hit enemies).

HIAWATHA (hero)

ARMOR CLASS: 5
MOVE: 15''
HIT POINTS: 200
NO. OF ATTACKS: 2
DAMAGE/ATTACK: 2-20 or by
    weapon type
SPECIAL ATTACKS: Nil
SPECIAL DEFENSES: Nil
MAGIC RESISTANCE: Standard
SIZE: M (6½')
ALIGNMENT: Lawful good
CLERIC/DRUID: 8th level druid
FIGHTER: 15th level paladin/10th
    level ranger
MAGIC-USER/ILLUSIONIST: Nil
THIEF/ASSASSIN: Nil
MONK/BARD: Nil
PSIONIC ABILITY: Nil
    Attack/Defense Modes: Nil
S: 21 (+4, +9) I: 18 W: 18 D: 19 C: 19 CH: 18

Possibly the greatest of all Indian heroes, this warrior can be found (with many other names) in many of the cultures of America. He is often depicted battling monsters and even gods on behalf of mankind.

Hiawatha travels the rivers on a canoe that moves by itself, and the animals of the area talk to him warning him of possible dangers.

He fights with bow and spear, but his favorite battle tactic is to wrestle his enemy and bear-hug him to death (causing 2-20 points of damage per melee round).

Hiawatha seems to be a loner. He transcends the normal boundaries of tribal feuds in that he will help all people in trouble. He is a great peacemaker and defender of the weak. He fought the great bear of death and won through hand-to-hand combat. He brought the plant maize to the starving by defeating the god who guarded its secret.

HOTORU (wind god)

Lesser god

ARMOR CLASS: −2
MOVE: 12''/24''
HIT POINTS: 200
NO. OF ATTACKS: 3/2
DAMAGE/ATTACK: By weapon type
SPECIAL ATTACKS: Lightning
SPECIAL DEFENSES: Nil
MAGIC RESISTANCE: 30%
SIZE: L (20')
ALIGNMENT: Chaotic good
WORSHIPER'S ALIGN: Chaotic good
SYMBOL: Clouds
PLANE: Elemental Plane of Air
CLERIC/DRUID: Nil
FIGHTER: 10th level fighter
MAGIC-USER/ILLUSIONIST: 10th level
    in each
THIEF/ASSASSIN: Nil
MONK/BARD: Nil
PSIONIC ABILITY: VI
S: 23 (+5, +11) I: 23 W: 20 D: 23 C: 23 CH: 20

This being can sometimes be influenced by the needs of humans for certain types of weather or the growth of crops. On the other side of the coin, he can utterly destroy those same crops and humans for any slight to his priesthood.

He casts three lightning bolts per round for 2-20 points of damage each, for a range of 900 yards. If lightning does not work on his enemies, the god will use any fallen weapon he can pick up in battle.

The god takes on the form of the chief of any village that he is near. While Hotoru is in this form, that chief will have a bonus of +1 added to all of his saving throw rolls.

QAGWAAZ *(hero)*

ARMOR CLASS: 6
MOVE: 15''
HIT POINTS: 150
NO. OF ATTACKS: 3/2
DAMAGE/ATTACK: By weapon type
SPECIAL ATTACKS: Nil
SPECIAL DEFENSES: Nil
MAGIC RESISTANCE: Standard
SIZE: M (6')
ALIGNMENT: Neutral good
CLERIC/DRUID: Nil
FIGHTER: 12th level ranger
MAGIC-USER/ILLUSIONIST: Nil
THIEF/ASSASSIN: Nil
MONK/BARD: 5th level bard
PSIONIC ABILITY: Nil
    Attack/Defense Modes: Nil
S: 19 (+3, +7)   I: 18   W: 19   D: 18   C: 18   CH: 18

This powerful warrior can be found chasing and capturing horses and buffalo on the plains for sport, and entering villages to test his strength against the best warriors there. He fights with a huge wooden club, letting his strength do the talking for him. A hero of the plains, he seems to exist to set an example for the best warriors of any given tribe to copy. Always the first in battle, Qagwaaz is also a favorite among women.

SHAKAK *(winter spirit)*

Greater god

ARMOR CLASS: −2
MOVE: 12''
HIT POINTS: 390
NO. OF ATTACKS: 2
DAMAGE/ATTACK: 3-30 (+9)
SPECIAL ATTACKS: Nil
SPECIAL DEFENSES: Cold aura,
    regeneration
MAGIC RESISTANCE: 90% versus fire
    only
SIZE: L (10')
ALIGNMENT: Chaotic evil
WORSHIPER'S ALIGN: See below
SYMBOL: Ice spear
PLANE: Prime Material Plane
CLERIC/DRUID: Nil
FIGHTER: 12th level ranger
MAGIC-USER/ILLUSIONIST: 15th level
    magic-user
THIEF/ASSASSIN: Nil
MONK/BARD: Nil
PSIONIC ABILITY: VI
S: 21 (+4, +9)   I: 19   W: 19   D: 20   C: 24   CH: 6

This white-skinned deity is able to bring on any kind of cold weather at will. Those that sacrifice to him can often lessen the force of winter, but no one prays to this evil being for fear that he will come. Sacrifices always take the form of burning precious possessions during the dead of winter. While his form is usually human, his face is demonic with fangs and blazing white eyes.

His body radiates cold and those within 30 yards of him suffer 20 points of damage per melee round (no saving throw). His spear is made of ice and does 3-30 points of damage per strike. When the temperature is below freezing he regenerates 10 points per melee round.

SNAKE-MAN

Greater god

ARMOR CLASS: −2
MOVE: 12''/18''
HIT POINTS: 350
NO. OF ATTACKS: 0
DAMAGE/ATTACK: Nil
SPECIAL ATTACKS: Spells
SPECIAL DEFENSES: See below
MAGIC RESISTANCE: 75%
SIZE: M (6')
ALIGNMENT: Chaotic good
WORSHIPER'S ALIGN: Chaotic good
SYMBOL: Snake on sand
PLANE: Prime Material Plane
CLERIC/DRUID: 10th level in each
FIGHTER: Nil
MAGIC-USER/ILLUSIONIST: 15th level
    in each
THIEF/ASSASSIN: 8th level thief
MONK/BARD: 5th level bard
PSIONIC ABILITY: III
S: 24   I: 24   W: 19   D: 23   C: 24   CH: 20

This god appears in the shape of a man with rainbow-colored skin. He always wears 75,000 gold pieces worth of jewelry. He ages at will, and often visibly turns younger or older in long conversations with other beings. He can control all reptiles, and no reptile type will attack him, even if they are magically controlled in some fashion. This defense extends to fantastic reptilian beings such as certain devils, demons, dragons, and the like. Instantly, he can summon 5-500 random types of snakes to serve him (once per day).

Snake-Man has never been known to attack beings with other than spells; if assaulted by creatures that are impervious to magic, he will summon snakes to fight for him instead of personally attacking.

STONERIBS *(hero)*

ARMOR CLASS: 6
MOVE: 15''
HIT POINTS: 150
NO. OF ATTACKS: 3/2
DAMAGE/ATTACK: By weapon type
SPECIAL ATTACKS: Nil
SPECIAL DEFENSES: Nil
MAGIC RESISTANCE: Standard
SIZE: M (5½')
ALIGNMENT: Lawful good
CLERIC/DRUID: Nil
FIGHTER: 10th level ranger
MAGIC-USER/ILLUSIONIST: Nil
THIEF/ASSASSIN: Nil
MONK/BARD: Nil
PSIONIC ABILITY: Nil
    Attack/Defense Modes: Nil
S: 19 (+3, +7)   I: 15   W: 14   D: 18   C: 19   CH: 15

This Indian hero has a cloak that enables him to turn into a halibut at will, and he is also able to shrink to any size he chooses. He attacks with a bow or club.

This hero is famed for his great strength and will wander from tribe to tribe and fight the best each tribe has. Sometimes he will lose, and when this happens he will stay with the tribe for one year and fight in their battles.

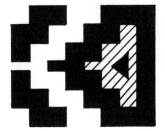
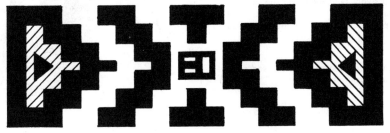
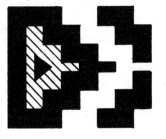

THUNDER BIRD

FREQUENCY: *Unique*
NO. APPEARING: *1*
ARMOR CLASS: *–2*
MOVE: *15"/24"*
HIT DICE/POINTS: *200*
% IN LAIR: *25%*
TREASURE TYPE: *U (X 3)*
NO. OF ATTACKS: *2*
DAMAGE/ATTACK: *2-20/1-10*
SPECIAL ATTACKS: *Lightning*
SPECIAL DEFENSES: *Never surprised*
MAGIC RESISTANCE: *32%*
INTELLIGENCE: *Genius*
ALIGNMENT: *Chaotic good*
SIZE: *L (12')*
PSIONIC ABILITY: *Nil*
　　Attack/Defense Modes: *Nil*
LEVEL/X.P. VALUE: *X/22,600*

This great bird attacks by biting with its beak for 1-10 points and bludgeon-ing with its wings for 2-20 points of damage. It can cast one *lightning bolt* per round at any target from 50 to 300 yards away. Each bolt does 30 points of damage (save for half damage). It is never surprised because of the warning that its superb senses give the creature. When it is ready to attack, its wings beat together and thunder sounds.

The Thunder Bird warns of great disaster and is often found fighting evil creatures of great power that have been summoned by the enemies of good tribes. This creature is never invoked. It always comes of its own will and does not leave until the battle is done. It has been known to die in several battles against powerful beings, only to appear again years later to confront another evil.

TOBADZISTSINI *(war spirit)*

Lesser god

ARMOR CLASS: *–2*
MOVE: *15"*
HIT POINTS: *344*
NO. OF ATTACKS: *2*
DAMAGE/ATTACK: *1-10/3-30 (+14)*
SPECIAL ATTACKS: *See below*
SPECIAL DEFENSES: *See below*
MAGIC RESISTANCE: *30%*
SIZE: *M (6½')*
ALIGNMENT: *Neutral evil*
WORSHIPER'S ALIGN: *Warriors*
SYMBOL: *Crossed spear and shield*
PLANE: *Prime Material Plane*
CLERIC/DRUID: *10th level in each*
FIGHTER: *18th level ranger*
MAGIC-USER/ILLUSIONIST: *10th level*
　　in each
THIEF/ASSASSIN: *10th level assassin*
MONK/BARD: *8th level monk*
PSIONIC ABILITY: *IV*
S: *25 (+7, +14)* I: *20* W: *19* D: *25* C: *25* CH: *20*

This god usually appears as a massively built male, but he can *shape change* at will. He occasionally, on a whim, enters into battles between tribes that interest him, either by personally taking a hand or increasing the abilities of one side or another.

His arrows strike for 1-10 points of damage and his spear is used only for hand-to-hand combat and strikes for 3-30 points of damage.

Worshiping warriors promise him kills in battle, which are burned after the victory.

YANAULUHA *(first priest)*

ARMOR CLASS: *3*
MOVE: *12"*
HIT POINTS: *200*
NO. OF ATTACKS: *3/2*
DAMAGE/ATTACK: *By weapon type*
SPECIAL ATTACKS: *Nil*
SPECIAL DEFENSES: *See below*
MAGIC RESISTANCE: *30%*
SIZE: *M (6')*
ALIGNMENT: *Neutral*
CLERIC/DRUID: *13th level druid/20th*
　　level cleric
FIGHTER: *10th level ranger*
MAGIC-USER/ILLUSIONIST: *9th level*
　　in each
THIEF/ASSASSIN: *Nil*
MONK/BARD: *Nil*
PSIONIC ABILITY: *Nil*
　　Attack/Defense Modes: *Nil*
S: *14* I: *20* W: *20* D: *18* C: *19* CH: *18*

Yanauluha was the first of all tribal clerics, and he is able to summon any spirit (god) of this pantheon to his people. The priest is now classified as a friendly spirit and is invoked by Indian priests whenever they need an es-pecially large boon from the gods. He is not worshiped as a god, but sacri-fices in the form of magic items are made to him and there is a 10% chance at each occurrence that he will appear and personally help out in the situation. He appears as an old man in rich Indian garb and talks very slowly.

Arthurian Heroes

Sir Thomas Malory's *Le Morte D'Arthur* collected all the legends and tales of Arthur and his Knights of the Round Table, and first presented the stories in the forms we are familiar with today. Arthur's knights represent the concept of chivalry to modern readers more than any other person or group. Chivalrous conduct basically means playing fair. Taking advantage of your opponent's misfortune is dishonorable, as is fighting him at better-than-even odds. A chivalrous knight shows respect to ladies and good clerics, but is suspicious of sorcery, and will avoid it if possible. To win fame and prove their virtue, knights will often undertake quests, usually swearing an oath that their efforts will be unceasing until their goal is achieved.

The knights of the Round Table may not fit into some **AD&D** worlds, but DMs may find it interesting to spice up their campaign with a trip to Arthur's Britain. More useful information can be found in TSR's **KNIGHTS OF CAMELOT**™ Fantasy Boardgame.

THE AVERAGE KNIGHT OF RENOWN

ARMOR CLASS: *3 to −2*
MOVE: *12'' (6'' in armor)*
HIT POINTS: *Variable with level, but
   never less than 60*
NO. OF ATTACKS: *3/2*
DAMAGE/ATTACK: *By weapon type*
SPECIAL ATTACKS: *Nil*
SPECIAL DEFENSES: *Nil*
MAGIC RESISTANCE: *Standard*
SIZE: *M (5½-6')*
ALIGNMENT: *Variable (but 80% law-
   ful)*
CLERIC/DRUID: *Nil*
FIGHTER: *8th through 10th level
   fighter*
MAGIC-USER/ILLUSIONIST: *Nil*
THIEF/ASSASSIN: *Nil*
MONK/BARD: *Nil*
PSIONIC ABILITY: *Nil*
   Attack/Defense Modes: *Nil*
S: *Special** I: * W: * D: * C: * CH: *

* These ''specials'' relate to variable numbers, which may never be below 10, and most average 15.

Knights always have a high quality heavy war-horse, use a lance, a bastard sword, a two-handed sword, or a morningstar in battle. They always have a lesser beast to ride when not fighting, and a squire of some type to aid them with their equipment. There is a 5% chance that the squire is better at fighting than the knight he serves. Squires cannot use swords in battle nor fight from horseback until they have been made knights. Average knights will most often kill their defeated opponents, rather than grant mercy.

KNIGHT OF QUALITY

ARMOR CLASS: *3 to −2*
MOVE: *12'' (6'' in armor)*
HIT POINTS: *Variable with level, but
   never less than 70*
NO. OF ATTACKS: *3/2*
DAMAGE/ATTACK: *By weapon type*
SPECIAL ATTACKS: *Nil*
SPECIAL DEFENSES: *Nil*
MAGIC RESISTANCE: *Standard*
SIZE: *M (6½')*
ALIGNMENT: *Variable (but 85% law-
   ful)*
CLERIC/DRUID: *Nil*
FIGHTER: *10th through 13th level
   fighter*
MAGIC-USER/ILLUSIONIST: *Nil*
THIEF/ASSASSIN: *Nil*
MONK/BARD: *Nil*
PSIONIC ABILITY: *Nil*
   Attack/Defense Modes: *Nil*
S: *Special** I: * W: * D: * C: * CH: *

* These ''specials'' relate to variable numbers, which may never be below 13, and most average about 16.

Knights of this type often (60%) have 1-4 squires and a group of 1-10 men-at-arms to serve them as they travel. These knights will usually (75% of the time) grant mercy to all those that ask for it during battle.

The following are all good or neutral knights of the Arthurian legends. All practiced chivalry in some form or degree:

Abellius
Ablamor o' the Marsh
Accolon o' Gaul*
Aglovale
Agravaine (brother of Gawaine, betrayer of Launcelot)*
Alisander
Allardin o' the Isles

Bagdemagus, King
Balin*
Barant Les Apres (King of the Hundred Knights)*
Bedivere*
Belleus o' the Pavilion
Berel
Blamor
Bleoberis
Bohort*
Bors de Ganis*
Brandiles
Breunor
Brian o' the Forest
Bruin le Noire (La Cote Male Taile)*

Cador o' Cornwall
Caradoc
Carados, King of Scotland
Chestelaine
Clairemonde
Clegis

Dagonet (Arthur's court jester)
Darras
Dinadan*
Dodinas le Savage

17

Ebel
Ector de Maris*
Edward
Elias
Epinogris
Ewaine

Feldenak
Felot o' Langdue
Florence*
Floridas

Gahalatine
Gaheris (brother of Gawaine)*
Gainus
Galagers
Gaunter
Gilbert
Gilmere
Gouvernail (Tristram's squire)
Griflet

Hector
Helior le Preuse
Herlen
Hervis de Revel
Hontzlake o' Wentland

Ider

Kay (Arthur's seneschal)*
Kehydius

Lanceor
Lavaine*
Lionel*
Lucan de Butterlere

Mador de la Porte
Managgen
Marhaus*
Melias
Meliot de Logres
Miles o' the Lands*

Naram

Ontzlake

Patrice
Pelleas*
Pelles, King
Percard (knight of the black lawns)*
Percivale*
Perimones (the red knight)*
Persante of Inde (the blue knight)
Persides
Pertelope (the green knight)*
Priamus the Saracen

Sadok
Safere
Sagramour le Desirous*
Segwarides
Sorlons

Trantrist o' the White*

Ulfius*
Uriens, king of Gore
Uwaine*

Wisshard

*Indicates a knight of quality.

The following knights are evil through and through, and will go to any length to win a battle. They can be counted on to have a wide variety of dirty tricks up their metal sleeves. The concept of chivalry means very little to them and it is to be used solely for the advantage it gives them over others.

Andred
Breunis Sans Pite*
Damas
Edward the Knight Perilous*
Gringamore
Helius
Hue the Knight Perilous
King Mark
Meleagrance
Mordred*
Phelot
Pinell
Turquine*

*Indicates a knight of quality.

KING ARTHUR

ARMOR CLASS: 0
MOVE: 12'' (6'' in armor)
HIT POINTS: 123
NO. OF ATTACKS: 2
DAMAGE/ATTACK: By weapon type
SPECIAL ATTACKS: Magic sword (see below)
SPECIAL DEFENSES: Magic scabbard (see below)
MAGIC RESISTANCE: Standard
SIZE: M (6')
ALIGNMENT: Lawful good
CLERIC/DRUID: Nil
FIGHTER: 14th level paladin
MAGIC-USER/ILLUSIONIST: Nil
THIEF/ASSASSIN: Nil
MONK/BARD: 5th level bard
PSIONIC ABILITY: Nil
    Attack/Defense Modes: Nil
S: 18 (52) (+2, +3)   I: 18   W: 19   D: 16   C: 18   CH: 18

According to legends, King Uther Pendragon (Arthur's father) died when Arthur was just a boy and Merlin the Prophet and Wizard took the babe and hid him away in the keeping of the knight Sir Ector, who knew nothing of the boy's royal heritage. While growing up, Arthur was trained in war by Ector and trained in kingliness by Merlin. Sir Ector and his son Sir Kay were at a tourney with Arthur as their squire when Arthur was sent back for a sword for Sir Kay. Wanting to get back to see the action as soon as possible, Arthur happened by a church and a sword embedded in a stone. He pulled it out, and thus identified himself as the rightful king of all England. Arthur lived on to fight all who opposed him, aided by Merlin and many strong and brave men. He married his lady Gwynevere and organized the Knights of the Round Table to fight for all that is right and proper. Arthur upholds the idea of lawful righteousness and fair play.

He wields the sword Excalibur, a +5 lawful good sword of sharpness, that has a scabbard that prevents him from being cut by any attack. Thrusting and slashing attacks against Arthur do half damage (from the force of the blow), and bludgeoning attacks do full damage. His shield device is a gold dragon.

SIR BERNLAD DE HAUTDESERT (the magical green knight)

ARMOR CLASS: See below
MOVE: 12''
HIT POINTS: 99
NO. OF ATTACKS: 2
DAMAGE/ATTACK: By weapon type
SPECIAL ATTACKS: Nil
SPECIAL DEFENSES: Impervious to physical weaponry
MAGIC RESISTANCE: Standard
SIZE: M (7')
ALIGNMENT: Chaotic good
CLERIC/DRUID: Nil
FIGHTER: 14th level fighter
MAGIC-USER/ILLUSIONIST: Nil
THIEF/ASSASSIN: Nil
MONK/BARD: Nil
PSIONIC ABILITY: Nil
  Attack/Defense Modes: Nil
S: 18 (77) (+2, +4)   I: 17   W: 14   D: 13   C: 18   CH: 12

As long as he wears his bright green armor, Bernlad cannot be hurt by physical weapons. This armor is enchanted for Bernlad only, and is normal plate mail for anyone else. This knight was one of the few powerful good knights that would not side with Arthur (though he also would not side with Arthur's enemies) and he was fond of baiting knights of the Round Table to test their courage. He wields a +3 axe.

SIR GALAHAD

ARMOR CLASS: −4
MOVE: 12'' (6'' in armor)
HIT POINTS: 120
NO. OF ATTACKS: 3
DAMAGE/ATTACK: By weapon type
SPECIAL ATTACKS: Nil
SPECIAL DEFENSES: Nil
MAGIC RESISTANCE: Standard
SIZE: M (7')
ALIGNMENT: Lawful good
CLERIC/DRUID: Nil
FIGHTER: 20th level paladin
MAGIC-USER/ILLUSIONIST: Nil
THIEF/ASSASSIN: Nil
MONK/BARD: Nil
PSIONIC ABILITY: Nil
  Attack/Defense Modes: Nil
S: 18 (00) (+3, +6)   I: 15   W: 18   D: 18   C: 18   CH: 18

Dressed in white armor, this bastard son of Sir Launcelot and Princess Elaine was the perfect representation of knighthood in that he was a paragon of purity and invincibility. It was he who successfully completed the quest for the Holy Grail.

SIR GARETH OF ORKNEY (knight of the many colors)

ARMOR CLASS: −2
MOVE: 12'' (6'' in armor)
HIT POINTS: 105
NO. OF ATTACKS: 2
DAMAGE/ATTACK: By weapon type
SPECIAL ATTACKS: Nil
SPECIAL DEFENSES: Nil
MAGIC RESISTANCE: Standard
SIZE: M (6')
ALIGNMENT: Neutral good
CLERIC/DRUID: Nil
FIGHTER: 17th level fighter
MAGIC-USER/ILLUSIONIST: Nil
THIEF/ASSASSIN: Nil
MONK/BARD: Nil
PSIONIC ABILITY: Nil
  Attack/Defense Modes: Nil
S: 18 (52) (+2, +3)   I: 12   W: 11   D: 18   C: 18   CH: 12

The young son of King Lot, Gareth served in the kitchens of King Arthur and became the enemy of Sir Kay, who called him "Beaumains". He was the most modest of all the knights and used his great fighting skills to help many a lady in distress, especially one Lady Lyoness. He was noted for the many colors he used on his armor and shield.

SIR GARLON (the invisible knight)

ARMOR CLASS: 1 (effectively −3, due to invisibility)
MOVE: 12'' (6'' in armor)
HIT POINTS: 80
NO. OF ATTACKS: 1
DAMAGE/ATTACK: By weapon type
SPECIAL ATTACKS: Able to fight invisibly
SPECIAL DEFENSES: Invisibility
MAGIC RESISTANCE: Standard
SIZE: M (5½')
ALIGNMENT: Chaotic evil
CLERIC/DRUID: Nil
FIGHTER: 13th level fighter
MAGIC-USER/ILLUSIONIST: Nil
THIEF/ASSASSIN: 3rd level thief
MONK/BARD: Nil
PSIONIC ABILITY: Nil
  Attack/Defense Modes: Nil
S: 15   I: 15   W: 9   D: 15   C: 17   CH: 15

This knight would always fight invisibly and was only defeated by the combined might of several knights of quality acting in concert. He was given the power of invisibility by a witch of the fens for the promise to only use the power for evil.

SIR GAWAINE

ARMOR CLASS: −2
MOVE: 12'' (6'' in armor at normal strength)
HIT POINTS: 112
NO. OF ATTACKS: 2
DAMAGE/ATTACK: By weapon type
SPECIAL ATTACKS: Nil
SPECIAL DEFENSES: Nil
MAGIC RESISTANCE: Standard
SIZE: M (6')
ALIGNMENT: Neutral
CLERIC/DRUID: Nil
FIGHTER: 17th level fighter
MAGIC-USER/ILLUSIONIST: Nil
THIEF/ASSASSIN: Nil
MONK/BARD: Nil
PSIONIC ABILITY: Nil
  Attack/Defense Modes: Nil
S: 18 (30) (+1, +3)   I: 16   W: 13   D: 18   C: 18   CH: 16

Gawaine has been given a magical gift of an unusual nature. From 9 in the morning till 12 noon, he gains in strength. From 9-10 he has a 19 strength; from 10-11 he has a 20 strength; and from 11-12 his strength is 21. After 12 his strength returns to normal.

The favorite cousin of King Arthur, this man was a revengeful knight and would travel to the ends of the earth to right some supposed wrong done to him or his family. His sword, Galatine, is a +2 weapon.

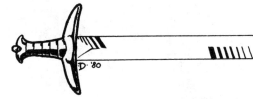

SIR LAMORAK

ARMOR CLASS: –2
MOVE: 12'' (6'' in armor)
HIT POINTS: 99
NO. OF ATTACKS: 1
DAMAGE/ATTACK: By weapon type
SPECIAL ATTACKS: Nil
SPECIAL DEFENSES: Nil
MAGIC RESISTANCE: Standard
SIZE: M (6½')
ALIGNMENT: Neutral
CLERIC/DRUID: Nil
FIGHTER: 15th level fighter
MAGIC-USER/ILLUSIONIST: Nil
THIEF/ASSASSIN: Nil
MONK/BARD: Nil
PSIONIC ABILITY: Nil
    Attack/Defense Modes: Nil
S: 18 (00) (+3, +6) I: 13 W: 8 D: 18 C: 18 CH: 17

The son of King Pellinore, and a constant champion at many tournaments held by Queen Margawse (Lamorak's lover), this knight was the death of several members of the Round Table. His greatest enemy was Sir Gawaine and his brothers. Sir Lamorak was noted for a battle in which he killed 12 renegade knights of Morgan le Fay.

SIR LAUNCELOT DU LAKE

ARMOR CLASS: –3
MOVE: 12'' (6'' in armor)
HIT POINTS: 141
NO. OF ATTACKS: 2
DAMAGE/ATTACK: By weapon type
SPECIAL ATTACKS: Nil
SPECIAL DEFENSES: Nil
MAGIC RESISTANCE: Standard
SIZE: M (6½')
ALIGNMENT: Lawful good
CLERIC/DRUID: Nil
FIGHTER: 20th level paladin
MAGIC-USER/ILLUSIONIST: Nil
THIEF/ASSASSIN: Nil
MONK/BARD: Nil
PSIONIC ABILITY: Nil
    Attack/Defense Modes: Nil
S: 19 (+3, +7) I: 14 W: 13 D: 18 C: 18 CH: 18

This mighty knight was the best of the best in the circle of the Round Table and was able to use all the powers of a Paladin, until he fell from grace by being tricked into loving King Pelles' daughter, the lovely Elaine (who bore him a son, the knight Sir Galahad). While he was forced to leave the side of King Arthur, who had until then treated Launcelot as the king's champion, he would never fail to aid the king in time of need. He went on all of the most important quests for the king and it was his weapons skills that defended the King's side in major battles.

D. '80

MERLIN

ARMOR CLASS: 2 (due to bracers)
MOVE: 15''
HIT POINTS: 175
NO. OF ATTACKS: 1
DAMAGE/ATTACK: 1-10
SPECIAL ATTACKS: See below
SPECIAL DEFENSES: See below
MAGIC RESISTANCE: Standard
SIZE: M (6')
ALIGNMENT: Neutral good
CLERIC/DRUID: 14th level druid
FIGHTER: Nil
MAGIC-USER/ILLUSIONIST: 15th level
    magic-user/10th level illusionist
THIEF/ASSASSIN: Nil
MONK/BARD: Nil
PSIONIC ABILITY: 300
    Attack/Defense Modes: B, C, E/-
    All
S: 15 I: 19 W: 19 D: 18 C: 18 CH: 18

The son of a sorceress and an incubus (a succubus shape-changed into male form), Merlin has a combination of powers and abilities far beyond those of mortals. There is a great deal of evidence to support the concept that Merlin is a being as powerful as the Great Druid with magical powers thrown in. While he never uses armor or normal physical weapons, his staff is as a *staff of many spell storings* and acts as a *staff of striking*. With this device, Merlin can absorb spells thrown at him and turn the power of these into spells to his own needs (like a *staff of the magi*).

Merlin can foresee the future in a random manner. There are times when his inability to see what lies just ahead in the future causes him great problems. He always teleports away from danger that could cause him a quick death. While he doesn't want to take part in battles, there are times when it is necessary in order to advise Arthur and others closely, and on several occasions he was attacked and suffered damage that would kill a mortal man. His demonic heritage allows him to regenerate 1 hit point per melee round and his magical skills allow him to heal the remainder. He is a very earthy being and a pretty face may cause him to act rather boyish in order to impress a lady.

MORGAN LE FAY

ARMOR CLASS: 4
MOVE: 12''
HIT POINTS: 39
NO. OF ATTACKS: 1
DAMAGE/ATTACK: 1-4
SPECIAL ATTACKS: Poisoned dagger
SPECIAL DEFENSES: Nil
MAGIC RESISTANCE: Standard
SIZE: M (5½')
ALIGNMENT: Chaotic evil
CLERIC/DRUID: Nil
FIGHTER: Nil
MAGIC-USER/ILLUSIONIST: 12th level
    in each
THIEF/ASSASSIN: Nil
MONK/BARD: Nil
PSIONIC ABILITY: Nil
    Attack/Defense Modes: Nil
S: 10 I: 18 W: 7 D: 17 C: 18 CH: 18

The half sister to King Arthur, this sorceress constantly uses the powers of illusion to attempt to become queen of the British Isles. Arthur was aware of her evil, but never acted openly against her because of their blood tie. As her name indicates (Fay = Faerie), Morgan is at least partially nonhuman. She wears a +3 *ring of protection*.

She is sometimes able to trick knights of the Round Table into her castle and either seduce them to evil ways or imprison them for a time.

SIR PALOMIDES THE SARACEN

ARMOR CLASS: 2
MOVE: 12'' (9'' in chain armor)
HIT POINTS: 93
NO. OF ATTACKS: 2
DAMAGE/ATTACK: *By weapon type*
SPECIAL ATTACKS: *Nil*
SPECIAL DEFENSES: *Nil*
MAGIC RESISTANCE: *Standard*
SIZE: M (5¼')
ALIGNMENT: *Neutral*
CLERIC/DRUID: *Nil*
FIGHTER: *16th level fighter*
MAGIC-USER/ILLUSIONIST: *Nil*
THIEF/ASSASSIN: *Nil*
MONK/BARD: *3rd level in each*
PSIONIC ABILITY: *Nil*
    Attack/Defense Modes: *Nil*
S: *17 (+1, +1)* I: *18* W: *11* D: *18* C: *17* CH: *18*

A bitter rival of Sir Tristram, Palomides was noted for the quickness of his scimitar and his courage in battle. The man was also noted for his use of the composite bow (a weapon not usually used by knights of any order).

KING PELLINORE *(knight of the questing beast)*

ARMOR CLASS: −2
MOVE: 12'' (6'' in armor)
HIT POINTS: 65
NO. OF ATTACKS: 1
DAMAGE/ATTACK: *By weapon type*
SPECIAL ATTACKS: *Nil*
SPECIAL DEFENSES: *Nil*
MAGIC RESISTANCE: *Standard*
SIZE: M (6½')
ALIGNMENT: *Lawful neutral*
CLERIC/DRUID: *Nil*
FIGHTER: *12th level fighter*
MAGIC-USER/ILLUSIONIST: *Nil*
THIEF/ASSASSIN: *Nil*
MONK/BARD: *Nil*
PSIONIC ABILITY: *Nil*
    Attack/Defense Modes: *Nil*
S: *18 (01) (+1, +3)* I: *15* W: *10* D: *18* C: *18* CH: *15*

This knight fought with King Arthur and almost defeated him. He later joined the Round Table and became one of the Queen's Guards. Pellinore hunts a strange unique creature, the Questing Beast, which his family is fated to pursue, though neither they nor anybody else will ever catch it. At the time of Arthur's court, Pellinore is just past middle age, though still a stout fighter.

SIR TRISTRAM OF LYONESS

ARMOR CLASS: −3
MOVE: 12'' (6'' in armor)
HIT POINTS: 120
NO. OF ATTACKS: 2
DAMAGE/ATTACK: *By weapon type*
SPECIAL ATTACKS: *Nil*
SPECIAL DEFENSES: *Nil*
MAGIC RESISTANCE: *Standard*
SIZE: M (6')
ALIGNMENT: *Neutral*
CLERIC/DRUID: *Nil*
FIGHTER: *17th level fighter*
MAGIC-USER/ILLUSIONIST: *Nil*
THIEF/ASSASSIN: *Nil*
MONK/BARD: *Nil*
PSIONIC ABILITY: *Nil*
    Attack/Defense Modes: *Nil*
S: *18 (99) (+2, +5)* I: *16* W: *13* D: *19* C: *18* CH: *17*

Known for his skill of arms and savagery in battle, this knight was considered by many to be second only to Launcelot in battle skills. Tristram is well-known for his ill-fated romance with the beautiful Lady Isolde, who is married to the evil and cowardly King Mark. The insanely jealous King searches constantly for ways to discredit or destroy the noble Tristram.

BABYLONIAN MYTHOS

The origins of Babylonian mythology are extremely ancient. Because of this, misconceptions, duality among the gods and goddesses, and similarities between their deities and those of other pantheons exist. In formulating this list for your use, we have consulted many sources, and some of these conflict with each other. This version is designed to be close to historically accurate and still playable in **AD&D** terms.

(NOTE: If you wish to look hard enough, we are sure that you will find many points of disagreement with certain historical sources. This is unavoidable, when so many sources conflict.)

The high priest of this religion is often the king of the country and must be a combination magic-user/cleric of great power. All clerical types must remain aloof from the normal populace in temples or shrines and work to further the state politically as well as spiritually.

Through Anu and the priest-king, all money collected by the shrines and temples is dealt out. The ruler also distributes all political power through appointments. The new moon is looked on as a time of great ceremony, and also a time for the people to pay money to the temples as a sort of tithe to appease the gods. Kings are expected to go forth occasionally on quests with other clerics of differing levels and bring back riches (usually through conquest) to further the sect.

Punishment for failing in duties is always severe for the cleric. The breaking of minor laws requires fasting, prayers, meditation, and sacrifices of animals and goods the cleric owns until the deity makes it known through the higher-level clerics that everything is forgiven. Sacrifices are commonly made in gold or precious jewels. Major clerical transgressions include helping the enemies of the sect, communicating with intelligent creatures or demi-humans (all of whom are considered "demons") other than humans, and dealing with humans of the opposite alignment. These crimes are all dealt with in the same manner, by complete denial of spells at all levels and excommunication from the sect, unless the erring one will take up a quest which will greatly aid the sect (either in terms of monetary riches or loss of power to other cults).

The traditional attire of all Babylonian clerics is a wraparound kilt of white with red cuneiform writing along the hem. They have been known to enter battle, but always in the rear of the action as support. Advancement within a sect is through the payment of gold to the high priest's court. Note that this is not the same as level advancement. Increase in ability does not guarantee increase in temporal power. Priests of a successful nature were known to be given great (and highly dangerous) quests to prove their worthiness to stand by the King.

ANU *(god of the sky) "Chief of all the Babylonian Deities"*

Greater god

ARMOR CLASS: −4
MOVE: 12″
HIT POINTS: 400
NO. OF ATTACKS: 2
DAMAGE/ATTACK: 2-20 (+7)
SPECIAL ATTACKS: Command power
SPECIAL DEFENSES: See below
MAGIC RESISTANCE: 80%
SIZE: M (6½')
ALIGNMENT: Lawful neutral
WORSHIPER'S ALIGN: All alignments
SYMBOL: Gold sun partially blocked
    by a gray cloud
PLANE: Nirvana
CLERIC/DRUID: 20th level cleric
FIGHTER: 18th level fighter
MAGIC-USER/ILLUSIONIST: See
    below
THIEF/ASSASSIN: Nil
MONK/BARD: Nil
PSIONIC ABILITY: VI
S: 19 (+3, +7)   I: 25   W: 25   D: 25   C: 25   CH: 25

This god appears as a man. A strong breeze constantly blows in the direction of his gaze. Beings casting things at this god must make a saving throw against *disintegration* at −4 for both the being and the thing cast. His voice is the voice of all leaders, and *any* being must make a saving throw versus magic at −4 to resist his commands. He can summon any dragon type (except for the king and queen and any other types of dragon royalty) to fight for him once a week, per dragon type.

He uses a brass mace in battle that strikes for 2-20 points of damage plus his bonus of 7 points.

Anu is said to have created the heavens and the earth. All of the other Babylonian gods bow to his authority.

ANSHAR *(god of darkness and the night)*

Lesser god

ARMOR CLASS: 2
MOVE: 12″
HIT POINTS: 300
NO. OF ATTACKS: 0
DAMAGE/ATTACK: Nil
SPECIAL ATTACKS: Beam of darkness
SPECIAL DEFENSES: See below
MAGIC RESISTANCE: 50%
SIZE: M (6')
ALIGNMENT: Chaotic evil
WORSHIPER'S ALIGN: Neutral evil
    and chaotic evil
SYMBOL: Black sphere
PLANE: Pandemonium
CLERIC/DRUID: 20th level cleric
FIGHTER: 18th level fighter
MAGIC-USER/ILLUSIONIST: See
    below
THIEF/ASSASSIN: Nil
MONK/BARD: Nil
PSIONIC ABILITY: VI
S: 16 (0, +1)   I: 20   W: 12   D: 18   C: 22   CH: 18

This deity always appears as a dark-skinned human and only appears at night or in deep darkness. He casts his darkness beam for a maximum range of 300 yards, once per melee round, and this ray affects any flesh for 40 points of damage per strike. Body parts hit may never be regenerated or healed. Anshar can only teleport into areas of shadow or darkness. The god is unaffected by any source of light or light reflector. The god can grasp spells out of the air as they pass or hit him, and save these spells (as a *ring of spell storing*) or toss them back right away. He can alter one spell effect per melee round in this manner, and the chosen spell will have no effect on him. When preparing for battle, he usually stores one of every ninth level spell (given to him by some other god) so that he starts out with something to cast. This storing or returning ability comes from a godly attribute that lets him sense what spells are passing through his area. There is a 200 spell level storage limit to this attribute.

DAHAK *(three-headed dragon spirit of death)*

FREQUENCY: *Unique*
NO. APPEARING: *1*
ARMOR CLASS: *1 or ethereal*
MOVE: *9"/15"*
HIT DICE/POINTS: *200 hp*
% IN LAIR: *25%*
TREASURE TYPE: *U, Z, (X 3)*
NO. OF ATTACKS: *3*
DAMAGE/ATTACK: *3-30/3-30/3-30*
SPECIAL ATTACKS: *See below*
SPECIAL DEFENSES: *See below*
MAGIC RESISTANCE: *55%*
INTELLIGENCE: *Average*
ALIGNMENT: *Chaotic evil*
SIZE: *L (72' long)*
PSIONIC ABILITY: *Nil*
   Attack/Defense Modes: *Nil*
LEVEL/X.P. VALUE: *X/24,000*

This monster has no corporeal form unless it is attacking with its bite; the rest of the time it is ethereal. It appears to the world as a huge three-headed dragon (the color of the scales depending on its whim at the time). It will only eat the flesh of lawful or good creatures, and it never goes hungry. The monster can breathe any type of dragon breath at any time (but the creature enjoys crunching things with its teeth). It is able to negate any magical device permanently with a touch of all three of its heads at the same time.

DRUAGA *(ruler of the devil world)*

Lesser god

ARMOR CLASS: *-1*
MOVE: *21"/45"*
HIT POINTS: *230*
NO. OF ATTACKS: *2*
DAMAGE/ATTACK: *35 points*
SPECIAL ATTACKS: *See below*
SPECIAL DEFENSES: *Immune to*
   breath weapons
MAGIC RESISTANCE: *75%*
SIZE: *L (9')*
ALIGNMENT: *Lawful evil*
WORSHIPER'S ALIGN: *Lawful evil*
SYMBOL: *Ruby mace*
PLANE: *Nine Hells*
CLERIC/DRUID: *Nil*
FIGHTER: *15th level fighter*
MAGIC-USER/ILLUSIONIST: *15th level*
   magic-user
THIEF/ASSASSIN: *15th level assassin*
MONK/BARD: *Nil*
PSIONIC ABILITY: *Nil*
S: *24 (+6, +12)*   I: *18*   W: *13*   D: *23*   C: *25*   CH: *-4*

This being generally never appears to anyone the same way twice. The creature's real form has 8 arms ending in talons, is scaled with ruby red hide, and has 4 legs ending in snakey masses, while the head is that of a beautiful boy. The combination is so hideous that it often causes enemies to be paralyzed with fear. It can *shape change* at will, call on any type of

devil (except for the arch-devils) once a day in numbers from 2-20, and it is not affected by breath weapons from any creature.

Druaga only fights in person when his soul object (always put in a living being) is threatened. The soul object is the total essence of his being. If Druaga's bodily form is destroyed, the soul object will begin regenerating a whole new being with all the memories of the old devil. The human that has Druaga's soul implanted in him or her has no knowledge of this, and will die at the same time the devil's body dies, so that when the human's body is buried, there will be a safe place for the new devil to grow.

Druaga will very occasionally send a group of devils out to aid his worshipers, especially those that have recently sacrificed a virgin to their deity.

His mace does 35 points of damage every time it hits and turns all beings it hits into devils (random type) under his command if they do not make their magic saving throw.

GILGAMESH *(hero)*

ARMOR CLASS: *6*
MOVE: *15"*
HIT POINTS: *180*
NO. OF ATTACKS: *2*
DAMAGE/ATTACK: *2-20 (+8)*
SPECIAL ATTACKS: *See below*
SPECIAL DEFENSES: *Cannot be*
   charmed
MAGIC RESISTANCE: *10%*
SIZE: *M (6')*
ALIGNMENT: *Neutral good*
CLERIC/DRUID: *5th level in each*
FIGHTER: *12th level ranger*
MAGIC-USER/ILLUSIONIST: *10th level*
   magic-user
THIEF/ASSASSIN: *Nil*
MONK/BARD: *11th level monk/5th*
   level bard
PSIONIC ABILITY: *Nil*
   Attack/Defense Modes: *Nil*
S: *20 (+3, +8)*   I: *18*   W: *17*   D: *18*   C: *19*   CH: *18*

This hero of legend was the warrior/necromancer/high priest ruler of his land. He is noted for going out and getting things done when others were unable.

While his +2 mace is able to hit with brutal force (2-20), Gilgamesh loves to attack by wrestling, and stories abound of him wrestling a mighty bull or god to destruction.

Gilgamesh is a great king, noted for his tyrannical rule. Although he governs well and maintains peace, he uses his authority to satisfy his personal pleasures. He is a great lover of all types of earthly pleasure. He is stubborn and prefers the direct method for solving problems whenever possible. He is a great wrestler, using this attack mode in preference to all others.

Gilgamesh has a great fear of death. If he learns of any way to avoid death, he will do whatever is required to gain it. One oddity, however, is that his fear of death seldom occurs to him when facing a terrible foe. At such times, his courage will hearten him and he will fight without wavering.

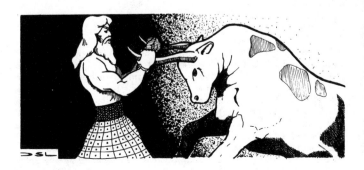

GIRRU *(god of fire)*

Lesser god

ARMOR CLASS: –2
MOVE: 18″
HIT POINTS: 280
NO. OF ATTACKS: 2
DAMAGE/ATTACK: 1-8 (+12) / 2-20
   (+12)
SPECIAL ATTACKS: Poison, stunning
SPECIAL DEFENSES: See below
MAGIC RESISTANCE: 50%
SIZE: M (6′)
ALIGNMENT: Lawful good
WORSHIPER'S ALIGN: Lawful good
   and neutral good
SYMBOL: Fire-enwrapped axe
PLANE: Seven Heavens
CLERIC/DRUID: Nil
FIGHTER: 16th level fighter
MAGIC-USER/ILLUSIONIST: See
   below
THIEF/ASSASSIN: Nil
MONK/BARD: Nil
PSIONIC ABILITY: Nil
S: 24 (+6, +12) I: 20 W: 14 D: 18 C: 23 CH: 18

Girru usually manifests himself as a man. He hates all things evil and will destroy such whenever he comes in contact with them. The god casts all fire spells as a 40th level magic-user, and is himself totally unaffected by fire. He can *shape change* and *teleport* (though only to places with flame in the area). All those that come within 10 feet of him will suffer 10 points of damage per melee round from heat (no saving throw). He fights with a mace that does 1-8 plus 12 points for his strength, plus a poisoned barb breaks off the mace and is embedded in the victim with each hit (save vs. poison at –4). His +3 axe hits for 2-20, plus his strength bonus, plus the target must save vs. petrification or be stunned for 2-8 rounds. Any weapon that touches the god's body will *disintegrate*, no saving throw applicable. This happens after the damage has been done by the weapon.

ISHTAR *(goddess of love and war)*

Greater goddess

ARMOR CLASS: –4
MOVE: 12″
HIT POINTS: 250
NO. OF ATTACKS: 2
DAMAGE/ATTACK: See below
SPECIAL ATTACKS: Suggestion
SPECIAL DEFENSES: Nil
MAGIC RESISTANCE: 75%
SIZE: M (6′)
ALIGNMENT: Neutral
WORSHIPER'S ALIGN: All alignments
SYMBOL: Female hand grasping a
   blue crystal rod
PLANE: Elysium
CLERIC/DRUID: 15th level cleric
FIGHTER: 20th level ranger
MAGIC-USER/ILLUSIONIST: 25th level
   magic-user
THIEF/ASSASSIN: Nil
MONK/BARD: Nil
PSIONIC ABILITY: Nil
S: 25 (+7, +14) I: 22 W: 12 D: 25 C: 23 CH: 25

Ishtar never appears to her worshipers in any form other than that of a beautiful woman. She has the strength of a titan, the ability to *shape change* at will, and she uses her voice as a constant *suggestion* spell. She wears the *headdress of love and war*. When she is interested in a male, the headdress forces him to become passionately in love with the wearer (no saving throw applicable), but she must really be interested in that male. When fighting an enemy, this headdress gives the wearer the same powers her enemy(s) has. Ishtar drives a flying chariot, pulled by 7 enchanted lions. The lions have 50 hit points each, an armor class of –2, 11 hit dice each, attack for 1-8/1-8, and cannot be controlled by any being

(using magic or otherwise) except for the goddess herself. The chariot travels at a speed of 21″, and when in the chariot, no metal can touch the goddess.

She is able to cast 2 spells per melee round, and when facing beings that are not affected by magic, she strikes with a *blue crystal rod* that is able to transform any spell level into direct energy times ten, e.g. she is able to strike for 90 points of damage when expending a ninth level spell through the rod and 10 points when using a first level spell through the rod. She is limited to the number and level of spells she can cast as a 15th level cleric/25th level magic-user.

MARDUK *(god of the city, wind, thunder, storms, & rain)*

Greater god

ARMOR CLASS: 1
MOVE: Infinite
HIT POINTS: 350
NO. OF ATTACKS: 2
DAMAGE/ATTACK: See below
SPECIAL ATTACKS: See below
SPECIAL DEFENSES: +3 or better
   weapon to hit
MAGIC RESISTANCE: 50%
SIZE: L (9′)
ALIGNMENT: Lawful neutral
WORSHIPER'S ALIGN: Lawful neutral
SYMBOL: Silvery net
PLANE: Arcadia
CLERIC/DRUID: Nil
FIGHTER: 19th level fighter
MAGIC-USER/ILLUSIONIST: 16th level
   magic-user
THIEF/ASSASSIN: Nil
MONK/BARD: 15th level bard
PSIONIC ABILITY: Nil
S: 24 (+6, +12) I: 23 W: 24 D: 20 C: 24 CH: 23

This god is one of the few nonhuman-appearing beings in this pantheon. He is always shown with four eyes, four ears, flames shooting from his mouth when he speaks, and a reddish tinge to his skin. He occasionally assumes the leadership of the Babylonian gods when Anu is preoccupied. This god can borrow any single ability from any one other deity in the pantheon (no saving throw applicable) and use it as he sees fit. This ability is effective on anything within sight of the god and can be given back at any time from any distance. In battle, he uses a net made out of the four winds that, when striking, binds the target until Marduk releases the net. The strands cannot be broken, but the god must remain within 50 feet of the net at all times for it to function. The god may create any type of weather condition in an instant and summon 20 dice *lightning bolts* from the sky at any time.

Marduk is called "the justice bringer" and "lord of pure incantations". His battles with Tiamat are legendary.

NERGAL *(god of the underworld)*

Lesser god

ARMOR CLASS: *1*
MOVE: *12″/12″*
HIT POINTS: *300*
NO. OF ATTACKS: *2*
DAMAGE/ATTACK: *See below*
SPECIAL ATTACKS: *See below*
SPECIAL DEFENSES: *Uses a special shield*
MAGIC RESISTANCE: *See below*
SIZE: *M (6′)*
ALIGNMENT: *Neutral evil*
WORSHIPER'S ALIGN: *Evil alignments*
SYMBOL: *Dark-skinned man holding a jet black shield*
PLANE: *Hades*
CLERIC/DRUID: *25th level cleric*
FIGHTER: *12th level fighter*
MAGIC-USER/ILLUSIONIST: *20th level magic-user*
THIEF/ASSASSIN: *Nil*
MONK/BARD: *Nil*
PSIONIC ABILITY: *Nil*
S: *19 (+3, +7)* I: *20* W: *20* D: *19* C: *23* CH: *24*

This deity rules over all things that are dead and never uses any form but a human one. His favorite tactic is to revive the 5 most powerful dead enemies of his foe or foes and have them fight for him. When he goes into personal combat, he uses a night-black shield that is both a weapon and a means of defense. The shield has a bonus of +5; when in use, no being can attack the god from behind. It also casts a *death spell* aura (saving throw applicable) in a 30 foot radius around the god, and no spell of less than the eighth level can affect the user of the shield.

His worshipers (those that wish success in evil deeds) sacrifice good creatures on his altar of black basalt, or dedicate the proceeds of evil actions to the church in a type of promised sacrifice.

RAMMAN *(god of storms and thunder)*

Lesser god

ARMOR CLASS: *−4*
MOVE: *12″/48″*
HIT POINTS: *325*
NO. OF ATTACKS: *2*
DAMAGE/ATTACK: *30 points*
SPECIAL ATTACKS: *Lightning*
SPECIAL DEFENSES: *See below*
MAGIC RESISTANCE: *50% + special (see below)*
SIZE: *M (7′)*
ALIGNMENT: *Neutral*
WORSHIPER'S ALIGN: *All neutrals + special (see below)*
SYMBOL: *Lighting bolt through a storm cloud*
PLANE: *Concordant Opposition*
CLERIC/DRUID: *Nil*
FIGHTER: *17th level fighter*
MAGIC-USER/ILLUSIONIST: *15th level in each*
THIEF/ASSASSIN: *Nil*
MONK/BARD: *Nil*
PSIONIC ABILITY: *Nil*
S: *22 (+4, +10)* I: *20* W: *16* D: *21* C: *24* CH: *16*

This god appears on the earth in human form, with a massive build and a rather homely face. When anything hits him, sparks will fly doing 30 points of damage to anything within 3″ of his body (no saving throw applicable). His *lightning bolts* are cast two per round, and do 30 points of damage each. Spells must be of the fifth level or greater to affect him. His +4 ring mail is made out of cloud vapor, and his mallet, ten feet long, is often thrown, doing 30 points of damage every time it hits. It returns by itself to Ramman's hand. This weapon is usually only used against creatures that resist his lightning strikes.

His neutral worshipers always perform their services at night, but there are many other beings who wish rain that are not of his alignment, and they usually sacrifice expensive liquids to the god to bring on rain for their crops or just to bring cooler weather.

DSL

Celtic Mythos

The Celtic mythology is by no means confined to the British Isles. The beings listed are all in human form, unlike some of the other pantheons in this work. They all have spheres of influence and these spheres are areas of control for the deities. Any major manipulations of these areas by humans or other life forms will cause the god or goddess in question to take an interest (in force) and attempt to put a stop to it.

The clerics of most of these deities are druids, which are fully detailed in **PLAYERS HANDBOOK**. All religious services are performed by these druids in wooded areas made holy by the planting of mistletoe and holly. In these areas are deep natural wells or dug pits where sacrifices are thrown. Human sacrifices are made 4 times a year. These human sacrifices are made on November 1 (called Samain) celebrating winter's start; February 1 (called Imbalc) celebrating winter's leavetaking; May 1 (called Beltane) celebrating spring's planting; and August 1 (called Lugnasad) celebrating the time of harvest. Condemned criminals are typical sacrifices.

Druid groves are the only places where druids can use their *commune with nature* spell. These places are often guarded by a group of wild boars and their mates. The larger and more important the grove, the larger the pack of wild boars. These animals are under the complete control of the druids that use the grove.

Druids of the sixth level or less wear light blue robes, while druids of higher levels always wear white. Every druid wears a *torc* (ornamental neck ring), and it represents the god or goddess most favored by the druid. It is a work of respect to their deity, and the more powerful the druid, the better he or she makes the *torc*. The best ones are encrusted with precious gems and imparted with magical powers by their high-level owners (along the lines of a +1 or +2 protection ring or a talisman of some sort). Every druid has his or her own cauldron that they made as a first level druid. This is used to catch all the blood or sap of a sacrifice. The cauldrons of tenth level or higher druids act as *crystal balls* when filled with human blood. All druids of the eleventh, twelfth, thirteenth, and fourteenth levels will have the symbol of the wheel with a crossed spiral on all their tools, weapons, clothes, and anything else they use.

Celtic gods are very tolerant of the actions of their priests as long as such actions further the sect. Regard for nature is their prime concern and trifling with nature in any way harmful is reason for punishment.

Druids consider themselves an elite group, separate from all other humans. They do not mingle with others, and are only allowed to mate with worshipers within their sect.

DAGDA *(dozen king)*

Greater god

ARMOR CLASS: −4
MOVE: 12''
HIT POINTS: 400
NO. OF ATTACKS: 2
DAMAGE/ATTACK: 5-50 (+14)
SPECIAL ATTACKS: See below
SPECIAL DEFENSES: Nil
MAGIC RESISTANCE: 80%
SIZE: M (6')
ALIGNMENT: Neutral
WORSHIPER'S ALIGN: All types of
  neutral beings
SYMBOL: Bubbling cauldron
PLANE: Concordant Opposition
CLERIC/DRUID: 15th level cleric/14th
  level druid
FIGHTER: 18th level fighter
MAGIC-USER/ILLUSIONIST: 15th level
  in each
THIEF/ASSASSIN: Nil
MONK/BARD: 20th level bard
PSIONIC ABILITY: II
S: 25 (+7, +14) I: 25 W: 25 D: 23 C: 25 CH: 25

This god is the ruler of a very loose pantheon of gods. His two primary attributes are the ability to separate himself into 12 distinct and powerful entities. All 12 are fully aware and mobile, but 11 are ethereal in nature and roam the earth with unlimited range, constantly supplying information to Dagda. These beings have all the qualities of the original, but they must stay in the ethereal state at all times.

His other attributes include unlimited use of *shape change*, *telepathy*, and *legend lore*. He is very fond of walking the earth in the form of a shabbily dressed man with a large club.

Dagda has the strength to break anything in his two hands. He uses his club in all battles and while it does 5-50 when striking plus his strength bonus of 14 points, it is also magical in that when the large end touches a being it acts as a *death spell*. The small end is able to raise the dead, no matter how long ago the being died. Only a portion of the body is needed.

He can summon forth a cauldron that enables him to brew any nonmagical liquid or food, and he sings with a sentient harp that talks in the common tongue and can *control weather*.

ARAWN *(god of the dead)* ''The Dark One''

Greater god

ARMOR CLASS: −4
MOVE: 15''
HIT POINTS: 325
NO. OF ATTACKS: 2
DAMAGE/ATTACK: 2-20 (+11)
SPECIAL ATTACKS: See below
SPECIAL DEFENSES: See below
MAGIC RESISTANCE: 75%
SIZE: M (7')
ALIGNMENT: Lawful evil
WORSHIPER'S ALIGN: All beings
  worshiping death
SYMBOL: A black star on a gray background
PLANE: The Prime Material Plane
CLERIC/DRUID: 20th level cleric/14th
  level druid
FIGHTER: 17th level ranger
MAGIC-USER/ILLUSIONIST: See
  below
THIEF/ASSASSIN: Nil
MONK/BARD: 15th level bard
PSIONIC ABILITY: VI
S: 23 (+5, +11) I: 24 W: 23 D: 25 C: 24 CH: 20

Arawn appears as a normal man and lives upon an island in the sea that only the dead can find. His main attribute is the ability to flash 2 *death spells* from his eyes at any time, striking independent targets if he chooses. He is able to use any spell of up to the third level as a 20th level magic-user. The god will appear if someone restores to life a person he wants to stay in his domain (a 2% chance of this per level of the dead person, if he or she worshiped one of the Celtic gods), and he will either fight for the dead person or offer a substitute from the vast ranks of the dead (there is a 25% chance of this offer being made). He is immune to any magical or clerical spell causing direct damage to the body.

He fights with a +3 club that strikes for 2-20 points of damage plus his strength bonus of 11 points. Any being touching him with a magical weapon dies (saving throw applicable).

BRIGIT (goddess of fire and poetry)

Lesser goddess

ARMOR CLASS: −4
MOVE: 12''
HIT POINTS: 325
NO. OF ATTACKS: 3/2
DAMAGE/ATTACK: 2-20 (+14)
SPECIAL ATTACKS: See below
SPECIAL DEFENSES: See below
MAGIC RESISTANCE: 50%
SIZE: M (6')
ALIGNMENT: Neutral
WORSHIPER'S ALIGN: Beings
    worshiping fire and poetry
SYMBOL: Female form bathed in fire
PLANE: Concordant Opposition
CLERIC/DRUID: 14th level druid
FIGHTER: 12th level fighter
MAGIC-USER/ILLUSIONIST: See
    below
THIEF/ASSASSIN: Nil
MONK/BARD: 18th level bard
PSIONIC ABILITY: VI
S: 25 (+7, +14) I: 22 W: 22 D: 25 C: 24 CH: 25

Brigit appears as a tall woman with flame-colored hair. She can use any fire spell as a 35th level spell-caster. She has +5 armor in the form of tongues of flame. She loves to hear poetry sung on the battlefield and there is a 5% chance that she will favor a singer of an original composition by raising him 1 level for the length of the battle. Brigit is immune to any attack involving fire, cold, petrification, or dragon breath.

In battle, she becomes surrounded with flame that will cause 30 points of damage to all who come within 30 feet of her. All weapons that are less than +3 will melt when touching her. She carries a staff that turns into a tongue of flame at her command and it does 2-20 points of damage when striking.

Note: if any players wish to worship Brigit (and possibly catch her attention) by singing during battle, the DM should require that the player make up an original battle-song on the spot and sing it while engaging in strenuous activity.

CU CHULAINN (hero)

ARMOR CLASS: −1
MOVE: 15''
HIT POINTS: 150
NO. OF ATTACKS: 2
DAMAGE/ATTACK: 4-40 (+8)
SPECIAL ATTACKS: Nil
SPECIAL DEFENSES: See below
MAGIC RESISTANCE: 20%
SIZE: M (6½')
ALIGNMENT: Neutral good
CLERIC/DRUID: Nil
FIGHTER: 18th level ranger
MAGIC-USER/ILLUSIONIST: 12th level
    illusionist
THIEF/ASSASSIN: Nil
MONK/BARD: 8th level bard
PSIONIC ABILITY: Nil
    Attack/Defense Modes: Nil
S: 20 (+3, +8) I: 17 W: 16 D: 19 C: 18 CH: 17

Cu Chulainn in battle always uses his spear called Gae Bolg, made from the bones of a sea dragon. The spear is a +4 weapon, and when holding it he cannot be surprised. None but Cu Chulainn can wield Gae Bolg. It does 4-40 points of damage. In battle, he shines with a brilliance that makes it impossible for his mortal enemies to look directly at him (−4 on their chances to hit).

The hero exists to fight giants and right wrongs all over the countryside. He often appears when all hope is lost.

DIANCECHT (physician of the gods)

Lesser god

ARMOR CLASS: −1
MOVE: 12''
HIT POINTS: 300
NO. OF ATTACKS: 1
DAMAGE/ATTACK: 3-30 (+10)
SPECIAL ATTACKS: Nil
SPECIAL DEFENSES: See below
MAGIC RESISTANCE: 100%
SIZE: M (6')
ALIGNMENT: Lawful good
WORSHIPER'S ALIGN: Beings that use
    the healing arts
SYMBOL: Crossed oak and mistletoe
    branches
PLANE: Concordant Opposition
CLERIC/DRUID: 25th level cleric/14th
    level druid
FIGHTER: 14th level fighter
MAGIC-USER/ILLUSIONIST: 12th level
    magic-user
THIEF/ASSASSIN: Nil
MONK/BARD: 10th level bard
PSIONIC ABILITY: VI
S: 22 (+4, +10) I: 25 W: 25 D: 20 C: 23 CH: 24

Diancecht appears as a young man. He can heal any wound or restore any dead being, no matter how long dead. The god will appear whenever any Celtic deity summons him to help. Clerics of the Celtic gods with great power (12th level or above) have a 10% chance of summoning him if they swear to take a year-long pilgrimage to heal *all* things knowing hurt, including beings of opposite alignment). Failure to fulfill this will result in the god's revenge. His power will not work on beings who have had their head taken away. He never fights in large battles, but has fought with Arawn over some of his dead. In these battles, Diancecht has always won. He is immune to anything that does less than one-fourth of his hit points in damage to his body in one strike.

He fights with a +3 spear that does 3-30 points when it hits, but he is hardly ever attacked because he will heal friends and enemies alike during a battle.

DUNATIS (god of the mountains and peaks)

Lesser god

ARMOR CLASS: −10
MOVE: 24''
HIT POINTS: 350
NO. OF ATTACKS: 2
DAMAGE/ATTACK: 8-80 or by
    weapon type
SPECIAL ATTACKS: See below
SPECIAL DEFENSES: See below
MAGIC RESISTANCE: 10%
SIZE: M (6')
ALIGNMENT: Neutral
WORSHIPER'S ALIGN: Neutral
SYMBOL: A red sun-capped mountain
    peak
PLANE: Concordant Opposition
CLERIC/DRUID: 15th level cleric
FIGHTER: 18th level fighter
MAGIC-USER/ILLUSIONIST: Nil
THIEF/ASSASSIN: Nil
MONK/BARD: 20th level bard
PSIONIC ABILITY: VI
S: 25 (+7, +14) I: 20 W: 22 D: 20 C: 24 CH: 23

This god always appears as a normal man. His main attribute is the power to raise a mountain peak from a flat plain, or flatten a giant mountain into a prairie. This is done instantaneously and was often done to destroy forts and the like.

He enters battle using +4 armor and shield, and his weapons are boulders he forms instantly from thin air. He throws these up to 1,000 yards with great accuracy, doing 8-80 points of damage. He is immune to paralysis, petrification, and attacks involving *charming*.

GOIBHNIE *(blacksmith of the gods)*

Lesser god

ARMOR CLASS: —4
MOVE: 9''
HIT POINTS: 329
NO. OF ATTACKS: 2
DAMAGE/ATTACK: 3-30 (+14)
SPECIAL ATTACKS: See below
SPECIAL DEFENSES: *Immune to physical weapons*
MAGIC RESISTANCE: 75%
SIZE: M (6')
ALIGNMENT: *Neutral*
WORSHIPER'S ALIGN: *Neutrals and workers of metal*
SYMBOL: *Giant mallet over sword*
PLANE: *Concordant Opposition*
CLERIC/DRUID: *14th level druid*
FIGHTER: *18th level fighter*
MAGIC-USER/ILLUSIONIST: *Nil*
THIEF/ASSASSIN: *Nil*
MONK/BARD: *15th level bard*
PSIONIC ABILITY: *VI*
S: 25 (+7, +14) I: 24 W: 23 D: 20 C: 25 CH: 19

This god appears as a hugely proportioned man. His main attribute is the ability to make weapons and amulets of great power for the gods and the very few mortals he favors. The weapons he makes never miss their target and the amulets have the power to nullify any one specific spell. If Goibhnie's weapons are used to attempt an impossible hit (like a sword strike from 200 yards away), the weapon will hit, but will then shatter and bring on the wielder the instant wrath of the god in the form of a thunder bolt (doing 50 points of damage, no saving throw).

It is impossible to wear more than one of Goibhnie's amulets at a time, and if this is attempted, the amulets will shatter. Effects of the spell which an amulet is designed to protect against will never appear, or (in the case of something solid, such as a *wall of iron*) will turn to dust. An amulet can protect up to 500 persons and anything they carry, if their hands are linked in series.

Goibhnie's +4 spear does 3-30 points of damage plus his strength bonus of 14 points. The god has made himself immune to any damage done by physical weaponry of any type.

LUGH *"long handed" (god of generalities)*

Greater god

ARMOR CLASS: 0
MOVE: 12''
HIT POINTS: 375
NO. OF ATTACKS: 2
DAMAGE/ATTACK: See below
SPECIAL ATTACKS: See below
SPECIAL DEFENSES: See below
MAGIC RESISTANCE: 90%
SIZE: M (7')
ALIGNMENT: *Neutral*
WORSHIPER'S ALIGN: *Neutral*
SYMBOL: *A pair of long hands*
PLANE: *Concordant Opposition*
CLERIC/DRUID: *Nil/see below*
FIGHTER: *19th level ranger*
MAGIC-USER/ILLUSIONIST: *Nil*
THIEF/ASSASSIN: *Nil*
MONK/BARD: *19th level bard*
PSIONIC ABILITY: *VI*
S: 23 (+5, +11) I: 25 W: 24 D: 25 C: 24 CH: 24

This god is unique among the gods in that he can use any one attribute of *any being* he has ever met. He appears as a tall man with very large hands.

He never uses armor, and in battle he depends on his one power to defeat his foe. He is immune to any type of *control, petrification,* or *paralyzation*.

Lugh is a druidical ideal, and more fully understands druidism than any other entity. He casts druidical spells at the 30th level of magic use (an unattainable level for any other being), and has an unlimited number of these spells.

MANANNAN MAC LIR *(god of the sea)*

Greater god

ARMOR CLASS: —2
MOVE: 12''//48''
HIT POINTS: 389
NO. OF ATTACKS: 2
DAMAGE/ATTACK: See below
SPECIAL ATTACKS: *Summon sea creatures*
SPECIAL DEFENSES: See below
MAGIC RESISTANCE: 75%
SIZE: M (6')
ALIGNMENT: *Chaotic neutral*
WORSHIPER'S ALIGN: *Beings using the sea*
SYMBOL: *A wave of white water on a green background*
PLANE: *Concordant Opposition*
CLERIC/DRUID: *25th level cleric*
FIGHTER: *16th level fighter*
MAGIC-USER/ILLUSIONIST: *See below*
THIEF/ASSASSIN: *Nil*
MONK/BARD: *Nil*
PSIONIC ABILITY: *VI*
S: 24 (+6, +12) I: 24 W: 23 D: 21 C: 24 CH: 22

This god appears as a large red-bearded man. He commonly goes into battle wearing +5 armor of sea shells. He uses a trident that absorbs moisture from the bodies that it hits (draining ¼ of the total amount of the victim's original hit points). When fighting his enemies, the fire giants, he uses a sword called Retaliator, that kills every time it hits (magic saving throw applicable), and does 3-30 points of damage (plus strength bonus) even if the save is made.

His main attribute is the power to call on any non-godlike creature of the sea to fight for him at any time and in numbers up to 50. These creatures must, however, get to the battle under their own power. He is immune to any type of magical device attack while in salt water.

MATH *(magic-user)*

ARMOR CLASS: 6
MOVE: 12''
HIT POINTS: 100
NO. OF ATTACKS: 1
DAMAGE/ATTACK: See below
SPECIAL ATTACKS: See below
SPECIAL DEFENSES: *Nil*
MAGIC RESISTANCE: 35%
SIZE: M (5½')
ALIGNMENT: *Neutral*
CLERIC/DRUID: *6th level druid*
FIGHTER: *4th level fighter*
MAGIC-USER/ILLUSIONIST: *30th level magic-user/10th level illusionist*
THIEF/ASSASSIN: *Nil*
MONK/BARD: *Nil*
PSIONIC ABILITY: *200*
   Attack/Defense Modes: *A, B, C,/ F, G, H, I*
S: 18 (+1, +2) I: 18 W: 18 D: 18 C: 18 CH: 18

Math is the greatest of all the legendary wizards in Celtic myth. He has given himself the power to hear anything said in a breeze anywhere in the world. He has done so much for the gods that he has been given a *Torc of the Gods* (q.v.).

When forced to fight, he uses a rod that turns any being touched by it into a pool of water (permanently), magic saving throw applicable. He also enjoys using *polymorph others* to turn opponents into animals.

MORRIGAN (goddess of war)

Lesser goddess

ARMOR CLASS: —4
MOVE: *Variable (see below)*
HIT POINTS 388
NO. OF ATTACKS: 2
DAMAGE/ATTACK: 3-36 (+14)
SPECIAL ATTACKS: *See below*
SPECIAL DEFENSES: *Nil*
MAGIC RESISTANCE: 50%
SIZE: *M (6')*
ALIGNMENT: *Neutral*
WORSHIPER'S ALIGN: *All beings living by war*
SYMBOL: *2 crossed spears*
PLANE: *Concordant Opposition*
CLERIC/DRUID: *10th level druid*
FIGHTER: *20th level ranger*
MAGIC-USER/ILLUSIONIST: *Nil*
THIEF/ASSASSIN: *15th level assassin*
MONK/BARD: *10th level bard*
PSIONIC ABILITY: *VI*
S: 25 (+7, +14) I: 22 W: 19 D: 25 C: 24 CH: 21 or —1

This goddess appears as a well-proportioned woman with a hideous face. She has the power to deprive all who face her of their courage (as the *fear* spell). She can fight invisibly, see clearly over 15 miles, and travel on land at any speed she wishes when chasing a foe. It is said that she will strike dead (5% chance) any one of her worshipers who runs away from a battle she is watching (there is a 10% chance she is watching any given battle).

She uses 2 spears, one with a red head and one with a yellow head, that strike for 3-36 points each and never miss. She is immune to any attack by a magic-using being not of godlike power while she is in battle.

Morrigan's servants include four demi-goddesses of war, Fen, Neman, Badb, and Macha, who are identical to her in all regards save hit points (they each have 200).

NUADA (god of war) ''god of the Silver Hand''

Greater god

ARMOR CLASS: —4
MOVE: *15''*
HIT POINTS: 390
NO. OF ATTACKS: 3
DAMAGE/ATTACK: *See below*
SPECIAL ATTACKS: *See below*
SPECIAL DEFENSES: *Immune to charm-type spells*
MAGIC RESISTANCE: 10%
SIZE: *M (6')*
ALIGNMENT: *Neutral*
WORSHIPER'S ALIGN: *Warriors*
SYMBOL: *A silver hand on a black background*
PLANE: *Concordant Opposition*
CLERIC/DRUID: *10th level druid*
FIGHTER: *20th level ranger*
MAGIC-USER/ILLUSIONIST: *Nil*
THIEF/ASSASSIN: *12th level assassin*
MONK/BARD: *10th level bard*
PSIONIC ABILITY: *VI*
S: 25 (+7, +14) I: 22 W: 19 D: 25 C: 25 CH: 24

This god appears as a man with an artificial silver hand. He has the ability to give any weapon he holds a +3 bonus to hit and double the weapon's normal damaging power. When in battle, he detaches his hand of silver, and it will enter battle with a weapon as a *dancing sword*, hitting for 6-36 points of damage. He commonly uses a +4 suit of studded leather armor and a +5 sword that has the power to fend off any 3 weapons used against its master, no matter how powerful the weapons, and still attack without difficulty. The god is immune to any type of magical control spell.

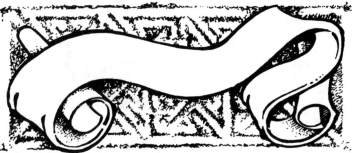

OGHMA (god of knowledge) ''The Binder, Patron of all Bards''

Greater god

ARMOR CLASS: —6
MOVE: *12''*
HIT POINTS: 310
NO. OF ATTACKS: 2
DAMAGE/ATTACK: *See below*
SPECIAL ATTACKS: *Nil*
SPECIAL DEFENSES: *Nil*
MAGIC RESISTANCE: 85%
SIZE: *M (6')*
ALIGNMENT: *Neutral*
WORSHIPER'S ALIGN: *Neutral*
SYMBOL: *An unfurled scroll*
PLANE: *Concordant Opposition*
CLERIC/DRUID: *15th level in each*
FIGHTER: *15th level fighter*
MAGIC-USER/ILLUSIONIST: *18th level in each*
THIEF/ASSASSIN: *Nil*
MONK/BARD: *20th level bard*
PSIONIC ABILITY: *IV*
S: 25 (+7, +14)* I: 25 W: 25 D: 22 C: 20 CH: 23

   *See below

Oghma looks like an aged, white-haired man. He is the best wrestler of all the gods and considered their champion when fights with giants occur. He is also patron of things creative and beautiful in man and woman alike. His love of song, story, and poetry causes him to often visit the earth in human shape and travel from hold to hold seeking especially gifted people. There is a 1% chance that he is listening to an original composition when it is sung, and there is a 5% chance that if a song or tale was spread by others he would hear it and reward the creator with great wealth in the form of gold "strangely" given by the lord of the particular hold that the person was visiting and performing at.

His two main powers are the ability to answer any question after a short period of study (the more difficult the question, the longer it takes) and the fact that he knows the secret name of any non-godlike creature. In Celtic mythology, everything has a name it gives to the world, and another secret name that links it to its soul. If any being knows the secret name, he or she can control the creature or being or simply make them die (save vs. death applicable).

In battle he wears +4 chainmail and demands that all his enemies wrestle (grapple) with him. If they win, he leaves the battle. If he wins, they are forced to leave the battle. His strength is such that when facing any being, he will have equal to that being's strength plus his own.

Oghma is known as *The Binder* for his ability to successfully force demons and devils into a special prison of his making where they stay imprisoned until he wishes to bring them out.

SILVANUS *(god of the forests and nature)*

Greater god

ARMOR CLASS: –4
MOVE: 18" (48" through forests)
HIT POINTS: 333
NO. OF ATTACKS: 3/2
DAMAGE/ATTACK: 5-50 (+14)
SPECIAL ATTACKS: Nil
SPECIAL DEFENSES: Wolfhound (see below)
MAGIC RESISTANCE: 30%
SIZE: M (7')
ALIGNMENT: Neutral
WORSHIPER'S ALIGN: Dwellers of the forest
SYMBOL: A summer oak tree
PLANE: Concordant Opposition
CLERIC/DRUID: 14th level in each
FIGHTER: 13th level fighter
MAGIC-USER/ILLUSIONIST: 19th level illusionist
THIEF/ASSASSIN: Nil
MONK/BARD: 15th level bard
PSIONIC ABILITY: VI
S: 25 (+7, +14) I: 24 W: 25 D: 24 C: 25 CH: 23

Silvanus looks like a man with very long legs. He can control any number of animals and creatures of the forest with the sound of his voice. He has the power to make plants grow and/or shrink at any rate he wills. He wears armor made of leaves that act like +5 plate mail and his mallet is constantly with him. This +5 wooden weapon strikes for 5-50 points in his hands. A giant wolfhound fights at his side (AC 3, HD 10, hp 100, #AT 1, D 2-20; regenerates 5 hit points per melee round). It is so fast that no matter how many beings strike at his master, the dog will take the damage. It cannot block spells.

Silvanus is worshiped by druids and their followers, and he is a protector of the places of the druids: their groves, their villages and colleges, and their paths through the woods. There is a 1% chance that he will appear whenever harm is done to a high level druid or his or her grove.

TATHLUM

This weapon of war with magical properties can be made by anyone of the Celtic religions. First, cut off the head of an enemy and coat it with lime gotten from a lime pool in the former territory of the dead person, allowing several coats to dry to a rock hard ball. It takes one day to do each coat, and each coat takes one week to dry. When thrown at friends of the former owner of the head under bright sunshine, it will have the effect of doing damage up to ¼ of the original hit points of the person hit. If the person hit is a relative of the head, one-half of the hit points are taken away. This weapon is usable only once.

TORC OF THE GODS

This magical device made by Goibhnie allows the holder to *shape change* or *polymorph others*. This is similar to the other druidical torcs, but it is made of rare metals and bears a large gem (of a random type) set into the front.

THE WILD HUNT

The Wild Hunt exists in all the lands where Druids and their deities dwell. It is a physical manifestation of "life force" that always takes on the same form. The Hunt is made up of one huge black-skinned man with antlers growing from his head and his pack of hounds.

The Hunt appears whenever there is evil in the land (as in the case of an evil temple or an evil priest of the 12th level or greater coming into the area, or what the DM decides is a grossly evil act).

When the Hunt passes, the noise of the howling dogs or the Hunt Master's horn can be heard for miles in the night. If this noise is actively pursued by any being, they will become part of the Hunt when they sight the pack and its master! If the Hunt passes by any given being they must make a magic saving throw (on a 25% chance they will look at the pack) or join the Hunt. When any given being becomes part of the Hunt they may take on one of two roles: they will be the hunters or the hunted!

The Hunt always begins ten miles from the source of evil that "summons" it, and for each mile nearer the source of evil when the Hunt is spotted there is a 10% chance that the observing being will be the object of the Hunt instead of the hunter. The Hunt will always pass close by the source of evil that has created it (never going into a building, but going within inches of the building and passing by). After passing by, it will travel on in a random direction for ten more miles.

There will only be one Hunt on the Prime Material Plane on any given night, and it will always be drawn to the greatest evil in the Celtic area (decided upon by the referee). If the Hunt finds a being to hunt before finding the source of evil, it will attack that being to kill it, and then disappear as it reaches its summoning source. If the Hunt does not find a victim before it reaches the source, it will travel on for another ten miles and every being that sees it and does not make their saving throw vs. magic will have a 90% chance of becoming the hunted!

If after ten miles, no being becomes the hunted, the entire pack will turn on the nearest big game creature around (deer, stag, bear or anything partially dangerous and non-intelligent). All during this hunt, the beings that have come along with the Hunt must travel with the Master, and they must attack whatever becomes the hunted, even if it goes against their alignment! Thus, paladins might have to attack helpless women or the like. All beings that have been taken in as hunters will attack the quarry (whatever it may be) and if they do not succeed in killing the being, the Master and his hounds will take over (but only when all other hunters have been incapacitated) and they will either kill or be killed.

The magic of the Hunt will catch up and sweep along any who become part of it, so that, whether mounted or on foot, they will be able to keep up with the fast pace that the hounds set.

The Hunt generally pursues on the ground, but it has the ability to run right into the air to fly over obstacles or especially difficult terrain.

When the hunted being has been run down, there is an instant melee to the death. All participants must fight on to the death to the best of their abilities (no holding back).

The only ways to prevent being killed as the object of the Hunt are to run out of the 10 mile radius of the source of evil, to elude the pack until morning, or to slay the Master and his pack.

All beings that have been in any part of the Hunt have a 50% chance of becoming ensnared again with every sighting of the Master and his pack.

There have been legends of epic battles between the Master and his hounds and some of the greater heroes of the past. In these legends, the Master and his pack have been slain, only to disappear in the darkness and appear somewhere else the next night, proving that the force that creates the Hunt is eternal.

THE MASTER OF THE HUNT

ARMOR CLASS: *0*
MOVE: *18"*
HIT POINTS: *100*
NO. OF ATTACKS: *2*
DAMAGE/ATTACK: *By weapon type*
SPECIAL ATTACKS: *Nil*
SPECIAL DEFENSES: *Nil*
MAGIC RESISTANCE: *25%*
SIZE: *M (7')*
ALIGNMENT: *Neutral*
CLERIC/DRUID: *Nil*
FIGHTER: *15th level ranger*
MAGIC-USER/ILLUSIONIST: *Nil*
THIEF/ASSASSIN: *Nil*
MONK/BARD: *Nil*
PSIONIC ABILITY: *Nil*
   Attack/Defense Modes: *Nil*
S: *18 (00) (+3, +6)* I: *18* W: *18* D: *18* C: *18* CH: *15*

The Master has jet black skin and glowing green eyes. His head is crowned by a set of stag antlers, and he wears a suit of black leather. The Master never speaks.

He runs a few feet behind his pack of hounds and will sound his horn at every 1 mile increment in his chase. He uses a +3 spear in battle.

THE PACK OF THE WILD HUNT

FREQUENCY: *Uncommon*
NO. APPEARING: *20*
ARMOR CLASS: *5*
MOVE: *18"*
HIT DICE/POINTS: *30 hp*
% IN LAIR: *0%*
TREASURE TYPE: *Nil*
NO. OF ATTACKS: *1*
DAMAGE/ATTACK: *2-8*
SPECIAL ATTACKS: *Nil*
SPECIAL DEFENSES: *Nil*
MAGIC RESISTANCE: *15%*
INTELLIGENCE: *Average*
ALIGNMENT: *Neutral*
SIZE: *L (4' at shoulder)*
PSIONIC ABILITY: *Nil*
   Attack/Defense Modes: *Nil*
LEVEL/X.P. VALUE: *VI/950 per hound*

These huge black hounds have licks of green fire for tongues and green fire for eyes. These flames do no damage but they make the whole Hunt cast an eerie green glow. The beasts will never attack the hunted until all the beings that have drawn themselves into the Hunt have had their chance to kill. If the pack is killed, the Master will then battle the being. The death of any member of the pack goes unnoticed by the rest and it disappears after the battle is over. The hounds attack as 8 hit dice monsters.

CENTRAL AMERICAN MYTHOS

The Aztec and Maya presented the world with an interesting set of closely related gods, goddesses and creatures that have a moral background similar to that of other ancient mythoi. The beings are just as evil or just as good; the difference seems to be that they are not moved by anything resembling human thoughts and feelings, unlike the deities of other mythoi. They act only upon their own inscrutable motives.

These beings are said to have come from the stars, and their "plane of origin" is not the same as other mythologies. For the purposes of this work, we will assume that these gods come from the Prime Material Plane of a parallel universe. *Commune* or *gate* spells used by the clerics of these deities will only connect with this parallel universe and the plane where their gods dwell. There is no way that others can summon these deities if they do not know the special ceremonies used in contacting them. Also, these deities' unusual nature makes it impossible for them to travel on any planes but the ones that they have worshipers on.

The clerics of this mythos are the elite of the populace, and even the lowest levels have absolute authority over any of the peasants. Along the same lines, any cleric of a higher level may give orders to lesser clerics of the same deity with complete freedom. Though all sects must usually work together, there is much clandestine infighting between groups for followers among the rich and poor alike.

Rituals are performed every 20 days, and sacrifices take many forms, from food in the spring and fall seasons to humans before and after battles and during the rainy winter months. The public is forced to attend these rituals, and they are always held at the temple of the appropriate god. All temples are built on the step pyramid design, with entrances at the bottom at the four compass points and east of the altar at the top.

Divine punishment of erring clerics is swift. Small mistakes, like the breaking of clerical laws or defeats in personal combat (duels) result in immediate loss of some wealth and/or experience points. Major failures, in the form of lost battles, failed quests, or alignment changes, will cause a cleric to be stripped of all possessions and levels and require him or her to start again from the first level of experience.

First level clerics must choose a compass direction for their own (east, west, north or south), and this is the direction that they pray to, meditate towards, and start their quests towards. From then on, any attacks they make or spells they cast in that direction will have +1 added to their chance of success, i.e. a +1 chance to hit, or –1 subtracted from a target's saving throw. When in combat or other situations where the direction is not chosen or dictated by circumstances, the DM should roll a 4-sided die to determine which compass point the cleric is facing. Clerics of the east must wear red clothes at all times, clerics of the south must wear yellow, clerics of the west must wear black, and clerics of the north must wear white.

QUETZALCOATL (god of the air) "Law Giver"

Greater god

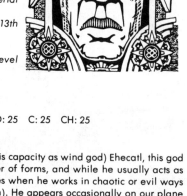

ARMOR CLASS: –2
MOVE: *Infinite*
HIT POINTS: *400*
NO. OF ATTACKS: *Variable*
DAMAGE/ATTACK: *Variable*
SPECIAL ATTACKS: *See below*
SPECIAL DEFENSES: *See below*
MAGIC RESISTANCE: *75%*
SIZE: *L (15')*
ALIGNMENT: *Lawful neutral*
WORSHIPER'S ALIGN: *All alignments*
SYMBOL: *Feathered serpent*
PLANE: *A parallel Prime Material Plane*
CLERIC/DRUID: *25th level cleric/13th level druid*
FIGHTER: *20th level paladin*
MAGIC-USER/ILLUSIONIST: *20th level in each*
THIEF/ASSASSIN: *20th level thief*
MONK/BARD: *20th level bard*
PSIONIC ABILITY: *I*
S: 25 (+7, +14) I: 25 W: 25 D: 25 C: 25 CH: 25

Also known as Kukulcan, or (in his capacity as wind god) Ehecatl, this god appears in a bewildering number of forms, and while he usually acts as per his alignment, there are times when he works in chaotic or evil ways (making it very hard to align him). He appears occasionally on our plane and works closely with his worshipers against other gods. When in battle, the god will usually assume a monster form and use that to attack with, but if he suffers a great loss of hit points, he will take the form that he had assumed at the beginning of the battle and quadruple its powers and re-attack. He fights until his side has won the battle or until he has been personally defeated in combat.

He cannot be hurt by creatures of the same form he is using; in other words, when he is in the form of a dragon, he cannot be hurt by any dragon type, and when he is in the form of a magic-user, he cannot be hurt by magical spells.

Quetzalcoatl was the mightiest god of the mythos, though his claim is disputed by the followers of Tezcatlipoca, his arch-enemy. Quetzalcoatl is patron of the arts and the founder of metallurgy.

CAMAXTLI (god of fate)

Greater god

ARMOR CLASS: −2
MOVE: 15"/24"
HIT POINTS: 350
NO. OF ATTACKS: 0
DAMAGE/ATTACK: Nil
SPECIAL ATTACKS: See below
SPECIAL DEFENSES: See below
MAGIC RESISTANCE: 50%
SIZE: L (15')
ALIGNMENT: Neutral
WORSHIPER'S ALIGN: All alignments
SYMBOL: Human figure holding the
    sun
PLANE: A parallel Prime Material
    Plane
CLERIC/DRUID: 20th level cleric
FIGHTER: 12th level paladin
MAGIC-USER/ILLUSIONIST: 18th level
    magic-user
THIEF/ASSASSIN: Nil
MONK/BARD: Nil
PSIONIC ABILITY: I
S: 23   I: 24   W: 23   D: 23   C: 23   CH: 23

This human-appearing god is able to see the past and future of any being and put this information to use in his own way. He is not allowed to kill any being, but he can look into that being's past and discover what force caused the most physical damage to that being, and then recreate that force exactly to again do the same amount of damage.

If the proper sacrifices are made in precious metals in an amount of 500,000 gold pieces or more, there is a 25% chance that the god will look favorably upon the sacrificer and do what he can to help for a short period. The sacrifice is always cast into the beyond by the most powerful means available (i.e. a random *teleport* spell, a *limited wish*, or the like).

In the presence of any light, Camaxtli regenerates 5 hit points per melee round.

CAMAZOTZ (bat god)

Lesser god

ARMOR CLASS: −2
MOVE: Infinite
HIT POINTS: 362
NO. OF ATTACKS: 3
DAMAGE/ATTACK: 2-20/2-20/3-30
SPECIAL ATTACKS: Paralysis
SPECIAL DEFENSES: See below
MAGIC RESISTANCE: 50%
SIZE: L (15')
ALIGNMENT: Chaotic evil
WORSHIPER'S ALIGN: Chaotic evil
SYMBOL: Giant bat
PLANE: A parallel Prime Material
    Plane
CLERIC/DRUID: 15th level cleric
FIGHTER: 10th level fighter
MAGIC-USER/ILLUSIONIST: 20th level
    in each
THIEF/ASSASSIN: 15th level assassin
MONK/BARD: Nil
PSIONIC ABILITY: I
S: 19 (+3, +7)   I: 20   W: 18   D: 20   C: 24   CH: −2

This god appears as a huge bat and is always found with 1,000 normal bats flying around him. He may be tempted to comply to a *summons* by a being that offers many insects for his followers. Priests can actually appease this deity by offering him *insect plagues*.

His claws do 2-20/2-20 and a save is necessary versus (paralytic) poison; his bite does 3-30 with the same save. Any weapons cast in the darkness at him will not touch or harm him.

CHALCHIUHTLICUE (goddess of running water and love)

Lesser goddess

ARMOR CLASS: −2
MOVE: Infinite
HIT POINTS: 200
NO. OF ATTACKS: 3/2
DAMAGE/ATTACK: 1-4
SPECIAL ATTACKS: See below
SPECIAL DEFENSES: Nil
MAGIC RESISTANCE: 95%
SIZE: M (6½')
ALIGNMENT: Chaotic good
WORSHIPER'S ALIGN: All alignments
SYMBOL: Jade fish
PLANE: A parallel Prime Material
    Plane
CLERIC/DRUID: 20th level cleric
FIGHTER: 12th level paladin
MAGIC-USER/ILLUSIONIST: 20th level
    magic-user
THIEF/ASSASSIN: Nil
MONK/BARD: 15th level bard
PSIONIC ABILITY: I
S: 15   I: 24   W: 25   D: 25   C: 23   CH: 25

Also known as the "goddess of the jade petticoat", this goddess is not only a water deity, she is the goddess of life and chaste love. In any of these aspects, she uses her power for the good of the beings that she is favoring at the time. Those that sacrifice to her (of any alignment) can expect her help if the proper forms are observed. She is especially eager to aid when healing or love are the factors to be dealt with. She also has the unusual ability to transform 3-300 beings into any single form she wishes (usually fish). This ability is used only to save the lives of devout worshipers.

The proper ritual sacrifice to her requires the tossing of jade (the higher the quality the better the response) into a bottomless pool of water in one of several such areas in the mountains. This is done by the light of the full moon, and there must be no other being within a mile of the area. Clerics that perform this ceremony for the needy have a 25% chance of success, while normal worshipers have only a 1% chance. It may be attempted four times a year.

Chalchiutlicue is the wife of Tlaloc.

HUHUETEOTL (fire god)

Greater god

ARMOR CLASS: −2
MOVE: 18"/24"
HIT POINTS: 373
NO. OF ATTACKS: 0
DAMAGE/ATTACK: Nil
SPECIAL ATTACKS: Light beam
SPECIAL DEFENSES: Nil
MAGIC RESISTANCE: 80%
SIZE: L (15')
ALIGNMENT: Chaotic evil
WORSHIPER'S ALIGN: Chaotic evil
SYMBOL: Image of the god
PLANE: A parallel Prime Material
    Plane
CLERIC/DRUID: 15th level cleric/10th
    level druid
FIGHTER: 10th level fighter
MAGIC-USER/ILLUSIONIST: 15th level
    in each
THIEF/ASSASSIN: 15th level assassin
MONK/BARD: 10th level monk
PSIONIC ABILITY: I
S: 23   I: 23   W: 23   D: 23   C: 23   CH: 9

Physically, Huhueteotl appears to be a demon with a humanoid body, reptilian facial features, flames shooting all around him, and hair patches where his red gem armor does not cover him.

The god requires frequent human sacrifices and will punish his erring worshipers with destructive flames whenever a whim takes him. Sacrifices are in the form of valuable articles of clothing or gems and jewels, and they are always thrown into molten areas in mountains. Sacrifices are usually made in the waning of the moon.

The god may cast a beam of searing light once per round that does 50 points of damage per strike and has a range of 2 miles.

The god is also in charge of keeping time in motion, and in this capacity must have a special sacrifice of gems, feather robes, and humans every 52 years. During the fifty-second year, the god has the ability to stop the motion of any one thing in any single day. In this stopped state, that thing cannot be harmed by any force in the Prime Material Plane.

HUITZILOPOCHTLI *(god of war)*

Lesser god

ARMOR CLASS: –3
MOVE: 12''/24''
HIT POINTS: 389
NO. OF ATTACKS: 3
DAMAGE/ATTACK: 3-30 (+14)
SPECIAL ATTACKS: Nil
SPECIAL DEFENSES: See below
MAGIC RESISTANCE: 50%
SIZE: L (15')
ALIGNMENT: Neutral
WORSHIPER'S ALIGN: Warriors
SYMBOL: Eagle
PLANE: A parallel Prime Material Plane
CLERIC/DRUID: 13th level in each
FIGHTER: 20th level ranger
MAGIC-USER/ILLUSIONIST: 8th level in each
THIEF/ASSASSIN: 15th level assassin
MONK/BARD: 10th level monk
PSIONIC ABILITY: I
S: 25 (+7, +14) I: 23 W: 20 D: 25 C: 25 CH: 25

This god may appear on any battlefield where his worshipers are fighting and aid them, but this will not be in such a manner as to make sure his side will win. He can rarely be called upon for any non-warlike situation and can never be *communed* with.

His battle axe does 3-30 points (plus strength bonus) with each of his 3 strikes per melee round. All attacks on his rear will return on the attacker and never miss.

The god is usually depicted fully armed in blue jade armor. His axe is bright red and his headdress is made of hummingbird feathers.

Sacrifices are made to him only in battle and only by fighting clerics. When the god chooses to appear for that battle (on a 5% chance) he will take the body of a dead warrior that won great victories either during that battle or in the past. No matter what the outcome of the battle (i.e. win, lose, or draw) that warrior will be raised and live a long and lucky life. This luck takes the form of +3 on all saving throws.

HUNAPU AND XBALANQUE *(twin heroes)*

ARMOR CLASS: 2
MOVE: 12''
HIT POINTS: 150 each
NO. OF ATTACKS: 3/2
DAMAGE/ATTACK: 1-10 (+6)
SPECIAL ATTACKS: Poisoned blow gun darts
SPECIAL DEFENSES: Resistant to cold and fire
MAGIC RESISTANCE: Standard
SIZE: M (5½')
ALIGNMENT: Lawful good
CLERIC/DRUID: 10th level druids
FIGHTER: 10th level rangers
MAGIC-USER/ILLUSIONIST: 8th level magic-users
THIEF/ASSASSIN: Nil
MONK/BARD: Nil
PSIONIC ABILITY: Nil
    Attack/Defense Modes: Nil
S: 18 (00) (+3, +6) I: 16 W: 12 D: 18 C: 18 CH: 18

These twin brothers are legendary for their thirst for revenge. Their father was killed by beings of the underworld and so they went down and defeated these beings in games and battle. They were expert with the blow gun and could shoot their darts up to 200 yards away with accuracy (short range = 50 yards, medium range = 135 yards).

In hand-to-hand combat they use axes which inflict 1-10 points of damage, but they try hard not to get close enough to be forced into that situation. They are resistant to cold and fire so that one point is subtracted from every die of damage they take.

ITZAMNA *(god of medicine)*

Greater god

ARMOR CLASS: –3
MOVE: Infinite
HIT POINTS: 369
NO. OF ATTACKS: 2
DAMAGE/ATTACK: 3-24
SPECIAL ATTACKS: See below
SPECIAL DEFENSES: See below
MAGIC RESISTANCE: 85%
SIZE: Variable
ALIGNMENT: Neutral good
WORSHIPER'S ALIGN: Good
SYMBOL: Red hand
PLANE: A parallel Prime Material Plane
CLERIC/DRUID: 22nd level cleric
FIGHTER: 13th level paladin
MAGIC-USER/ILLUSIONIST: 15th level magic-user
THIEF/ASSASSIN: Nil
MONK/BARD: Nil
PSIONIC ABILITY: VI
S: 21 (+4, +9) I: 24 W: 25 D: 17 C: 21 CH: 23

Itzamna normally appears to men in the guise of a toothless old man, with sunken cheeks and a Roman nose, leaning on a crooked staff. However, he may also assume the form of light in one of its myriad aspects, e.g. a blazing globe, a fading ember, or a dusty moonbeam, and when in this guise he may take on any size. Itzamna often travels in the world of men. He may see everything that transpires in the world if there is a light source present, much like a *wizard eye* spell.

Itzamna is the friend and benefactor of men, instructing mankind in medicine, drawing and letters. He is often called upon by his clerics to intercede for man with the other gods in times of calamities and sicknesses. In his dealings with other gods he rarely relies on the strength of his arms, using his wits to cause his fellow deities to react favorably towards man.

Itzamna is the son of the sun-god, Tezcatlipoca, and tries to temper his father's harsh dealings with man. If Itzamna is ever in a desperate situation he will call upon his father for help. The god of medicine is by no means a weakling and if battle is forced upon him he will strike with either his staff or with scintillating beams of light (depending upon his form) for 3-24 points of damage. Whenever he is attacked he will become surrounded by a nimbus of light which acts as a *protection from evil 6" radius* and as a *robe of scintillating colors*. In light form, Itzamna is intangible, and it requires +2 or better magical weapons to strike him. He is also capable of drawing any one *symbol* per round in the air.

Clerics of Itzamna will deal only with spells to bless and heal (abjuration and necromancy) or spells of a written nature (symbols). They are friends to all good creatures and are loath to do combat unless there is no other recourse. These clerics wear few garments or just a coarse robe and carry a staff and medicine pouch. Often they may be identified by a necklace with a red hand ornament. They are usually excellent scribes.

Ceremonies to Itzamna are held throughout the year, particularly in relation to the planting of crops. Sweet balsam is burned and squirrels are sacrificed to him.

MICTLANTECUHTLI (god of death)

Greater god

ARMOR CLASS: -2
MOVE: *Infinite*
HIT POINTS: 339
NO. OF ATTACKS: 2
DAMAGE/ATTACK: *See below*
SPECIAL ATTACKS: *See below*
SPECIAL DEFENSES: *Death aura*
MAGIC RESISTANCE: 95%
SIZE: *L (15')*
ALIGNMENT: *Lawful evil*
WORSHIPER'S ALIGN: *All alignments*
SYMBOL: *Dog totem (itzcuintli)*
PLANE: *A parallel Prime Material Plane*
CLERIC/DRUID: *14th level in each*
FIGHTER: *15th level ranger*
MAGIC-USER/ILLUSIONIST: *18th level in each*
THIEF/ASSASSIN: *15th level assassin*
MONK/BARD: *Nil*
PSIONIC ABILITY: *I*
S: 25 (+7, +14)   I: 24   W: 19   D: 23   C: 24   CH: -4

The god usually appears in a lich form, and no undead is able to resist his commands. At any given time, he can instantly summon 20-200 skeletons, 10-100 ghouls, 6-36 wights, and 2-5 spectres. He can be summoned only after at least 50 live human sacrifices have been given the god in worship. The god demands these lives during the dark of the moon and requires them from the ranks of his worshipers.

In battle, touching his body with anything causes the toucher to make a saving throw versus death. The god will usually attack with spells when personally in battle, but if enemies dare touch him, he will draw out a red jade rod that acts as a *hammer of thunderbolts* as per the **DUNGEON MASTERS GUIDE.**

TEZCATLIPOCA (sun god)

Greater god

ARMOR CLASS: -2
MOVE: *Infinite*
HIT POINTS: 400
NO. OF ATTACKS: 2
DAMAGE/ATTACK: 3-30
SPECIAL ATTACKS: *Nil*
SPECIAL DEFENSES: *Nil*
MAGIC RESISTANCE: 85%
SIZE: *Variable*
ALIGNMENT: *Chaotic evil*
WORSHIPER'S ALIGN: *Chaotic evil*
SYMBOL: *Jaguar*
PLANE: *A parallel Prime Material Plane*
CLERIC/DRUID: *9th level cleric*
FIGHTER: *20th level fighter*
MAGIC-USER/ILLUSIONIST: *15th level magic-user*
THIEF/ASSASSIN: *15th level assassin*
MONK/BARD: *6th level bard*
PSIONIC ABILITY: *II*
S: 25 (+7, +14)   I: 25   W: 24   D: 25   C: 25   CH: 25

Tezcatlipoca (which means "the smoking mirror") is the god of the sun who ripens the crops but also brings drought and famine. Conversely, he is also the god of the moon and the night. Tezcatlipoca and his followers are always plotting the overthrow of Quetzalcoatl, and this god is the patron of treacherous schemings and betrayals.

Tezcatlipoca rarely takes on physical form, preferring to remain invisible and ethereal, but when he does it is usually as a giant jaguar or bear. In these forms he strikes with his claws for 3-30 points of damage each. He occasionally takes human form to masquerade as someone else in the furtherance of one of his schemes.

Once a year, at a great religious gathering, Tezcatlipoca's priests sacrifice a young, perfect human male and offer the god his heart. These sacrifices (usually war prisoners) are pampered and feted for a full year before the ritual. Though they are given almost anything they might desire during this period, they always end up on the altar.

Tezcatlipoca is a spreader of disorder and war, but also an originator of wealth.

TLALOC (rain god)

Greater god

ARMOR CLASS: -2
MOVE: 12"/24"
HIT POINTS: 377
NO. OF ATTACKS: 3/2
DAMAGE/ATTACK: *See below*
SPECIAL ATTACKS: *See below*
SPECIAL DEFENSES: *Nil*
MAGIC RESISTANCE: 50%
SIZE: *L (15')*
ALIGNMENT: *Lawful evil*
WORSHIPER'S ALIGN: *All who need rain*
SYMBOL: *Deer totem (mazatl)*
PLANE: *A parallel Prime Material Plane*
CLERIC/DRUID: *20th level cleric*
FIGHTER: *10th level fighter*
MAGIC-USER/ILLUSIONIST: *20th level magic-user*
THIEF/ASSASSIN: *Nil*
MONK/BARD: *Nil*
PSIONIC ABILITY: *I*
S: 20 (+3, +8)   I: 24   W: 23   D: 24   C: 24   CH: 19

With his great tusks and goggle eyes, Tlaloc's appearance is quite impressive. He wears all black but for a garland of white feathers.

At each full moon, a priest of Tlaloc sacrifices a child or baby to Tlaloc. Once a year, there is a great festival held in his honor. Numerous babies are bought or taken from the populace. These babies are sacrificed to Tlaloc, after which the priests cook and eat them. If the babies cry during the sacrifice, this is taken as a good sign that rain will be abundant during the coming year.

If the proper rituals and sacrifices have been followed to the letter, Tlaloc will usually grant his worshipers the rain they need. However, if he thinks his requirements have not been met, the people will be punished. Tlaloc has four pitchers of water: one filled with good water to make crops grow properly, one filled with water that contains spiders' eggs and webs and causes blight, one filled with water that turns to frost, and one with water that rots all fruit.

If pressed hard in battle, Tlaloc will summon a bolt of lightning, and he will fight with this against all comers. The bolt of lightning will do 40 points of damage to all those in armor, 30 points of damage to all those wearing clothes, and 20 points of damage to all naked flesh it hits. He uses the lightning bolt as if it were a weapon instead of a spell.

TLAZOLTEOTL (goddess of vice)

Lesser goddess

ARMOR CLASS: −3
MOVE: Infinite
HIT POINTS: 211
NO. OF ATTACKS: 0
DAMAGE/ATTACK: Nil
SPECIAL ATTACKS: Nil
SPECIAL DEFENSES: See below
MAGIC RESISTANCE: 25%
SIZE: L (15')
ALIGNMENT: Chaotic evil
WORSHIPER'S ALIGN: Chaotic evil
SYMBOL: Ocelot totem (ocelotl)
PLANE: A parallel Prime Material
    Plane
CLERIC/DRUID: 14th level in each
FIGHTER: Nil
MAGIC-USER/ILLUSIONIST: 15th level
    magic-user/25th level illusionist
THIEF/ASSASSIN: 15th level assassin
MONK/BARD: 15th level bard
PSIONIC ABILITY: I
S: 10 I: 25 W: 18 D: 25 C: 25 CH: 24/−5

When this goddess is under stress, rushed, or being attacked, she appears as an incredible monster, with a humanoid body, demonic face with fangs and blazing eyes, talons for the ends of her feet and hands, and a black warty skin with a slick, greasy look. This is an illusion, however. When she is at ease, before her worshipers, working on a victim, or in front of many strangers for one reason or another, she appears as a beautiful woman capable of inspiring desire in any male and jealous respect from any female. She tries very hard to ruin lawful good beings all over the Prime Material Plane, by tempting them and then destroying them when they succumb.

Though she may assassinate, she will never fight physically, and if met with beings that cannot be hurt by spells, she will teleport away. Her favorite attack is to use charm spells of all sorts. No evil being can even think of harming her, even if they are magically controlled.

XOCHIPILLI (god of gambling and chance) "Lord of Flowers"

Lesser god

ARMOR CLASS: −5
MOVE: Infinite
HIT POINTS: 381
NO. OF ATTACKS: 3/2
DAMAGE/ATTACK: 3-30
SPECIAL ATTACKS: Never misses
SPECIAL DEFENSES: See below
MAGIC RESISTANCE: 25%
SIZE: L (16')
ALIGNMENT: Neutral
WORSHIPER'S ALIGN: All alignments
SYMBOL: Monkey totem (ozomahtli)
PLANE: A parallel Prime Material
    Plane
CLERIC/DRUID: 12th level in each
FIGHTER: 12th level paladin
MAGIC-USER/ILLUSIONIST: 12th level
    in each
THIEF/ASSASSIN: 12th level thief
MONK/BARD: 12th level in each
PSIONIC ABILITY: I
S: 24 (+6, +12) I: 24 W: 20 D: 25 C: 24 CH: 25

Xochipilli almost always appears as a young man, and can often be found wandering among the people bestowing good and bad luck in the form of lost or granted saving throws. He is predominantly a peaceful being that gives a great deal of happiness to his followers. The god is most pleased with beings that take a large calculated risk.

His hand axe causes 3-30 points of damage per strike and he doesn't miss. Any weapon that has a chance of missing him will miss.

CHINESE MYTHOS

The title of this section is somewhat misleading, as the mythology of the Chinese is so vast and varied that it is impossible to cover it adequately and remain within our size restrictions. We have chosen the deities we feel most appropriate for inclusion.

The Chinese image of the Heavens is that of a great bureaucracy. Many of the deities exist to perform a special task and watch over a special area of life. Each god is supervised by a more important deity, who is responsible for seeing that things are done correctly. Every being is accountable to the Emperor of the Heavens. Every year the gods send reports to their supervisors, and it is not uncommon to be promoted or demoted for work done during the year.

Clerics play several roles in this master plan. They support the existing mortal government and preach the divinity of their emperor. The emperor in every case is not only the head of the state, but also the head of the church (thus gifted with high priest powers by the gods). The atonement for all sins by both the clerical staff and mortal worshipers is a matter of sacrificing items of value commensurate with the improper act. If the deed was severe enough (judge's option as to this in **AD&D** terms) the atonement might even be death. Clerics must travel about the countryside preaching to rich and poor alike.

CANON OF CHANGES

This is a book of the gods that deals with redistribution of matter and motion. It allows the reader to create any nonmagical object instantly when the command words are spoken. It takes 72 hours of constant reading to learn the words for any one given thing, and after uttering them it takes another 72 hours for another creation of even the same thing to take place. Only immortals have the constitutional stamina to read the passages for the length of time required.

DANCING SWORD OF LIGHTNING

This weapon behaves as a *dancing sword* as per the **DUNGEON MASTERS GUIDE**, except that its powers include shooting one lightning bolt from the tip per melee round which does 30 points per strike (saving throw applicable). It has unlimited charges and is the favorite weapon of the demigods of the air (when they can use it in their turn). It performs as a normal sword when held by mortals.

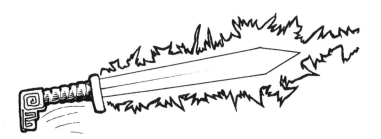

FIRE GEMS

These are extremely rare and magical hand-sized gems that shoot flame, doing 6-60 points of damage per strike. They have a maximum range of 50 yards and fire once per turn when the command words are spoken. Each gem has 2-12 charges.

GIANT BLACK PEARL

This 3 foot sphere negates all wind and earth turbulence in a one mile radius. It does this of its own accord and cannot be controlled to make it stop.

IRON WAND

This device makes all invisible things appear if within a 30' radius of the wand. It can make one object disappear as *dust of disappearance*; it also acts as a *staff of striking* with unlimited charges, and will grow to a length of 100' upon command and become roughened for easy climbing.

JADE SCEPTER OF DEFENDING

This device will defend the user from any number of material weapons, not permitting any one to strike its master while the holder concentrates on defense. While this concentration is going on, no other action may even be contemplated.

WIND FIRE WHEELS

There are 25 of these devices and they are used in large battles where the gods fear that they might be defeated. They are handed out by Shang-Ti to the demi-deities and their servants. They shoot fire and/or wind as a *staff of the magi*. For every 5 charges expended one hit point is drawn from the using being. They are 1 foot circular fans and are started by a command word from the holder.

SHANG-TI (*supreme god of the heavens, god of the sky and agriculture*)

Greater god

ARMOR CLASS: –2
MOVE: 24''/24''
HIT POINTS: 400
NO. OF ATTACKS: 2
DAMAGE/ATTACK: 3-36
SPECIAL ATTACKS: *Nil*
SPECIAL DEFENSES: *See below*
MAGIC RESISTANCE: 50%
SIZE: M (5½')
ALIGNMENT: *Lawful neutral*
WORSHIPER'S ALIGN: *All alignments*
SYMBOL: *Shaft of yellow light in a fist*
PLANE: *Nirvana*
CLERIC/DRUID: *13th level cleric*
FIGHTER: *15th level paladin*
MAGIC-USER/ILLUSIONIST: *20th level in each*
THIEF/ASSASSIN: *Nil*
MONK/BARD: *15th level bard*
PSIONIC ABILITY: *I*
S: 20 (+3, +8) I: 25 W: 25 D: 25 C: 25 CH: 20

Shang-Ti can sometimes be found travelling among mortals. On these occasions he appears to be an aged man with a long white beard, dressed in tattered robes. He also likes to float in the air ethereally, viewing cities and towns and the manner in which he is or isn't being worshiped.

All physical weapon attacks sent through the air at the god will turn and strike the sender. He uses a shaft of light as a weapon that does 3-36 points of damage per strike. Its range is sight.

In his aspects as god of the sky and agriculture, Shang-Ti has complete control over weather. He can instantly summon or banish any type of weather he desires.

Shang-Ti is the head of the Celestial Bureaucracy, and all the other deities ultimately report to him. His word is law among all of the gods and goddesses, regardless of their alignment, and he is the final arbiter in any dispute among them.

CHAO KUNG MING (demigod of war)

Demigod

ARMOR CLASS: −4
MOVE: 15″
HIT POINTS: 199
NO. OF ATTACKS: 2
DAMAGE/ATTACK: 10-60 (+14)
SPECIAL ATTACKS: Nil
SPECIAL DEFENSES: Nil
MAGIC RESISTANCE: 5%
SIZE: M (6½′)
ALIGNMENT: Neutral good
WORSHIPER'S ALIGN: Warriors
SYMBOL: Black pearl
PLANE: Elemental Plane of Air
CLERIC/DRUID: Nil
FIGHTER: 17th level ranger
MAGIC-USER/ILLUSIONIST: Nil
THIEF/ASSASSIN: 10th level assassin
MONK/BARD: 7th level monk
PSIONIC ABILITY: II
S: 25 (+7, +14)   I: 18   W: 14   D: 20   C: 20   CH: 20

This god appears as a very muscular man with bright red skin. He wears special +3 scale mail that does not interfere with the use of his monk abilities. He rides a giant flying tiger into battle (AC 3, MV 24″/24″, HD 11, hp 50, #AT 3, D 1-8/1-8/2-16). This god is able to travel from plane to plane with however many beings he wishes. He strikes with a spear of power for 10-60 points of damage.

CHIH-CHIANG FYU-YA (god of archers, punisher of the gods)

Demigod

ARMOR CLASS: −7
MOVE: 12″/30″
HIT POINTS: 287
NO. OF ATTACKS: 2
DAMAGE/ATTACK: 2-24 (+11) or 2-20
SPECIAL ATTACKS: Magic bow
SPECIAL DEFENSES: See below
MAGIC RESISTANCE: 20%
SIZE: L (8′)
ALIGNMENT: Lawful evil
WORSHIPER'S ALIGN: Lawful evil and archers
SYMBOL: Green longbow
PLANE: Gehenna
CLERIC/DRUID: Nil
FIGHTER: 18th level fighter
MAGIC-USER/ILLUSIONIST: Nil
THIEF/ASSASSIN: Nil
MONK/BARD: 10th level in each
PSIONIC ABILITY: VI
S: 23 (+5, +11)   I: 22   W: 22   D: 25   C: 22   CH: −2

This god has fiery red skin resembling scales, a black demonic head with tusks, elephant ears, a large set of leathery wings with a span of 40 feet, a humanoid body, and cloven hooves. With his bow he can hit any target within sight, and is able to reverse any weapon thrown through the air at him and send it back at its caster.

His bow is magicked so that use of it by anyone else will cause the arrows to fly at the user. The god can shape change at will and wears green +4 plate mail in battle. His arrows inflict 2-20 points of damage when they hit and his sword strikes for 2-24 points in hand-to-hand combat.

It is the duty of Chih-Chiang Fyu-Ya to avenge offenses against the gods, particularly desecration of temples.

CHIH SUNG-TZU (lord of rain)

Greater god

ARMOR CLASS: −2
MOVE: 12″/24″
HIT POINTS: 388
NO. OF ATTACKS: 2
DAMAGE/ATTACK: 3-30 (+11)
SPECIAL ATTACKS: Nil
SPECIAL DEFENSES: See below
MAGIC RESISTANCE: Standard
SIZE: M (6¼′)
ALIGNMENT: Neutral
WORSHIPER'S ALIGN: Neutral and all beings needing rain
SYMBOL: Small red bird with one leg
PLANE: Elemental Plane of Air
CLERIC/DRUID: 20th level cleric
FIGHTER: 13th level fighter
MAGIC-USER/ILLUSIONIST: 20th level magic-user
THIEF/ASSASSIN: Nil
MONK/BARD: Nil
PSIONIC ABILITY: VI
S: 23 (+5, +11)   I: 20   W: 24   D: 19   C: 23   CH: 23

This god appears as a very muscular man. He always wears a blue war helm, giving him the power of constant haste and flying at twice the speed he could attain by himself (i.e., 48″). He prefers to ride a storm cloud that travels at 24″ and is able to support up to 10 beings of any size. Like Shang-Ti, he can create weather of any type upon command.

His suit of +3 scale mail appears to be badly rusted, and when any other metal touches it, that metal completely rusts away (no saving throw). His +3 mace strikes for 3-30 points per hit.

CHUNG KUEL (god of truth and testing)

Greater god

ARMOR CLASS: −2
MOVE: 12″/12″
HIT POINTS: 319
NO. OF ATTACKS: 2
DAMAGE/ATTACK: Variable (usually by weapon type)
SPECIAL ATTACKS: See below
SPECIAL DEFENSES: See below
MAGIC RESISTANCE: 80%
SIZE: M (6′)
ALIGNMENT: Lawful good
WORSHIPER'S ALIGN: Lawful good
SYMBOL: Open book
PLANE: Seven Heavens
CLERIC/DRUID: 20th level cleric/14th level druid
FIGHTER: 20th level ranger
MAGIC-USER/ILLUSIONIST: 15th level in each
THIEF/ASSASSIN: 15th level assassin
MONK/BARD: 10th level in each
PSIONIC ABILITY: II
S: 20 (+3, +8)   I: 25   W: 25   D: 20   C: 20   CH: 19

This god is always dressed in costly robes, and his primary ability is to draw from a well of knowledge so that he can meet any test with success, if given time to visit his well. In any physical contest, if his normal powers will not let him immediately win (and he will know if this is possible), he will always run and secure the materials that will allow him to win, and he will do nothing else until he does win.

He carries a +3 sword of sharpness and a rod of cancellation at all times.

This god occasionally travels around the Prime Material Plane dressed as an old pot-bellied man with a long grey beard. He asks beings riddles, and if they answer correctly, he may grant them a reward, perhaps even a limited wish. The more difficult the riddle, the greater the reward.

FEI LIEN & FENG PO "Counts of the Wind"

Demigods

ARMOR CLASS: −4
MOVE: 24''/24''
HIT POINTS: 150
NO. OF ATTACKS: 3/2
DAMAGE/ATTACK: 2-20 (+6)
SPECIAL ATTACKS: Wind control
SPECIAL DEFENSES: Nil
MAGIC RESISTANCE: Standard
SIZE: M (6')
ALIGNMENT: Neutral good
WORSHIPER'S ALIGN: Neutral good
    and farmers
SYMBOL: Lightning bolt on a black
    background
PLANE: Elemental Plane of Air
CLERIC/DRUID: Nil
FIGHTER: 10th level ranger
MAGIC-USER/ILLUSIONIST: Nil
THIEF/ASSASSIN: 10th level thief
MONK/BARD: 5th level monk
PSIONIC ABILITY: V
S: 14   I: 14   W: 14   D: 19   C: 20   CH: 9

These man-shaped beings wear +2 plate mail into battle. They each ride a piece of the wind; these take 10 melee rounds to conjure up and are easily negated by any spell affecting weather or wind. They each have a large sack of leather; when opened, these sacks blow whirlwinds like those of the djinn. These whirlwinds last two rounds, and can only be conjured up once per day.

These beings figure prominently in all major battles of the gods, and are often used as go-betweens for gods and men.

They appear to be demonic creatures in that their skin is jet black, their eyes blaze fire and they are tusked. Their swords not only strike for 2-20, they do an additional 6 points of electrical damage per blow (no saving throw).

HUAN-TI (god of war)

Lesser god

ARMOR CLASS: −7
MOVE: 18''
HIT POINTS: 380
NO. OF ATTACKS: 2 or 4
DAMAGE/ATTACK: 3-30 (+14)
SPECIAL ATTACKS: See below
SPECIAL DEFENSES: See below
MAGIC RESISTANCE: 50%
SIZE: M (7')
ALIGNMENT: Chaotic good
WORSHIPER'S ALIGN: Chaotic good
    and warriors
SYMBOL: Black-winged chariot
PLANE: Limbo
CLERIC/DRUID: Nil
FIGHTER: 20th level ranger
MAGIC-USER/ILLUSIONIST: Nil
THIEF/ASSASSIN: 15th level assassin
MONK/BARD: 12th level monk
PSIONIC ABILITY: VI
S: 25 (+7, +14)   I: 23   W: 18   D: 25   C: 25   CH: 10

Huan-Ti appears as a heavily-muscled man in red +3 plate mail. When pressed by more than one enemy, he will simultaneously use both his +2 halberd (doing 3-30 points of damage) and +3 sword (which also does 3-30 points of damage).

When flying in his chariot, pulled by 4 Pegasi at 24''/48'', no magic spell can affect him or the steeds.

He watches every battle in which his worshipers take part, and when any

mortal dedicates the last ten slain enemies to him he may (on a 1% chance) destroy utterly the very next enemy that being faces. Slain enemies dedicated to Huan-Ti must have their heads taken off and burned, or the sacrifices will not be received. Clerics of this god must always wear red armor or clothes.

KUAN YIN (goddess of mercy and child bearing)

Greater goddess

ARMOR CLASS: −3
MOVE: 12''/12''
HIT POINTS: 376
NO. OF ATTACKS: 0
DAMAGE/ATTACK: Nil
SPECIAL ATTACKS: Nil
SPECIAL DEFENSES: See below
MAGIC RESISTANCE: 100%
SIZE: M (5')
ALIGNMENT: Lawful good
WORSHIPER'S ALIGN: Lawful good
    and all suffering beings
SYMBOL: Image of the goddess
    holding a child
PLANE: Seven Heavens
CLERIC/DRUID: 25th level cleric/14th
    level druid
FIGHTER: Nil
MAGIC-USER/ILLUSIONIST: See
    below
THIEF/ASSASSIN: Nil
MONK/BARD: 15th level bard
PSIONIC ABILITY: VI
S: 8   I: 25   W: 25   D: 12   C: 22   CH: 25

Kuan Yin appears as a slim young woman wearing a green satin dress. Her main attribute is the ability to negate any single act of violence directed at anyone, once per melee round. When a being accomplishes a good act affecting 50 or more worshipers of Kuan Yin, and if the goddess is near, that being may be granted a wish (5% chance).

No act of violence can be directed towards her by any being in the universe. For example, she could walk safely through 500 different types of demons and devils and never be harmed.

She has the powers of a 20th level magic-user, though she will never use her spells to cause harm.

Her main following is with the common folk and all may work in her cause and expect to be rewarded someday. Her clerics are the peacemakers of the world and work diligently for the end of violence.

LEI KUNG *(duke of thunder)*

Greater god

ARMOR CLASS: –4
MOVE: 12"/24"
HIT POINTS: 354
NO. OF ATTACKS: 2
DAMAGE/ATTACK: 7-42 or special
  (see below)
SPECIAL ATTACKS: See below
SPECIAL DEFENSES: See below
MAGIC RESISTANCE: 5%
SIZE: M (6')
ALIGNMENT: Lawful evil
WORSHIPER'S ALIGN: Lawful evil
SYMBOL: Storm cloud with lightning
  bolt through it
PLANE: Acheron
CLERIC/DRUID: 10th level druid
FIGHTER: 14th level fighter
MAGIC-USER/ILLUSIONIST: 14th level
  in each
THIEF/ASSASSIN: Nil
MONK/BARD: Nil
PSIONIC ABILITY: VI
S: 23 (+5, +11)   I: 23   W: 17   D: 20   C: 23   CH: 7

Lei Kung appears as a man with smoking black skin and eyes with pupils like lightning bolts. He has 2 large tusks and a huge nose. He has red spotted wings with a span of 40 feet. When battling large numbers of opponents he uses a set of green drums that act as a *horn of blasting* and *drums of panic* combined. In hand-to-hand combat he uses his fists for 7-42 points of damage. When not using his fists, he uses a +4 hammer that strikes for 25 points of electrical damage per hit (no saving throw).

Anything touching his +3 plate mail suffers 10 points of electrical damage, no saving throw.

Lei Kung exists to make foul weather of one type or another at the request of the other gods of the pantheon. These gods will request such when they feel that their worshipers need a lesson. Lei Kung particularly delights in creating wind storms that destroy fragile things of beauty or value.

LU YUEH *(god of epidemics)*

Lesser god

ARMOR CLASS: –2
MOVE: 12"/12"
HIT POINTS: 367
NO. OF ATTACKS: 6
DAMAGE/ATTACK: 1-10 each
SPECIAL ATTACKS: Disease
SPECIAL DEFENSES: See below
MAGIC RESISTANCE: Standard
SIZE: L (10')
ALIGNMENT: Chaotic evil
WORSHIPER'S ALIGN: Chaotic evil
SYMBOL: 3 demon heads
PLANE: Abyss
CLERIC/DRUID: 20th level cleric
FIGHTER: 15th level fighter
MAGIC-USER/ILLUSIONIST: 19th level
  in each
THIEF/ASSASSIN: 19th level thief
MONK/BARD: Nil
PSIONIC ABILITY: VI
S: 20 (+3, +8)   I: 17   W: 5   D: 17   C: 25   CH: –3

This god has 3 demon-like heads, 6 arms ending in claws, and green scaled skin. He has a look of death about him and an odor of putrescence. His main attribute is the ability to cast a *rotting sickness* as a spell that will kill his enemies who fail to make their saving throw versus poison in 2 melee rounds. Besides his damage done by clawing, his touch causes the Red Fever that will subtract 3 hit points from those hit every melee round until cured.

He never wears armor because all wounds instantly close themselves after being made (i.e., Lu Yueh *regenerates*, at a rate of 25 points per round), and those hitting him from less than 10 feet away will suffer the *rotting sickness* (no saving throw applicable).

He can wave his hand and cast a sickness in a cloud 3" x 3" x 3" that will cause the Red Fever to all who breathe it.

Lu Yueh bestows gifts on those he deems evil enough. This is decided whenever an evil act affects more than 500 people. If the god is watching (on a 1% chance) there is a 5% chance he will give the evil being a disease-causing present with no strings attached.

MA YUAN *(killer of the gods)*

FREQUENCY: Unique
NO. APPEARING: 1
ARMOR CLASS: –4
MOVE: 24"/24"//24"
HIT DICE/POINTS: 300 hp
% IN LAIR: 10%
TREASURE TYPE: A (X 5)
NO. OF ATTACKS: 5
DAMAGE/ATTACK: 3-30 (X 4)/5-40
SPECIAL ATTACKS: See below
SPECIAL DEFENSES: +3 or better
  weapon to hit
MAGIC RESISTANCE: 65%
INTELLIGENCE: High
ALIGNMENT: Chaotic evil
SIZE: L (70')
PSIONIC ABILITY: Nil
  Attack/Defense Modes: Nil
LEVEL/X.P. VALUE: X/32,300

This monster has 3 eyes in his tyrannosaurus-shaped head, and has 4 large humanoid arms. He has the strength of a storm giant, but rarely relies on this in battle. He also has a powerful magical device shaped in the form of a small triangular piece of stone that has the power to turn into any weapon the holder wishes, magical or otherwise. This monster's favorite tactic is to make a weapon from his stone that is double the power of the one being used against him. The creature is known to have killed at least 10 minor deities. It attacks as a 16+ hit dice monster. The existence of Ma Yuan prevents complacency among the gods.

NO CHA *(demigod of thieves)*

Demigod

ARMOR CLASS: –2
MOVE: 15"/48"
HIT POINTS: 239
NO. OF ATTACKS: 8
DAMAGE/ATTACK: Variable
SPECIAL ATTACKS: See below
SPECIAL DEFENSES: Nil
MAGIC RESISTANCE: 10%
SIZE: L (60')
ALIGNMENT: Neutral evil
WORSHIPER'S ALIGN: Thieves
SYMBOL: Silver bracelet
PLANE: Nine Hells
CLERIC/DRUID: 10th level druid
FIGHTER: 12th level fighter
MAGIC-USER/ILLUSIONIST: 17th level
  illusionist
THIEF/ASSASSIN: 20th level thief
MONK/BARD: Nil
PSIONIC ABILITY: VI
S: 25 (+7, +14)   I: 25   W: 7   D: 25   C: 20   CH: 10

The god appears as a three-headed, eight-armed man, with silvery scaled skin, eyes that blaze like fire, and the ability to grow or shrink in size.

He often fights with a +3 flaming spear that hits for 30 points of damage plus a *disintegrate* spell (save applicable). He also uses a small brick of gold that he throws for 5-50 points of damage up to 100 yards away. He has a panther skin bag that blows a whirlwind like that of a djinni. He uses a bracelet which, if it is thrown and strikes an enemy, attaches itself to the neck of its target and strangles him or her in 5 melee rounds unless they are able to alter their form or teleport themselves to another plane. He also has the power to throw one 30 point *fireball* per round.

No Cha is the patron of thieves, and there are many tales of his famous thieving exploits.

SHAN HAI CHING (god of wind & sea)

Greater god

ARMOR CLASS: −2
MOVE: 6″/48″
HIT POINTS: 366
NO. OF ATTACKS: 2
DAMAGE/ATTACK: 3-18/3-18
SPECIAL ATTACKS: Hurricanes, sum-
    moning
SPECIAL DEFENSES: See below
MAGIC RESISTANCE: 35%
SIZE: L (60′ + wingspread)
ALIGNMENT: Lawful neutral
WORSHIPER'S ALIGN: Lawful
    neutral, those who depend on
    the sea
SYMBOL: Three huge waves
PLANE: Nirvana
CLERIC/DRUID: 10th level cleric
FIGHTER: 15th level fighter
MAGIC-USER/ILLUSIONIST: 10th level
    in each
THIEF/ASSASSIN: Nil
MONK/BARD: Nil
PSIONIC ABILITY: VI
S: 24 (+6, +12) I: 21 W: 23 D: 17 C: 24 CH: 19

This god has a roc's body with the oversized head of a man. He has 2 main attributes: the power to raise up a hurricane wind (doing 5-50 points of damage per melee round) and the power to call forth any creature of the sea (of non-divine nature) to do his bidding. His wind force is said to be able to last a full day when "great wrath is upon the deity". His summoning power will seem to create beings from the very water.

One spell attack against Shan Hai Ching per round will be turned back upon the caster. If multiple spells are cast, the one turned is chosen at random.

The god and his clerics serve all beings using the sea, and any trip out into the oceans requires a sacrifice to this deity for good winds and the like.

SPIRITS OF THE AIR

FREQUENCY: Very rare
NO. APPEARING: 1-100
ARMOR CLASS: 4
MOVE: 12″/24″
HIT DICE/POINTS: 50 hp
% IN LAIR: 75%
TREASURE TYPE: Nil
NO. OF ATTACKS: 2
DAMAGE/ATTACK: 2-20/2-20
SPECIAL ATTACKS: Nil
SPECIAL DEFENSES: +1 or better
    weapon to hit
MAGIC RESISTANCE: Standard
INTELLIGENCE: Average
ALIGNMENT: Neutral
SIZE: L (8′)
PSIONIC ABILITY: Nil
    Attack/Defense Modes: Nil
LEVEL/X.P. VALUE: VII/3,650

These minions of the wind gods can be summoned by them in numbers of up to 100 every day. They have black skin, large bat wings, clawed feet (which they use in battle), and a tusked monkey's head. They exist to fight for the gods, attacking as 11 hit dice monsters.

TOU MU (goddess of the north star)

Lesser goddess

ARMOR CLASS: −3
MOVE: 24″/24″
HIT POINTS: 300
NO. OF ATTACKS: 8
DAMAGE/ATTACK: Variable
SPECIAL ATTACKS: See below
SPECIAL DEFENSES: See below
MAGIC RESISTANCE: 25%
SIZE: L (20′)
ALIGNMENT: Chaotic evil
WORSHIPER'S ALIGN: Evil beings
SYMBOL: Lotus and bow
PLANE: Abyss
CLERIC/DRUID: 20th level cleric
FIGHTER: 15th level ranger
MAGIC-USER/ILLUSIONIST: 6th level
    in each
THIEF/ASSASSIN: Nil
MONK/BARD: Nil
PSIONIC ABILITY: II
S: 23 (+5, +11) I: 25 W: 3 D: 25 C: 19 CH: 5

Tou Mu appears on the earth with 16 massive arms, 3 eyes in her barely human head, and red scaly skin. She uses many weapons in battle: a magical bow that never misses anything within 100 yards, the arrows of which do 1-10 points of damage per strike; a +3 spear that hits for 3-30 points per strike; a +3 *dancing sword*; a large red flag that projects 3 *death spells* from its folds every melee round; a living red dragon's head that breathes fire as a normal dragon with 80 hit points; a piece of the moon that is able to block any single hit directed at her person in any given melee round; and a lotus flower that heals all wounds at a touch. Her free claws do 1-10 points of damage per hit. She may make up to 8 attacks per melee round.

She has 5 chariots at her disposal that fly through the air at 24″ and move at her command even though there is no visible force to pull them. The chariots are all of adamant with gold figures of dragons decorating the sides of each. The chariot tongues appear to be made of solid diamond and are 32 feet long. The wheels are of unbreakable green jade and sparks fly from them whenever they are used to run over beings in battle. This overrun inflicts 2-12 points of damage.

WEN CHUNG *(minister of thunder)*

Demigod

ARMOR CLASS: −2
MOVE: 12''/21''
HIT POINTS: 213
NO. OF ATTACKS: 3/2
DAMAGE/ATTACK: 3-30 (+12)
SPECIAL ATTACKS: See below
SPECIAL DEFENSES: See below
MAGIC RESISTANCE: 15%
SIZE: L (8')
ALIGNMENT: Chaotic neutral
WORSHIPER'S ALIGN: Chaotic
    neutral
SYMBOL: Crossed sword and thunder
    bolt
PLANE: Elemental Plane of Air
CLERIC/DRUID: Nil
FIGHTER: 10th level ranger
MAGIC-USER/ILLUSIONIST: 15th level
    in each
THIEF/ASSASSIN: Nil
MONK/BARD: Nil
PSIONIC ABILITY: VI
S: 24 (+6, +12)   I: 20   W: 22   D: 21   C: 19   CH: 15

Wen Chung has 3 eyes in his head and a massive dark-skinned body. He summons weather for Lei Kung and for his chaotic worshipers.

His third eye can cast a 20 point *lightning bolt* to a range of 180 yards or closer (ten times a day) and his +3 sword does 3-30 points of damage.

Wen Chung is totally immune to lightning, cold, or light attacks.

YEN-WANG-YEH *(judge of the dead)*

Greater god

ARMOR CLASS: −5
MOVE: 12''/12''
HIT POINTS: 349
NO. OF ATTACKS: 2
DAMAGE/ATTACK: 2-20
SPECIAL ATTACKS: Death ray
SPECIAL DEFENSES: See below
MAGIC RESISTANCE: 75%
SIZE: M (6')
ALIGNMENT: Neutral
WORSHIPER'S ALIGN: Neutral
SYMBOL: Red helm wrapped with
    orange ribbons on a yellow back-
    ground
PLANE: Concordant Opposition
CLERIC/DRUID: 20th level cleric
FIGHTER: 18th level fighter
MAGIC-USER/ILLUSIONIST: 15th level
    magic-user
THIEF/ASSASSIN: 15th level assassin
MONK/BARD: 12th level monk
PSIONIC ABILITY: VI
S: 14   I: 24   W: 20   D: 25   C: 23   CH: 19

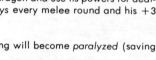

Yen-Wang-Yeh appears as a warrior with black skin. When in battle, he likes to *shape change* into an oriental dragon and use its powers for dealing out death. His eyes cast 2 *death rays* every melee round and his +3 broad sword does 2-20 points per strike.

Anyone touching his body with anything will become *paralyzed* (saving throw applicable).

This god collects all the souls and spirits of the dead and makes sure that they are transported to the proper plane and do not roam the earth at will. He tracks down spirits that do and makes them suffer for eternity. He has no power over the dead who have risen to a higher plane through their good deeds.

EGYPTIAN MYTHOS

The ancient Egyptians developed a culture lasting over 3,000 years. It is only natural that their faith would undergo a change in that time. Their deities aged, with Ra starting as the ruler and growing senile and Osiris taking over after being killed by Set and being brought back to life. The pantheon presented is one with Ra in prominence only because there are more beings of power in this early grouping.

Temples were many in Egyptian society, but each city had only one major deity. All the other deities could be worshiped, but only in an inferior position. Temples always follow the same design and differ only in size and splendor. They are shaped in a large rectangle, and enclosed with high walls. The entrance (only one obvious one, though there are several secret ones) is supported by 2 large pylons that are marked with the symbol of the god of the city. There is always a large public hall whose walls are covered with hieroglyphics depicting the story of the deity of the temple, but no image of that being is permitted here. There is always an inner sanctuary where the deity's image is presented in the best materials the sect can afford (marble, alabaster, silver, gold, and the like). Near the temple is a cultivated garden where the priests and priestesses of the temple have to bathe every day.

This area is holy, and if desecrated, the entire temple is rendered useless. Offerings are always objects that are pleasing to the eye and made to dress up the altar, either in the outer hall or the inner court. Only priests and priestesses are allowed in the inner sanctuary.

Clerics of less than the fourth level are expected to serve their deity by serving the people with their knowledge, healing, or the like. Clerics of the fourth through the sixth level serve the needs of the temple, either by being messengers, using their powers to fight for the sect, or whatever else the higher clerics need. Female clerics can rise no higher than the 9th level in ability, but it is necessary for all 11th level males or higher to take on a female cleric as a consort and advisor, and these women often rule in the stead of their male counterparts when the males have to be away from the temple. The female clerics keep all official temple records. All clerics wear white in some part of their dress, and it is a great sin to be stripped of white for any reason and is cause for going on a major quest of redemption if it happens. Otherwise, clerics are as other humans, save that the males shave their heads upon attaining the fourth or higher levels, while the females wear long hair at all times. Egyptian clerics can only rise in levels by donating large sums to the sect for its use (in **AD&D** terms it is necessary to donate the equivalent of the needed experience points in gold in order to rise in levels).

RA (sun god) "Pharaoh to the Gods"

Greater god

ARMOR CLASS: −3
MOVE: 24"/24"
HIT POINTS: 400
NO. OF ATTACKS: 0
DAMAGE/ATTACK: Nil
SPECIAL ATTACKS: Heat rays
SPECIAL DEFENSES: Anti-magic shell,
   +3 or better weapon to hit
MAGIC RESISTANCE: 80%
SIZE: M (6')
ALIGNMENT: Neutral good
WORSHIPER'S ALIGN: Neutral good
SYMBOL: Solar disk encircled by a
   serpent
PLANE: Prime Material Plane
CLERIC/DRUID: 20th level cleric
FIGHTER: 16th level fighter
MAGIC-USER/ILLUSIONIST: 19th level
   magic-user
THIEF/ASSASSIN: Nil
MONK/BARD: Nil
PSIONIC ABILITY: VI
S: 20   I: 25   W: 25   D: 20   C: 25   CH: 25

Ra usually appears with the body of a man and the head of a hawk, surmounted by a solar disk. Often he can be seen in the shape of a hawk. He can *shape change* at will, and has a permanent *anti-magic shell* which prevents the entrance of others' spell effects but allows Ra to cast his own spells. He can cast the light of day into any area he wishes. He rides through the air in a huge war galley made of part of the sun and called the Matet (this galley changes into a simple barge at night called the Semktet). It travels at a rate of 24", is surrounded by flames (which inflict 40 points of searing damage on contact), and is never affected by magic.

In battle, Ra has the power to shoot rays of intense heat from his hands, two at a time, to a range of 500 yards. These rays inflict 4-40 points of damage, and cannot be negated by any power in the universe.

This god prevents fighting among the other beings of the pantheon and is able to reduce all conflict to a state where only the clerics of each sect are able to do battle, with their respective gods never taking a hand, unless Ra himself is out of commission.

ANHUR (god of war)

Lesser god

ARMOR CLASS: −5
MOVE: 15"/24"
HIT POINTS: 345
NO. OF ATTACKS: 2
DAMAGE/ATTACK: 6-60 (+14)
SPECIAL ATTACKS: See below
SPECIAL DEFENSES: Ability negation
   (see below); +2 or better
   weapon to hit
MAGIC RESISTANCE: 20%
SIZE: M (7')
ALIGNMENT: Chaotic good
WORSHIPER'S ALIGN: Warriors
SYMBOL: A cord
PLANE: Prime Material Plane
CLERIC/DRUID: Nil
FIGHTER: 20th level ranger
MAGIC-USER/ILLUSIONIST: 8th level
   in each
THIEF/ASSASSIN: 10th level assassin
MONK/BARD: 7th level monk
PSIONIC ABILITY: VI
S: 25 (+7, +14)   I: 19   W: 12   D: 25   C: 25   CH: 12

Anhur is unusually tall and always appears as a human. He *shape changes*, but only when attacked by more than one being. He will sometimes take forms with more than two arms to allow him to use more weapons. He commonly fights in +4 scale mail and his lance (the tip of which is made out of a part of the sun) is a +5 weapon that hits for 6-60 points of damage plus his strength bonus of 14 points. It destroys all undead within 50 yards, no matter what is shielding them. In combat, Anhur always magically negates his enemy's strongest ability (no saving throw applicable).

A worshiper of Anhur offers sacrifices to him in battle, in the form of powerful enemies. If a follower of Anhur promises the god a foe's life as a sacrifice, and the foe is at least twice as powerful as the worshiper (considering levels, hit points, special abilities, etc.), then if the worshiper is successful, there is a 1% chance that Anhur will immediately grant him or her sufficient experience to raise one level of experience.

ANUBIS (guardian of the dead)

Lesser god

ARMOR CLASS: −2
MOVE: 12″
HIT POINTS: 300
NO. OF ATTACKS: 3/2
DAMAGE/ATTACK: 3-30
SPECIAL ATTACKS: See below
SPECIAL DEFENSES: Blink ability; +2
  or better weapon to hit
MAGIC RESISTANCE: 80%
SIZE: M (6′)
ALIGNMENT: Lawful good
WORSHIPER'S ALIGN: All alignments
SYMBOL: Black jackal
PLANE: Astral Plane
CLERIC/DRUID: 20th level cleric
FIGHTER: 12th level paladin
MAGIC-USER/ILLUSIONIST: 20th level
  magic-user
THIEF/ASSASSIN: Nil
MONK/BARD: Nil
PSIONIC ABILITY: III
S: 24 (+6, +12) I: 24 W: 24 D: 19 C: 22 CH: 19

Anubis appears as a man with the head of a jackal. He can animate any statue of himself, cast 2 *charm monster* spells at the same time, *shape change* at will, and short range *teleport* like a blink dog. The god hates all thieves, and if a tomb with his image within is being robbed, there is a 5% chance that he will come and kill the robber(s).

If this tomb has been consecrated especially to Anubis, there is a 10% chance that he will come, but this involves the intercession of a 10th level priest and the sacrifice to Anubis of 50,000 gp worth of precious gems.

In his role as the collector of souls for transportation to the house of the dead, there is a 20% chance that a dead being (worshiping any Egyptian deity) will, while in the process of being raised from the dead by a cleric, attract the anger of the god, and as a result that cleric will be forced to go on a quest for the purpose of increasing the power of the cult of Anubis (no saving throw; judge's option as to the quest).

While the god is perfectly able to use spells or the like on his enemies, he particularly likes to bite them to death and does 3-30 points of damage when he attacks.

APEP (king of serpents)

FREQUENCY: Unique
NO. APPEARING: 1
ARMOR CLASS: −4
MOVE: 18″
HIT DICE/POINTS: 250 hp
% IN LAIR: 70%
TREASURE TYPE: H (X 3)
NO. OF ATTACKS: 2
DAMAGE/ATTACK: 3-30 (bite)/4-24
  (constriction)
SPECIAL ATTACKS: Poison, breath
  weapon
SPECIAL DEFENSES: +3 or better
  weapon to hit
MAGIC RESISTANCE: 40%
INTELLIGENCE: High
ALIGNMENT: Chaotic evil
SIZE: L (300′ long)
PSIONIC ABILITY: Nil
  Attack/Defense Modes: Nil
LEVEL/X.P. VALUE: X/28,350

This creature of the Abyss is the deadly enemy of the gods, particularly Osiris. Apep is the physical embodiment of chaotic evil in the Egyptian mythos. He is usually attended by 5-50 flame snakes (q.v.), who act at his will.

This great serpent not only has a poisonous bite (3-30 points damage and save at −4 or die), he can breathe 6-60 points of flame every other melee round in a 10″ long by 4″ wide cone. Apep attacks as a 16+ HD monster, with the ability to constrict for 4-24 points of damage. His scaly hide is so tough that +3 or better weapons are required to hit him, and nonmagical weapons shatter when they strike.

APSHAI (god of insects)

Demigod

ARMOR CLASS: 3
MOVE: 21″/21″
HIT POINTS: 289
NO. OF ATTACKS: 1
DAMAGE/ATTACK: 6-60
SPECIAL ATTACKS: See below
SPECIAL DEFENSES: +1 or better
  weapon to hit
MAGIC RESISTANCE: 10%
SIZE: L (15′)
ALIGNMENT: Neutral
WORSHIPER'S ALIGN: Farmers
SYMBOL: Praying mantis
PLANE: Prime Material Plane
CLERIC/DRUID: Nil
FIGHTER: 15th level fighter
MAGIC-USER/ILLUSIONIST: Nil
THIEF/ASSASSIN: Nil
MONK/BARD: Nil
PSIONIC ABILITY: VI
S: 20 (+3, +8) I: 17 W: 25 D: 18 C: 19 CH: −3

Apshai is a great praying mantis, able to *shape change* at will and call an *insect plague* on a person, town, or country. He can control any type of insect (of a non-divine nature).

His bite does 6-60 points of damage and he never misses his prey.

BAST (cat goddess)

Lesser goddess

ARMOR CLASS: −2
MOVE: 24″
HIT POINTS: 300
NO. OF ATTACKS: 2
DAMAGE/ATTACK: 5-50/5-50
SPECIAL ATTACKS: Shape change
SPECIAL DEFENSES: +2 or better
  weapon to hit; also see below
MAGIC RESISTANCE: 45%
SIZE: M (6′)
ALIGNMENT: Chaotic good
WORSHIPER'S ALIGN: Chaotics of all
  types
SYMBOL: Cat
PLANE: Gladsheim
CLERIC/DRUID: 15th level cleric
FIGHTER: 10th level fighter
MAGIC-USER/ILLUSIONIST: 15th level
  in each
THIEF/ASSASSIN: Nil
MONK/BARD: Nil
PSIONIC ABILITY: II
S: 25 (+7, +14) I: 24 W: 10 D: 23 C: 20 CH: 22

Bast's bitter enemies are Set and his minions. When fighting evil with her claws, she often *teleports* about and *shape changes* so that she can use more claws in battle. She can sense evil within 100 yards. She is the protector of all cat kind, and there is a 2% chance that she will see a being killing one of the cat race. When this happens, she may (5%) do one of the following: come and kill the slayer, or demand that he or she devote one-half of the rest of his or her life to Bast.

All of her priests have a special power vs. snakes of all types. They gain +1 when trying to strike them, and they gain a bonus of one point to every die of damage they do to them. All snakes save at –2 vs. their snake charm spells, but the priests may never summon them in a spell.

Weapons striking at Bast's body have a 75% chance of shattering with every attempt, before they do damage. The goddess is also never surprised by anything.

BES *(god of luck)*

Lesser god

ARMOR CLASS: –3
MOVE: 6''/24''
HIT POINTS: 210
NO. OF ATTACKS: 3/2
DAMAGE/ATTACK: 4-24
SPECIAL ATTACKS: Never misses
SPECIAL DEFENSES: See below
MAGIC RESISTANCE: 100%
SIZE: S (4')
ALIGNMENT: Neutral
WORSHIPER'S ALIGN: Beings
  wishing for luck
SYMBOL: Dwarf wearing a panther's
  skin and tail
PLANE: Concordant Opposition
CLERIC/DRUID: Nil
FIGHTER: 10th level fighter
MAGIC-USER/ILLUSIONIST: 15th level
  in each
THIEF/ASSASSIN: 15th level thief
MONK/BARD: 8th level bard
PSIONIC ABILITY: VI
S: 24 (+6, +12) I: 25 W: 10 D: 24 C: 25 CH: 15

Bes appears as a mountain dwarf as described in the **MONSTER MANUAL**. He is often found *shape changing* to watch and aid all types of creatures. Bes looks favorably upon all gambles and the greater the risk (excepting foolhardy ones) the better he likes it. There is a 5% chance that the god will, if really pleased (judge's option), give the being a *luck stone*, no strings attached. (DMs must exercise discretion with this.)

His sword is a +2 weapon and does 4-24 points of damage, and it always hits. He always makes his saving throws; any weapon striking him needs a score of at least a natural 17, no matter what the pluses are; and he often fights while *invisible* (not appearing for the strike as others do).

FLAME SNAKE

FREQUENCY: Rare
NO. APPEARING: 1
ARMOR CLASS: 2
MOVE: 3''
HIT DICE/POINTS: 1 HD
% IN LAIR: 80%
TREASURE TYPE: H
NO. OF ATTACKS: 1
DAMAGE/ATTACK: 1-2
SPECIAL ATTACKS: Breath weapon
SPECIAL DEFENSES: Nil
MAGIC RESISTANCE: 85%
INTELLIGENCE: Low
ALIGNMENT: Chaotic evil
SIZE: S (1' long)
PSIONIC ABILITY: Nil
  Attack/Defense Modes: Nil
LEVEL/X.P. VALUE: II/45 + 1 per hp

This creature is an enemy of the gods, and is related to the great serpent Apep. It appears as a small harmless grass snake and is most often found sitting coiled on the highest pile of treasure in a tomb. 5 times in a 24 hour period it can blast flame up to 3'', inflicting 15 points of fire damage (save vs. breath weapon for half damage). The Egyptian hells swarm with flame snakes.

GEB *(god of the earth) also known as Seb or Qeb*

Greater god

ARMOR CLASS: –3
MOVE: 12'' (48'')
HIT POINTS: 339
NO. OF ATTACKS: 2
DAMAGE/ATTACK: 6-60/6-60
SPECIAL ATTACKS: See below
SPECIAL DEFENSES: +3 or better
  weapon to hit; also see below
MAGIC RESISTANCE: 30%
SIZE: L (70')
ALIGNMENT: Neutral
WORSHIPER'S ALIGN: Neutral beings
SYMBOL: Earth hieroglyph
PLANE: Elemental Plane of Earth
CLERIC/DRUID: Nil
FIGHTER: 17th level fighter
MAGIC-USER/ILLUSIONIST: 15th level
  magic-user
THIEF/ASSASSIN: Nil
MONK/BARD: Nil
PSIONIC ABILITY: VI
S: 25 (+7, +14) I: 22 W: 20 D: 23 C: 25 CH: 22

Geb appears as a heavily muscled man. He is not affected by any physical weapon while he is standing on the ground. He can *shape change* at will, negate any spell having to do with earth (no save), and call up 2-12 earth elementals to fight for him, once per day. He uses 2 magical devices that he is never without. The first is a crown that can summon 2-8 random monsters to fight for him once a day. The other is a staff that regenerates lost hit points for the holder at the rate of 25 per melee round, and drains 5 energy levels per strike from any enemy it hits. Geb can strike with his fists for 6-60 points of damage each.

HORUS *(son of Osiris) "The Avenger"*

Lesser god

ARMOR CLASS: –2
MOVE: 15''/15''
HIT POINTS: 359
NO. OF ATTACKS: 2
DAMAGE/ATTACK: 3-36 (+14:
  spear)/3-30 (+14: sword)
SPECIAL ATTACKS: See below
SPECIAL DEFENSES: See below
MAGIC RESISTANCE: 75%
SIZE: M (6½')
ALIGNMENT: Lawful neutral
WORSHIPER'S ALIGN: Lawful neutral
  and anyone seeking vengeance
SYMBOL: Hawk
PLANE: Nirvana
CLERIC/DRUID: Nil
FIGHTER: 19th level paladin
MAGIC-USER/ILLUSIONIST: 16th level
  magic-user
THIEF/ASSASSIN: Nil
MONK/BARD: Nil
PSIONIC ABILITY: VI
S: 25 (+7, +14) I: 25 W: 21 D: 25 C: 23 CH: 24

Horus appears on the earth as a muscular man with a hawk's head, and his main attribute is the ability to triple the power of any weapon or magic item he uses. He uses a *wand of fire*, which in his hands shoots an 18 dice *fireball*, and he can cast *monster summoning VII*, *shape change*, and *project image* at will. His sword nullifies all first through fifth level spells used against him and is a +3 weapon striking for 3-30 points of damage. His 30 foot spear strikes for 3-36 points of damage and will instantly kill any being that is in *shape changed* form (no saving throw). Note that the effects of these weapons if used by others are much less: the sword would be +1, do 1-10 points of damage, and only nullify first and second level spells; the lance will do 1-12 and only paralyze the *shape changed*, etc.

Horus is not affected by the first blow of any given weapon used against him.

This god is very aware of any avenging human. When a "good" person seeks righteous revenge, there is a 5% chance that the god will aid by increasing all of the being's ability scores to 19 until the deed is done.

ISIS *(goddess of magic and fertility)*

Greater goddess

ARMOR CLASS: −2
MOVE: 12''/24''
HIT POINTS: 300
NO. OF ATTACKS: 3/2
DAMAGE/ATTACK: 1-10
SPECIAL ATTACKS: See below
SPECIAL DEFENSES: +3 or better
   weapon to hit; also see below
MAGIC RESISTANCE: 90%
SIZE: M (5½')
ALIGNMENT: Neutral good
WORSHIPER'S ALIGN: Neutral good
   and beings dealing with magic
SYMBOL: Ankh and star
PLANE: Elysium
CLERIC/DRUID: See below
FIGHTER: 10th level fighter
MAGIC-USER/ILLUSIONIST: See
   below
THIEF/ASSASSIN: Nil
MONK/BARD: Nil
PSIONIC ABILITY: I
S: 10 I: 25 W: 25 D: 20 C: 19 CH: 25

Isis usually appears as a beautiful well-proportioned female. She can use any spell as a 20th level spell-caster an unlimited number of times. She wears a magical headdress that puts her in contact with any Egyptian god any time she wills. She understands the fashioning of magical charms as no other being, and is able to form these so that each resists the effects of one spell only. She gives these to beings she particularly favors of the good or neutral alignments. The giving of these charms often does not depend on actions, just her whims. They are usually given (5% chance) upon the creation of a new spell or magic item not known before.

NEPHTHYS *(goddess of wealth and protector of the dead)*

Lesser goddess

ARMOR CLASS: 2
MOVE: 12''/12''
HIT POINTS: 200
NO. OF ATTACKS: 3/2
DAMAGE/ATTACK: By weapon type
SPECIAL ATTACKS: Death rays
SPECIAL DEFENSES: +2 or better
   weapon to hit
MAGIC RESISTANCE: 40%
SIZE: M (5½')
ALIGNMENT: Chaotic good
WORSHIPER'S ALIGN: Chaotic good
SYMBOL: Horns around a lunar disk
PLANE: Olympus
CLERIC/DRUID: 15th level cleric
FIGHTER: 8th level fighter
MAGIC-USER/ILLUSIONIST: 17th level
   magic-user
THIEF/ASSASSIN: Nil
MONK/BARD: Nil
PSIONIC ABILITY: VI
S: 17 (+1, +1) I: 21 W: 18 D: 23 C: 20 CH: 22

Nephthys is the twin sister to Isis, and appears as a beautiful woman. She protects chaotic good souls (of the Egyptian cults) after death. She hates evil of any sort, and will attempt to destroy it by means of the twin *death rays* she can project from her eyes (save at −6 applicable) to a range of 12''. Nephthys was once married to Set, but she left him when that god turned to evil.

Nephthys is also a goddess of wealth and the protector of the edge of civilization, where fields meet deserts. Nephthys' clerics are expected to protect her worshipers and diligently root out evil. In return, they expect monetary support from the worshipers to enable them to continue their crusades.

OSIRIS *(god of nature and the dead)*

Greater god

ARMOR CLASS: −2
MOVE: 24''/48''
HIT POINTS: 400
NO. OF ATTACKS: 2
DAMAGE/ATTACK: 3-30 (+12)
SPECIAL ATTACKS: See below
SPECIAL DEFENSES: +3 or better
   weapon to hit; also see below
MAGIC RESISTANCE: 80%
SIZE: M (7')
ALIGNMENT: Lawful good
WORSHIPER'S ALIGN: Lawful good
   and farmers
SYMBOL: White crown
PLANE: Prime Material Plane
CLERIC/DRUID: 20th level cleric/14th
   level druid
FIGHTER: 16th level ranger
MAGIC-USER/ILLUSIONIST: 20th level
   magic-user
THIEF/ASSASSIN: Nil
MONK/BARD: 15th level bard
PSIONIC ABILITY: V
S: 24 (+6, +12) I: 25 W: 25 D: 19 C: 25 CH: 24

Osiris usually appears as a muscular green man. He is the lord and protector of the dead. Vegetation or anything made out of vegetation has no effect on the god. His also is the power to raise the dead, no matter how long in that condition.

Anyone touching his body in battle instantly dies (saving throw vs. death applicable). At will, he *shape changes*, controls all forms of vegetation (making it shrink or grow), and he can use any weapon even if that weapon is magically tied to its owner. He has a crown with the power to see all invisible objects and illusions for what they are, and negate all fourth or lower level spells cast at him (no saving throw). He uses a scepter in battle that acts as a *rod of cancellation* with unlimited charges, and strikes for 3-30 points of damage.

This god is very aware of his clerical worshipers, and if one does a great deed for the religion (judge's option), that cleric may (5%) be given a *wish*. Osiris is second only to Ra in power and rules in Ra's absence.

PHOENIX

FREQUENCY: Unique
NO. APPEARING: 1
ARMOR CLASS: 3
MOVE: 12''/24''
HIT DICE/POINTS: 50 hp
% IN LAIR: 50%
TREASURE TYPE: H (× 2)
NO. OF ATTACKS: 3
DAMAGE/ATTACK: 3-18/3-18/4-24
SPECIAL ATTACKS: Flame
SPECIAL DEFENSES: See below
MAGIC RESISTANCE: See below
INTELLIGENCE: Low
ALIGNMENT: Neutral
SIZE: L (60' + wingspread)
PSIONIC ABILITY: Nil
   Attack/Defense Modes: Nil
LEVEL/X.P. VALUE: IX/not applicable

The phoenix was said to exist and be watching at the time of the creation of the universe, and it stands for everlasting life beyond even the power of

JEFF DEE 1980

gods to attain. It regenerates 5 points per melee round and no magical spell can affect the creature. The bird is constantly burning, and anything within 10 yards of it takes 25 points of fire damage per melee round (no saving throw) even if resistant to fire and heat. Any weapon less than +4 will melt when striking the body of the creature, doing no damage.

If assaulted the phoenix will defend itself, attacking as a 12 hit dice monster with its wings (for 3-18) and its beak (4-24), plus its heat damage.

If killed, the phoenix's body is consumed by its own flames in a great explosion of heat that incinerates everything within 5". If creatures within this radius save (vs. breath weapons, or magical fire, if an object), they only take 10-100 points of damage from the explosion.

3-18 rounds after its death, the phoenix will be reborn whole from its own ashes. There is no way by which the phoenix can be killed permanently. Even if its ashes are destroyed, it will rise again, seemingly out of nothingness.

PTAH *(creator of the universe) "Opener of the Ways"*

Greater god

ARMOR CLASS: −5
MOVE: Infinite
HIT POINTS: 390
NO. OF ATTACKS: 2
DAMAGE/ATTACK: 1-100 (+9)
SPECIAL ATTACKS: See below
SPECIAL DEFENSES: +3 or better
    weapon to hit
MAGIC RESISTANCE: 70%
SIZE: S (4')
ALIGNMENT: Lawful neutral
WORSHIPER'S ALIGN: Lawful neutral
SYMBOL: Apis bull
PLANE: Ethereal
CLERIC/DRUID: 20th level cleric
FIGHTER: 14th level fighter
MAGIC-USER/ILLUSIONIST: 25th level
    magic-user
THIEF/ASSASSIN: Nil
MONK/BARD: Nil
PSIONIC ABILITY: II
S: 21 (+4, +9) I: 25 W: 25 D: 18 C: 23 CH: 20

Ptah appears as a dwarf with eyes that reflect the universe. He exudes a feeling of great power. According to legend, Ptah formed the Prime Material Plane out of the Ethereal, and created the Egyptian pantheon of gods. However, he is not really a member of their group, and generally makes his own way.

Ptah is a master of planar travel. His gaze can force others out of the Prime Material Plane to a plane of Ptah's choice, one being per round (save vs. spells at −6). He can teleport anywhere in the multiverse with accuracy, and there is no limit to the speed with which he can travel through any medium. In combat he never uses armor and fights with the *Scepter of the Gods*. This weapon tells its user of the strong points of any enemy faced, is able to nullify one of any type spell or magical device used against it per melee round, and also hits for 1-100 points of damage per strike.

Ptah enjoys new ideas and devices. When a being creates a device that is highly useful there is a 5% chance that the god will reward that being with a *Thet*. This chance goes up by 5% if that being is a worshiper of the cult and 10% if that being is a cleric. The *Thet* is an amulet geared to do one of two things: it can project an *anti-magic shell* around the user which does not effect the user's ability to cast spells, or it enables the wearer to become *ethereal* once a week. In either form, a *Thet* has 2-12 charges.

SEKER *(god of light)*

Lesser god

ARMOR CLASS: −2
MOVE: 24"
HIT POINTS: 300
NO. OF ATTACKS: 2
DAMAGE/ATTACK: 3-30 (+14:
    halberd) or 2-24 (+14: mace)
SPECIAL ATTACKS: See below
SPECIAL DEFENSES: +2 or better
    weapon to hit
MAGIC RESISTANCE: 40%
SIZE: M (6½')
ALIGNMENT: Neutral good
WORSHIPER'S ALIGN: Worshipers of
    light
SYMBOL: Hawk-headed mummy
    with an ankh in his right hand
PLANE: Elysium
CLERIC/DRUID: 13th level in each
FIGHTER: 15th level paladin
MAGIC-USER/ILLUSIONIST: 12th level
    in each
THIEF/ASSASSIN: Nil
MONK/BARD: Nil
PSIONIC ABILITY: VI
S: 25 (+7, +14) I: 18 W: 18 D: 25 C: 24 CH: 24

Cousin to Shu, Seker appears as a rather ordinary man. This god is relentless in his efforts to destroy all evil on the earth. He always fights with his halberd, which does 3-30 points of damage. He also uses a +3 *mace of disintegration;* anything it hits must save vs. spells or be disintegrated. If the save is successful, the mace still inflicts 2-24 points of damage.

He casts shafts of light from his hands that kill any undead they touch (range 500 yards), and he *shape changes* at will.

Seker is one of the gods of the afterworld, and protects neutral good souls (of the Egyptian cults) after death.

SET *(god of evil and the night)*

Greater god

ARMOR CLASS: −4
MOVE: 18"
HIT POINTS: 378
NO. OF ATTACKS: 2
DAMAGE/ATTACK: 7-70
SPECIAL ATTACKS: Alignment
    change
SPECIAL DEFENSES: Poison skin; +3
    or better weapon to hit
MAGIC RESISTANCE: 59%
SIZE: M (7')
ALIGNMENT: Lawful evil
WORSHIPER'S ALIGN: Evil beings
SYMBOL: Coiled cobra
PLANE: Nine Hells
CLERIC/DRUID: 15th level cleric
FIGHTER: 17th level fighter
MAGIC-USER/ILLUSIONIST: 30th level
    illusionist
THIEF/ASSASSIN: 15th level assassin
MONK/BARD: Nil
PSIONIC ABILITY: II
S: 14 I: 25 W: 23 D: 20 C: 25 CH: −2

Set is a scaled humanoid with the head of a fierce jackal. He is totally dedicated to the spreading of evil and has attributes to match. He can change any being's alignment from neutral or good to lawful evil with a touch (saving throw applicable); these changed beings become Minions of Set (see below). He uses a *Spear of Darkness* that is a jet black +4 spear that hits for 7-70 points of damage. His skin is also deadly poisonous to the touch.

There is a 5% chance that Set may be watching when one of his worshipers does a highly evil act, and if so, Set will lend that being 2-20 Minions of Set for 12 weeks.

Set is the implacable enemy of Osiris and Horus, and will attempt to thwart them through others whenever possible.

Minions of Set

FREQUENCY: *Uncommon*
NO. APPEARING: *1-20*
ARMOR CLASS: *−2*
MOVE: *12''*
HIT DICE/POINTS: *25 hp*
% IN LAIR: *0%*
TREASURE TYPE: *Nil*
NO. OF ATTACKS: *3/2*
DAMAGE/ATTACK: *1-12 (bite), by*
    weapon type, or by form
SPECIAL ATTACKS: *See below*
SPECIAL DEFENSES: *Save as 10th*
    level fighters
MAGIC RESISTANCE: *10%*
INTELLIGENCE: *High*
ALIGNMENT: *Lawful evil*
SIZE: *M (6½')*
PSIONIC ABILITY: *Nil*
    Attack/Defense Modes: Nil
LEVEL/X.P. VALUE: *V/500*

Minions are able to *polymorph* themselves into giant snakes that bite for 1-12 points of damage. They fight and save as 10th level fighters. They appear in black scaly plate mail and use broadswords. They are fully intelligent and act as go-betweens for Set and mankind. These beings never need to check morale.

Some minions are also able to *polymorph* themselves into cave bears, giant crocodiles, or giant scorpions.

SHU (god of the sky)

Lesser god

ARMOR CLASS: *−6*
MOVE: *12''/48''*
HIT POINTS: *346*
NO. OF ATTACKS: *3/2*
DAMAGE/ATTACK: *See below*
SPECIAL ATTACKS: *See below*
SPECIAL DEFENSES: *+2 or better*
    weapon to hit; also see below
MAGIC RESISTANCE: *69%*
SIZE: *M (6')*
ALIGNMENT: *Lawful good*
WORSHIPER'S ALIGN: *Good beings*
SYMBOL: *Ostrich feather*
PLANE: *Elemental Plane of Air*
CLERIC/DRUID: *15th level cleric*
FIGHTER: *12th level paladin*
MAGIC-USER/ILLUSIONIST: *15th level*
    magic-user
THIEF/ASSASSIN: *Nil*
MONK/BARD: *Nil*
PSIONIC ABILITY: *VI*
S: *16 (0, +1)* I: *20* W: *23* D: *20* C: *23* CH: *19*

Twin brother to Tefnut, this god appears as a normal man. At will he can *levitate, shape change,* create the light of day as Ra, and call forth 1-10 16 HD air elementals once per day. He is not affected by any form of heat. He wears +5 scale mail made of phoenix feathers, which enables him to surround himself in flames which cause 25 points of damage to any who come in contact with them (no saving throw).

He uses a double strength *staff of the magi* in battle. A touch of his skin causes things to wither (saving throw vs. spells applicable): metal turns weak and shatters, flesh rots, and vegetable matter dries and turns to dust.

TEFNUT (goddess of storms and flowing water)

Lesser goddess

ARMOR CLASS: *−2*
MOVE: *24''*
HIT POINTS: *223*
NO. OF ATTACKS: *3/2*
DAMAGE/ATTACK: *By weapon type*
SPECIAL ATTACKS: *See below*
SPECIAL DEFENSES: *+2 or better*
    weapon to hit
MAGIC RESISTANCE: *69%*
SIZE: *M (6')*
ALIGNMENT: *Lawful good*
WORSHIPER'S ALIGN: *Lawful good*
SYMBOL: *Lioness head*
PLANE: *Elemental Plane of Water*
CLERIC/DRUID: *18th level cleric*
FIGHTER: *8th level fighter*
MAGIC-USER/ILLUSIONIST: *13th level*
    magic-user
THIEF/ASSASSIN: *Nil*
MONK/BARD: *Nil*
PSIONIC ABILITY: *VI*
S: *16 (0, +1)* I: *20* W: *23* D: *20* C: *23* CH: *18*

Tefnut has the power to call up wind storms, *shape change* at will, *speak with the dead,* and summon water monsters (depending on what is in the one mile radius around her).

This goddess will attack with 2 lightning bolts per melee round, each doing 24 points of damage up to a maximum range of 1,000 yards. If these do not work she will *teleport* away from the scene of battle.

Shu is Tefnut's brother, and he is very protective of his sister. Anything that dares to harm her will suffer his immediate vengeance, and there is a 75% chance that Horus will also help.

THOTH (god of knowledge)

Greater god

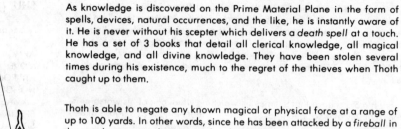

ARMOR CLASS: −4
MOVE: 12''/24''
HIT POINTS: 389
NO. OF ATTACKS: 1
DAMAGE/ATTACK: By weapon type
SPECIAL ATTACKS: See below
SPECIAL DEFENSES: See below
MAGIC RESISTANCE: 98%
SIZE: M (6½')
ALIGNMENT: Neutral
WORSHIPER'S ALIGN: Seekers of
   knowledge
SYMBOL: Ibis
PLANE: Concordant Opposition
CLERIC/DRUID: Nil
FIGHTER: 5th level fighter
MAGIC-USER/ILLUSIONIST: 30th level
   in each
THIEF/ASSASSIN: Nil
MONK/BARD: Nil
PSIONIC ABILITY: 1
S: 20 (+3, +8) I: 25 W: 25 D: 20 C: 24 CH: 18

Thoth was the teacher of the gods, and this role allows him full knowledge of *everything* and *anything*, particularly magic. His spells always inflict maximum possible damage (saving throws are still applicable).

As knowledge is discovered on the Prime Material Plane in the form of spells, devices, natural occurrences, and the like, he is instantly aware of it. He is never without his scepter which delivers a *death spell* at a touch. He has a set of 3 books that detail all clerical knowledge, all magical knowledge, and all divine knowledge. They have been stolen several times during his existence, much to the regret of the thieves when Thoth caught up to them.

Thoth is able to negate any known magical or physical force at a range of up to 100 yards. In other words, since he has been attacked by a *fireball* in the past he negates the power of such things automatically within that 100 yard radius. He can negate only one such power per round.

Worshipers of Thoth are primarily interested in the acquisition and spread of knowledge.

TRUE ANKH

This magical device, carried by all of the gods of the Nile at one time or another, enables them to raise any dead creature fully (as the spell) as long as all of the body pieces are present at the time of the raising. The device will kill by fire any non-divine being that touches it. It is about one foot long, with a cross shape, having a loop on the top. It is usually bright blue in color. There are only 7 of these in any given plane at any one time.

Non-magical ankhs are used as holy symbols by many clerics of Egyptian deities.

HIEROGLYPHS

Egyptian written language did not use an alphabet as we know it; rather, ideas were conveyed by means of *hieroglyphs*, or word-pictures. Each hieroglyph could mean one simple word, or it could stand for a whole phrase or concept. A hieroglyph could be altered slightly with the effect of negating, emphasizing, or otherwise modifying the meaning of the base hieroglyph; however, this practice tended to confuse meanings when artists couldn't agree on their depictions. Later, archaeologists would face these same difficulties in trying to uncover the meanings of the hiero-

glyphs they found.

DMs using the Egyptian pantheon may wish to use hieroglyphs on maps, scrolls, temple writings, and anywhere else runes might be found (warning of danger ahead, etc.). These hieroglyphs can be combined to make phrases and sentences; for more information consult *The Book of the Dead*, a translation of ancient hieroglyphs found in Egyptian tombs.

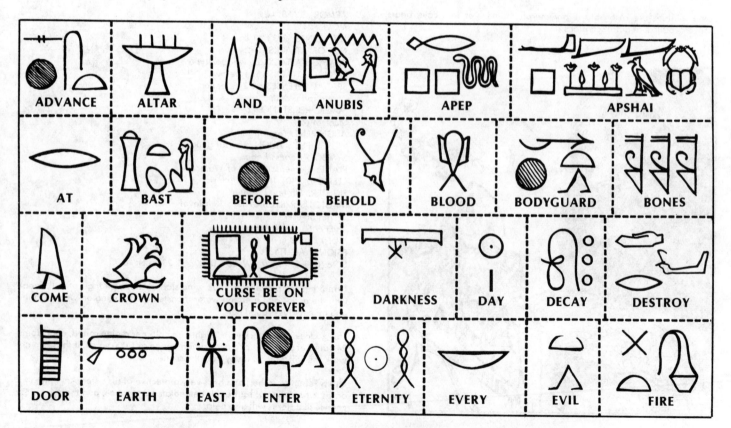

GEB	TO GIVE	GOD	GOLD	GREAT	HAIL	HE	HEAD
HEAVEN	HIDDEN	HIS	HORIZON	HORUS	HOUSE	I AM
IN	IS	ISIS	KILLED	LIFE	LIVING	MAGIC
MAGICAL CHARM	MAGICAL POWERS	MAKING	MEN	MIGHTY	NEPHTHYS
NORTH	NOT	NOW	OF	ON	OSIRIS	OVER
PAIN	PASSAGE	PEACE	PHOENIX	POWER	PROTECT	PTAH
RA	RIGHT	RULE	SEE	SEKER	SET	SHOOTING
SHU	SORROW	SOUL	SOUTH	STRENGTH	THIS	TERROR
THOTH	UNDER	VICTORY	WEAPON	WEST	WHAT
WHEN	WILL	WIND	WITH	WITHIN	YESTERDAY	YOU

Finnish Mythos

The stories of this mythos are magnificently told in *The Kalevala*, the Finnish national epic. These tales focus on the exploits of the heroes, rather than the gods. The heroes of *The Kalevala* are very powerful; they possess abilities beyond those of mortal men, and most have divine ancestors. They even have brushes with the gods (though only Vainamoinen is powerful and skillful enough to successfully meddle with the gods).

The core of the epic is the continuing conflict between Kalevala, the land of good heroes, and Pohjola, the land of evil and wizardry. All of the heroes are great bards, and make mighty magics with their songs. The clerics of the gods consider themselves above normal men, and are generally well-respected and/or feared. They have no qualms about using spells to chastise those who offend them or threaten their power.

GREAT TREE

The fragments of this tree can be used to make various magic items. Each branch can be made into 1-10 magic arrows or a +1 magical spear. The wood of this tree merely supplies the raw materials for these items. It cannot just be cut into the shape of magic weapons; it still must be enchanted properly.

MAGIC WOOL

Certain mighty persons of Pohjola have some of this material which, when rubbed against the flesh, produces a flock of 30 sheep once a month.

RAKE OF IRON

This item appears 3' in length but, because of its magical nature and purpose, it can elongate to as far as the user wishes (up to 200 yards). This rake was used by Lemminkainen's mother in recovering his body, which was deep under water. There is a 10% chance per stroke of raking out a specific item from under the water if its approximate location is known.

VAINAMOINEN *(hero)*

ARMOR CLASS: −4
MOVE: 15''
HIT POINTS: 250
NO. OF ATTACKS: 2
DAMAGE/ATTACK: *By weapon type*
SPECIAL ATTACKS: *See below*
SPECIAL DEFENSES: *Immune to charm and disease*
MAGIC RESISTANCE: *Standard*
SIZE: *M (7')*
ALIGNMENT: *Lawful good*
CLERIC/DRUID: *12th level cleric*
FIGHTER: *20th level paladin*
MAGIC-USER/ILLUSIONIST: *12th level illusionist*
THIEF/ASSASSIN: *Nil*
MONK/BARD: *23rd level bard*
PSIONIC ABILITY: *Nil*
    Attack/Defense Modes: *Nil*
S: 19 (+3, +7) I: 18 W: 18 D: 24 C: 20 CH: 18

Vainamoinen is the Kalevala's greatest hero and minstrel. His mother is Ilmatar (q.v.), so Vainamoinen has divine ancestors (like many of the Finnish heroes). He is called "Son of the Wind" by his friends and enemies alike.

Vainamoinen appears as an elderly fighter wearing +5 leather armor. He has two weapons which he wields alternately: a +5 battle axe and an intelligent +3 *sword of sharpness*. This sword talks, and it can cast a *fear* spell once per day. He wears a *girdle of cloud giant strength* (which gives him a strength of 23). He has two magical crossbows: one combines the

abilities of crossbows of *accuracy*, *distance* and *speed*, and the other, once started, loads and fires itself at Vainamoinen's enemies until stopped (much like the way a *dancing sword* fights by itself).

In addition to his clerical, illusionist and bardic spell powers, Vainamoinen can *shape change*, *dispel magic*, and use *monster summoning I-IV* at will. He is immune to the effects of *charm*-type spells and disease.

Vainamoinen has two special methods of transportation. He has a special horse (AC 3, MV 24'', HD 10, hp 59, #AT 3, D 1-10/1-10/1-6, immune to magical attacks) that can pull his sledges across land or water, drawing weights of up to 300,000 gp with no appreciable loss of speed. He has a canoe-sized boat that can carry huge quantities of objects in much the same manner as a *bag of holding*: it can hold up to 60,000 gp of weight in a volume of 1,000 cubic feet.

AHTO *(god of the seas and waters)*

Greater god

ARMOR CLASS: −2
MOVE: 18''/24''/ /24''
HIT POINTS: 324
NO. OF ATTACKS: 3/2
DAMAGE/ATTACK: 2-20 (+12)
SPECIAL ATTACKS: *Wind and water spells*
SPECIAL DEFENSES: *+3 or better weapon to hit*
MAGIC RESISTANCE: *100% in water; 50% otherwise*
SIZE: *M (7')*
ALIGNMENT: *Neutral good*
WORSHIPER'S ALIGN: *Neutral good*
SYMBOL: *Rippling water wave*
PLANE: *Elemental Plane of Water*
CLERIC/DRUID: *10th level cleric*
FIGHTER: *12th level fighter*
MAGIC-USER/ILLUSIONIST: *15th level in each*
THIEF/ASSASSIN: *Nil*
MONK/BARD: *10th level bard*
PSIONIC ABILITY: *IV*
S: 24 (+6, +12) I: 22 W: 24 D: 22 C: 23 CH: 23

Ahto appears to the world as a green-bearded man, but he rarely reveals himself to mortals. When called on to aid them, he sends the Water Dwarf (q.v.). He can use any spell involving wind or water as a 40th level spell caster. He fights with a +4 sickle that strikes for 2-20 points of damage. Sacrifices are made to Ahto by placing the objects into deep water and calling on him.

Water Dwarf (Ahto's shield man)

ARMOR CLASS: –2
MOVE: 12''
HIT POINTS: 99
NO. OF ATTACKS: 2
DAMAGE/ATTACK: By weapon type
SPECIAL ATTACKS: Magical crossbow
SPECIAL DEFENSES: Regeneration
MAGIC RESISTANCE: Standard
SIZE: S (4')
ALIGNMENT: Lawful good
CLERIC/DRUID: Nil
FIGHTER: 16th level fighter
MAGIC-USER/ILLUSIONIST: Nil
THIEF/ASSASSIN: Nil
MONK/BARD: Nil
PSIONIC ABILITY: Nil
   Attack/Defense Modes: Nil
S: 18 (37) (+1, +3) I: 16 W: 15 D: 18 C: 18 CH: 7

This dwarf is often sent on missions for Ahto, and at these times he is carefully observed by the god. There is a 25% chance that Ahto will aid him in any difficulties he encounters and 100% chance that the god will appear if the dwarf is slain.

He uses a *crossbow of accuracy* at twice the usual rate of fire. For hand-to-hand combat he uses a +3 mace. Ahto has given him the ability to regenerate 5 points per melee round when within 50 feet of a body of water.

HIISI (god of evil)

Greater god

ARMOR CLASS: 2
MOVE: 18''
HIT POINTS: 333
NO. OF ATTACKS: 2
DAMAGE/ATTACK: 4-40 (+12)
SPECIAL ATTACKS: Nil
SPECIAL DEFENSES: See below
MAGIC RESISTANCE: 45%
SIZE: M (7')
ALIGNMENT: Chaotic evil
WORSHIPER'S ALIGN: Chaotic evil
SYMBOL: Lightning bolt in the night
   sky
PLANE: Prime Material Plane
CLERIC/DRUID: 15th level cleric
FIGHTER: 15th level fighter
MAGIC-USER/ILLUSIONIST: 15th level
   illusionist
THIEF/ASSASSIN: 15th level assassin
MONK/BARD: 15th level bard
PSIONIC ABILITY: VI
S: 24 (+6, +12) I: 22 W: 10 D: 21 C: 22 CH: 23

This god always appears as a huge, richly robed man with coarse features. His giant club does 4-40 points per strike. He constantly aids evil creatures, but does not like to directly enter battle, preferring to sit on the sidelines while sending in a group of 1-10 evil heroes (AC 2, 4th level, armed with swords).

Evil beings are unable to do any damage to him either directly or indirectly.

ILMARINEN (hero)

ARMOR CLASS: 0
MOVE: 15''
HIT POINTS: 167
NO. OF ATTACKS: 2
DAMAGE/ATTACK: 1-10 (+7)
SPECIAL ATTACKS: See below
SPECIAL DEFENSES: Nil
MAGIC RESISTANCE: Standard
SIZE: M (6')
ALIGNMENT: Neutral good
CLERIC/DRUID: 5th level druid
FIGHTER: 15th level fighter
MAGIC-USER/ILLUSIONIST: 9th level
   in each
THIEF/ASSASSIN: Nil
MONK/BARD: 15th level bard
PSIONIC ABILITY: Nil
   Attack/Defense Modes: Nil
S: 19 (+3, +7) I: 18 W: 17 D: 18 C: 19 CH: 17

Ilmarinen is a blacksmith of great magical power, with the ability to create mighty magic items of many sorts. He is a massively built man who wears +4 leather armor and wields a +4 hammer that strikes for 1-10 points of damage. He has a magical sledge that pulls itself at a rate of 21'' and can travel over land or water. When traveling incognito or among enemies, Ilmarinen will yoke deer to the front of this sledge to conceal its magical nature.

ILMATAR (goddess of mothers)

Lesser goddess

ARMOR CLASS: 4
MOVE: 12''/24''
HIT POINTS: 200
NO. OF ATTACKS: 1
DAMAGE/ATTACK: By weapon type
SPECIAL ATTACKS: Nil
SPECIAL DEFENSES: Nil
MAGIC RESISTANCE: 50%
SIZE: M (5')
ALIGNMENT: Lawful good
WORSHIPER'S ALIGN: Lawful beings
   of all types
SYMBOL: Looped cross
PLANE: Prime Material Plane
CLERIC/DRUID: 13th level in each
FIGHTER: 10th level paladin
MAGIC-USER/ILLUSIONIST: 20th level
   magic-user
THIEF/ASSASSIN: Nil
MONK/BARD: 9th level bard
PSIONIC ABILITY: Nil
S: 14 I: 19 W: 22 D: 20 C: 22 CH: 19

Ilmatar is Vainamoinen's mother and is described as the Daughter of the Air. She can instantly *gate* in any Finnish god or goddess, and they will help her or her son, as they all owe her favors. She has a hand-sized ball that she carries in a copper box. This ball has written upon it all of the legends of creation and the spells used in that formation. She is able to use this thing to know all of the powers and abilities of any being that ever existed. She also has a sledge that moves by itself on the land, air, and water at a rate of 24''.

KIPUTYTTO (goddess of sickness) "Mother of the Plague"

Demigoddess

ARMOR CLASS: 2
MOVE: 12"/24"
HIT POINTS: 189
NO. OF ATTACKS: 1
DAMAGE/ATTACK: By weapon type
SPECIAL ATTACKS: Disease
SPECIAL DEFENSES: See below
MAGIC RESISTANCE: 25%
SIZE: M (5')
ALIGNMENT: Chaotic evil
WORSHIPER'S ALIGN: Chaotic evil
SYMBOL: Battered metal bowl over
   a flame
PLANE: Tarterus
CLERIC/DRUID: 14th level in each
   (harming spells only)
FIGHTER: 4th level fighter
MAGIC-USER/ILLUSIONIST: 15th level
   in each
THIEF/ASSASSIN: Nil
MONK/BARD: Nil
PSIONIC ABILITY: Nil
S: 19 (+3, +7) I: 19 W: 19 D: 19 C: 19 CH: 6

Kiputytto is able to cast a sickness (saving throw applicable) that will take away 5 hit points from its victim per turn until dead or cured. Anything that touches her will rot away, including swords, armor, claw, or fang. She is very fond of floating above a battle invisibly and affecting those that have minor wounds and are forced to retreat.

She appears to the world most often as a black skinned, twisted old crone with a scarred face. The members of her cult seem to have all suffered from some wasting disease and bear the marks on their faces.

KULLERVO (hero)

ARMOR CLASS: 1
MOVE: 15"
HIT POINTS: 119
NO. OF ATTACKS: 2
DAMAGE/ATTACK: 1-10 (+7)
SPECIAL ATTACKS: See below
SPECIAL DEFENSES: Impervious to
   fire
MAGIC RESISTANCE: Standard
SIZE: M (6½')
ALIGNMENT: Chaotic neutral (evil)
CLERIC/DRUID: Nil
FIGHTER: 19th level fighter
MAGIC-USER/ILLUSIONIST: 8th level
   in each
THIEF/ASSASSIN: 10th level thief
MONK/BARD: 5th level bard
PSIONIC ABILITY: Nil
   Attack/Defense Modes: Nil
S: 19 (+3, +7) I: 15 W: 6 D: 18 C: 19 CH: 14

Kullervo is the foil of the good heroes of Kalevala. He is doomed to eventually betray Kalevala and become evil, and acts as if he knows it.

Kullervo wields a +2 axe of sharpness (as the sword of the same name) that strikes for 1-10 points of damage. In addition to his other spell abilities, Kullervo can shape change. He is immune to fire-based attacks.

LEMMINKAINEN (hero)

ARMOR CLASS: −2
MOVE: 12"
HIT POINTS: 149
NO. OF ATTACKS: 2
DAMAGE/ATTACK: By weapon type
SPECIAL ATTACKS: See below
SPECIAL DEFENSES: See below
MAGIC RESISTANCE: Standard
SIZE: M (6½')
ALIGNMENT: Neutral good
CLERIC/DRUID: 8th level druid
FIGHTER: 18th level fighter
MAGIC-USER/ILLUSIONIST: 10th level
   magic-user/15th level illusionist
THIEF/ASSASSIN: Nil
MONK/BARD: 15th level bard
PSIONIC ABILITY: Nil
   Attack/Defense Modes: Nil
S: 18 (09) (+1, +3) I: 18 W: 18 D: 18 C: 20 CH: 18

Lemminkainen is jovial and reckless, constantly getting himself into serious scrapes. He has mastered the art of shape changing, and bears and wolves will not attack him. He is immune to poisons of all types.

In combat he has use of the following weapons: a +3 javelin of distance with a range of 36"; a +3 bow with a quiver of animal slaying arrows; and his +5 sword is both a sword of sharpness and a flaming sword. He has a +3 dagger, uses a girdle of frost giant strength, and wears +4 chainmail.

He has been known to wear a pair of snowshoes of speed and traveling that enables him to proceed at a rate of 24" on snow-covered ground. He has a magical brush which he leaves at home when he goes on an adventure. This brush sheds blood when Lemminkainen is in trouble, by which token his mother (a mighty magic-user in her own right) knows that she should send aid.

Tiera (Lemminkainen's shield man)

ARMOR CLASS: 4
MOVE: 12"
HIT POINTS: 66
NO. OF ATTACKS: 3/2
DAMAGE/ATTACK: 1-10 (+1)
SPECIAL ATTACKS: Nil
SPECIAL DEFENSES: Nil
MAGIC RESISTANCE: Standard
SIZE: M (5½')
ALIGNMENT: Lawful good
CLERIC/DRUID: Nil
FIGHTER: 9th level ranger
MAGIC-USER/ILLUSIONIST: Nil
THIEF/ASSASSIN: Nil
MONK/BARD: 5th level bard
PSIONIC ABILITY: Nil
   Attack/Defense Modes: Nil
S: 17 (+1, +1) I: 17 W: 17 D: 17 C: 18 CH: 17

This fighter will always aid his master to the best of his ability. He uses a +3 spear that does 1-10 points of damage and glows when a lie is told in its presence.

LOUHI *(old crone of Pohjola)*

ARMOR CLASS: 8
MOVE: 9''
HIT POINTS: 110
NO. OF ATTACKS: 1
DAMAGE/ATTACK: *By weapon type*
SPECIAL ATTACKS: *See below*
SPECIAL DEFENSES: *Nil*
MAGIC RESISTANCE: 15%
SIZE: *M (5')*
ALIGNMENT: *Lawful evil*
CLERIC/DRUID: *10th level in each*
FIGHTER: *Nil*
MAGIC-USER/ILLUSIONIST: *15th level
    magic-user/10th level illusionist*
THIEF/ASSASSIN: *Nil*
MONK/BARD: *Nil*
PSIONIC ABILITY: *Nil*
    Attack/Defense Modes: Nil
S: 8 I: 19 W: 14 D: 18 C: 19 CH: 7

Louhi rules the evil land of Pohjola with an iron hand. She opposes all of the good heroes of Kalevala, and works continuously for their downfall.

Louhi can summon four invisible fighters (AC 7/effectively 3 because invisible, LVL 6, hp 27 each, armed with spears) at will to defend her; two will guard her while two attack the enemy. Louhi is very adept at the creation of poison and sleep potions, which she uses on guests she wants to eliminate.

MIELIKKI *(goddess of nature)* "Mistress of the Forest"

Lesser goddess

ARMOR CLASS: -4
MOVE: *Infinite*
HIT POINTS: 322
NO. OF ATTACKS: 3/2
DAMAGE/ATTACK: *By weapon type*
SPECIAL ATTACKS: *See below*
SPECIAL DEFENSES: *See below*
MAGIC RESISTANCE: 50%
SIZE: *M (5½')*
ALIGNMENT: *Neutral good*
WORSHIPER'S ALIGN: *Good align-
    ments*
SYMBOL: *Evergreen*
PLANE: *Prime Material Plane*
CLERIC/DRUID: *14th level in each*
FIGHTER: *10th level ranger*
MAGIC-USER/ILLUSIONIST: *12th level
    in each*
THIEF/ASSASSIN: *Nil*
MONK/BARD: *12th level bard*
PSIONIC ABILITY: *I*
S: 15 I: 22 W: 25 D: 19 C: 23 CH: 23

The goddess is always dressed in a green gossamer gown, even in the coldest of winters, and is always surrounded with summer songbirds. She watches over rangers and all creatures of the forest (especially dryads). There is a 1% chance that she will aid her dryads when they are in extreme danger within the bounds of the forest. There is a 5% chance that she will attack those that try to destroy her domain, for whatever reason. Because of this, men like woodcutters must plant two trees for every one that they cut down, or eventually face her wrath.

She automatically negates all *charm*-type spells within a 30 yard radius of her body. No creature that lives in the wilds is able to hurt her, even if controlled. She is not affected by clerical spells of any type. When magic has failed to hurt her enemies, she has been known to *summon* huge packs of wolves and flights of hawks to attack despoilers of the forest.

LOVIATAR *(goddess of hurt)* "Maiden of Pain"

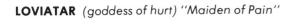

Demigoddess

ARMOR CLASS: 2
MOVE: 24''/48''
HIT POINTS: 227
NO. OF ATTACKS: 1
DAMAGE/ATTACK: *By weapon type*
SPECIAL ATTACKS: *See below*
SPECIAL DEFENSES: *See below*
MAGIC RESISTANCE: 25%
SIZE: *M (5')*
ALIGNMENT: *Lawful evil*
WORSHIPER'S ALIGN: *Evil align-
    ments*
SYMBOL: *White dagger held in a
    pallid hand*
PLANE: *Gehenna*
CLERIC/DRUID: *12th level in each*
FIGHTER: *5th level fighter*
MAGIC-USER/ILLUSIONIST: *10th level
    magic-user/15th level illusionist*
THIEF/ASSASSIN: *10th level assassin*
MONK/BARD: *10th level bard*
PSIONIC ABILITY: *VI*
S: 16 (0, +1) I: 20 W: 20 D: 16 C: 22 CH: 20

Loviatar, described as a beautiful cold maiden, is usually dressed in white silks, and when she speaks a cold wind blows. Her main concern is the inflicting of pain. She owns a *dagger of ice* that makes her immune to all magical spells. When she is attacked or magic is used against her, the attacker will once again re-experience the worst pain he or she has ever suffered. In other words, if the worst thing that ever happened to a character was to take 49 hit points of damage from a *fireball*, then that will happen to him or her again (no saving throw). A second attack on the part of this character would result in the second most painful thing hurting him, etc.

SON OF POHJOLA (evil hero)

ARMOR CLASS: 4
MOVE: 15''
HIT POINTS: 119
NO. OF ATTACKS: 3/2
DAMAGE/ATTACK: 2-20 (+6)
SPECIAL ATTACKS: Nil
SPECIAL DEFENSES: Nil
MAGIC RESISTANCE: Standard
SIZE: M (7')
ALIGNMENT: Lawful evil
CLERIC/DRUID: 5th level druid
FIGHTER: 12th level fighter
MAGIC-USER/ILLUSIONIST: 10th level
    illusionist
THIEF/ASSASSIN: 8th level assassin
MONK/BARD: 5th level bard
PSIONIC ABILITY: Nil
    Attack/Defense Modes: Nil
S: 18 (00) (+3, +6) I: 15 W: 15 D: 19 C: 19 CH: 17

This son of Louhi was a leader of the people of Pohjola and a savage enemy to Lemminkainen and the other good heroes of Kalevala. His sword does 2-20 points of damage per strike and is a +3 weapon.

His mother has given him a giant wolf (AC 5, MV 18'', HD 6, hp 40, #AT 1, D 1-10, immune to cold attacks) that obeys his every command.

SURMA (demigod of death)

Demigod

ARMOR CLASS: -2
MOVE: 18''
HIT POINTS: 224
NO. OF ATTACKS: 2
DAMAGE/ATTACK: 3-30 (+14)
SPECIAL ATTACKS: Nil
SPECIAL DEFENSES: +1 or better
    weapon to hit
MAGIC RESISTANCE: 40%
SIZE: M (6')
ALIGNMENT: Neutral evil
WORSHIPER'S ALIGN: Evil align-
    ments
SYMBOL: Withered oak branch
PLANE: Tarterus
CLERIC/DRUID: 14th level in each
    (harming spells only)
FIGHTER: 15th level ranger
MAGIC-USER/ILLUSIONIST: 12th level
    in each (harming spells only)
THIEF/ASSASSIN: 15th level assassin
MONK/BARD: Nil
PSIONIC ABILITY: VI
S: 25 (+7, +14) I: 19 W: 19 D: 23 C: 22 CH: 18

Surma occasionally travels about the country challenging all he meets to combat, and if they refuse, he lets them go only to follow them and kill them in their sleep. He often appears as a slightly aging warrior in leather buckskins and red boots. He uses a club in battle that strikes for 3-30 points of damage; only Surma can wield this weapon.

TUONETAR (goddess of the underworld)

Greater goddess

ARMOR CLASS: 6
MOVE: 9''
HIT POINTS: 340
NO. OF ATTACKS: 1
DAMAGE/ATTACK: 4-40
SPECIAL ATTACKS: Nil
SPECIAL DEFENSES: Fear aura
MAGIC RESISTANCE: 70%
SIZE: M (5')
ALIGNMENT: Chaotic evil
WORSHIPER'S ALIGN: Chaotic evil
SYMBOL: Decapitated head
PLANE: Pandemonium
CLERIC/DRUID: 15th level cleric
FIGHTER: Nil
MAGIC-USER/ILLUSIONIST: 20th level
    in each
THIEF/ASSASSIN: Nil
MONK/BARD: 5th level bard
PSIONIC ABILITY: II
S: 15 I: 18 W: 21 D: 17 C: 25 CH: -6

The wife of Tuoni, Tuonetar appears to the world as an incredibly ugly old crone. Any creature that comes within 30' of her must save vs. spells or be affected by her fear aura, fleeing until exhaustion sets in. Tuonetar's merest touch inflicts 4-40 points of damage. She is an implacable enemy of Vainamoinen.

TUONI (god of the underworld)

Greater god

ARMOR CLASS: -2
MOVE: 18''/18''//48''
HIT POINTS: 389
NO. OF ATTACKS: 2
DAMAGE/ATTACK: 3-30 (+14)
SPECIAL ATTACKS: See below
SPECIAL DEFENSES: Immune to
    charm/enchantment and death
    spells
MAGIC RESISTANCE: 64%
SIZE: L (10')
ALIGNMENT: Chaotic neutral (evil)
WORSHIPER'S ALIGN: Chaotic align-
    ments
SYMBOL: His club in a clenched fist
PLANE: Pandemonium
CLERIC/DRUID: 20th level cleric
FIGHTER: 15th level fighter
MAGIC-USER/ILLUSIONIST: 15th level
    in each
THIEF/ASSASSIN: Nil
MONK/BARD: 10th level bard
PSIONIC ABILITY: Nil
S: 25 (+7, +14) I: 20 W: 19 D: 18 C: 24 CH: 14

This god is usually dressed in dark furs. At will he can constantly shape change and cast death and prismatic wall spells. He is immune to all death and charm-type spells. The god will always appear as if in a vision when a being who worships the Finnish pantheon is raised from the dead, and there is a 1% chance that he will actually come in person to reclaim the raised person's soul.

His club (which only he can lift) does 3-30 points of damage, and always disenchants one randomly-determined magic item on the being hit (no saving throw).

Tuoni's clerics go about the battlefield and aid those that are near death to reach the land of the dead. They have been noted for sending the near-dead off a bit too soon. After they administer these rites, they take the dead person's valuables as recompense for their aid in helping the person to go to the land of the dead.

UKKO *(supreme god of the Kalevala)*

Greater god

ARMOR CLASS: −2
MOVE: *Infinite*
HIT POINTS: 400
NO. OF ATTACKS: 2
DAMAGE/ATTACK: 3-30 (+14)
SPECIAL ATTACKS: *See below*
SPECIAL DEFENSES: *Nil*
MAGIC RESISTANCE: 85%
SIZE: *M (7')*
ALIGNMENT: *Lawful good*
WORSHIPER'S ALIGN: *Good align-*
  ments
SYMBOL: *Flaming sword*
PLANE: *Twin Paradises*
CLERIC/DRUID: *20th level cleric*
FIGHTER: *20th level paladin*
MAGIC-USER/ILLUSIONIST: *25th level*
  magic-user
THIEF/ASSASSIN: *Nil*
MONK/BARD: *15th level bard*
PSIONIC ABILITY: *VI*
S: 25 (+7, +14) I: 24 W: 25 D: 23 C: 25 CH: 23

Ukko is represented as an old man. He is very supportive of all the good heroes in the mythos. While he usually uses a magic attack, when hard pressed in battle he uses a *flaming sword* that does 3-30 points of damage and has the power to slay anything it hits (as a *death* spell; saving throw at −6 applicable).

This god is master of the sky and air, and supports the world. He thus is responsible for all weather and protects all avian life.

Because Ukko is the supreme god he will never directly intervene in worldly affairs unless there is a strong possibility of the world being destroyed by evil (especially chaotics). Instead, when a devout follower of his calls his name he is likely (30%) to send a warrior maiden: first to advise, then to rescue the imperiled believer. These powerful warriors will be sent by Ukko only when his worshipers face certain death at the hands of demons, devils or very powerful evil characters.

AIR MAIDEN *(Ukko's warrior)*

ARMOR CLASS: −5
MOVE: *48"*
HIT POINTS: 85
NO. OF ATTACKS: 2
DAMAGE/ATTACK: *1-8 (+7)*
SPECIAL ATTACKS: *Sword*
SPECIAL DEFENSES: *None*
MAGIC RESISTANCE: 50%
SIZE: *M (6')*
ALIGNMENT: *Lawful Good*
CLERIC/DRUID: *7th level cleric*
FIGHTER: *16th level fighter*
MAGIC-USER/ILLUSIONIST: *7th level*
  magic-user
THIEF/ASSASSIN: *Nil*
MONK/BARD: *Nil*
PSIONIC ABILITY: *Nil*
  Attack/Defense Modes: *Nil*
S: 19 (+3, +7) I: 19 W: 19 D: 19 C: 19 CH: 19

An air maiden appears as a winged human with a sword, garbed in flowing robes, and glowing with a brilliant light. Only one air maiden will appear at a time. Each maiden is armed with a +3 *frost brand* sword. When sent by Ukko, a maiden will first advise the worshiper as to the best course of action, using telepathy; if necessary, a maiden will enter combat thereafter. Although having few magical abilities, each maiden is 50% magic resistant, and may fly (at up to 48") without tiring. Should an air maiden be slain before her mission is completed, another will immediately appear. If a maiden is slain, she and all her possessions (including the sword) will vanish.

UNTAMO *(god of sleep and dreams)*

Lesser god

ARMOR CLASS: 0
MOVE: *18"/36"*
HIT POINTS: 319
NO. OF ATTACKS: 3/2
DAMAGE/ATTACK: 3-30 (+7)
SPECIAL ATTACKS: *Sleep aura*
SPECIAL DEFENSES: *Sleep aura*
MAGIC RESISTANCE: 25%
SIZE: *M (7')*
ALIGNMENT: *Neutral*
WORSHIPER'S ALIGN: *Neutral*
SYMBOL: *Closed eyes*
PLANE: *Concordant Opposition*
CLERIC/DRUID: *15th level cleric*
FIGHTER: *10th level fighter*
MAGIC-USER/ILLUSIONIST: *25th level*
  illusionist
THIEF/ASSASSIN: *Nil*
MONK/BARD: *10th level bard*
PSIONIC ABILITY: *Nil*
S: 19 (+3, +7) I: 25 W: 23 D: 24 C: 24 CH: 20

This god is very mild in all of his actions and dislikes being summoned for any reason. He cannot be hurt by any being that has not recently slept for 13 hours or more, as they will otherwise go to sleep instantly in his presence. Those that summon him must agree to serve his needs for one year to receive his help in any matter.

His club strikes for 3-30 points of damage and those that do not make their saving throw vs. spells will fall instantly asleep.

·GREEK·MYTHOS·

The Greek assembly of gods is probably more familiar to most readers than others of the groups in this work, because they were woven into a literature that has lasted down through the ages. Many of our civil concepts can be traced from the assumed actions of the gods and their mates.

Many of the gods of Greece descended from the greater titans, who were elder beings before the time of mortals and therefore did not need worshipers to make them strong. The worship by man gave power to the sons and daughters of the titans of a type that was not known to their elders. This enabled them to throw down the titans and gain mastery of the Prime Material Plane.

Because of their need for human worship, the Greek gods show all the traits of the mortals that they claim to be so high above. The gods are highly jealous, envious, petty, and fly into blind rages in an instant.

The first places of worship for the Greek gods were areas of natural beauty: a bubbling spring, a grove of oak trees, and the like. As large city states were created, large elaborate temples were built to honor the gods. If clerics of this pantheon live in a city, they must build or work in temples within the city. If these clerics live in the country or sparsely populated areas, they must find a natural setting for the worship of their deity.

Only clerics worshiping Poseidon may ride horses; all others must walk or ride in wagons or chariots. No cleric may have dealings with the clerics of other sects for any reason (on non-hostile terms) as this is considered a minor transgression by their deity and punishable by the stripping away of the third and higher levels of spells for a lunar month.

All clerics must permanently attach themselves to one temple, and this temple is the only place where they will be able to *commune* and where they must be drawn back to in their *word of recall* spell. While they may travel from this temple (or gladed area if they have chosen a more natural setting) they can only receive their sixth and seventh level spells from meditation in that area. If that natural area or that temple gets sacked or despoiled in any way the cleric loses his or her higher level spell abilities until the area is reconsecrated.

AEGIS

This magical shield can throw *fear* into the heart of any beings coming within 10 yards of it if they do not make their save vs. spells. It is a +5 shield and the *fear* ability must be activated by the desire of the holder. The shield also has the power to form itself into a *displacer cloak* with the same *fear* power at a word command. Its primary owner is Zeus, though Athena often has custody of it. It is used by Zeus in all of his major battles, though very occasionally he lends it to mortals he favors.

ZEUS *(god of the air) "ruler of the gods"*

Greater god

ARMOR CLASS: –2
MOVE: 18''/24''
HIT POINTS: 400
NO. OF ATTACKS: 2
DAMAGE/ATTACK: 6-60 (+14)
SPECIAL ATTACKS: *Lightning bolts*
SPECIAL DEFENSES: *See below*
MAGIC RESISTANCE: 75%
SIZE: M (6½')
ALIGNMENT: *Chaotic good*
WORSHIPER'S ALIGN: *All good alignments*
SYMBOL: *A fist full of lightning bolts on a black background*
PLANE: *Olympus*
CLERIC/DRUID: *25th level cleric*
FIGHTER: *17th level fighter*
MAGIC-USER/ILLUSIONIST: *20th level in each*
THIEF/ASSASSIN: *Nil*
MONK/BARD: *15th level bard*
PSIONIC ABILITY: *II*
S: 25 (+7, +14)   I: 25   W: 25   D: 25   C: 25   CH: 25

This god usually appears as a human bearded male of powerful physique. He often *shape changes*. He disdains the use of armor, but will use a +5 shield, his *Aegis*. Zeus is able to simultaneously attack and cast a 30 point *lightning bolt* each melee round. He wields a spear that does 6-60 points of damage.

When his wounds spill blood on the earth, the blood forms a random sixth level monster. This can happen once per round. The monster will then fight for Zeus until dead or 48 hours elapse.

A giant white eagle is always at the god's side, and one of its type is occasionally given to those the god favors.

Clerics that preach the god's ways use symbols of an eagle, ram, and an oak tree in their teachings. These symbols are also incorporated in the clerics' vestments and holy relics.

Zeus is the son of the titans Kronos and Rhea. He led the gods in their overthrow of the titans, and became their general ruler. He is the lord of the upper air and the major ruler of the plane of Olympus. However, his rule is not always absolute, and the other gods and goddesses may argue his decisions.

THE WHITE EAGLE OF ZEUS

FREQUENCY: *Unique*
NO. APPEARING: *1*
ARMOR CLASS: *2*
MOVE: *6''/48''*
HIT DICE/POINTS: *100 hp*
% IN LAIR: *25%*
TREASURE TYPE: *Nil*
NO. OF ATTACKS: *3*
DAMAGE/ATTACK: *1-10/1-10/3-30*
SPECIAL ATTACKS: *Nil*
SPECIAL DEFENSES: *Nil*
MAGIC RESISTANCE: *10%*
INTELLIGENCE: *Very*
ALIGNMENT: *Neutral good*
SIZE: *L (50' wing span)*
PSIONIC ABILITY: *Nil*
    Attack/Defense Modes: *Nil*
LEVEL/X.P. VALUE: *X/14,100*

This bird is very special, and though it appears to be a normal giant of its breed, it is not. The creature can teleport from plane to plane, it talks to Zeus, and is often used to carry large loads of the god's thunder bolts into battle. It acts as Zeus' messenger and symbol. In battle, it attacks as a 16+ hit dice monster with its two claws and its huge beak.

ACHILLES *(hero)*

ARMOR CLASS: 0
MOVE: 18''
HIT POINTS: 90
NO. OF ATTACKS: 2
DAMAGE/ATTACK: 1-10
SPECIAL ATTACKS: *Nil*
SPECIAL DEFENSES: *See below*
MAGIC RESISTANCE: *Standard*
SIZE: M (5½')
ALIGNMENT: *Neutral good*
CLERIC/DRUID: *Nil*
FIGHTER: *15th level fighter*
MAGIC-USER/ILLUSIONIST: *Nil*
THIEF/ASSASSIN: *Nil*
MONK/BARD: *Nil*
PSIONIC ABILITY: *Nil*
   Attack/Defense Modes: *Nil*
S: *18 (51%) (+2, +3)* I: *12* W: *10* D: *18* C: *18* CH: *18*

Achilles is the son of King Peleus and the sea nymph Thetis. He wears +2 chainmail and a +2 shield into battle, all gold plated. He is a charioteer who uses immortal horses to pull his chariot at 24'' per turn.

His skin cannot be pierced by edged weapons (except at his left heel); only bludgeon-type weapons can harm him in battle.

ANTAEUS *(giant)*

FREQUENCY: *Unique*
NO. APPEARING: *1*
ARMOR CLASS: *4*
MOVE: *15''*
HIT DICE/POINTS: *100 hp*
% IN LAIR: *50%*
TREASURE TYPE: *Q (× 3)*
NO. OF ATTACKS: *1*
DAMAGE/ATTACK: *2-16/3-18/4-24/*
   5-30/6-36/7-42/8-48 (see below)
SPECIAL ATTACKS: *See below*
SPECIAL DEFENSES: *Growth,*
   regeneration (see below)
MAGIC RESISTANCE: *Standard*
INTELLIGENCE: *Low*
ALIGNMENT: *Chaotic evil*
SIZE: *L (11'-21')*
PSIONIC ABILITY: *Nil*
   Attack/Defense Modes: *Nil*
LEVEL/X.P. VALUE: *X/14,000 + 35*
   per hp when killed

This giant is the offspring of Poseidon and Gaia, the original earth-deity. He grows stronger each round he fights, as long as he remains on the earth. Antaeus starts similar to a hill giant in size and appearance, but every round he fights he grows, gaining the size and strength each round of the next largest giant type, until he reaches titan strength and size. Each time he grows, all damage he has taken is healed, and he increases a further 25 hit points (up to 250 total). Even after he ceases growing, all damage he takes in one round is healed in the next as long as he remains on the earth. Antaeus will remain at titan size as long as he fights, gradually shrinking when the battle is over. If Antaeus is lifted off the ground, he loses strength and size at the same rate he gained it, and will no longer heal. He always attacks as a 16+ hit dice monster.

APHRODITE *(goddess of love, beauty and passion)*

Greater goddess

ARMOR CLASS: 4
MOVE: 12''/24''
HIT POINTS: 259
NO. OF ATTACKS: 1
DAMAGE/ATTACK: 1-10
SPECIAL ATTACKS: *Charm*
SPECIAL DEFENSES: *Nil*
MAGIC RESISTANCE: 50%
SIZE: M (5½')
ALIGNMENT: *Chaotic good*
WORSHIPER'S ALIGN: *Chaotic beings*
SYMBOL: *Sea shell*
PLANE: *Olympus*
CLERIC/DRUID: *10th level cleric*
FIGHTER: *Nil*
MAGIC-USER/ILLUSIONIST: *12th level*
   magic-user/15th level illusionist
THIEF/ASSASSIN: *Nil*
MONK/BARD: *10th level bard*
PSIONIC ABILITY: *VI*
S: *19 (+3, +7)* I: *20* W: *20* D: *23* C: *21* CH: *25*

The goddess of love and beauty, Aphrodite's main ability is to generate strong passion in mortals and gods alike. In every one of her *shape changed* forms she is beautiful. She is able to *charm* either sex, and once a person has viewed her and not made their saving throw against her *charm*, they can never attack her again.

The simple wave of her hand causes 1-10 hit points of pain to any who would harm her, no saving throw.

Her clerics sacrifice doves to her every 10 days and objects of art and lovely pieces of jewelry are destroyed on her altar every new moon. All of her female clerics must have a 15 or greater charisma and her male clerics must have a constitution of 16 or better.

Aphrodite is an extremely vain and jealous goddess. If any character should unfavorably compare Aphrodite's charm to his or her own, there is a 10% chance that the goddess will hear and seek vengeance.

APOLLO *(god of the sun, prophecy, music and archery)*

Greater god

ARMOR CLASS: 1
MOVE: 15''
HIT POINTS: 376
NO. OF ATTACKS: 2
DAMAGE/ATTACK: *By weapon type*
SPECIAL ATTACKS: *Bow; also see*
   below
SPECIAL DEFENSES: *Protective haze*
MAGIC RESISTANCE: 56%
SIZE: L (20')
ALIGNMENT: *Chaotic good*
WORSHIPER'S ALIGN: *Chaotic good,*
   music lovers, archers, sun worship-
   ers
SYMBOL: *Lyre*
PLANE: *Olympus*
CLERIC/DRUID: *20th level cleric/14th*
   level druid
FIGHTER: *15th level ranger*
MAGIC-USER/ILLUSIONIST: *15th level*
   in each
THIEF/ASSASSIN: *15th level thief*
MONK/BARD: *23rd level bard*
PSIONIC ABILITY: *I*
S: *25 (+7, +14)* I: *24* W: *23* D: *25* C: *24* CH: *25*

Apollo appears as an incredibly handsome young man. At will, he can *shape change, polymorph others, turn flesh to stone, cause diseases, cure diseases,* and *cure serious wounds* (one per round).

The range of his +4 bow is that of his line of sight, and his +3 arrows are made of adamantite. Apollo has a lyre that is able to raise a friendly being's strength to that of a storm giant for as long as the god plays, if he so desires. It also bestows *curses* and casts *disintegrate* spells (one at a time, up to once per round).

If Apollo is especially fond of a human (judge's option), he may indirectly aid him or her in a battle or give needed advice.

In battle, he casts a purple haze around any single being (usually himself) that will act as a +5 *ring of protection*.

Apollo has been known to lend his aid in several ways: giving his archery skill to mortals for special battles; giving his arrows as gifts; healing heroes in the thick of battle; and using his prophetic power to advise.

Apollo is also the sun god, and it is said that he carries the sun across the sky each day in his solar chariot.

Apollo and his sister Artemis are close companions. If either is in need of aid, there is a 60% chance that the other will come to help.

All of Apollo's clerics must wear leaves of laurel on their vestments and must use laurel wood in their devices. The laurel wreath and the sun chariot are also Apollo's symbols.

ARES *(god of war)*

Greater god

ARMOR CLASS: −2
MOVE: 26''/24''
HIT POINTS: 333
NO. OF ATTACKS: 2
DAMAGE/ATTACK: 5-50 (+9) or 3-30 (+9)
SPECIAL ATTACKS: Nil
SPECIAL DEFENSES: See below
MAGIC RESISTANCE: 59%
SIZE: M (6')
ALIGNMENT: Chaotic evil
WORSHIPER'S ALIGN: Neutral and evil (warriors)
SYMBOL: Spear
PLANE: Olympus
CLERIC/DRUID: Nil
FIGHTER: 20th level ranger
MAGIC-USER/ILLUSIONIST: 10th level illusionist
THIEF/ASSASSIN: 12th level assassin
MONK/BARD: 12th level monk
PSIONIC ABILITY: V
S: 21 (+4, +9) I: 20 W: 9 D: 25 C: 24 CH: 22

Ares appears as a normal man wearing +5 chainmail. He often flies into battle, and can *shape change* at will.

His +3 spear does 5-50 points of damage and causes *fear* (as the spell) within 10 yards of it; his +5 sword does 3-30 points of damage per strike and creates an *anti-magic shell* around the god at will. It also makes him invulnerable to poison or petrification. No being in the Prime Material Plane but Ares can pick up his spear, and with the spear in hand the god can move as a blink dog. Ares can use either the spear or the sword; never both at once.

There is a great rivalry between Athena and Ares because of their conflicting roles in combat. Ares is the god of total battle lust and love of killing and fighting, while Athena is a goddess of war and a love of style and battle art. Both clerical groups will oppose each other at every opportunity.

ARTEMIS *(goddess of the hunt)*

Lesser goddess

ARMOR CLASS: 1
MOVE: 18''
HIT POINTS: 219
NO. OF ATTACKS: 2
DAMAGE/ATTACK: 1-10 (+5) or 2-20 (+9)
SPECIAL ATTACKS: +3 bow
SPECIAL DEFENSES: See below
MAGIC RESISTANCE: See below
SIZE: M (5½')
ALIGNMENT: Neutral
WORSHIPER'S ALIGN: Neutral
SYMBOL: Bow of ivory in front of the moon
PLANE: Olympus
CLERIC/DRUID: 14th level druid
FIGHTER: 16th level ranger
MAGIC-USER/ILLUSIONIST: 10th level illusionist
THIEF/ASSASSIN: Nil
MONK/BARD: 5th level bard
PSIONIC ABILITY: V
S: 21 (+4, +9) I: 23 W: 24 D: 24 C: 19 CH: 25

Artemis appears in the form of a slim young girl with an obvious maidenly way about her. She *shape changes* at will, and any magical spell sent to hurt her will reflect back to the sender. Whenever she is transformed into animal shape she is *hasted* as the spell.

Arrows shot from her +3 bow do 1-10 points of damage, and she only uses +2 arrows. Her maximum range is 1,000 yards. Any magical creature that fights with fang and claw cannot hurt her after seeing her once. She has absolute power over all nonmagical animals of the forest. In hand-to-hand combat she uses a slim dagger that is a +3 weapon, inflicting 2-20 points of damage when in her hands.

All of the clerics in her sect are druids, and they must be pure of body as well as spirit.

While she is a huntress and chases down all types of animals, this is only done for eating purposes and never for mere sport. The animals she hunts are always the ones that have gained a slight upper hand in the ecological balance of nature.

Artemis is the sister twin of Apollo, daughter of Zeus and Leto. She is also associated with the moon.

ATHENA *(goddess of wisdom and combat)*

Greater goddess

ARMOR CLASS: −2
MOVE: 15''/24''
HIT POINTS: 329
NO. OF ATTACKS: 2
DAMAGE/ATTACK: 5-50 (+11)
SPECIAL ATTACKS: Petrification, never misses target
SPECIAL DEFENSES: Anti-magic shell
MAGIC RESISTANCE: 80%
SIZE: M (6')
ALIGNMENT: Lawful good
WORSHIPER'S ALIGN: Lawful good, fighters
SYMBOL: An owl
PLANE: Olympus
CLERIC/DRUID: 20th level cleric/14th level druid
FIGHTER: 20th level fighter
MAGIC-USER/ILLUSIONIST: 12th level in each
THIEF/ASSASSIN: Nil
MONK/BARD: 12th level bard
PSIONIC ABILITY: VI
S: 23 (+5, +11) I: 25 W: 25 D: 22 C: 23 CH: 21

Athena usually appears as a beautiful woman wearing a war helm and carrying a spear and shield. She is often seen with an owl on her shoulder.

She *shape changes* at will, moves as a blink dog, and she never misses her target. Her weapon does 5-50 points of damage per strike. Her shield has a medusa head upon it, and those looking at it may be turned to stone just as if it were alive. Her helm creates an *anti-magic shell* whenever she wishes, through which she can cast spells.

Athena's clerics are aggressive in their attempts to spread her worship, and are contemptful of all other clerics. Whenever possible, they will act to oppose clerics of Ares.

ATLAS *(greater titan, "strength personified")*

ARMOR CLASS: -3
MOVE: 24''/30''
HIT POINTS: 350
NO. OF ATTACKS: 2
DAMAGE/ATTACK: 10-100/10-100
SPECIAL ATTACKS: See below
SPECIAL DEFENSES: Nil
MAGIC RESISTANCE: 95%
SIZE: L (50')
ALIGNMENT: Chaotic evil
PLANE: Tarterus
CLERIC/DRUID: Nil
FIGHTER: 19th level fighter
MAGIC-USER/ILLUSIONIST: Nil
THIEF/ASSASSIN: Nil
MONK/BARD: 10th level monk
PSIONIC ABILITY: V
S: 25 (+7, +14) I: 12 W: 12 D: 20 C: 23 CH: 20

This greater titan is massively built, and his primary attribute is his great strength. This strength is drawn from the Prime Material Plane. When the titan is on other planes he only has strength of 25, but when on the Prime Material Plane there is nothing he can't lift, nothing he can't bend, and nothing he can't break!

Despite his alignment, if he gives his word on a matter, he will keep it even unto death!

BELLEROPHON *(hero)*

ARMOR CLASS: 4
MOVE: 12''
HIT POINTS: 69
NO. OF ATTACKS: 3/2
DAMAGE/ATTACK: By weapon type
SPECIAL ATTACKS: Nil
SPECIAL DEFENSES: See below
MAGIC RESISTANCE: Standard
SIZE: M (5½')
ALIGNMENT: Lawful good
CLERIC/DRUID: Nil
FIGHTER: 10th level ranger
MAGIC-USER/ILLUSIONIST: Nil
THIEF/ASSASSIN: Nil
MONK/BARD: Nil
PSIONIC ABILITY: Nil
    Attack/Defense Modes: Nil
S: 18 (00) (+3, +6) I: 17 W: 17 D: 18 C: 17 CH: 18

Bellerophon is the son of Glaucus, a king. He is credited with defeating the king of the chimerae. He rode a pegasus into battle against several other enchanted monsters and defeated them all with his javelins and war spear.

There is a 25% chance that at any given time a god or goddess of Olympus is watching over him, and if so, there is a 75% chance that he will be saved by the watcher if Bellerophon is in mortal danger.

CERBERUS *(guardian of Hades)*

FREQUENCY: Unique
NO. APPEARING: 1
ARMOR CLASS: 1
MOVE: 24''
HIT DICE/POINTS: 30 hp per head/
    100 hit points for the body
% IN LAIR: 99%
TREASURE TYPE: Nil
NO. OF ATTACKS: 3
DAMAGE/ATTACK: 3-30/3-30/3-30
SPECIAL ATTACKS: See below
SPECIAL DEFENSES: Regeneration
MAGIC RESISTANCE: 25%
INTELLIGENCE: Very
ALIGNMENT: Neutral evil
SIZE: L (30')
PSIONIC ABILITY: Nil
    Attack/Defense Modes: Nil
LEVEL/X.P. VALUE: X/26,240

This beast is always found guarding the doorway to the House of Hades. It is a monstrous dog with 3 mastiff heads and a huge body. He not only keeps beings out, he keeps them in, and cannot be magicked away from his post by any force.

Each head bites for 3-30 points; the middle head spews forth a powerful poisonous spittle up to 30' which kills on contact (no saving throw); the collective gaze of all 3 heads turns mortals to stone (one per round, saving throw applies). It attacks as a 16+ hit dice monster. Cerberus may only use one attack form per head per round. The creature regenerates 5 points per melee round.

CIRCE *(the black sorceress)*

ARMOR CLASS: 10
MOVE: 12''
HIT POINTS: 51
NO. OF ATTACKS: 1
DAMAGE/ATTACK: 1-4
SPECIAL ATTACKS: Nil
SPECIAL DEFENSES: Nil
MAGIC RESISTANCE: Standard
SIZE: M (5')
ALIGNMENT: Chaotic evil
CLERIC/DRUID: 15th level cleric
FIGHTER: Nil
MAGIC-USER/ILLUSIONIST: 12th level
    magic-user/9th level illusionist
THIEF/ASSASSIN: Nil
MONK/BARD: 5th level bard
PSIONIC ABILITY: Nil
    Attack/Defense Modes: Nil
S: 10 I: 17 W: 9 D: 17 C: 18 CH: 18

Circe's main magical attacks all deal with polymorphing humans into animals of one type or another. Towards this end she has every magical device capable of turning creatures into other creatures (polymorph wands, polymorph potions, polymorph scrolls, and the like).

She is the one who intercepted the hero Odysseus and his crew, changed the crew into pigs, and fell in love with Odysseus. She always wears revealing black gowns to meet mortals. She is almost immortal and does not appear to age. Circe also possesses great prophetic powers and can give useful advice if she wishes.

COEUS (greater titan of fear)

ARMOR CLASS: 2
MOVE: 24''
HIT POINTS: 344
NO. OF ATTACKS: 2
DAMAGE/ATTACK: 5-30 (+12)
SPECIAL ATTACKS: Fear
SPECIAL DEFENSES: Fear aura
MAGIC RESISTANCE: 50%
SIZE: L (21')
ALIGNMENT: Chaotic evil
PLANE: Tarterus
CLERIC/DRUID: Nil
FIGHTER: 16th level fighter
MAGIC-USER/ILLUSIONIST: 15th level
    magic-user
THIEF/ASSASSIN: Nil
MONK/BARD: Nil
PSIONIC ABILITY: V
S: 24 (+6, +12) I: 20 W: 14 D: 20 C: 23 CH:−4

Coeus appears as a horrifying greater titan, and he kills by fear. All those that do not make their saving throw versus magic will be struck with a loss of 25% of their total original hit points every time they see him angry. Coeus can shape change at will.

When first coming within 20 yards of him, a saving throw vs. spells must be made or the being will die of fright! After that it is necessary to make a saving throw every 4 melee rounds or run in fear for 10 turns.

He uses a +5 sword in battle that strikes for 5-30 points of damage. Coeus travels only at night and never fights during the day.

CRIUS (greater titan of density and gravity)

ARMOR CLASS: −3
MOVE: 24''
HIT POINTS: 390
NO. OF ATTACKS: 2
DAMAGE/ATTACK: 10-60/10-60
SPECIAL ATTACKS: See below
SPECIAL DEFENSES: See below
MAGIC RESISTANCE: 50%
SIZE: L (100')
ALIGNMENT: Chaotic evil
PLANE: Tarterus
CLERIC/DRUID: 15th level cleric
FIGHTER: 16th level fighter
MAGIC-USER/ILLUSIONIST: 15th level
    magic-user
THIEF/ASSASSIN: Nil
MONK/BARD: Nil
PSIONIC ABILITY: V
S: 25 (+7, +14) I: 23 W: 19 D: 23 C: 23 CH: 23

Crius can increase the weight of objects at will, and he can make things weightless. He is able to make any one non-living object too heavy to lift for a period of 1-4 melee rounds; this power can be increased to permanency if the titan is allowed to work on the object for one full turn (saving throw vs. the permanency applicable).

In battle, the titan creates a field of gravity that causes anything launched at him of a physical nature (arrows, spears, etc.) to fall short. All attackers will be at −4 on their chances to hit and −1 on their armor classes while in this field. Likewise, dexterity bonuses do not apply.

CYCLOPS, Greater

FREQUENCY: Very rare
NO. APPEARING: 1-4
ARMOR CLASS: −4
MOVE: 15''
HIT DICE/POINTS: 15 HD + 1-8 hit
    points
% IN LAIR: 55%
TREASURE TYPE: E, Q (× 10), S
NO. OF ATTACKS: 1
DAMAGE/ATTACK: 7-42
SPECIAL ATTACKS: Nil
SPECIAL DEFENSES: Immune to fire
MAGIC RESISTANCE: 25%
INTELLIGENCE: Exceptional
ALIGNMENT: Chaotic good
SIZE: L (21')
PSIONIC ABILITY: Nil
    Attack/Defense Modes: Nil
LEVEL/X.P. VALUE: IX/7,800 + 20
    per hp

These giants were a gift to Hephaestus by his mother Hera. These are much more intelligent than the lesser cyclopes, and serve the blacksmith god in his mountain and in underwater caves near the shores of some major city-states.

These cyclopes are able to live very well on land or in the water, and spend most of their time making javelins of lightning, magic armor and shields, etc. They are immune to all fire attacks, accustomed as they are to the great heat of Hephaestus' forge. If a mortal brings them gifts they can use, there is a 20% chance that they will reward the mortal with one of their magic items; there is an 80% chance they will kill the gift bringer for his presumption. They have no qualms about using their own magic items in attack or defense. Each greater cyclops wears a personal set of magical scale mail.

CYCLOPS, Lesser

FREQUENCY: Very rare
NO. APPEARING: 1-2
ARMOR CLASS: 2
MOVE: 15''
HIT DICE/POINTS: 13 HD
% IN LAIR: 85%
TREASURE TYPE: E, S
NO. OF ATTACKS: 1
DAMAGE/ATTACK: 6-36
SPECIAL ATTACKS: Hurl rocks
SPECIAL DEFENSES: Nil
MAGIC RESISTANCE: Standard
INTELLIGENCE: Low
ALIGNMENT: Chaotic evil
SIZE: L (20')
PSIONIC ABILITY: Nil
    Attack/Defense Modes: Nil
LEVEL/X.P. VALUE: VIII/3,950 + 18
    per hp

These brutes appear as extremely ugly and huge hill giant types with one eye under a beetling brow. They are usually solitary creatures and react violently to any mortal who dares to disturb them. Originally created by Poseidon, they usually inhabit islands.

They always have a supply of huge boulders at hand to hurl for 4-40 points of damage, and they can toss these rocks up to 50''.

DEMETER *(goddess of agriculture)*

Lesser goddess

ARMOR CLASS: 1
MOVE: 15''
HIT POINTS: 219
NO. OF ATTACKS: 3/2
DAMAGE/ATTACK: 2-20 (+9)
SPECIAL ATTACKS: See below
SPECIAL DEFENSES: See below
MAGIC RESISTANCE: 29%
SIZE: M (5')
ALIGNMENT: Neutral good
WORSHIPER'S ALIGN: Neutral good
  and all farmers
SYMBOL: Mare's head
PLANE: Olympus
CLERIC/DRUID: 14th level druid
FIGHTER: 12th level ranger
MAGIC-USER/ILLUSIONIST: 15th level
  illusionist
THIEF/ASSASSIN: Nil
MONK/BARD: 10th level bard
PSIONIC ABILITY: VI
S: 21 (+4, +9) I: 24 W: 24 D: 25 C: 21 CH: 25

This goddess appears in the form of a beautiful woman. She *shape changes* at will, can create any type of weather for any length of time, can summon and control any type of plant or animal she wills, and can *polymorph* others at will.

Demeter rides a chariot pulled by two ancient green dragons. In battle she uses a +2 spear of ash wood that strikes for 2-20 points of damage.

Demeter is the goddess of agriculture, specifically grain, and no grain will grow on the earth if she neglects her duties.

DIONYSUS *(god of wine)*

Greater god

ARMOR CLASS: 4
MOVE: 15''
HIT POINTS: 380
NO. OF ATTACKS: 2
DAMAGE/ATTACK: 4-40
SPECIAL ATTACKS: See below
SPECIAL DEFENSES: Immune to illusions and magical control
MAGIC RESISTANCE: 45%
SIZE: M (7')
ALIGNMENT: Chaotic neutral
WORSHIPER'S ALIGN: Chaotic (good, neutral or evil)
SYMBOL: Thyrsus
PLANE: Olympus
CLERIC/DRUID: 15th level cleric
FIGHTER: 14th level fighter
MAGIC-USER/ILLUSIONIST: 13th level in each
THIEF/ASSASSIN: Nil
MONK/BARD: 19th level bard
PSIONIC ABILITY: III
S: 24 (+6, +12) I: 22 W: 20 D: 23 C: 25 CH: 23

As the god of wine, Dionysus has a dual nature: on the one hand, he represents joy, pleasure and camaraderie; on the other hand, savage, mindless, bloodthirsty violence. He represents the fact that wine can induce both happiness and madness.

While Dionysus most often appears as a young man in a purple robe, he also likes to appear in lion, panther, dolphin, and bear shapes. He can *shape change* at will, cast any *polymorph* spell whenever he wishes, and can control any type of feline or ursine creature. He savagely inflicts madness upon anyone who attacks or discomforts him (save vs. spells at −4). He is also protective of his temples and high level clerics, and may, if greatly outraged, inflict this same madness upon defilers of his holy places.

Dionysus rides a panther-drawn chariot which moves at 24''. Panthers: AC 2, HD 11, hp 50 each, #AT 3, D 1-8/1-8/3-18 (claw/claw/bite).

Dionysus uses his *thyrsus* in battle, which inflicts 4-40 points of damage at a touch. A thyrsus is a staff tipped with a pine cone and twined with ivy. It is the symbol of Dionysus and all his clerics. The god's thyrsus has the following powers: it can restore all dead things to life (as a *raise dead*), it allows the holder to *teleport* from any plant he or she is touching to any other plant, and it acts as a *mirror of life trapping* (at a touch instead of a gaze).

ENCELADUS *(giant)*

FREQUENCY: Unique
NO. APPEARING: 1
ARMOR CLASS: 1
MOVE: 15''
HIT DICE/POINTS: 219 hp
% IN LAIR: 85%
TREASURE TYPE: Nil
NO. OF ATTACKS: 2
DAMAGE/ATTACK: 7-70/7-70
SPECIAL ATTACKS: See below
SPECIAL DEFENSES: See below
MAGIC RESISTANCE: Standard
INTELLIGENCE: Low
ALIGNMENT: Chaotic evil
SIZE: L (85')
PSIONIC ABILITY: Nil
  Attack/Defense Modes: Nil
LEVEL/X.P. VALUE: X/21,175

This giant has huge snake bodies and tails for legs. It is known to live alone in a desolate swamp. Enceladus is so horrifying that any who come within 100 yards of him must save vs. spells or flee in *fear* (as the spell).

There is a power in this being's hands that allows it to grab spells out of the air and negate them before they have time to function. Enceladus can grab up to four spells directed at him per melee round. If he does not grab spells, he can strike with his fists for 7-70 points of damage each. He can grab two spells with one hand and strike with the other, if he chooses. The giant fights as a 16+ hit dice monster, and he has been known to fight against the gods of Olympus if given the chance.

EPIMETHEUS *(greater titan)* "Afterthought"

ARMOR CLASS: −3
MOVE: 24''
HIT POINTS: 345
NO. OF ATTACKS: 2
DAMAGE/ATTACK: 9-90
SPECIAL ATTACKS: Nil
SPECIAL DEFENSES: Nil
MAGIC RESISTANCE: 50%
SIZE: L (100')
ALIGNMENT: Chaotic good
PLANE: Twin Paradises
CLERIC/DRUID: 10th level in each
FIGHTER: 14th level fighter
MAGIC-USER/ILLUSIONIST: 15th level
  magic-user
THIEF/ASSASSIN: Nil
MONK/BARD: Nil
PSIONIC ABILITY: V
S: 25 (+7, +14) I: 21 W: 19 D: 23 C: 22 CH: 22

The bumbling brother of Prometheus, this greater titan means well but is not very careful with his creations. He can create as does Prometheus, but there is a 45% chance that the creature he makes will fight him! He is fond of mankind, and if he is paying attention when a person does a particularly difficult act (judge's option) there is a 5% chance that the god will reward the being with a ball of clay. This ball can be made into any 4th level creature, but there is a 60% chance that the creature will try to kill, rather than obey, its maker. All that is necessary is for the mortal to toss the ball to the ground and call on the creature that is desired. If it does not attack the person, it will obey him or her until its death.

Epimetheus can strike with his fists for 9-90 points of damage each.

FURIES *(Alecto, Tisiphone, Megarea)*

FREQUENCY: *Unique*
NO. APPEARING: *3*
ARMOR CLASS: *−1*
MOVE: *18″/24″*
HIT DICE/POINTS: *200 hp each*
% IN LAIR: *1%*
TREASURE TYPE: *Nil*
NO. OF ATTACKS: *1*
DAMAGE/ATTACK: *5-30*
SPECIAL ATTACKS: *Ability reduction*
SPECIAL DEFENSES: *Nil*
MAGIC RESISTANCE: *100%*
INTELLIGENCE: *High*
ALIGNMENT: *Neutral*
SIZE: *M (5′)*
PSIONIC ABILITY: *V*

These 3 spirits are the punishment force of the gods. Mortals who perform an act that the gods determine must be punished will face the wrath of the Furies. They appear as old winged crones carrying metal-barbed whips and attack as 16+ HD monsters. Their main attribute is the power to find anyone or anything on any plane they are on (as long as he, she, or it is not hidden by magical means).

Their punishments cannot be appealed, and the whips have the power to strip away points in a being's ability categories with every hit (intelligence points, strength points, and the like) besides doing hit point damage. The amount and type of ability points lost is always commensurate with the victim's crime against the gods.

HADES *(god of the underworld and death)*

Greater god

ARMOR CLASS: *−1*
MOVE: *29″*
HIT POINTS: *390*
NO. OF ATTACKS: *2*
DAMAGE/ATTACK: *5-50 (+12)*
SPECIAL ATTACKS: *See below*
SPECIAL DEFENSES: *See below*
MAGIC RESISTANCE: *75%*
SIZE: *M (6½′)*
ALIGNMENT: *Neutral evil*
WORSHIPER'S ALIGN: *Neutral evil*
SYMBOL: *Black ram*
PLANE: *Hades*
CLERIC/DRUID: *20th level cleric*
FIGHTER: *15th level fighter*
MAGIC-USER/ILLUSIONIST: *25th level illusionist*
THIEF/ASSASSIN: *15th level assassin*
MONK/BARD: *15th level monk*
PSIONIC ABILITY: *III*
S: *24 (+6, +12)* I: *24* W: *20* D: *24* C: *25* CH: *24 (−9)*

The plane where Hades resides is known to most mortals by the name of its most powerful ruler. Hades appears as a heavily muscled, dark skinned man. When in a pleasant mood and talking to mortals, he appears handsome and kind, but when fighting, the god appears as a hideous humanoid with fangs and flame for eyes! Hades *shape changes* at will, and his eyes can cast 2 *death spells* every melee round, up to a range of 120′, if he is not engaged in hand-to-hand combat.

To touch his body with any nonmetal object will cause an explosion of *death rays* to strike all those in a 30′ radius (saving throw applicable).

He has complete control over all things made of the earth and can alter the form of any amount of earth with a word. With this power, the god can make a sword turn into dust or a suit of armor turn into gold (saving throw applicable).

The house of Hades is a dark underground place with eternal fires of lava burning in pools. The dead move to the god's command and mortals do not see them unless Hades wills it so. In this place are several items of note such as his *chair of forgetfulness* which was designed to cause a being to

forget his or her past and become devoted to Hades when sat in (he often tricked powerful mortals and lesser gods and goddesses into the chair, and there they remained until freed). His jet black chariot is pulled by nightmares, and while in this vehicle he cannot be touched by mortals or gods alike. The god also possesses a helm that renders him invisible to *all beings*, even in battle, though he is only allowed to use this device in service against the enemies of the gods of Olympus. There is only one entrance to the House of Hades and that one is guarded by Cerberus (cf.).

The god uses a +4 sword in battle that does 5-50 hit points of damage per strike.

HECATE *(goddess of magic)*

Lesser goddess

ARMOR CLASS: *−2*
MOVE: *12″*
HIT POINTS: *289*
NO. OF ATTACKS: *1*
DAMAGE/ATTACK: *See below*
SPECIAL ATTACKS: *See below*
SPECIAL DEFENSES: *See below*
MAGIC RESISTANCE: *89%*
SIZE: *M (5¼′)*
ALIGNMENT: *Lawful evil*
WORSHIPER'S ALIGN: *Any being working with magic*
SYMBOL: *Setting moon*
PLANE: *Nine Hells*
CLERIC/DRUID: *14th level druid*
FIGHTER: *Nil*
MAGIC-USER/ILLUSIONIST: *Special*
THIEF/ASSASSIN: *Nil*
MONK/BARD: *Nil*
PSIONIC ABILITY: *I*
S: *12* I: *25* W: *9* D: *20* C: *22* CH: *25*

Hecate appears as a beautiful woman and is able to use any magic-user or illusionist spell as often as she likes without restriction as if she were 20th level. From sunset to sunrise, she is able to cast two spells per melee round in any combination. During the day, she casts one per round.

She has twin *spheres of annihilation* with her at all times that move to attack her enemies. These devices move by themselves after being started and cannot be controlled by mortals.

She has 9 hell hounds as servants (with maximum hit points and abilities). These creatures are sent out to hunt down all those who would desecrate her temples or attack her clerics of greater than 10th level (a 10% chance of this happening with every such act). All of her clerics have a special rapport with hell hounds. Hell hounds will never attack them in any case, and Hecate's clerics have a chance of controlling them equal to their chance of affecting "special" undead.

Hecate's clerics sacrifice to her on the night of the full moon. Her images often have three faces.

HECATONCHEIRE *(hundred handed one)*

FREQUENCY: *Very rare*
NO. APPEARING: *1*
ARMOR CLASS: *5*
MOVE: *15″*
HIT DICE/POINTS: *300 hp*
% IN LAIR: *89%*
TREASURE TYPE: *H*
NO. OF ATTACKS: *10*
DAMAGE/ATTACK: *3-30 each*
SPECIAL ATTACKS: *Hurled boulders*
SPECIAL DEFENSES: *Nil*
MAGIC RESISTANCE: *25%*
INTELLIGENCE: *Low*
ALIGNMENT: *Chaotic neutral*
SIZE: *L (100′)*
PSIONIC ABILITY: *Nil*
    Attack/Defense Modes: *Nil*
LEVEL/X.P. VALUE: *X/29,300*

These beings are giants that have 100 arms and 50 heads each, with an unusually high manual dexterity. All are bitter enemies of the gods of Olympus. If a hecatoncheire decides to grab a being, a strength of 18 (50%) will give the grabbed being a 10% chance of pulling free, with a 1% increase for every percentage point of strength over 50.

These creatures hurl groups of boulders at their enemies which act as the *meteor swarm* spell for damaging effects. Their maximum range is 30''.

Opponents who get close to a hecatoncheire may be struck by up to ten fists simultaneously. Huge opponents (20' or greater) can be struck by an additional 3-30 more. They strike as 16+ hit dice monsters.

HEPHAESTUS *(god of blacksmiths)*

Lesser god

ARMOR CLASS: −5
MOVE: 9''
HIT POINTS: 312
NO. OF ATTACKS: 2
DAMAGE/ATTACK: 20-80 (+14)
SPECIAL ATTACKS: See below
SPECIAL DEFENSES: Nil
MAGIC RESISTANCE: 50%
SIZE: L (20')
ALIGNMENT: Neutral
WORSHIPER'S ALIGN: All workers of metal, including dwarves
SYMBOL: Hammer and anvil
PLANE: The Prime Material Plane
CLERIC/DRUID: Nil
FIGHTER: 18th level fighter
MAGIC-USER/ILLUSIONIST: 18th level magic-user
THIEF/ASSASSIN: Nil
MONK/BARD: Nil
PSIONIC ABILITY: IV
S: 25 (+7, +14)   I: 25   W: 20   D: 22   C: 23   CH: 9

Hephaestus looks like a tall hill giant with a humped back and a club foot. He is the only being able to easily work the extremely hard metal adamant. This god has so few worshipers that any being doing a great service (judge's option) for his sect, on a 5% chance, will be given a +5 shield especially made to be useable by any class and not hamper him in battle.

He uses a nine foot long hammer in battle that strikes for 20-80 points of damage.

The god works in a volcanic mountain with his helpers: greater cyclopes, fire elementals, efreet, and some of the lesser types of intelligent demons. The god is friend to the dwarves and has been known to personally teach their most talented smiths. A red dragon guards the tunnel entrance to his mountain. This ancient creature will always talk to those who seek entrance to discover if they are merely curious (and therefore edible) or have actual business with the god. His clerics above 10th level are allowed to commune with him in the caves for advice and the like.

HERA *(goddess of marriage and intrigue)*

Greater goddess

ARMOR CLASS: 2
MOVE: 12''
HIT POINTS: 300
NO. OF ATTACKS: 3/2
DAMAGE/ATTACK: 2-20 (+1)
SPECIAL ATTACKS: Voice (see below)
SPECIAL DEFENSES: Nil
MAGIC RESISTANCE: 50%
SIZE: M (5½')
ALIGNMENT: Neutral
WORSHIPER'S ALIGN: Variable (wives and intriguers)
SYMBOL: Peacock
PLANE: Olympus
CLERIC/DRUID: 15th level cleric
FIGHTER: 10th level fighter
MAGIC-USER/ILLUSIONIST: 12th level in each
THIEF/ASSASSIN: Nil
MONK/BARD: Nil
PSIONIC ABILITY: VI
S: 17 (+1, +1)   I: 20   W: 25   D: 23   C: 23   CH: 23

Hera looks like a very tall woman, but she *shape changes* at will. The wife of Zeus, she is the patron of all married women. If a woman prays to the goddess about husband problems while the goddess is listening (a 5% chance) the goddess may react with a curse thrown at the offending male (save vs. spells negates).

As the wife of Zeus, she is constantly killing or attacking his paramours. Attempting to keep track of them has caused her to develop methods of spying and watching that are unparalleled.

Because of her very strong desire for vengeance, her clerics have a revenge drive of their own. For the slightest imagined or real wrong doing to her or them, the clerics will work to the utmost to cause the death of the offender, sometimes taking years to plan the defeat of the more powerful beings.

While Hera can strike with her rod for 2-20 points of damage, she sometimes uses her special voice for attacking. When she is angry her voice does 20 points of damage to all within 50 yards of her because of its harshness (no saving throw). Those who do not make their saving throw vs. spells will be forced to flee in terror from the sound of her screaming (as the *fear* spell).

HERACLES *(demigod)*

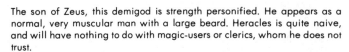

ARMOR CLASS: −2
MOVE: 15''
HIT POINTS: 187
NO. OF ATTACKS: 2
DAMAGE/ATTACK: 5-50 (+14)
SPECIAL ATTACKS: Bow
SPECIAL DEFENSES: See below
MAGIC RESISTANCE: Standard
SIZE: M (6')
ALIGNMENT: Chaotic neutral
PLANE: The Prime Material Plane
CLERIC/DRUID: Nil
FIGHTER: 15th level ranger
MAGIC-USER/ILLUSIONIST: Nil
THIEF/ASSASSIN: Nil
MONK/BARD: 3rd level bard
PSIONIC ABILITY: Nil
S: 25 (+7, +14)   I: 11   W: 9   D: 19   C: 20   CH: 17

The son of Zeus, this demigod is strength personified. He appears as a normal, very muscular man with a large beard. Heracles is quite naive, and will have nothing to do with magic-users or clerics, whom he does not trust.

He uses a special bow at the beginning of every battle, a bow which only he can use effectively. It has a range of 1 mile, and it cannot miss at

distances of up to ½ mile. When he battles giants and other enchanted monsters, he uses poisoned arrows. He also wields a huge club which does 5-50 points of damage on a hit. Heracles wears the skin of the magical Nemean lion, and it cannot be pierced by anything. Thrusting weapons do but one point of damage (plus bonuses, if any), slashing weapons do half damage, but crushing or bludgeoning weapons do full damage. When he suffers more than half his hit points in damage, Heracles flies into a blind berserker's rage, and this causes him to attack all who are within striking distance of him, friend and foe alike. When in this state, his damage bonus from strength is +25 points.

It is dangerous to have dealings with this hero, as the slightest insult or affront is liable to cause him to lose his temper. At such times, he will act in the most direct and aggressive manner. If he is tricked by double-dealing, lies, or ingratitude, he will certainly exact vengeance, although it might be years before he has the chance.

HERMES (god of thieves, liars, gamblers and arbitrators)

Greater god

ARMOR CLASS: 2
MOVE: 18''/48''
HIT POINTS: 340
NO. OF ATTACKS: 2
DAMAGE/ATTACK: 5-30
SPECIAL ATTACKS: See below
SPECIAL DEFENSES: See below
MAGIC RESISTANCE: 35%
SIZE: M (6¼')
ALIGNMENT: Neutral
WORSHIPER'S ALIGN: Neutral and
   thieves
SYMBOL: Caduceus
PLANE: Olympus
CLERIC/DRUID: 14th level druid
FIGHTER: 15th level ranger
MAGIC-USER/ILLUSIONIST: 15th level
   illusionist
THIEF/ASSASSIN: 25th level thief
MONK/BARD: 15th level bard
PSIONIC ABILITY: IV
S: 22 (+4, +10) I: 25 W: 19 D: 25 C: 24 CH: 24

Appearing as a handsome teenager, this god has maximum thieving abilities. He moves as a blink dog, is always *hasted*. Hermes wears a pair of

winged sandals that allow him to fly, has a *helm of invisibility* (as the ring of the same name), and he carries a *white caduceus*, a winged rod with two entwined serpents. This device was given to him by the god Apollo and became Hermes' symbol. It gives the god complete control over all non-magical creatures other than man (no saving throw).

One of Hermes' functions is that of messenger of the gods to mortals, and in this capacity he will occasionally be seen by high level clerics of the various Olympian sects, bringing messages from their deities. He also acts as arbiter of disputes between the gods.

All of Hermes' clerics must keep physically fit and be able to run long distances, no matter how important their position. They must also carry a white rod as a symbol of their devotion. Clerics of Hermes often act as professional arbitrators. Their reputation for fair settlement of disputes keeps them busy in this line of work. Hermetic arbiters who accept bribes or other graft may (15% chance per offense) be punished by the god.

JASON (hero)

ARMOR CLASS: 3
MOVE: 12''
HIT POINTS: 129
NO. OF ATTACKS: 2
DAMAGE/ATTACK: By weapon type
SPECIAL ATTACKS: Nil
SPECIAL DEFENSES: Nil
MAGIC RESISTANCE: Standard
SIZE: M (6')
ALIGNMENT: Neutral good
CLERIC/DRUID: Nil
FIGHTER: 16th level ranger
MAGIC-USER/ILLUSIONIST: Nil
THIEF/ASSASSIN: 4th level thief
MONK/BARD: 7th level bard
PSIONIC ABILITY: Nil
   Attack/Defense Modes: Nil
S: 18 (00) (+3, +6) I: 16 W: 14 D: 18 C: 18 CH: 19

Jason is noted for his leadership ability and his strength. He roamed over the seas in his ship, the Argo, and succeeded in the quest for the *golden fleece*. This item is able to heal any wound instantly and raise the recently deceased (less than 3 days) by placing the fleece on the body overnight. However, after each time it is used, there is a 10% chance that it will disappear forever.

KRONOS *(former ruler of the gods and greater titans)*

ARMOR CLASS: 2
MOVE: 24''
HIT POINTS: 400
NO. OF ATTACKS: 2
DAMAGE/ATTACK: 5-50 (+14)
SPECIAL ATTACKS: Lava balls
SPECIAL DEFENSES: Nil
MAGIC RESISTANCE: 50%
SIZE: L (100')
ALIGNMENT: Chaotic evil
PLANE: Tarterus
CLERIC/DRUID: 25th level cleric
FIGHTER: 17th level fighter
MAGIC-USER/ILLUSIONIST: Nil
THIEF/ASSASSIN: Nil
MONK/BARD: Nil
PSIONIC ABILITY: V
S: 25 (+7, +14)　I: 25　W: 14　D: 25　C: 25　CH: 25

Kronos appears as a handsome giant. He *shape changes* at will, and at the beginning of any battle, he hurls lava balls (created out of thin air) up to a maximum range of 200 yards, each doing 4-40 points of damage per strike.

His sickle of adamant strikes as a +5 weapon for 5-50 points of damage.

NIKE *(goddess of victory)*

Lesser goddess

ARMOR CLASS: −4
MOVE: 24''/36''
HIT POINTS: 357
NO. OF ATTACKS: 2
DAMAGE/ATTACK: 5-50
SPECIAL ATTACKS: See below
SPECIAL DEFENSES: Cancellation
MAGIC RESISTANCE: 85%
SIZE: M (7')
ALIGNMENT: Lawful neutral
WORSHIPER'S ALIGN: Lawful neutral,
　　and those wishing victory
SYMBOL: Winged woman
PLANE: Olympus
CLERIC/DRUID: Nil
FIGHTER: 20th level fighter
MAGIC-USER/ILLUSIONIST: See
　　below
THIEF/ASSASSIN: Nil
MONK/BARD: Nil
PSIONIC ABILITY: VI
S: 23 (+5, +11)　I: 23　W: 23　D: 23　C: 24　CH: 25

This unusually stubborn goddess appears as a very tall woman with wings. She always uses her divine awe power to stun lesser creatures, not caring what happens to the poor mortals that see her. At will, she *shape changes*.

In close combat, she uses a *rod of power* that inflicts 5-50 points of damage at a touch (no saving throw).

She is able to destroy any device used against her (saving throw applicable) with a touch of her hand.

The goddess has a very stern way of looking at things and her clerics are not allowed to transgress against their alignments or sect even once. If they do, they suffer death from a *lightning bolt* large enough to destroy them totally.

OCEANUS *(greater titan of the sea and water areas)*

ARMOR CLASS: −3
MOVE: 24''
HIT POINTS: 390
NO. OF ATTACKS: 2
DAMAGE/ATTACK: 7-70/7-70
SPECIAL ATTACKS: See below
SPECIAL DEFENSES: See below
MAGIC RESISTANCE: 50%
SIZE: L (100')
ALIGNMENT: Chaotic evil
PLANE: Tarterus
CLERIC/DRUID: 10th level in each
FIGHTER: 15th level fighter
MAGIC-USER/ILLUSIONIST: Nil
THIEF/ASSASSIN: Nil
MONK/BARD: Nil
PSIONIC ABILITY: V
S: 25 (+7, +14)　I: 24　W: 10　D: 24　C: 25　CH: 20

This greater titan always has a green shimmer around his body. He is able to raise hurricane winds with a motion of his hand and create waves of great force where there is water. All creatures of water of less than divine status must obey his commands, though Poseidon outranks him on the Prime Material Plane since the greater titans were defeated.

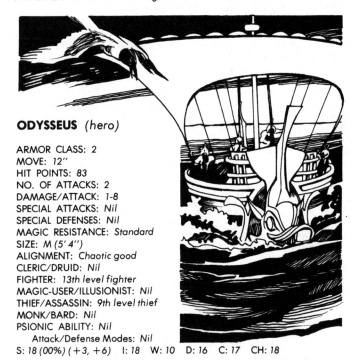

ODYSSEUS *(hero)*

ARMOR CLASS: 2
MOVE: 12''
HIT POINTS: 83
NO. OF ATTACKS: 2
DAMAGE/ATTACK: 1-8
SPECIAL ATTACKS: Nil
SPECIAL DEFENSES: Nil
MAGIC RESISTANCE: Standard
SIZE: M (5' 4'')
ALIGNMENT: Chaotic good
CLERIC/DRUID: Nil
FIGHTER: 13th level fighter
MAGIC-USER/ILLUSIONIST: Nil
THIEF/ASSASSIN: 9th level thief
MONK/BARD: Nil
PSIONIC ABILITY: Nil
　　Attack/Defense Modes: Nil
S: 18 (00%) (+3, +6)　I: 18　W: 10　D: 16　C: 17　CH: 18

Odysseus, while below average height, is an extremely muscular man. He is a renowned bowman and wields a bow which has such a powerful pull that only he can string it. Odysseus gains his strength bonuses "to hit" and damage when using this bow. Though possessing great strength, Odysseus prefers to use his wit and cunning to extricate himself from sticky situations, as he has found intelligence more universally useful than strength.

During the Trojan War, Odysseus added to his reputation of craftiness and cunning with various strategems. He is credited with the idea of the wooden horse ruse used to take the city. When returning home from Troy, Odysseus was blown off course and landed on an island of the lesser cyclopes. To escape from the human-eating Polyphemus, Odysseus had to blind the giant. As Polyphemus was Poseidon's child, this act brought about Poseidon's curse and forced Odysseus to wander for 10 years, never quite able to return home.

Some of the dangers Odysseus overcame were: the land of the lotus eaters, Circe the sorceress, a journey to Hades, the Sirens, stealing the cattle of the sun-titan Hyperion, sailing between the monsters Scylla and Charybdis, and enchantment by the nymph Calypso. Eventually Odysseus reached his home of the island of Ithaca, only to find his faithful wife beseiged by suitors who were convinced that Odysseus was dead. In a fit of rage, Odysseus slew all the suitors almost single-handedly.

PAN *(god of nature and wild passion)*

Lesser god

ARMOR CLASS: -2
MOVE: 18''
HIT POINTS: 359
NO. OF ATTACKS: 3/2
DAMAGE/ATTACK: 3-30
SPECIAL ATTACKS: *Fear and beguiling*
SPECIAL DEFENSES: *Nil*
MAGIC RESISTANCE: 89%
SIZE: M (5')
ALIGNMENT: *Chaotic neutral*
WORSHIPER'S ALIGN: *Chaotic neutral*
SYMBOL: *Syrinx*
PLANE: *The Prime Material Plane*
CLERIC/DRUID: *14th level druid*
FIGHTER: *13th level ranger*
MAGIC-USER/ILLUSIONIST: *15th level illusionist*
THIEF/ASSASSIN: *15th level thief*
MONK/BARD: *15th level bard*
PSIONIC ABILITY: *I*
S: 25 (+7, +14) I: 18 W: 18 D: 25 C: 25 CH: 22

As god of nature, Pan has two aspects. On the one hand he represents the beneficence and fertility of nature, and on the other the fearsome indifferent destructiveness of natural forces. Depending upon his mood, an encounter with Pan can be terrifying or delightful.

In appearance, Pan has the trunk of a human with small goat horns on his head and his legs and hooves are like those of a large goat. His main power comes from the sound of his voice. He has an intense dislike for Apollo and is constantly playing practical jokes on the god of music.

His fist strikes for 3-30 points of damage; his voice is able to cause *fear* as the spell within a range of 50 yards (saving throw applicable).

His *syrinx* is a set of reed pipes that he plays as a *rod of beguiling*. This instrument is able to cause any beings who fail their saving throw to become the blindly loving friends of the god. In times of danger and when he has suffered the loss of more than 25% of his hit points, he is able to shout so that all beings within 100' must run in *fear* for 4 melee rounds (no saving throw).

Pan and Apollo are enemies because Apollo replaced Pan in several areas (particularly music), and this caused Pan to lose some worshipers to Apollo. Their rivalry extends to the Prime Material Plane, where their clerics are often at cross purposes.

PERSEUS *(hero)*

ARMOR CLASS: 3
MOVE: 12''/24''
HIT POINTS: 112
NO. OF ATTACKS: 2
DAMAGE/ATTACK: *By weapon type*
SPECIAL ATTACKS: *See below*
SPECIAL DEFENSES: *See below*
MAGIC RESISTANCE: *Standard*
SIZE: M (6')
ALIGNMENT: *Lawful good*
CLERIC/DRUID: *Nil*
FIGHTER: *15th level paladin*
MAGIC-USER/ILLUSIONIST: *Nil*
THIEF/ASSASSIN: *Nil*
MONK/BARD: *5th level bard*
PSIONIC ABILITY: *Nil*
Attack/Defense Modes: *Nil*
S: 18 (89%) (+2, +4) I: 14 W: 12 D: 18 C: 18 CH: 18

This hero was responsible for taking the head of the first and most powerful medusa, and was favored by many of the gods. Hades loaned him his *helm of invisibility*, Hermes gave him a pair of *winged sandals* and a

vorpal blade, and Athena lent him the bright *Aegis* shield (cf.), though all of these were later returned.

POSEIDON *(god of seas, oceans, streams, and earthquakes)*

Greater god

ARMOR CLASS: 3
MOVE: 18''
HIT POINTS: 390
NO. OF ATTACKS: 2
DAMAGE/ATTACK: 4-40 (+14)/4-40 (+14)
SPECIAL ATTACKS: *See below*
SPECIAL DEFENSES: *See below*
MAGIC RESISTANCE: 75%
SIZE: L (30')
ALIGNMENT: *Chaotic neutral*
WORSHIPER'S ALIGN: *Chaotic neutral, and all who depend on the sea*
SYMBOL: *Trident*
PLANE: *Olympus*
CLERIC/DRUID: *12th level in each*
FIGHTER: *13th level fighter*
MAGIC-USER/ILLUSIONIST: *17th level in each*
THIEF/ASSASSIN: *Nil*
MONK/BARD: *10th level bard*
PSIONIC ABILITY: *VI*
S: 25 (+7, +14) I: 20 W: 22 D: 24 C: 25 CH: 22

This god appears as a huge human and may command any non-divine creature of the water. At will, he *shape changes, summons* water beings, and creates life in any form (often originating new life forms at a whim).

His anger at coastal towns who fail to sacrifice to him monthly may cause him to react in one of three ways: he may take all of the young males of the town in blood sacrifice, he may reduce the town to rubble in an earthquake, or he may flood the town and the surrounding countryside.

Poseidon is responsible for the creation of all horses and he rewards his high priests and high priestesses for exceptional services with a paladin-quality horse for their use.

Poseidon fights with a +5 trident that hits for 4-40 points twice per melee round; this weapon can absorb any single spell in any given melee round and return a like spell at the desire of the god. In battle, the god often puts a watery haze around his body that acts like a +5 *ring of protection*.

This god rewards the prayers of his clerics with material things like springs in dry lands, water when needed in the form of rain, or too much water to his clerics' enemies. He has also been known to plague the worshipers of his sect with enchanted monsters of random types when they have transgressed in some way.

Poseidon is the son of Kronos and Rhea and brother of Zeus and Hades.

PROMETHEUS (greater titan) "Forethought"

Lesser god

ARMOR CLASS: −2
MOVE: 15''/24''
HIT POINTS: 388
NO. OF ATTACKS: 2 (fists)
DAMAGE/ATTACK: 5-50/5-50
SPECIAL ATTACKS: See below
SPECIAL DEFENSES: Nil
MAGIC RESISTANCE: 50%
SIZE: L (100')
ALIGNMENT: Neutral good
WORSHIPER'S ALIGN: Good (human)
SYMBOL: Torch
PLANE: Olympus
CLERIC/DRUID: 13th in each
FIGHTER: 16th level ranger
MAGIC-USER/ILLUSIONIST: 15th level
   magic-user
THIEF/ASSASSIN: 10th level thief
MONK/BARD: 10th level bard
PSIONIC ABILITY: V
S: 24 (+6, +12)   I: 25   W: 20   D: 24   C: 24   CH: 25

Prometheus is the son of Iapetus and Clymene, and the brother of Atlas and Epimetheus. When the gods revolted against the titans, Prometheus sided with the gods since he correctly deduced the outcome of the struggle. Prometheus is credited with making the first man and woman from clay, and he has made it his task to help mankind whenever possible. Prometheus taught humans many of the civilized arts, including the medicinal use of plants, cultivation of grains, and domestication of wild animals.

Prometheus stole fire from the sun and gave it to humankind. For this affront, Zeus ordered Prometheus chained to a mountain top where his perpetually-regenerating liver was torn out afresh each day by a griffon-vulture. Zeus repented after 30 years and allowed Heracles to free Prometheus. After he was freed, Prometheus was invited to Olympus to join the gods.

Prometheus is the only titan worshiped as a god. As a token of his punishment, Zeus ordered Prometheus to wear a ring made from his chains. Prometheus' clerics also wear an iron ring set with a chip of stone supposedly from the mountain where Prometheus was chained. Prometheus expects his clerics to be self-reliant, but not self-centered. Trickery and cunning are fair weapons but only if the end serves the human race as a whole. Prometheus will side with faithful clerics against any force, even the most powerful god, but he takes a dim view of clerics calling upon him unless they have absolutely no chance of survival otherwise.

The clerics of Prometheus will take any available opportunity to kill a griffon. They will also do all in their power to prevent humans from attacking any titan, and will actually side with Atlas or Epimetheus if they see either titan under attack.

Prometheus can create any mortal creature from clay in 2 melee rounds. This creature will serve him until it dies, though Prometheus usually sets it free after a specific service. In return for extraordinary service by one of his clerics, Prometheus may reward the cleric with a companion creature suitable to the cleric's level of experience.

THESEUS (hero)

ARMOR CLASS: 4
MOVE: 12''
HIT POINTS: 103
NO. OF ATTACKS: 2
DAMAGE/ATTACK: By weapon type
SPECIAL ATTACKS: Nil
SPECIAL DEFENSES: Nil
MAGIC RESISTANCE: Standard
SIZE: M (6')
ALIGNMENT: Lawful good
CLERIC/DRUID: Nil
FIGHTER: 13th level paladin
MAGIC-USER/ILLUSIONIST: Nil
THIEF/ASSASSIN: Nil
MONK/BARD: 9th level bard
PSIONIC ABILITY: Nil
   Attack/Defense Modes: Nil
S: 18 (76) (+2, +4)   I: 18   W: 17   D: 18   C: 18   CH: 18

This hero was credited with defeating the first and most powerful minotaur. He was noted for his bravery and fearlessness, but often lost struggles for power because of his refusal to deal on anything but an honest and open level with his enemies. He can be counted on to know the habits and weaknesses of all enemies he faces, both magical and non-magical.

TYCHE (goddess of good fortune)

Lesser goddess

ARMOR CLASS: −3
MOVE: 12''/36''
HIT POINTS: 200
NO. OF ATTACKS: 1
DAMAGE/ATTACK: See below
SPECIAL ATTACKS: Nil
SPECIAL DEFENSES: See below
MAGIC RESISTANCE: 100%
SIZE: M (5')
ALIGNMENT: Neutral
WORSHIPER'S ALIGN: Neutral, or
   those wishing luck
SYMBOL: Red pentagram
PLANE: Olympus
CLERIC/DRUID: Nil
FIGHTER: Nil
MAGIC-USER/ILLUSIONIST: 15th level
   in each
THIEF/ASSASSIN: Nil
MONK/BARD: 10th level bard
PSIONIC ABILITY: I
S: 20 (+3, +8)   I: 25   W: 25   D: 25   C: 22   CH: 25

Tyche appears as a rather small, slim, elfin human. She is able to cast "good luck" as a spell. The recipient of this spell will always win any single contest, no matter what the odds. She can also *shape change* at will and speak with anything. If threatened, her touch drains one-half the total original hit points of her attacker (no saving throw).

She has a small *blue sphere* that is able to absorb any one single attack in any given melee round and reflect the total damage that the attack would have done back at any being within touching distance of her person. This device is a function of her luck, and will not work for anyone else.

The goddess is not treated very well in the pantheon, as the other deities think of her as a poor relative and not really of divine caliber. She is therefore not often willing to aid them in their struggles against giants, titans, and the like.

Indian Mythos.

The translation of these beings into **AD&D** terms was one of the more difficult tasks of this work. They were very hard to categorize in the lawful or chaotic sense because of the diversity of their worldly actions. The pantheon that resulted is a mixture of Vedic and Hindu concepts, usually leaning toward the Vedic. These gods and goddesses maintain an aloofness greater than normal when compared with some of the other pantheons.

There are several concepts that are original with this section that must be dealt with for gaming purposes. The culture that created this mythos also created one of the most rigid caste systems ever known, where one is born to his or her station in life and learns to live with it. In a campaign under the influence of these gods, a character may be born a cleric, magic-user or a fighter. One does not switch from class to class or overlap into other areas (which usually prevents any characters from having two classes). The caste system also modifies the behavior of players toward one another and toward non-player characters. Persons of higher status are to be treated with respect and honor and either obeyed or left strictly alone. Those of the magic-user caste are deemed superior to all other castes, including the warriors. All of this is followed strictly by those who obey any sort of lawful code.

There is also a belief that all prayers will be answered if the proper sacrifices are made to the gods. If the prayer is not immediately answered, then some impropriety was made and the prayers must be done again (and again) until the desired result is achieved.

Worshipers are identified by marks they wear. For example, the followers of Vishnu have two parallel lines of a special white earth drawn from the hair-line to the bridge of the nose, with a perpendicular line connecting them at the bottom. All worshipers have marks of this type somewhere on their persons.

Probably the most difficult concept this mythos presents, at least in **AD&D** terms, is that of the "avatar". An avatar is a physical manifestation of a deity upon the Prime Material Plane. An avatar usually has lesser powers and a different appearance than the deity it has sprung from. Avatars often represent one particular aspect or side of a deity, and may have been created to perform a specific function. A deity may have several avatars simultaneously co-existent, each one different and uninvolved with the others. Vishnu, in particular, has many avatars.

Temples and cultural trappings within this pantheon vary from one extreme to another. On one hand, there are awesomely huge shrines to single gods that are many stories high, and in the same area there are tiny shrines dedicated to all of the gods that a single worshiper can use.

The deities of this mythos are often described as having many heads and/or arms. This multiplicity is somewhat representative of the powers of the deity. For example, if a deity has seven important abilities, he or she will probably have seven arms. This number may vary from one account to another. Given most of the deities' ability to shape change, it is only logical that they have as many arms (or heads) as they need.

INDRA (god of the atmosphere, storms and rain)

Greater god

ARMOR CLASS: −12
MOVE: 18"/24"
HIT POINTS: 400
NO. OF ATTACKS: 2
DAMAGE/ATTACK: 3-30 (+14)
SPECIAL ATTACKS: See below
SPECIAL DEFENSES: +3 or better
   weapon to hit
MAGIC RESISTANCE: 80%
SIZE: M (6')
ALIGNMENT: Chaotic neutral
WORSHIPER'S ALIGN: Chaotic
   neutral and farmers
SYMBOL: White elephant
PLANE: Limbo
CLERIC/DRUID: 25th level cleric
FIGHTER: 14th level fighter
MAGIC-USER/ILLUSIONIST: 20th level
   in each
THIEF/ASSASSIN: Nil
MONK/BARD: 10th level bard
PSIONIC ABILITY: III
S: 25 (+7, +14) I: 25 W: 25 D: 25 C: 25 CH: 25

Indra, the first ruler of the gods, appears as a heavily muscled man. His main attribute is the ability to create and control any form of weather at will. He can also influence humans, animals, and plants as a *staff of command*. He can *shape change* at will.

Indra wears +4 plate mail and a +4 shield in battle. He plies a bow made out of rainbows which shoots lightning bolts at the rate of two per melee round, each doing 3-30 points of damage, with a 1,000 yard range (all of which is treated as *short* range). For hand-to-hand combat, he uses a +3 *flaming sword* that does 3-30 points of damage per hit.

Indra's Elephant

FREQUENCY: Unique
NO. APPEARING: 1
ARMOR CLASS: 0
MOVE: 18"/24"
HIT DICE/POINTS: 150 hp
% IN LAIR: Nil
TREASURE TYPE: Nil
NO. OF ATTACKS: 5
DAMAGE/ATTACK: 2-20 (× 5)
SPECIAL ATTACKS: Nil
SPECIAL DEFENSES: Nil
MAGIC RESISTANCE: 25%
INTELLIGENCE: Low
ALIGNMENT: Neutral
SIZE: L (20' tall)
PSIONIC ABILITY: Nil
   Attack/Defense Modes: Nil
LEVEL/X.P. VALUE: X/21,450

This huge white beast is able to carry any weight his master wishes through the air, through the planes, or on the ground. It attacks as a 16+ HD monster, stabbing with its tusks, constricting with its trunk, and trampling with its great columnar forelegs. Each of these attacks does 2-20 points of damage.

AGNI (god of fire and lightning)

Greater god

ARMOR CLASS: –2
MOVE: 18''/18''
HIT POINTS: 378
NO. OF ATTACKS: 2
DAMAGE/ATTACK: 3-30 (+12)
SPECIAL ATTACKS: *See below*
SPECIAL DEFENSES: *See below*
MAGIC RESISTANCE: 75%
SIZE: L (10')
ALIGNMENT: *Chaotic neutral*
WORSHIPER'S ALIGN. *Chaotic neutral*
SYMBOL: *Flames*
PLANE: *Limbo*
CLERIC/DRUID: *20th level cleric*
FIGHTER: *15th level fighter*
MAGIC-USER/ILLUSIONIST: *See below*
THIEF/ASSASSIN: *Nil*
MONK/BARD: *Nil*
PSIONIC ABILITY: *I*
S: 24 (+6, +12)   I: 21   W: 20   D: 25   C: 24   CH: 20

Agni has 3 legs, 7 arms, and as many as 3 heads. He is completely red. His main attribute is the control of all forms of fire. He is able to control any number of fire beings that are within 1 mile of his presence and cast all fire spells as if he were a 50th level spell-caster. He is able to cure or cause any disease.

He fights with an axe of flame that hits for 3-30 points of damage and slays lesser demons and devils if it hits them (no saving throw). His fire aura brightly illuminates his body and causes 25 points of flame damage to any who attack him in hand-to-hand combat. This aura will melt weapons of less than a +4 bonus when they strike the god (Agni will be damaged by such attacks, but the weapon will be destroyed). Agni has a breath weapon usable 3 times per day that shoots a red stream of flame up to 30 yards and does 5-50 points of damage (successful saving throw versus breath weapons negates). His voice charms as the *charm person* or *charm monster* spell. He can *shape change* at will.

He disdains the use of armor and attacks the strongest of any enemy group from his fire chariot. This is a one-wheeled device made out of the seven winds which appears to be made of red gold. It is pulled by 2 giant horses which are immune to all forms of heat. On the ground, it travels at a rate of 36'', and in the air it travels at a rate of 48''. (Red horses: AC 2, HD 10, hp 90, #AT 3, D 2-20/2-20/1-12.)

KALI (black earth mother)

Lesser goddess

ARMOR CLASS: –9
MOVE: 27''
HIT POINTS: 279
NO. OF ATTACKS: 4
DAMAGE/ATTACK: 4-40
SPECIAL ATTACKS: *See below*
SPECIAL DEFENSES: *Fear*
MAGIC RESISTANCE: 39%
SIZE: L (20')
ALIGNMENT: *Chaotic evil*
WORSHIPER'S ALIGN: *Chaotic evil*
SYMBOL: *Skull*
PLANE: *Abyss*
CLERIC/DRUID: *10th level in each*
FIGHTER: *20th level fighter*
MAGIC-USER/ILLUSIONIST: *15th level in each*
THIEF/ASSASSIN: *15th level assassin*
MONK/BARD: *13th level monk*
PSIONIC ABILITY: *III*
S: 25 (+7, +14)   I: 18   W: 5   D: 25   C: 24   CH: –7

Kali has night black skin, tusks, 3 eyes, and 4 arms ending in talons. She can *shape change* at will and her visage causes *fear* as the spell to any who look upon it (save vs. spells negates).

This goddess is destruction incarnate, the ruthless mother who can give life and then take it away. She eats her own children for sustenance. The other deities of this pantheon will allow her to lead them in battle against the most powerful of their enemies, because she is so awesome in her destructiveness that she is able to inspire fear in even the most gruesome demons and devils. Each of her taloned hands can strike for 4-40 points of damage. Sometimes she wields a sword in one hand that inflicts 2-24 points of damage (plus strength bonus) on a hit.

Her worship requires sacrifices of blood, and even an occasional human sacrifice. Her cult includes many assassins. Those sworn to defend her cult will often do so in a sort of berserk, suicidal manner, slaying all who oppose them until they themselves are slain.

KARTTIKEYA (demigod of war)

Demigod

ARMOR CLASS: –8
MOVE: 18''
HIT POINTS: 222
NO. OF ATTACKS: 10
DAMAGE/ATTACK: 2-12 (+14) each
SPECIAL ATTACKS: *See below*
SPECIAL DEFENSES: *Nil*
MAGIC RESISTANCE: 50%
SIZE: L (20')
ALIGNMENT: *Chaotic good*
WORSHIPER'S ALIGN: *Chaotic good and warriors*
SYMBOL: *Peacock*
PLANE: *Gladsheim*
CLERIC/DRUID: *Nil*
FIGHTER: *18th level fighter*
MAGIC-USER/ILLUSIONIST: *Nil*
THIEF/ASSASSIN: *10th level thief*
MONK/BARD: *Nil*
PSIONIC ABILITY: *VI*
S: 25 (+7, +14)   I: 20   W: 16   D: 25   C: 20   CH: 18

Karttikeya has 6 heads and 12 arms (with swords in 10 of them). Each of his swords strikes for 2-12 points of damage. This demigod was created to fight devils wherever they are found, and his clerics have a 2% chance of successfully requesting aid from him in battles against devils and their allies (e.g. rakshasas).

Karttikeya rides a giant peacock into battle, and this bird is his symbol to his worshipers and enemies alike.

Peacock of Karttikeya

FREQUENCY: *Unique*
NO. APPEARING: *1*
ARMOR CLASS: *2*
MOVE: *24''/36''*
HIT DICE/POINTS: *120 hp*
% IN LAIR: *Nil*
TREASURE TYPE: *Nil*
NO. OF ATTACKS: *1*
DAMAGE/ATTACK: *3-36*
SPECIAL ATTACKS: *Nil*
SPECIAL DEFENSES: *Nil*
MAGIC RESISTANCE: *Standard*
INTELLIGENCE: *Exceptional*
ALIGNMENT: *Lawful good*
SIZE: *L (20' tall)*
PSIONIC ABILITY: *Nil*
   Attack/Defense Modes: *Nil*
LEVEL/X.P. VALUE: *IX/12,200*

This huge bird is said to have feathers made of metal, while its beak is said to strike with the swiftness of lightning at the god's enemies. The creature attacks as a 16+ HD monster, striking with its beak for 3-36 points of damage, and while it does not speak, it obeys the commands of the god perfectly and can act independently of its master.

LAKSHMI *(goddess of fortune)*

Lesser goddess

ARMOR CLASS: –3
MOVE: 18"/75"
HIT POINTS: 300
NO. OF ATTACKS: 0
DAMAGE/ATTACK: Nil
SPECIAL ATTACKS: See below
SPECIAL DEFENSES: See below
MAGIC RESISTANCE: 100%
SIZE: M (6')
ALIGNMENT: Chaotic good
WORSHIPER'S ALIGN: Chaotic good,
   those seeking luck
SYMBOL: Lotus
PLANE: Gladsheim
CLERIC/DRUID: 20th level cleric
FIGHTER: Nil
MAGIC-USER/ILLUSIONIST: 20th level
   in each
THIEF/ASSASSIN: Nil
MONK/BARD: 10th level bard
PSIONIC ABILITY: VI
S: 10 I: 25 W: 25 D: 20 C: 23 CH: 24

Lakshmi is the wife of Vishnu. She appears as a golden-skinned woman and always sits on a giant floating lotus when traveling about on the Prime Material Plane. This device will carry only her and can travel at great speed (75").

When the goddess looks at beings with only her right eye, they will always make their saving throws in the next hour and always hit targets that are physically possible to hit in that time. The left eye has just the opposite effect, for the same amount of time (saving throw vs. spells negates either of these effects).

Lakshmi always makes her saving throws. She is immune to attacks from creatures that are flying.

MARUT *(wind spirit)*

FREQUENCY: Very rare
NO. APPEARING: 1-10 (10-100 in
   battles)
ARMOR CLASS: –2
MOVE: 9"/24"
HIT DICE/POINTS: 100 hp
% IN LAIR: 25%
TREASURE TYPE: Nil
NO. OF ATTACKS: 1
DAMAGE/ATTACK: By weapon type
SPECIAL ATTACKS: Nil
SPECIAL DEFENSES: See below
MAGIC RESISTANCE: 50%
INTELLIGENCE: Average
ALIGNMENT: Neutral
SIZE: M (6')
PSIONIC ABILITY: Nil
   Attack/Defense Modes: Nil
LEVEL/X.P. VALUE: X/16,700

These humanoids are creatures created out of the wind. They serve as troops for the gods, particularly Vishnu and Rudra, and are often led by one of the demigods of air when they enter battle. Maruts live in the clouds and help create weather for the gods. They are not subject to the will of any but divine beings (i.e. cannot be *charmed* or *enchanted*), and they are invisible unless attacking the enemies of the gods. They attack as 16+ HD monsters with their weapons, which are usually broadswords. As wind creatures, they naturally have the ability to fly.

RATRI *(goddess of the night, thieves, & robbers)*

Demigoddess

ARMOR CLASS: –2
MOVE: 18"
HIT POINTS: 250
NO. OF ATTACKS: 1
DAMAGE/ATTACK: 1-10
SPECIAL ATTACKS: See below
SPECIAL DEFENSES: See below
MAGIC RESISTANCE: 25%
SIZE: M (5')
ALIGNMENT: Neutral evil
WORSHIPER'S ALIGN: Neutral evil
   and thieves
SYMBOL: Image of a female in dark
   robes
PLANE: Hades
CLERIC/DRUID: 10th level cleric
FIGHTER: Nil
MAGIC-USER/ILLUSIONIST: 5th level
   magic-user/15th level illusionist
THIEF/ASSASSIN: 15th level assassin
MONK/BARD: Nil
PSIONIC ABILITY: V
S: 19(+3, +7) I: 22 W: 20 D: 19 C: 21 CH: 23

Ratri appears as a well-proportioned woman. She has the ability to cast an area of *darkness 15'* (as the spell) upon any opponent, with no saving throw. She also has the power to permanently *blind* any being that crosses her shadow (saving throw vs. spells).

Ratri wears a magical cloak that causes any objects or persons that touch it to be cast into the Ethereal Plane (no saving throw). Her attack of a physical nature takes the form of an angry look from her eyes that automatically does 1-10 points of damage — she can do this once per round.

RUDRA *(storm god, god of the dead)* "Lord of Animals"

Greater god

ARMOR CLASS: –2
MOVE: 18"/24"
HIT POINTS: 344
NO. OF ATTACKS: 2
DAMAGE/ATTACK: 2-20 (+9)
SPECIAL ATTACKS: See below
SPECIAL DEFENSES: Illusions
MAGIC RESISTANCE: 25%
SIZE: M (6')
ALIGNMENT: Lawful neutral
WORSHIPER'S ALIGN: Lawful neutral
SYMBOL: Black bow
PLANE: Nirvana
CLERIC/DRUID: 14th level druid
FIGHTER: 14th level fighter
MAGIC-USER/ILLUSIONIST: 25th level
   illusionist
THIEF/ASSASSIN: 15th level thief
MONK/BARD: Nil
PSIONIC ABILITY: V
S: 21(+4, +9) I: 23 W: 20 D: 25 C: 24 CH: 20

Rudra appears as a man with a red complexion and blue neck. He governs both the spread of disease and its remedies. He can also create and control storms. All of his treasure is kept in a special portable hole that opens into an extra-dimensional area approximately the same size as the Grand Canyon.

Rudra possesses a magical black bow from which he shoots his *arrows of disease*. These inflict 2-20 points of damage on a hit, and infect the victim with a *rotting disease* like that resulting from a mummy's touch. (Save vs. death at a –6 negates this effect.) With these arrows, he spreads disease among those whose time of death has come.

SURYA *(sun god)*

Greater god

ARMOR CLASS: −3
MOVE: 18″
HIT POINTS: 360
NO. OF ATTACKS: 2
DAMAGE/ATTACK: 4-40
SPECIAL ATTACKS: See below
SPECIAL DEFENSES: See below
MAGIC RESISTANCE: 50%
SIZE: L (10′)
ALIGNMENT: Lawful good
WORSHIPER'S ALIGN: Lawful good
SYMBOL: Sun disc
PLANE: Seven Heavens
CLERIC/DRUID: 20th level cleric
FIGHTER: 16th level paladin
MAGIC-USER/ILLUSIONIST: 15th level
    magic-user
THIEF/ASSASSIN: Nil
MONK/BARD: 8th level bard
PSIONIC ABILITY: VI
S: 24 (+6, +12)   I: 24   W: 24   D: 24   C: 24   CH: 20

Surya has dark red skin, long golden hair, 3 eyes in his semi-human head, and 4 arms on his humanoid trunk. His main attribute is the ability to *sleep* any number of 20th level or lesser beings (non-divine) with no saving throw; he can also affect any number of higher level creatures though they are given a save vs. spells. This ability has a range of 15″. He can see anything in the Prime Material Plane that has the sun shining on it. He disdains the use of armor, and will attack demons first in any given battle where they appear.

In battle he uses a shaft of light that no one else can grasp. It is a +4 swordlike weapon and does 4-40 points of damage per strike. It also automatically dispels all illusions and *darkness* within 1,000 yards of it, and acts as a non-negatable *continual light* spell.

SURYA'S CHARIOT: This one-wheeled device is made of a piece of the sun, and is pulled by 7 magical horses, each a different color of the rainbow. The vehicle is not corporeal unless Surya rides in it. The chariot travels with no limit to the speed it can attain. The horses are always incorporeal and are never affected by magic.

When in battle against demons, the chariot shines with intense light that causes 30 points of heat damage per round, with this heat only hurting demonic creatures (no saving throw).

TVASHTRI *(demigod of artifice and science)*

Demigod

ARMOR CLASS: −3
MOVE: 15″
HIT POINTS: 227
NO. OF ATTACKS: 1
DAMAGE/ATTACK: 4-40
SPECIAL ATTACKS: See below
SPECIAL DEFENSES: See below
MAGIC RESISTANCE: 65%
SIZE: M (6′)
ALIGNMENT: Neutral
WORSHIPER'S ALIGN: Neutral
SYMBOL: A pinwheel fan held on a
    jade rod
PLANE: Concordant Opposition
CLERIC/DRUID: 15th level cleric
FIGHTER: 11th level fighter
MAGIC-USER/ILLUSIONIST: 20th level
    magic-user
THIEF/ASSASSIN: Nil
MONK/BARD: Nil
PSIONIC ABILITY: I
S: 19 (+3, +7)   I: 25   W: 22   D: 21   C: 23   CH: 19

Tvashtri appears as a normal man. His is the ability to design objects of great utility and weapons of awesome power. Because of this, none of the weapons that the gods use that he designed (virtually all of them) have the power to hurt him. He carries a pinwheel device with him at all times, and when activated it is able to permanently nullify all magical devices in a 200 yard radius around it. This thing can also cast black beams of power (one per round) that do 4-40 points of damage and never miss their target, up to a range of 30″.

Tvashtri can regenerate 20 lost hit points per melee round by grabbing parts of the air and applying them to his (or anyone else's) wounds. This healing ability requires all of his attention; he cannot attack or defend while doing this.

Tvashtri is the patron of artisans and inventors. His clerics are expected to be resourceful and original in solving their problems.

USHAS *(goddess of the dawn)*

Lesser goddess

ARMOR CLASS: −2
MOVE: 18″/24″
HIT POINTS: 300
NO. OF ATTACKS: 0
DAMAGE/ATTACK: Nil
SPECIAL ATTACKS: Blindness, gaze
SPECIAL DEFENSES: See below
MAGIC RESISTANCE: 60%
SIZE: M (5½′)
ALIGNMENT: Neutral good
WORSHIPER'S ALIGN: Neutral good
SYMBOL: Rising sun
PLANE: Elysium
CLERIC/DRUID: 20th level cleric
FIGHTER: Nil
MAGIC-USER/ILLUSIONIST: 15th level
    illusionist
THIEF/ASSASSIN: Nil
MONK/BARD: Nil
PSIONIC ABILITY: VI
S: 17 (+1, +1)   I: 21   W: 23   D: 25   C: 22   CH: 23

Ushas, who appears as a woman wearing red and gold robes, is able to reincarnate any living thing into any other non-divine living form. This is because she is responsible (as goddess of the dawn) for the endless reincarnation of the daytime. She is able to send a brilliant light from her body that will blind all those looking at her for 1-4 turns (no saving throw). She can regenerate 30 hit points per round while the sun shines on her and she uses her gaze to inflict 1-10 points of damage upon any who offend her (she can do this once per round).

She fights the forces of darkness, as this is the only substance that resists her light. In this battle she rides a chariot like that of Surya's (q.v.), except that all of the horses that pull it are red. When fighting forces of darkness and evil, she uses her ability of *instant awakening*. This enables her to awaken all dormant or sleeping good creatures (so that they may come to her aid). It also enables her to automatically dispel all *charm/enchantment*-type spells or influences, and prevents her enemies from using these types of spells or abilities.

VARUNA (god of order & protector of oaths)

Greater god

ARMOR CLASS: −2
MOVE: 15''/24''
HIT POINTS: 329
NO. OF ATTACKS: 3/2
DAMAGE/ATTACK: 5-50 (+11)
SPECIAL ATTACKS: Nil
SPECIAL DEFENSES: See below
MAGIC RESISTANCE: 80%
SIZE: M (6½')
ALIGNMENT: Lawful neutral
WORSHIPER'S ALIGN: Lawful neutral
SYMBOL: Moon
PLANE: Nirvana
CLERIC/DRUID: 15th level cleric
FIGHTER: 14th level paladin
MAGIC-USER/ILLUSIONIST: 20th level
    magic-user
THIEF/ASSASSIN: Nil
MONK/BARD: 4th level bard
PSIONIC ABILITY: VI
S: 23 (+5, +11) I: 25 W: 25 D: 23 C: 22 CH: 18

Varuna is the god of physical and moral order, the personification of law-fulness. He is the protector of all oaths, and oathbreakers of the lawful alignments have reason to fear his wrath — there is a 1% chance per level of the oathbreaker that Varuna will cause him or her to be punished.

Varuna appears as a tall but ordinary man. He has the ability to become *ethereal* at will. His aura of lawfulness is so strong that no non-divine crea-ture of the chaotic alignment can approach within 5'' of his form. Varuna wields a jet black spear that strikes for 5-50 points of damage.

VISHNU (god of mercy and light)

Greater god

ARMOR CLASS: −5
MOVE: 18''/27''
HIT POINTS: 389
NO. OF ATTACKS: 2
DAMAGE/ATTACK: 1-10 (+11)
SPECIAL ATTACKS: See below
SPECIAL DEFENSES: See below
MAGIC RESISTANCE: 85%
SIZE: M (6')
ALIGNMENT: Lawful good
WORSHIPER'S ALIGN: All good
    alignments
SYMBOL: Sun-disc, seashell, lotus &
    mace
PLANE: Seven Heavens
CLERIC/DRUID: 15th level cleric
FIGHTER: 17th level paladin
MAGIC-USER/ILLUSIONIST: 25th level
    magic-user/18th level illusionist
THIEF/ASSASSIN: Nil
MONK/BARD: Nil
PSIONIC ABILITY: I
S: 23 (+5, +11) I: 23 W: 25 D: 24 C: 24 CH: 25

Vishnu most commonly appears as a normal man with four arms, but he is capable of *shape changing* at will into almost any form. His primary power is the ability to make any creature of intelligence (low or greater) unable to commit violence of any type within 30 yards of him (no saving throw). When exercising this ability, the god cannot do harm. He can also cast double strength *prismatic wall* spells at will, and undead turn to dust at his glance.

In battle he wields a mace that *disintegrates* anything it hits (saving throw vs. spells applicable) and does 1-10 points of damage per strike plus his strength bonus. He also has a disc weapon that is capable of shooting a stream of fire for 5-50 points of damage to a maximum range of 40 yards, and this can be discharged once per round. He is able to use both of these weapons simultaneously, striking twice per round with the mace and blast-ing with the sun disc.

Vishnu's magical sea shell automatically sends him into the *Ethereal Plane* when he is about to be killed, and his lotus flower can *heal* all of his lost hit points at a touch (up to three times per day). He rides Garuda, the king of all birds, into battle, and while on this creature he is not affected by *charm* spells of any type.

Vishnu is very helpful towards his worshipers, and there is a chance that he will aid them if they are in serious trouble. This is a percent chance equal to the number of worshipers in mortal danger, to a maximum of 20%. Vishnu may send one or more of his minions (the maruts) to aid them, or he may send part of himself in the form of an avatar. An avatar will probably have only one or two of Vishnu's character class levels plus the appropriate divine ability scores. For example, a clerical avatar would be 15th level, have a wisdom of 25, maximum hit points, and probably a special magic item or two.

Vishnu's clerics are expected to combat the forces of evil with determina-tion and persistence, but to show mercy to those defeated opponents who are redeemable.

Garuda "King of all Birds"

FREQUENCY: Unique
NO. APPEARING: 1
ARMOR CLASS: −1
MOVE: 18''/48''
HIT DICE/POINTS: 100 hp
% IN LAIR: 10%
TREASURE TYPE: Z (× 3)
NO. OF ATTACKS: 2
DAMAGE/ATTACK: 2-24/2-24
SPECIAL ATTACKS: Nil
SPECIAL DEFENSES: Sense evil
    creatures
MAGIC RESISTANCE: 75%
INTELLIGENCE: High
ALIGNMENT: Lawful good
SIZE: L (60')
PSIONIC ABILITY: Nil
    Attack/Defense Modes: Nil
LEVEL/X.P. VALUE: X/17,100

This half-man/half-bird hates all things evil with a mad passion. Garuda is said to be able to carry 5 gods in full battle armor and not be slowed in flight. He can sense any evil creatures or things within a 1 mile radius of himself. He can also summon 1-10 of any type of avian creature he chooses, even over the commands of other gods, and all avians will follow the commands of Garuda when they meet him. Garuda can perform this summons once per day.

He attacks by battering with his wings for 2-24 points of damage per wing and fights as a 16+ HD monster.

YAMA (demigod of death)

Demigod

ARMOR CLASS: −1
MOVE: 15″
HIT POINTS: 229
NO. OF ATTACKS: 2
DAMAGE/ATTACK: 2-12 (+9)
SPECIAL ATTACKS: *See below*
SPECIAL DEFENSES: *See below*
MAGIC RESISTANCE: 25% (100% in
    his robes)
SIZE: M (7′)
ALIGNMENT: *Lawful neutral*
WORSHIPER'S ALIGN: *Neutral
    alignments*
SYMBOL: *Red mace*
PLANE: *Nirvana*
CLERIC/DRUID: *10th level cleric*
FIGHTER: *14th level fighter*
MAGIC-USER/ILLUSIONIST: *See
    below*
THIEF/ASSASSIN: *Nil*
MONK/BARD: *Nil*
PSIONIC ABILITY: V
S: 21 (+4, +9) I: 24 W: 18 D: 18 C: 18 CH: 18

Yama started life as the first mortal, but so impressed the gods with his ability to cause destruction that they made him an immortal. He appears to the world with green skin, copper-colored eyes, and wearing red robes.

He enters battle wearing *armor of etherealness*. His +3 mace hits for 2-12 points of damage per strike. He uses a +5 magical noose as a weapon when he rides his giant water buffalo, which strangles those he catches in 3 melee rounds, no matter how many hit points they have. He has acquired the ability to cast any magic-user's spell as if he were 20th level as long as it does damage to his enemies.

His red robes are an artifact in themselves and have the following powers: they give him 100% magic resistance; they negate all damage from heat, cold, and light sources; they prevent him from being surprised from any source by flashing red 2 melee rounds before any attack; and they allow him to fly and travel in the water as fast as he can move on land (15″).

Yama is the judge of the dead: based on the record of a man's deeds in life, Yama decides which plane he will go to after death (in the case of those who worship a member of this pantheon).

Yama's Water Buffalo

FREQUENCY: *Unique*
NO. APPEARING: *1*
ARMOR CLASS: *3*
MOVE: *24″*
HIT DICE/POINTS: *100 hp*
% IN LAIR: *0%*
TREASURE TYPE: *Nil*
NO. OF ATTACKS: *1*
DAMAGE/ATTACK: *4-40*
SPECIAL ATTACKS: *Nil*
SPECIAL DEFENSES: *Nil*
MAGIC RESISTANCE: *Standard*
INTELLIGENCE: *Average*
ALIGNMENT: *Lawful neutral*
SIZE: *L (12′ tall at the shoulders)*
PSIONIC ABILITY: *Nil*
    Attack/Defense Modes: *Nil*
LEVEL/X.P. VALUE: *IX/11,500*

This beast can carry 2 gods dressed in full armor without strain, and it moves over land, air, water, or space with ease. This creature can pull any weight not attached to the earth. It is slavishly loyal to its master, Yama, and because of this will not allow itself to be used by others. It fights as a 16+ HD monster, goring for 4-40 points of damage, and can obey complicated orders from Yama.

JAPANESE MYTHOS.

The beings of this mythos present "ideal types" who give their worshipers models to live and grow by. As with one or two other mythoi, this allows the true believer to become as one of the gods with enough faith and natural ability (see **DIVINE ASCENSION**).

The first religion of Japan was Shintoism, and this faith centers around a deep love and affection for nature. Temples are arranged around trees and gardens. All temples have male and female clerics. There are also 8 million "Kami", or divine spirits, but none of these have images in the temples (see below). Shrines usually face the south and sometimes the east, but never the north or west as they are regarded as unlucky directions. There is always a gateway (Torii) to every shrine and sometimes there are whole clusters of these before the shrine.

Holy symbols do not abound in this religion, but there are three universal ones: the mirror (associated with Amaterasu Omikami), the sword, and a cluster of perfect gemstones.

Punishment for transgressions of any type is often through the stripping away of personal ability. A cleric who transgresses against the gods may lose points from abilities (like strength or dexterity) for slight sins and spell ability for greater sins, always with the provision that such things can be earned back with greater service.

The concept of "Kami" is one that prevails in all of Japanese thought throughout the several faiths of the island. It is sometimes translated to mean "divinity" or "spirit", but is a much more universal idea that is usually left untranslated by those that understand it. All things deserve to be revered and/or dreaded for their own sakes. The concept is applied to everything: all animals, all plants, seas, mountains, or any natural phenomena. Each of these has its own divine spirit — the larger (or more important) the place, the greater the Kami. If their "place" is threatened, the Kami may actually materialize as a person with druid or illusionist abilities.

AMATERASU OMIKAMI (goddess of the sun)

Greater goddess

ARMOR CLASS: –7
MOVE: Infinite
HIT POINTS: 400
NO. OF ATTACKS: 1
DAMAGE/ATTACK: 1–100
SPECIAL ATTACKS: Polymorphing
SPECIAL DEFENSES: Immune to heat and fire
MAGIC RESISTANCE: 75%
SIZE: M (5')
ALIGNMENT: Lawful good
WORSHIPER'S ALIGN: Lawful good
SYMBOL: Octagonal mirror
PLANE: Prime Material Plane
CLERIC/DRUID: 20th level cleric/14th level druid
FIGHTER: Nil
MAGIC-USER/ILLUSIONIST: 20th level in each
THIEF/ASSASSIN: Nil
MONK/BARD: 15th level in each
PSIONIC ABILITY: II
S: 25 (+7, +14) I: 25 W: 25 D: 25 C: 25 CH: 25

One of a trinity (with Susanowo and Tsukiyomi) of the most powerful of this group of deities, this human-seeming goddess was the mother of her pantheon. Amaterasu Omikami is able to touch anything and turn it into anything else (saving throw only applicable to divine beings, and then at a –8). One of her favorite tactics is to change weapons or monsters attacking her into small birds. Her fist does 1-100 points of damage per strike if she doesn't feel like *polymorphing* a being. She radiates a *continual light* like the spell.

AMA-TSU-MARA (god of blacksmiths)

Lesser god

ARMOR CLASS: –4
MOVE: 12"/12"
HIT POINTS: 299
NO. OF ATTACKS: 3/2
DAMAGE/ATTACK: 45 points
SPECIAL ATTACKS: See below
SPECIAL DEFENSES: Immune to heat and cold
MAGIC RESISTANCE: 50%
SIZE: M (6½')
ALIGNMENT: Neutral
WORSHIPER'S ALIGN: Workers of metal
SYMBOL: Double-edged axe
PLANE: Prime Material Plane
CLERIC/DRUID: 10th level cleric
FIGHTER: 12th level fighter
MAGIC-USER/ILLUSIONIST: 20th level magic-user
THIEF/ASSASSIN: Nil
MONK/BARD: 8th level bard
PSIONIC ABILITY: V
S: 25 (+7, +14) I: 24 W: 23 D: 25 C: 22 CH: 20

This massive human-appearing god is able to make any type of magical weapon in a week. He especially likes to make swords and spears that fight for themselves (as a *sword of dancing*). The god can create raw materials out of thin air, use any weapon known on any plane, and become astral or ethereal at will.

He favors blacksmiths, and there is a 2% chance that any weapon a blacksmith makes with extremely special care that is dedicated to Ama-Tsu-Mara (at referee's option), will be made into a +4 weapon by the god.

He uses a +4 double-edged axe that is 12 feet long and does 45 points of damage on a hit. It instantly slays any fire-type creature it strikes (saving throw vs. death applicable).

DAIKOKU (god of wealth and luck)

Lesser god

ARMOR CLASS: 2
MOVE: 9"/12"
HIT POINTS: 350
NO. OF ATTACKS: 2
DAMAGE/ATTACK: 20 points
SPECIAL ATTACKS: See below
SPECIAL DEFENSES: Etherealness, also see below
MAGIC RESISTANCE: 20%
SIZE: M (5½')
ALIGNMENT: Lawful good
WORSHIPER'S ALIGN: Those wishing luck and riches
SYMBOL: Three coins
PLANE: Prime Material Plane
CLERIC/DRUID: 10th level cleric/14th level druid
FIGHTER: 12th level fighter
MAGIC-USER/ILLUSIONIST: 12th level in each
THIEF/ASSASSIN: Nil
MONK/BARD: 10th level bard
PSIONIC ABILITY: VI
S: 22 (+4, +10) I: 23 W: 25 D: 24 C: 25 CH: 20

This god looks like a portly balding male with an easy grace about him. He is also known as the patron of all farmers, and in this aspect can be prayed to for weather of any type and hope for a good harvest. The god is noted for his good-natured outlook on all things and often uses his powers for the benefit of his clerics and worshipers. Besides being able to control all types of weather, he has complete control over the growth of plants and natural animal life (making them grow huge or shrink at will). He wanders the Prime Material Plane in ethereal form, observing his worshipers. Those who sacrifice great amounts of wealth to him at his temples will eventually be rewarded by the god (even if it is given to the descendants of the giver).

He fights with a wooden mallet that hits for 20 points of damage. It also shrinks any beings it hits (that do not make their magic saving throw) to half size. It will permanently negate any miscellaneous magic item used against its master (no saving throw), and will transport its master to a place of safety if the god is in mortal danger or becomes magically enspelled (charm, hold, etc.).

EBISU (god of luck through hard work)

Lesser god

ARMOR CLASS: −5
MOVE: 9″/12″
HIT POINTS: 313
NO. OF ATTACKS: 2
DAMAGE/ATTACK: 3-30 (+11)
SPECIAL ATTACKS: See below
SPECIAL DEFENSES: See below
MAGIC RESISTANCE: 50%
SIZE: M (5½′)
ALIGNMENT: Lawful good
WORSHIPER'S ALIGN: Lawful good
SYMBOL: Fishing rod or cane staff
PLANE: Seven Heavens
CLERIC/DRUID: 30th level cleric
FIGHTER: 10th level paladin
MAGIC-USER/ILLUSIONIST: 25th level
    magic-user
THIEF/ASSASSIN: Nil
MONK/BARD: 10th level bard
PSIONIC ABILITY: I
S: 23 (+5, +11) I: 25 W: 25 D: 22 C: 23 CH: 24

The deity appears as an elderly male, and is occasionally found floating over the earth rewarding those who work hard with bountiful harvests of foodstuffs or extra money for sale of goods.

He uses a *staff of striking* in battle that hits for 3-30 points of damage. He always makes his saving throw. His luck attribute affects all beings in the same way. Beings attacking the god will only be able to do half damage with any given hit and they will hit only one-half of the times they normally might have (i.e., every other hit will miss).

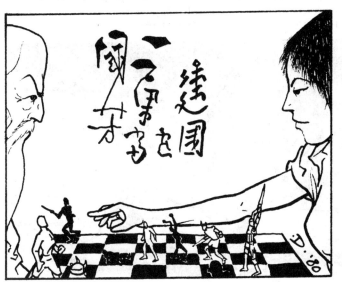

HACHIMAN (war god)

Demigod

ARMOR CLASS: −1
MOVE: 28″/21″
HIT POINTS: 300
NO. OF ATTACKS: 2 (3 open hand)
DAMAGE/ATTACK: 4-40 (+8) (5-20
    open hand)
SPECIAL ATTACKS: See below
SPECIAL DEFENSES: See below
MAGIC RESISTANCE: 35% (plus see
    below)
SIZE: M (6½′)
ALIGNMENT: Chaotic good
WORSHIPER'S ALIGN: Warriors
SYMBOL: Throwing dagger
PLANE: Gladsheim
CLERIC/DRUID: Nil
FIGHTER: 20th level ranger
MAGIC-USER/ILLUSIONIST: Nil
THIEF/ASSASSIN: 15th level assassin
MONK/BARD: 14th level monk
PSIONIC ABILITY: I
S: 20 (+3, +8) I: 21 W: 17 D: 25 C: 25 CH: 21

Hachiman has the following abilities: he *shape changes* at will, is not affected by any spell of the 7th level or less, and is never affected by any type of illusion.

The god has a throwing knife that turns into an ancient red dragon when cast in anger at an immortal. If the dragon dies in battle, it returns to dagger form, otherwise being forced to change back into dagger form for a 48 hour period after fighting up to 100 melee rounds.

In hand-to-hand combat, he uses his two-handed sword which only he can lift. This is a +3 weapon that acts as a *sword of sharpness* and also does 4-40 points of damage.

KISHIJOTEN (goddess of luck)

Lesser goddess

ARMOR CLASS: −10
MOVE: 12″/12″//12″
HIT POINTS: 311
NO. OF ATTACKS: 1
DAMAGE/ATTACK: 2-20
SPECIAL ATTACKS: See below
SPECIAL DEFENSES: See below
MAGIC RESISTANCE: 100%
SIZE: M (5′)
ALIGNMENT: Neutral good
WORSHIPER'S ALIGN: Any being
    wishing luck
SYMBOL: White diamond
PLANE: Prime Material Plane
CLERIC/DRUID: 25th level cleric
FIGHTER: Nil
MAGIC-USER/ILLUSIONIST: 20th level
    in each
THIEF/ASSASSIN: Nil
MONK/BARD: 15th level bard
PSIONIC ABILITY: II
S: 15 I: 25 W: 25 D: 20 C: 24 CH: 25

The goddess always appears as a human in any situation where she aids in a struggle. At will, she *shape changes*, always makes her saving throw, and can summon one of any good creature type to her presence once a month. With this last power she can summon, among other beings, a good dragon, a paladin, or a ranger to help her at any time she wills. These summoned beings are taken at random from the Prime Material Plane; she doesn't know who will come, and when arriving they are not under her dominance (they have free will).

She never physically takes part in battle, but observes and gives special luck to those she favors (at her whim and judge's option). This takes the form of that favored being making his or her saving throws and striking their enemies with every try. She also occasionally favors beings (not just humans) that take unusual chances (judge's option) in those situations where random chance plays a hand. There is a 2% chance of this happening in any given situation of great risk, if she is watching.

While the goddess prefers to use magic to attack her personal enemies, if pressed hard enough she will strike them with her gem, doing 2-20 points of damage.

OH-KUNI-NUSHI *(patron of heroes) "The Great Land Master"*

Demigod

ARMOR CLASS: −4
MOVE: 15"/12"
HIT POINTS: 200
NO. OF ATTACKS: 2
DAMAGE/ATTACK: 3-30 (+8)
SPECIAL ATTACKS: Nil
SPECIAL DEFENSES: See below
MAGIC RESISTANCE: 20%
SIZE: M (6')
ALIGNMENT: Chaotic good
WORSHIPER'S ALIGN: Chaotic and
  good heroes
SYMBOL: Red sword
PLANE: Gladsheim
CLERIC/DRUID: Nil
FIGHTER: 18th level fighter
MAGIC-USER/ILLUSIONIST: Nil
THIEF/ASSASSIN: Nil
MONK/BARD: 10th level in each
PSIONIC ABILITY: V
S: 20 (+3, +8) I: 20 W: 10 D: 20 C: 20 CH: 20

This god always appears human, and in his aspect as Land Master he is able to converse with all "natural" creatures, heal them and make them grow young or old at will. The very ground speaks to him and tells him who has passed or what is hidden underneath.

Oh-Kuni-Nushi wields a great red two-handed sword that strikes for 3-30 points of damage. He encourages his worshipers to actively seek heroic quests which they may attempt.

Clerics of Oh-Kuni-Nushi must attempt a heroic existence. These mortals travel the earth preaching a doctrine of the usefulness of bravery and courage to all walks of life. They may only rise to the next level if they have committed a heroic act on their own initiative (DM's discretion).

RAIDEN *(god of thunder & patron of fletchers)*

Greater god

ARMOR CLASS: −8
MOVE: 12"/24"
HIT POINTS: 337
NO. OF ATTACKS: 2
DAMAGE/ATTACK: 2-20 (+12) or 2-
  24/2-24
SPECIAL ATTACKS: See below
SPECIAL DEFENSES: See below
MAGIC RESISTANCE: 80% (plus see
  below
SIZE: M (7')
ALIGNMENT: Neutral
WORSHIPER'S ALIGN: Neutral
SYMBOL: Black spiked mace with a
  crossed lightning bolt
PLANE: Elemental Plane of Air
CLERIC/DRUID: 15th level cleric
FIGHTER: 13th level fighter
MAGIC-USER/ILLUSIONIST: 15th level
  in each
THIEF/ASSASSIN: Nil
MONK/BARD: Nil
PSIONIC ABILITY: V
S: 24 (+5, +12) I: 22 W: 19 D: 24 C: 24 CH: 19

Raiden has dark, roughened, scaled skin, with hands that end in talons that are capable of striking for 2-24 points of damage. The god also has a beard, pointed eyebrows and ears, heavily muscled arms and legs, and a large round belly. At will, he can *shape change*, cast 25 point *lightning bolts* as far as he can see, and create any type of weather. On rare occasions he will aid his mortal worshipers with their undertakings.

In battle he uses a +3 jet black mace that strikes for 2-20 points of damage every time it hits and disenchants other magical weapons and armor it comes in contact with (no saving throw). He wears +3 black splint mail and uses a +4 enchanted shield that prevents the success of any single weapon's attack in any given melee round (with the most powerful weapon being stopped in the case of more than one strike attempt against the deity). When Raiden battles, a wind storm always rages around him that does not allow missile weapons of any type to touch him. The god also has a shadowy aura about his body (at times when he is not wearing armor or using his shield) that negates the affects of any 8th or lower level magic-users' spell.

Besides his mace, Raiden uses a set of double-strength *drums of panic*. These will only affect the enemies of the god's allies.

In his aspect as patron of fletchers, the god will grant, to every worshiper who designs arrows, the ability in his or her lifetime to make ten *arrows of slaying mortals*. These shafts will not display their power or be detectable as magical. This may occur when a fletcher takes *extremely* special care with the crafting of an arrow; even the creator will not know these arrows for what they are. The maker will only prize them for the effort he or she put into them (the referee will know, however).

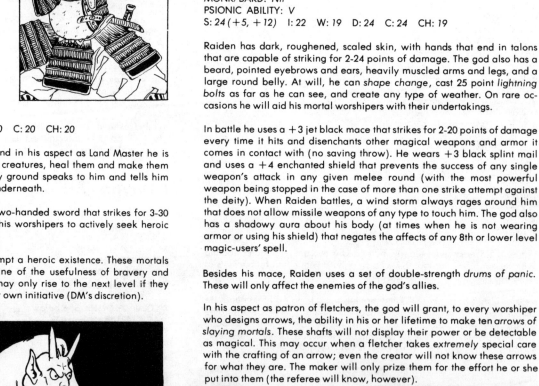

RAIKO (hero)

ARMOR CLASS: −1
MOVE: 29″
HIT POINTS: 180
NO. OF ATTACKS: 2 (or 3 with open
  hand)
DAMAGE/ATTACK: By weapon type
  (or 6-24 with open hand)
SPECIAL ATTACKS: Nil
SPECIAL DEFENSES: Nil
MAGIC RESISTANCE: Standard
SIZE: M (6′)
ALIGNMENT: Neutral good
CLERIC/DRUID: Nil
FIGHTER: 18th level ranger
MAGIC-USER/ILLUSIONIST: Nil
THIEF/ASSASSIN: 12th level assassin
MONK/BARD: 15th level monk
PSIONIC ABILITY: Nil
  Attack/Defense Modes: Nil
S: 18 (00) (+3, +6) I: 18 W: 11 D: 19 C: 18 CH: 18

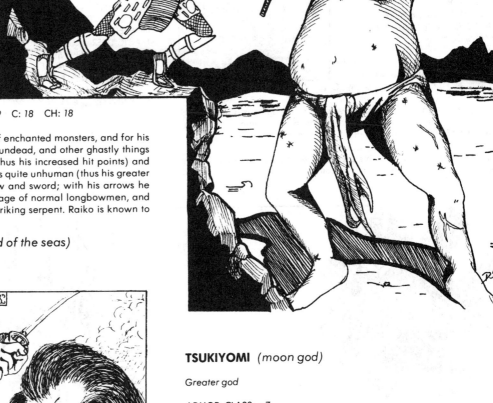

Raiko, favored of the gods, is a fighter of enchanted monsters, and for his many victories over giants, demons, the undead, and other ghastly things he has been given greater endurance (thus his increased hit points) and has achieved a speed of movement that is quite unhuman (thus his greater dexterity). His weapons are the longbow and sword; with his arrows he can achieve twice the distance and damage of normal longbowmen, and his sword is said to be swifter than the striking serpent. Raiko is known to some as Yorimitsu.

SUSANOWO (storm god and lord of the seas)

Greater god

ARMOR CLASS: −4
MOVE: 12″/36″//48″
HIT POINTS: 400
NO. OF ATTACKS: 2
DAMAGE/ATTACK: 3-30 (+14)
SPECIAL ATTACKS: See below
SPECIAL DEFENSES: See below
MAGIC RESISTANCE: 30% or 100%
  (see below)
SIZE: M (6½′)
ALIGNMENT: Chaotic neutral
WORSHIPER'S ALIGN: Chaotic
SYMBOL: Katana (sword)
PLANE: Limbo
CLERIC/DRUID: 10th level in each
FIGHTER: 13th level ranger
MAGIC-USER/ILLUSIONIST: 20th level
  magic-user
THIEF/ASSASSIN: Nil
MONK/BARD: Nil
PSIONIC ABILITY: V
S: 25 (+7, +14) I: 24 W: 20 D: 25 C: 25 CH: 22

A large bearded oriental with long flowing black hair, this deity can often be found riding a thunder cloud. He casts lightning bolts (doing 30 points of damage per strike) any time he wills. He *shape changes* at will, can summon any time 1-10 air or water elementals to do his bidding, and he can take away the power of flight from any being for up to 1 week (no saving throw). He wears yellow +4 splint mail into battle that emits blasts of heat once per round (doing 20 points of damage to all within 10 feet of the god, no saving throw).

He uses a +4 yellow sword that strikes for 3-30 points of damage with every hit, and if the weapon misses his enemy in any given melee round, the next closest enemy will be hit. While the god is in the water, he is 100% magic resistant, and all the nearby creatures of the sea will throw themselves in front of him so that they are hit instead of the god.

TSUKIYOMI (moon god)

Greater god

ARMOR CLASS: −7
MOVE: 12″/21″
HIT POINTS: 400
NO. OF ATTACKS: 3/2
DAMAGE/ATTACK: 40 points
SPECIAL ATTACKS: Nil
SPECIAL DEFENSES: See below
MAGIC RESISTANCE: 30%
SIZE: M (7′)
ALIGNMENT: Neutral good
WORSHIPER'S ALIGN: Good align-
  ments
SYMBOL: White disk
PLANE: Elysium
CLERIC/DRUID: 20th level cleric
FIGHTER: 12th level ranger
MAGIC-USER/ILLUSIONIST: 15th level
  in each
THIEF/ASSASSIN: 15th level assassin
MONK/BARD: 10th level bard
PSIONIC ABILITY: VI
S: 25 (+7, +14) I: 23 W: 23 D: 25 C: 25 CH: 25

This god has light blue skin, but otherwise appears to be a massively built human male. At will the god can *shape change*, and *summon* one of any type of flying creature (up to 5 times per day). He also has the ability to summon any object he sees to his hand (magic saving throw applicable) so that enemies' weapons and the like can be taken away from them.

He uses a +4 pike in battle that strikes for 40 points of damage with every hit and cannot be broken by any force on the Prime Material Plane. The weapon also makes the god immune to poison, petrification, and *magic jar* attacks.

YAMAMOTO DATE (hero)

ARMOR CLASS: 2
MOVE: 12''
HIT POINTS: 189
NO. OF ATTACKS: 2
DAMAGE/ATTACK: 3-18
SPECIAL ATTACKS: Nil
SPECIAL DEFENSES: Nil
MAGIC RESISTANCE: Standard
SIZE: M
ALIGNMENT: Lawful good
CLERIC/DRUID: Nil
FIGHTER: 15th level paladin
MAGIC-USER/ILLUSIONIST: Nil
THIEF/ASSASSIN: Nil
MONK/BARD: Nil
PSIONIC ABILITY: Nil
    Attack/Defense Modes: Nil
S: 17 (+1, +1) I: 17 W: 11 D: 19 C: 18 CH: 17

This hero, son of an emperor, is renowned for his ability as a fighter and loyalty to his emperor father. Many tales exist of his cunning and skill at disguise. He has the disguise skill of an 11th level assassin.

Yamamoto Date is known for his awesome speed and ability with any blade. He has a magic sword that is both a *dragon slaying blade* and *sword of sharpness*.

YOSHI-IYE (hero)

ARMOR CLASS: 2
MOVE: 19''
HIT POINTS: 109
NO. OF ATTACKS: 3/2
DAMAGE/ATTACK: 2-24 with arrow,
    otherwise by weapon type
SPECIAL ATTACKS: See below
SPECIAL DEFENSES: Nil
MAGIC RESISTANCE: Standard
SIZE: M
ALIGNMENT: Neutral good
CLERIC/DRUID: Nil
FIGHTER: 13th level ranger
MAGIC-USER/ILLUSIONIST: Nil
THIEF/ASSASSIN: Nil
MONK/BARD: 5th level in each
PSIONIC ABILITY: Nil
    Attack/Defense Modes: Nil
S: 18 (89) (+2, +4) I: 17 W: 15 D: 19 C: 19 CH: 18

This warrior holds the war god Hachiman as his patron, and his prayers for aid are occasionally answered personally by the god! He is a mighty fighter with any weapon, but his bow skills are legendary. His arrows are so powerfully launched that they can reputedly pierce rocks and so skillfully aimed that they do greater than normal damage with every hit.

Nehwon Mythos

The world of Nehwon is the creation of the famous fantasy author, Fritz Leiber. In it are a vast variety of gods, goddesses, and heroes of the best and worst sort. It is a world where magic is mixed with adventure to form a land that is very enjoyable to read about.

Striding through the pages of Leiber's books are two extraordinary characters: Fafhrd and the Gray Mouser. The first is a huge barbarian from the cold north, and the second is a swarthy man from the decadent depths of the city. These two combine to create a set of stories that delight and thrill all those who read them.

These characters live and play in the city of Lankhmar, the oldest center of civilization on the planet. Within the walls of the city lie everything an **AD&D** player could ask for.

This material includes the concept of Godsland. This is an area on the astral plane where most of the gods reside (irrespective of their alignment). From this area they keep an eye on, and are often called to help, the respective cults.

NOTE: Before developing the creatures and deities of this series, some attention should be given to a few of the organizations of the world of Nehwon.

THIEVES' GUILD OF LANKHMAR

This group is the perfection of the gangster's dream. It actively seeks to eliminate any thieves not of its membership and has the tacit support of the people of the city, who fear to report members of the Guild to law enforcement authorities. The members all study intensive training courses in all aspects of the thieving art, which means that instructors are always available for those studying to advance a level. The Guild is led by a 12th level Master Thief and he attempts to prevent other members from becoming as skilled as he is. At any given time, there are 3-24 members who are about the fifth level of ability (this does not include the many lesser thieves who are members). Their Guild Hall appears to be an old mansion, but has actually become a well-disguised fortress with many levels underground with escape tunnels which lead to exits all over Lankhmar.

SLAYERS' BROTHERHOOD

The Brotherhood passes as the bodyguard division of Lankhmar. Any type of fighter from the 1st level to the 10th can be hired for a price. All types of classes of people in Lankhmar use the Brotherhood for jobs. While openly it displays an uninspired, ignorant facade, in reality it is a subtle, powerful force in the city. Its leader and all the most powerful members are Expert or better assassins. The Guildmaster Assassin is also watchful of his subordinates and tries to kill those that advance to Prime Assassin level.

SNOW WITCHES

Many of the northern tribes have a group of women that have a measure of magical power. These women, after some preparation and working together, can control all forms of cold and ice spells. They also possess, among the strongest members, a limited telepathy when in direct eye contact with a human. Given a group of 5 women and 24 hours of time, limited weather control (chilling) is possible; this effect has a range of 5 miles.

FIRE SORCERERS OF THE EAST

These men come from the always uncertain East, and while never attaining high levels in the magical arts, they are still able to master fire spells and illusions of this type to a high level of excellence. They can use all fire-oriented spells at twice their level of ability, i.e. a 9th level spell caster of this type can use fire spells as an 18th level magic-user. To compensate for this specialization, they are limited to half their level of ability in all other spell areas.

GEMS

In Fritz Leiber's works, some gems have very special powers. A case in point are the jeweled skulls and hands of the dead masters of the Thieves Guild. The gems give the power of life and locomotion to these dead body parts. In the case of Urgaans of Angarngi's tower, for example, the gems placed at its center animated the structure, giving it the power to move itself internally and kill intruders. Gems are often magical containers of souls and life, or sources of strange powers.

CULTS OF THE BEAST

On the world of Nehwon there is a belief held in common by all of the mortals of the planet that there exist 13 perfect specimens of each of the animal creatures of the world. These 13 are fully intelligent and are the models for all the individual members of the species to look up to. They exist to aid either a pivotal member or a large group of a species that is threatened.

Belief in these perfect groups of 13 has caused some mortals to develop a worship of them in order to take advantage of the chance to sometimes use them to further mortal concerns.

It is said that to capture and control one of these 13 will result in the control of the whole species.

FAFHRD (hero)

ARMOR CLASS: 3
MOVE: 12''
HIT POINTS: 120
NO. OF ATTACKS: 2
DAMAGE/ATTACK: By weapon type
SPECIAL ATTACKS: Nil
SPECIAL DEFENSES: See below
MAGIC RESISTANCE: Standard
SIZE: M (6 feet, 11 inches)
ALIGNMENT: Neutral good
CLERIC/DRUID: Nil
FIGHTER: 15th level ranger
MAGIC-USER/ILLUSIONIST: Nil
THIEF/ASSASSIN: 13th level thief
MONK/BARD: 5th level bard
PSIONIC ABILITY: Nil
   Attack/Defense Modes: Nil
S: 18 (00) (+3, +6)   I: 17   W: 14   D: 18   C: 18   CH: 17

This Northern red-haired barbarian is the strong arm of the two-hero team. Taking special interest in languages, he can read and write all the major ones of Nehwon and there is an 80% chance that he will understand any obscure one he is exposed to. He always carries a bastard sword (which he always names Graywand) and a dirk (more short sword or poniard than anything else) he calls Heartseeker. He sometimes fights with a hand axe, balanced for throwing, in his left hand. He is also adept with a long bow. Fafhrd is able to climb walls and hide in shadows with a +20% over his usual thiefly base.

Coming from the frigid planes of the cold north, this barbarian hero is a hardy soul who withstands hardships with a grim smile. He loves sailing, as he went on many viking-like raids as a youth. It was in Lankhmar that he met the Gray Mouser. This hero is very emotional and willing to believe in wild tales and schemes far more readily than this shorter partner. Fafhrd has even gone so far as to take up religion upon one occasion, which was short lived but epic in the telling.

GRAY MOUSER (hero)

ARMOR CLASS: 2
MOVE: 12"
HIT POINTS: 96
NO. OF ATTACKS: 3/2 (or 3; see
    below)
DAMAGE/ATTACK: *By weapon type*
SPECIAL ATTACKS: *Nil*
SPECIAL DEFENSES: *Nil*
MAGIC RESISTANCE: *Standard*
SIZE: *M (5¼')*
ALIGNMENT: *Neutral*
CLERIC/DRUID: *Nil*
FIGHTER: *11th level fighter*
MAGIC-USER/ILLUSIONIST: *3rd level
    magic-user*
THIEF/ASSASSIN: *15th level thief*
MONK/BARD: *Nil*
PSIONIC ABILITY: *Nil*
    Attack/Defense Modes: *Nil*
S: *16 (0, +1)* I: *18* W: *14* D: *19* C: *17* CH: *18*

This short man of the western cities supplies the refinement and delicacy his brawny partner lacks. He calls his rapier Scalpel and the dagger he uses (balanced for throwing) Cat's Claw. The Gray Mouser is very fond of studying things arcane, but has not the magical skills to master his studies. He has a great aversion to *anything* sharp being pointed at him, an aversion that has saved his life many times. He generally fights with Scalpel in his right hand and Cat's Claw in his left, incurring no penalties to hit due to his phenomenal dexterity. When so armed, he strikes 3 times per melee round, with a 50% chance that the third strike will be with either weapon.

While the Mouser grew up on the streets (with all that that implies), his teen years were spent with an old hedge magician who taught him the ways of law and a little magic. It was these days spent in the forests with his mentor that gave Mouser his streak of morality. It was shortly after this time that the young man met his lifelong friend Fafhrd. While the Gray Mouser is a thief, a liar, and a trickster supreme, he can be relied upon to keep faith for causes he supports and people he favors.

AARTH

Demigod

ARMOR CLASS: 2
MOVE: 18"
HIT POINTS: 244
NO. OF ATTACKS: 3/2
DAMAGE/ATTACK: *By weapon type*
SPECIAL ATTACKS: *See below*
SPECIAL DEFENSES: *See below*
MAGIC RESISTANCE: *25%*
SIZE: *M (5½')*
ALIGNMENT: *Lawful neutral*
WORSHIPER'S ALIGN: *Lawful neutral*
SYMBOL: *Glowing gold rectangle
    on a field of black*
PLANE: *Godsland*
CLERIC/DRUID: *15th level cleric*
FIGHTER: *10th level fighter*
MAGIC-USER/ILLUSIONIST: *30th level
    magic-user*
THIEF/ASSASSIN: *Nil*
MONK/BARD: *Nil*
PSIONIC ABILITY: *Nil*
S: *20 (+3, +8)* I: *25* W: *24* D: *25* C: *23* CH: *22*

Aarth was once a powerful wizard, becoming so renowned that after his death, he achieved demigodhood. Because of the vast numbers of his worshipers, when the cult is suffering greatly, he will be brought to the Prime Material Plane to help his followers.

He instantly knows the powers of any device used against him and he has a special spell that can negate any magical device as a *rod of cancellation*. When he takes personal part in a battle, he fights invisibly.

His temples are among the mightiest in all of Lankhmar. It seems that the more powerful patrons are devoted to the cult more out of fear of "the revealing of information" than faith in the might of the religion. Clerics make it their personal duty to sneak about the town, learning all they can about the populace.

ASTRAL WOLF

FREQUENCY: *Very rare*
NO. APPEARING: *3-12*
ARMOR CLASS: *3 (on the astral
    plane)*
MOVE: *18"*
HIT DICE/POINTS: *3 HD*
% IN LAIR: *50%*
TREASURE TYPE: *Nil*
NO. OF ATTACKS: *1*
DAMAGE/ATTACK: *2-8*
SPECIAL ATTACKS: *See below*
SPECIAL DEFENSES: *Nil*
MAGIC RESISTANCE: *Standard*
INTELLIGENCE: *Animal*
ALIGNMENT: *Neutral evil*
SIZE: *L (4' at the shoulder)*
PSIONIC ABILITY: *Nil*
    Attack/Defense Modes: *Nil*
LEVEL/X.P. VALUE: *III/90 + 3 per hp*

These creatures are wolves that have died hungry and now roam about the wastelands in astral form, seeking to fill their now ever-empty bodies. All attacks are made in isolated areas. These creatures are able to force sleeping humans into the astral plane when there are 5 or more wolves concentrating on the act (save vs. spells applicable). When humans are attacked in this other plane, their earthly bodies will show the damage of the wolves' fangs.

BEHEMOTH

FREQUENCY: *Very rare*
NO. APPEARING: *1*
ARMOR CLASS: *4*
MOVE: *12"//18"*
HIT DICE/POINTS: *15 HD*
% IN LAIR: *30%*
TREASURE TYPE: *Nil*
NO. OF ATTACKS: *1*
DAMAGE/ATTACK: *4-40*
SPECIAL ATTACKS: *Nil*
SPECIAL DEFENSES: *Nil*
MAGIC RESISTANCE: *Standard*
INTELLIGENCE: *Animal*
ALIGNMENT: *Neutral*
SIZE: *L (40' long)*
PSIONIC ABILITY: *Nil*
    Attack/Defense Modes: *Nil*
LEVEL/X.P. VALUE: *VIII/4,000 + 20
    per hp*

Imagine a killer whale with four stubby legs and no fins and you have a perfect picture of a swamp behemoth. These fearsome mammals are easily capable of crossing water, marsh grass, and quicksand. A behemoth always attacks the largest thing in any given group. It has a white cousin of the snowy North which has a thick coat of fur and short claws on its feet. This snow beast is known to hunt during the fiercest of blizzards. There is also a jet black species with much longer legs that inhabits the plains and hills of Nehwon.

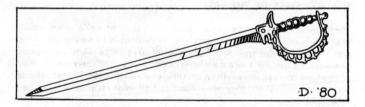

BIRD OF TYAA

FREQUENCY: *Rare*
NO. APPEARING: *3-30*
ARMOR CLASS: *7*
MOVE: *1"/18"*
HIT DICE/POINTS: *1-4 hp*
% IN LAIR: *10%*
TREASURE TYPE: *Q*
NO. OF ATTACKS: *1*
DAMAGE/ATTACK: *1-6*
SPECIAL ATTACKS: *20% have poison
    claws*
SPECIAL DEFENSES: *Nil*
MAGIC RESISTANCE: *Standard*
INTELLIGENCE: *Low*
ALIGNMENT: *Neutral evil*
SIZE: *S (1')*
PSIONIC ABILITY: *Nil*
    Attack/Defense Modes: *Nil*
LEVEL/X.P. VALUE: *II/30 + 1 per hp*

This avian is closely related to the raven, but has a much higher level of
sentience. It is commonly found in the mountains and hills. There is a 20%
chance that the bird's claws are poisoned, as it is able to crush some types
of deadly berries for that effect. The bird knows how to strike for exposed
body parts and uses a diving attack. These evil birds are among the followers of the goddess Tyaa (q.v.).

COLD WOMAN

FREQUENCY: *Unique*
NO. APPEARING: *1*
ARMOR CLASS: *-2*
MOVE: *9"*
HIT DICE/POINTS: *180 hp*
% IN LAIR: *10%*
TREASURE TYPE: *U (X 5)*
NO. OF ATTACKS: *1*
DAMAGE/ATTACK: *4-40*
SPECIAL ATTACKS: *See below*
SPECIAL DEFENSES: *See below*
MAGIC RESISTANCE: *25%*
INTELLIGENCE: *Very*
ALIGNMENT: *Neutral*
SIZE: *L (30' tall)*
PSIONIC ABILITY: *Nil*
    Attack/Defense Modes: *Nil*
LEVEL/X.P. VALUE: *X/28,500*

This creature is basically a huge white pudding. Her powers include *illusion generation*, and a *cold ray* with a range of 6" which does 7-70
points of damage if it hits. (Successful save vs. spells indicates a miss. Saving throw is adjusted by dexterity modifiers to AC, e.g. 17 dexterity gives a
+3). Cold Woman "bites" for 4-40, attacking as a 16+ hit dice monster,
and those bitten who fail to save are *paralyzed*.

Chopping or striking Cold Woman has no effect, as severed parts immediately rejoin the creature. Lightning has the same effect. Cold, of
course, does not bother her in the least. Her corrosive secretions dissolve
metal at the same rate as a black pudding: chainmail is destroyed in 1
round, plate mail in 2, with each magical plus of the armor adding a round
to the time needed to corrode.

Cold Woman lures persons into her lair with gems and jewelry, which are
scattered about her cave. She then paralyzes them and inserts one of her
eggs into the body. In a day's time the egg hatches and her spawn (a white
pudding) eats the host. The egg is easily removable and the spawn will die
if exposed to the air before hatching.

In the wastes, it is said that the excessively evil or greedy fall prey to her
power most often. She always abandons a lair after laying one batch of
eggs. Legend has it that there is only one Cold Woman at a time; all the
rest await her death, and then the strongest one becomes the mother. Her
young are known as Cold Spawn.

DEATH

Greater god

ARMOR CLASS: *-5*
MOVE: *Infinite*
HIT POINTS: *350*
NO. OF ATTACKS: *10 (1 per
    segment)*
DAMAGE/ATTACK: *Special*
SPECIAL ATTACKS: *See below*
SPECIAL DEFENSES: *Nil*
MAGIC RESISTANCE: *95%*
SIZE: *M (7')*
ALIGNMENT: *Neutral*
WORSHIPER'S ALIGN: *All alignments*
SYMBOL: *Death's head*
PLANE: *Prime Material Plane*
CLERIC/DRUID: *30th level cleric*
FIGHTER: *30th level fighter*
MAGIC-USER/ILLUSIONIST: *30th level
    in each*
THIEF/ASSASSIN: *15th level assassin*
MONK/BARD: *23rd level bard*
PSIONIC ABILITY: *I*
S: *24 (+6, +12)* I: *24* W: *24* D: *24* C: *24* CH: *21*

Referred to as a minor death, this deity is responsible for all the dying on
the world of Nehwon. He is given quotas to be met by the Lords of Neces-
sity (beings about which very little is known). He appears as a man with a
cadaverous skin color and he has the power to know the entire past history
of a being at a glance.

His sword slays anything it touches. On Nehwon, all beings are mortal. It
was pointed out that even Death is aware that at some future date, he will
die.

He lives in a huge fort in the heart of Shadowland, a land of perpetual twi-
light where the dead rest under the earth, to be called on at the will of
Death.

DEVOURER *(alien wizard)*

ARMOR CLASS: *7*
MOVE: *15"*
HIT POINTS: *50*
NO. OF ATTACKS: *1*
DAMAGE/ATTACK: *By weapon type*
SPECIAL ATTACKS: *Nil*
SPECIAL DEFENSES: *Nil*
MAGIC RESISTANCE: *24%*
SIZE: *Variable*
ALIGNMENT: *Lawful evil*
CLERIC/DRUID: *Nil*
FIGHTER: *5th level fighter*
MAGIC-USER/ILLUSIONIST: *13th level
    magic-user/25th level illusionist*
THIEF/ASSASSIN: *10th level thief*
MONK/BARD: *Nil*
PSIONIC ABILITY: *Nil*
    Attack/Defense Modes: *Nil*
S: *15* I: *19* W: *5* D: *17* C: *19* CH: *20*

Aliens of high magical ability, these creatures are totally occupied with
selling. This preoccupation forces them to any extreme in perfecting their
art. The best of them sell only junk they have magicked into something
appearing to be valuable.

They come from another Prime Material Plane of existence. Their usual
practice in any given place is to establish a sales beachhead and trick
whole nations and peoples into trading all of their valued items for the
Devourer's junk, until all the valuables are gone and they must work as the
Devourer's slaves to acquire the magicians' worthless wares.

GHOUL, Nehwon

FREQUENCY: *Rare*
NO. APPEARING: *1-100*
ARMOR CLASS: *10*
MOVE: *12"*
HIT DICE/POINTS: *3 HD*
% IN LAIR: *80%*
TREASURE TYPE: *A*
NO. OF ATTACKS: *1*
DAMAGE/ATTACK: *By weapon type*
SPECIAL ATTACKS: *Nil*
SPECIAL DEFENSES: *80% invisible in
    dark*
MAGIC RESISTANCE: *Standard*
INTELLIGENCE: *Average-Very*
ALIGNMENT: *Neutral evil*
SIZE: *M (5')*
PSIONIC ABILITY: *Nil*
    Attack/Defense Modes: *Nil*
LEVEL/X.P. VALUE: *II/50 + 3 per hp*

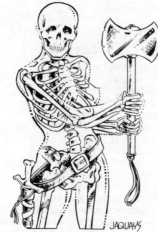

Nehwon's ghouls are not of the **AD&D** undead type, but are a species of humanoids unto themselves. They are almost totally transparent, except for their bones, which are grey. They are often mistaken for skeletons, and are almost invisible (80%) in the dark. Once detected, however, they are easily kept track of. They enjoy the taste of human flesh and sometimes raid human settlements for loot and food. It is said that some ride ghoulish horses, transparent to the bones like their masters.

GODS OF LANKHMAR

Demigods

ARMOR CLASS: *3*
MOVE: *9"*
HIT POINTS: *200*
NO. OF ATTACKS: *1*
DAMAGE/ATTACK: *3-30*
SPECIAL ATTACKS: *Withering*
SPECIAL DEFENSES: *Nil*
MAGIC RESISTANCE: *Standard*
SIZE: *M (6')*
ALIGNMENT: *Neutral evil*
WORSHIPER'S ALIGN: *Neutral evil
    and citizens of Lankhmar*
SYMBOL: *Skeleton holding a staff*
PLANE: *Prime Material Plane*
CLERIC/DRUID: *15th level cleric*
FIGHTER: *5th level fighter*
MAGIC-USER/ILLUSIONIST: *20th level
    magic-user*
THIEF/ASSASSIN: *Nil*
MONK/BARD: *Nil*
PSIONIC ABILITY: *V*
S: *19 (+3, +7)* I: *24* W: *9* D: *20* C: *23* CH: *−3*

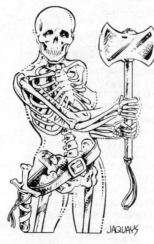

Ancient mummified skeletons sustaining themselves through the use of mighty magics, these beings are able to use spells twice as fast as mortal spell casters. They each carry a double-strength *staff of withering*. These gods appear only when their city is threatened with grave danger. When the problem is solved, they cast about the city wreaking havoc as a reminder that they are not to be called on too often. They inhabit one large temple at the end of the Street of the Gods.

The temple is a giant double-roomed structure with a set of 13 crypts underneath that hold the "gods"; the temple has no clerics. When worshipers wish a favor from the gods, they toss gifts into the door and hope for the best. The material is never there an hour later.

NOTE: The gods of Lankhmar are open to much free interpretation by the DM. There is a special difference between the gods of Lankhmar, the oldest city of Nehwon, and the gods "in" Lankhmar. The gods in Lankhmar

are those of the many religions in the many temples lining the Street of the Gods. Some are powerful, some are weak, and their fortunes change with the quantity and quality of their worshipers, who are a fickle lot. Though most Lankhmarts worship at one or another of the temples on the Street of the Gods, all secretly believe in and fear the gods of Lankhmar, who protect the city so that worship may continue. As long as this is the case, the gods of Lankhmar are indifferent to the existence of the gods in Lankhmar.

GODS OF TROUBLE

Lesser gods

ARMOR CLASS: *−2*
MOVE: *12"/24"*
HIT POINTS: *366*
NO. OF ATTACKS: *1*
DAMAGE/ATTACK: *See below*
SPECIAL ATTACKS: *Nil*
SPECIAL DEFENSES: *See below*
MAGIC RESISTANCE: *Special (see
    below)*
SIZE: *M (6')*
ALIGNMENT: *Chaotic evil*
WORSHIPER'S ALIGN: *Chaotic evil*
SYMBOL: *Three-pointed star*
PLANE: *Godsland*
CLERIC/DRUID: *15th level cleric*
FIGHTER: *Nil*
MAGIC-USER/ILLUSIONIST: *20th level
    in each*
THIEF/ASSASSIN: *15th level assassin*
MONK/BARD: *Nil*
PSIONIC ABILITY: *I*
S: *12* I: *23* W: *18* D: *18* C: *23* CH: *18*

These 3 beings of trouble have no constant form and are entities of energy that feed on all the trouble caused on the Prime Material Plane. Within 30 feet of their forms, no magic works, and when they gaze at a being, that being fails in whatever he or she or it is attempting (no saving throw). When under attack of any kind, they are immediately transported to the astral plane before any force can hurt them.

They enjoy roaming the world astrally, affecting all alignments equally. They have a very small sect of worshipers. The high priest of this cult has the gazing power of his god (saving throw vs. spells applicable). They care nothing for their worshipers, and inflict troubles upon them impartially if they should cross their path. The cult is quite naturally a rather fatalistic one.

HATE

Lesser god

ARMOR CLASS: *See below*
MOVE: *6"*
HIT POINTS: *0*
NO. OF ATTACKS: *6*
DAMAGE/ATTACK: *See below*
SPECIAL ATTACKS: *See below*
SPECIAL DEFENSES: *See below*
MAGIC RESISTANCE: *25%*
SIZE: *L (90' long)*
ALIGNMENT: *Chaotic evil*
WORSHIPER'S ALIGN: *Chaotic evil*
SYMBOL: *Foggy image with floating
    eyes*
PLANE: *Astral plane*
CLERIC/DRUID: *Nil*
FIGHTER: *Nil*
MAGIC-USER/ILLUSIONIST: *See
    below*
THIEF/ASSASSIN: *Nil*
MONK/BARD: *Nil*
PSIONIC ABILITY: *Nil*
S: *10* I: *10* W: — D: *10* C: — CH: —

KOS *(god of dooms)*

Greater god

ARMOR CLASS: –4
MOVE: 18"
HIT POINTS: 377
NO. OF ATTACKS: 2
DAMAGE/ATTACK: 8-80 (+14) or
   3-30 (+14)
SPECIAL ATTACKS: Nil
SPECIAL DEFENSES: See below
MAGIC RESISTANCE: 35%
SIZE: M (7')
ALIGNMENT: Neutral
WORSHIPER'S ALIGN: Neutral and
   fighters
SYMBOL: Crossed sword and axe
PLANE: Godsland
CLERIC/DRUID: 10th level druid
FIGHTER: 15th level ranger
MAGIC-USER/ILLUSIONIST: 20th level
   magic-user
THIEF/ASSASSIN: Nil
MONK/BARD: Nil
PSIONIC ABILITY: Nil
S: 25 (+7, +14) I: 24 W: 23 D: 25 C: 24 CH: 24

Hate manifests itself as a thick grey fog with a few red orbs resembling eyes in the density. This fog is able to control up to 6 beings (as in a *mass charm* spell) or manipulate up to 6 weapons in its tentacles as a set of 6th level fighters. The manifestation of the god must be generated at night by a high priest of at least the 10th level and 100 worshipers. The fog will appear from the worshipers and is able to travel a distance of 5 miles. Its only function is to do harm.

Hate's physical form is attached to its area of generation by a long, extremely tough silver-red cord, which is spun out behind it as it hunts for prey. The only way Hate can be damaged is by cutting this pulsing cord (which cannot be seen from in front of the Hate-cloud). The cord is AC –8, but any hit with a sharp weapon, or a spell such as *magic missile*, will cut it, dispelling Hate's physical form until the next night it can be summoned.

Kos appears as a northern barbarian of Nehwon dressed in furs of ancient monsters from the world's past. He fights with an intelligent +6 broadsword, doing 8-80 points of damage per strike, but his code of honor prevents him from using it on beings with less than 100 hit points. Against these he uses a +3 hand axe that does 3-30 points. His +6 weapon will not allow itself to be used by other beings; it does 50 points of damage to any other being trying to handle it.

The god is able to summon 9-90 berserkers per day for his purposes. He is said to exist in the cold wastes of the North, viewing battles all over the plane and destroying cowards amongst his worshipers as soon as they show fear.

ISSEK OF THE JUG

Demigod

ARMOR CLASS: –3
MOVE: 12"/12"
HIT POINTS: 210
NO. OF ATTACKS: 3/2
DAMAGE/ATTACK: 3-30
SPECIAL ATTACKS: Nil
SPECIAL DEFENSES: Nil
MAGIC RESISTANCE: Standard
SIZE: M (7')
ALIGNMENT: Lawful good
WORSHIPER'S ALIGN: Lawful good
SYMBOL: Man on a broken rack or a
   jug
PLANE: Godsland
CLERIC/DRUID: 15th level cleric
FIGHTER: 12th level paladin
MAGIC-USER/ILLUSIONIST: 10th level
   magic-user
THIEF/ASSASSIN: Nil
MONK/BARD: 15th level bard
PSIONIC ABILITY: Nil
S: 25 (+7, +14) I: 23 W: 25 D: 22 C: 24 CH: 24

LEVIATHAN

FREQUENCY: Very rare
NO. APPEARING: 1
ARMOR CLASS: –1
MOVE: 9"//15"
HIT DICE/POINTS: 40 HD
% IN LAIR: 15%
TREASURE TYPE: Nil
NO. OF ATTACKS: 8
DAMAGE/ATTACK: 4-40 or special
SPECIAL ATTACKS: See below
SPECIAL DEFENSES: See below
MAGIC RESISTANCE: Standard
INTELLIGENCE: Animal
ALIGNMENT: Neutral
SIZE: L (300' long)
PSIONIC ABILITY: Nil
   Attack/Defense Modes: Nil
LEVEL/X.P. VALUE: X/15,800 + 35
   per hp

Issek appears as a tall man with twisted wrists and ankles, and his manifestations are always in humans who are being tortured on the rack. These men will destroy the rack and those hurting them. He carries a jug which is able to pour out any liquid the god wishes.

His sect is a poor one and preaches the need to persevere under any hardships that life might bring. His clerics travel about always appearing to be one of the poor, even if they are not.

This squid-like creature lives on the bottom of the ocean and comes up once annually to feed on ships that travel over its territory. The thing's main attack form is to come up to a ship, crack it open and eat its softer contents. Each of its 8 tentacles does 4-40 points per strike, and when it grabs a ship or thing in the water with all 8 appendages it does 30 hull value points of damage per melee round. (See **DUNGEON MASTERS GUIDE**, *Waterborne Adventures*.)

Whenever the creature has taken more than half its hit points in damage, it retreats miles under the water.

MOVARL (hero)

ARMOR CLASS: 2
MOVE: 12"
HIT POINTS: 86
NO. OF ATTACKS: 3/2
DAMAGE/ATTACK: 2-20 (+3)
SPECIAL ATTACKS: Nil
SPECIAL DEFENSES: See below
MAGIC RESISTANCE: Standard
SIZE: M (6')
ALIGNMENT: Lawful good
CLERIC/DRUID: Nil
FIGHTER: 12th level paladin
MAGIC-USER/ILLUSIONIST: Nil
THIEF/ASSASSIN: Nil
MONK/BARD: Nil
PSIONIC ABILITY: Nil
   Attack/Defense Modes: Nil
S: 18 (51) (+2, +3) I: 14 W: 18 D: 17 C: 18 CH: 18

Movarl is the most influential of the heroes of the world of Nehwon, for he is (at least at times) overlord of the city of Kvarch Nar. However, he travels often amongst the cities and towns of the Great Forest to champion the cause of law and good. Movarl wields his great sword well enough to stand with the best of fighters, although he will not seek battle with any individuals except those who are evil. He fears to fight no one and is immune to *fear* spells. His +1 two-handed sword does 2-20 points of damage per strike. The man is instantly aware of any evil being within 20 feet of him.

NEHWON EARTH GOD

Lesser god

ARMOR CLASS: −2
MOVE: 12"
HIT POINTS: 300
NO. OF ATTACKS: 1
DAMAGE/ATTACK: 5-50
SPECIAL ATTACKS: Nil
SPECIAL DEFENSES: See below
MAGIC RESISTANCE: 50%
SIZE: L (15')
ALIGNMENT: Chaotic evil
WORSHIPER'S ALIGN: Chaotic evil
SYMBOL: Diamond eye
PLANE: Prime Material Plane
CLERIC/DRUID: 14th level druid
FIGHTER: 15th level fighter
MAGIC-USER/ILLUSIONIST: Nil
THIEF/ASSASSIN: Nil
MONK/BARD: Nil
PSIONIC ABILITY: VI
S: 25 (+7, +14) I: 10 W: 12 D: 18 C: 25 CH: 11

This god is an aware piece of molten earth, able to assume any shape in this molten form; no forged weapon can hurt it. The tropical priests of Klesh serve this deity, who wishes to return all of Nehwon to its molten state. The only thing preventing this deity from accomplishing its end is the hard crust of the world.

Its temples can be found in desolate areas all over Nehwon. These temples are usually rich in gems and gold. The god is able to control beings through a *mass charm* spell that it can cast through any gem consecrated to his sect. Its Kleshite clerics commonly use blow guns.

NINGAUBLE OF THE SEVEN EYES (wizard)

ARMOR CLASS: −2
MOVE: 9"
HIT POINTS: 150
NO. OF ATTACKS: Nil
DAMAGE/ATTACK: Nil
SPECIAL ATTACKS: See below
SPECIAL DEFENSES: See below
MAGIC RESISTANCE: Standard
SIZE: L (9')
ALIGNMENT: Neutral
CLERIC/DRUID: Nil
FIGHTER: Nil
MAGIC-USER/ILLUSIONIST: 20th level
   magic-user/12th level illusionist
THIEF/ASSASSIN: Nil
MONK/BARD: 10th level bard
PSIONIC ABILITY: Nil
   Attack/Defense Modes: Nil
S: 14 I: 19 W: 19 D: 16 C: 19 CH: 16

This being is Fafhrd's advisor and charges almost the same fees his arcane peer Sheelba charges, except that if the Mouser is called upon to kill a rare magical bird and bring back a feather or two, Fafhrd must kill a roc and bring back the whole body! Categories such as intelligence and the like, as with Sheelba, are subject to change, as the being's nature is not like that of humans. Though probably not originally of Nehwon, Ningauble inhabits a huge series of caves near the Sinking Lands. These caves are linked interdimensionally with other planes, other times of Nehwon and other multiverses. Only Ningauble, with his alien logic patterns, is able to fully comprehend the paths of his caves.

Ningauble is always wrapped in heavy robes with an empty cowl that displays seven constantly moving lights. Occasionally one will protrude from the cowl, and then it can be seen to be an eye upon the end of a snake-like tentacle. These eyes can see through all illusions.

Ningauble is known as the "gossiper of the gods" and loves nothing better than to listen to a good story about the powerful and mighty or the strange and unknown. He has informers in many different times and places, and sometimes makes use of other heroes in worlds other than Nehwon.

PULGH (hero)

ARMOR CLASS: 2
MOVE: 12"
HIT POINTS: 72
NO. OF ATTACKS: 2
DAMAGE/ATTACK: 2-12 (+1)
SPECIAL ATTACKS: Nil
SPECIAL DEFENSES: See below
MAGIC RESISTANCE: Standard
SIZE: M (6')
ALIGNMENT: Lawful evil
CLERIC/DRUID: 4th level cleric
FIGHTER: 15th level fighter
MAGIC-USER/ILLUSIONIST: Nil
THIEF/ASSASSIN: 5th level assassin
MONK/BARD: Nil
PSIONIC ABILITY: Nil
   Attack/Defense Modes: Nil
S: 17 (+1, +1) I: 14 W: 17 D: 17 C: 16 CH: 8

Pulgh does not appear in any of the currently published works about Nehwon, although a cousin, Pulg, is mentioned in "Lean Times in Lankhmar". Pulgh is the greatest warrior of Lankhmar (although when Fafhrd and Mouser are in the city, Pulgh would be hard pressed to claim he was the best *in* that place . . .). This title is based on the accomplishments of the warrior in getting impossible things done for the important personages of the city.

He favors using a great +3 spear which does 2-12 points of damage, although he can certainly employ any other weapon with skill. Prior to taking up the tools of the fighter's trade, Pulgh was an evil cleric (hence the clerical ability) and it is rumored that he still serves a cult of black evil within the city. He is a shadowy figure who avoids notice whenever possible, although he will emerge whenever circumstances warrant his doing so.

RAT GOD

Lesser god

ARMOR CLASS: 2
MOVE: 18''
HIT POINTS: 222
NO. OF ATTACKS: 2
DAMAGE/ATTACK: 4-40
SPECIAL ATTACKS: Nil
SPECIAL DEFENSES: See below
MAGIC RESISTANCE: 20%
SIZE: L (10' at the shoulder)
ALIGNMENT: Chaotic evil
WORSHIPER'S ALIGN: Chaotic evil
(and wererats)
SYMBOL: Two red eyes on a black
field
PLANE: Godsland
CLERIC/DRUID: 13th level cleric
FIGHTER: 15th level fighter
MAGIC-USER/ILLUSIONIST: Nil
THIEF/ASSASSIN: 12th level assassin
MONK/BARD: Nil
PSIONIC ABILITY: I
S: 20 (+3, +8) I: 18 W: 13 D: 23 C: 19 CH: –6

The rat god is the manifestation of all men's fears of its kind. All felines must run in fear from this apparition. It always walks erect, can shrink to normal rat size, and is able to summon 20 wererats to its side once per day.

The god's largest temple can be found in the port city of Ilthmar, where human sacrifices are held by the light of every full moon.

RED GOD

Lesser god

ARMOR CLASS: –2
MOVE: 18''
HIT POINTS: 311
NO. OF ATTACKS: 4
DAMAGE/ATTACK: 3-30 (+12)
twice/1-10 (+12) twice
SPECIAL ATTACKS: Nil
SPECIAL DEFENSES: See below
MAGIC RESISTANCE: 25%
SIZE: L (8')
ALIGNMENT: Neutral
WORSHIPER'S ALIGN: Neutral and
Eastern warriors
SYMBOL: Flame with a sword in its
midst
PLANE: Godsland
CLERIC/DRUID: 15th level cleric
FIGHTER: 20th level fighter
MAGIC-USER/ILLUSIONIST: 12th level
in each
THIEF/ASSASSIN: 10th level assassin
MONK/BARD: 10th level monk
PSIONIC ABILITY: VI
S: 24 (+6, +12) I: 22 W: 17 D: 25 C: 24 CH: 24

The war god of the East, this being appears with a +4 ring of protection, a helm of telepathy and teleportation, and a displacer cloak. He uses a +3 sabre in his right hand that does 3-30 points per strike and a +4 dirk in his left hand that does 1-10 points of damage. His sabre casts an anti-magic shell around his body that does not limit his own spell abilities.

This god is very protective of his more important worshipers, and when they are in foreign lands he will occasionally come to their aid in situations that he would not bother about in the East. This aid consists of an 8th level magic-user sent to help.

The god is a massive dark-skinned man with red studded leather armor carrying a bronze shield. He is always mustachioed and wears a pointed helm. His boots and belt shine as brightly as if a continual light spell had been placed on them.

SHEELBA OF THE EYELESS FACE (wizard)

ARMOR CLASS: 2
MOVE: 9''
HIT POINTS: 150
NO. OF ATTACKS: 1
DAMAGE/ATTACK: 1-10 (+8)
SPECIAL ATTACKS: See below
SPECIAL DEFENSES: See below
MAGIC RESISTANCE: Standard
SIZE: M
ALIGNMENT: Neutral
CLERIC/DRUID: Nil
FIGHTER: Nil
MAGIC-USER/ILLUSIONIST: 20th level
magic-user/5th level illusionist
THIEF/ASSASSIN: Nil
MONK/BARD: 10th level monk
PSIONIC ABILITY: Nil
Attack/Defense Modes: Nil
S: 20 (+3, +8) I: 19 W: 10 D: 16 C: 19 CH: 7

This being is the advisor to the Gray Mouser, charging for this advice the theft of seeming nonimportant and/or important objects and devices all over the world of Nehwon, and sometimes the other universes as the mood takes the being. While the books constantly refer to Sheelba as a he, the author of the series, Fritz Leiber, and his longtime friend Harry Fischer both maintain that Sheelba is a female. Whatever it is, it is clearly not a creature of Nehwon, but a being related to the lower planes. Sheelba appears to the world in a large monkish robe, with a full cowl that is totally dark inside (hence the name). It lives in the Great Salt Marsh in a magic hut with animated stilts. This hut moves at a rate of 24'' over the roughest landscape. Sheelba has a dislike for and rivalry with Ningauble of the Seven Eyes, but at times they are forced to help each other. Categories such as intelligence and the like change with the circumstances that the being finds itself in.

It is commonly known that demons (who can perceive its real form) scream in horror when facing Sheelba and leave instantly.

Sheelba is a greedy thing out to get all the profit out of life that it can. On the other hand it protects its investments by preventing bad things from happening to the heroic pair and their city.

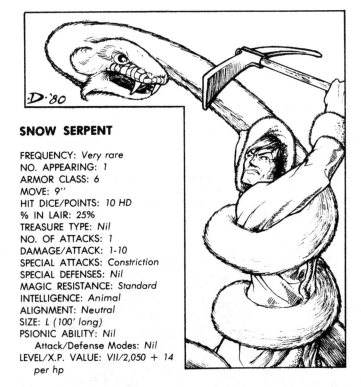

SNOW SERPENT

FREQUENCY: Very rare
NO. APPEARING: 1
ARMOR CLASS: 6
MOVE: 9''
HIT DICE/POINTS: 10 HD
% IN LAIR: 25%
TREASURE TYPE: Nil
NO. OF ATTACKS: 1
DAMAGE/ATTACK: 1-10
SPECIAL ATTACKS: Constriction
SPECIAL DEFENSES: Nil
MAGIC RESISTANCE: Standard
INTELLIGENCE: Animal
ALIGNMENT: Neutral
SIZE: L (100' long)
PSIONIC ABILITY: Nil
Attack/Defense Modes: Nil
LEVEL/X.P. VALUE: VII/2,050 + 14
per hp

This furred snake of enormous size commonly lies in wait near snow-piled mountain trails. Its bite does 1-10 points of damage, and it can constrict for 3-30 points of damage per melee round.

SPIDER GOD

Demigod

ARMOR CLASS: 2
MOVE: 18"
HIT POINTS: 249
NO. OF ATTACKS: 2
DAMAGE/ATTACK: 3-30
SPECIAL ATTACKS: Poison
SPECIAL DEFENSES: See below
MAGIC RESISTANCE: 10%
SIZE: L (18' at the shoulders)
ALIGNMENT: Chaotic evil
WORSHIPER'S ALIGN: Chaotic evil
SYMBOL: Black opal
PLANE: Godsland
CLERIC/DRUID: Nil
FIGHTER: 15th level fighter
MAGIC-USER/ILLUSIONIST: 15th level
    magic-users
THIEF/ASSASSIN: Nil
MONK/BARD: Nil
PSIONIC ABILITY: Nil
S: 22 (+4, +10) I: 18 W: 9 D: 22 C: 24 CH: –3

Appearing as a giant black spider, this deity is known for its delight in receiving human sacrifices. Its powers include the ability to summon 30 phase spiders per day, the power to make all arachnids obey, and the ability to transfer the powers of a spider to its most powerful high priest.

Its evil clerics work diligently to keep their god satisfied by way of human sacrifices. It rewards them with a gift of a pet large spider once per each ten sacrifices.

SPIDER, SALT

FREQUENCY: Rare
NO. APPEARING: 1-6
ARMOR CLASS: 6
MOVE: 15" * 18"
HIT DICE/POINTS: 3 HD
% IN LAIR: 25%
TREASURE TYPE: Nil
NO. OF ATTACKS: 1
DAMAGE/ATTACK: 1-8
SPECIAL ATTACKS: Poison
SPECIAL DEFENSES: Nil
MAGIC RESISTANCE: Standard
INTELLIGENCE: Animal
ALIGNMENT: Neutral
SIZE: M (4' long)
PSIONIC ABILITY: Nil
    Attack/Defense Modes: Nil
LEVEL/X.P. VALUE: III/105 + 3 per
    hp

This is a huge ugly spider about the size of a large pig. It has large suction pads on its feet allowing it to travel over any non-slippery surface. It lives in great salty swamps, where it makes complicated sticky web traps. It has a deadly poisonous bite.

TYAA (winged goddess of evil birds)

Lesser goddess

ARMOR CLASS: –3
MOVE: 9"/36"
HIT POINTS: 311
NO. OF ATTACKS: 1
DAMAGE/ATTACK: By weapon type
SPECIAL ATTACKS: Poisoned
    weapons
SPECIAL DEFENSES: Nil
MAGIC RESISTANCE: 32%
SIZE: M (5')
ALIGNMENT: Chaotic evil
WORSHIPER'S ALIGN: Chaotic evil
SYMBOL: Bird of Tyaa
PLANE: Godsland
CLERIC/DRUID: 15th level cleric
FIGHTER: 10th level fighter
MAGIC-USER/ILLUSIONIST: 15th level
    magic-user
THIEF/ASSASSIN: Nil
MONK/BARD: Nil
PSIONIC ABILITY: Nil
S: 18 (+1, +2) I: 19 W: 20 D: 25 C: 20 CH: 24

Tyaa has the power to manifest herself in her high priestess, though this is rare. She can summon 20 of any predatory birds, but prefers to use the Birds of Tyaa, of which she can summon 100 a day. If forced into combat she uses weapons that are poisoned, preferring a +2 longsword.

Tyaa's cult was banished from Lankhmar, but its worshipers can still be found in the mountains of Nehwon. Only women are permitted in the high priesthood and Tyaa demands the sacrifice of body parts from her more attractive worshipers. The Falconers of Tyaa are the male arm of the cult and always have some type of bird as a fighting companion. They, like the priestesses, are able to communicate with all avian life.

VOTISHAL

Demigod

ARMOR CLASS: –2
MOVE: 18"
HIT POINTS: 344
NO. OF ATTACKS: 3/2
DAMAGE/ATTACK: By weapon type
SPECIAL ATTACKS: Nil
SPECIAL DEFENSES: Nil
MAGIC RESISTANCE: 35%
SIZE: M (6')
ALIGNMENT: Lawful good
WORSHIPER'S ALIGN: Lawful good
SYMBOL: Leather pouch
PLANE: Godsland
CLERIC/DRUID: 13th level cleric
FIGHTER: 12th level fighter
MAGIC-USER/ILLUSIONIST: 15th level
    magic-user
THIEF/ASSASSIN: 25th level thief
MONK/BARD: 3rd level bard
PSIONIC ABILITY: V
S: 20 (+3, +8) I: 21 W: 19 D: 25 C: 20 CH: 20

Votishal appears as a normal thief in all of his idol representations. This is another case of a man of great ability becoming venerated by later generations. He was a master thief of the 14th level who reformed to the cause of good and law. His thieving abilities then went in the direction of robbing from evil groups to benefit the lawful good group he supported.

If he manifests himself on the Prime Material Plane, he will try to kill all evil beings he encounters. His clerics rise alternately in the clerical class and the thief class. They are very zealous in their efforts to rob all evil people (especially evil shrines). They are in direct opposition to the Thieves' Guild, and constantly try to get member thieves to join the sect by kidnapping them and brainwashing them in the temple crypts. The high clerics of this order are always 15th level patriarchs/12th level master thieves. No cleric can rise above the tenth level in this sect unless they have carried away some amount of riches from an evil temple.

WATER COBRA

FREQUENCY: *Uncommon*
NO. APPEARING: *1-8*
ARMOR CLASS: *8*
MOVE: *12''*
HIT DICE/POINTS: *3 + 3*
% IN LAIR: *0%*
TREASURE TYPE: *Nil*
NO. OF ATTACKS: *1*
DAMAGE/ATTACK: *1-4*
SPECIAL ATTACKS: *Poison*
SPECIAL DEFENSES: *See below*
MAGIC RESISTANCE: *Standard*
INTELLIGENCE: *Animal*
ALIGNMENT: *Neutral*
SIZE: *S (4' long)*
PSIONIC ABILITY: *Nil*
   Attack/Defense Modes: *Nil*
LEVEL/X.P. VALUE: *III/150 + 4 per*
   hp

The water cobra is invisible in the water because of its ability to change color to match the area underneath it. It only frequents fresh water rivers and creeks. Its bite is poisonous.

BIBLIOGRAPHY

Though the works of the esteemed author Fritz Leiber are numerous, only those referring to the gods, creatures, and heroes (Fafhrd and the Gray Mouser, in particular) of Nehwon were used in compiling this section. These are available in paperback editions from Ace books (New York), and include the following titles:

Swords Against Deviltry
Swords Against Death
Swords in the Mist
Swords Against Wizardry
The Swords of Lankhmar
Swords and Ice Magic

NEHWON ENCOUNTER TABLES

The following brief outdoor encounter tables are provided for referees who may wish to stage adventures upon the world of Nehwon.

COLD REGION

Creature Type	Dice Roll
Behemoth, snow*	01-02
Bugbear	03-08
Cold spawn (white pudding)	09-12
Dragon, white	13-17
Elf, winter (as wood elf)	18-21
Giant, frost	22-25
Giant, hill	26-31
Gnome, ice (northern gnome)	32-34
Griffon	35-40
Hydra, snow (as normal hydra, but furred)	41-43
Men, bandit	44-55
Men, barbarian	56-61
Men, berserker	62-65
Men, merchant	66-70
Ogre	71-77
Snake, giant, furred (constrictor)	78-82
Snow serpent*	83-85
Snow witch*	86-90
Tiger, ice (as normal tiger, but white)	91-96
Yeti	97-00

FOREST

Creature Type	Dice Roll
Centaur	01-06
Dryad	07-09
Elf, wood	10-18
Ghoul, Nehwon*	19-26
Lion	27-34
Men, bandit	35-50
Men, barbarian	51-58
Men, merchant	59-66
Ogre	67-82
Satyr	83-90
Snake, wood (spitting)	91-96
Unicorn	97-00

MARSH

Creature Type	Dice Roll
Behemoth, swamp*	01-03
Eel, giant	04-15
Ghoul, Nehwon*	16-20
Men, brigand	21-42
Men, merchant	43-50
Rat, swamp (giant)	51-70
Slug, swamp (giant)	71-80
Spider, salt*	81-85
Water cobra*	86-95
Worm, giant (purple)	96-00

MOUNTAINS

Creature Type	Dice Roll
Astral wolf*	01-02
Bird of Tyaa*	03-06
Ghoul, Nehwon*	07-15
Lion	16-24
Men, bandit	25-45
Men, barbarian	46-57
Men, merchant	58-66
Ogre	67-82
Satyr	83-90
Snake, wood (spitting)	91-96
Unicorn	97-00

PLAINS/HILLS

Creature Type	Dice Roll
Behemoth, black*	01-02
Bird of Tyaa*	03-07
Bugbear	08-16
Fire magician*	17-18
Ghoul, Nehwon*	19-27
Griffon	28-37
Hippogriff	38-43
Lion	44-52
Men, bandit	53-61
Men, barbarian	62-70
Men, merchant	71-90
Men, Mingol (as dervish)	91-00

WATERBORNE

Creature Type	Dice Roll
Behemoth*	01-03
Dragon, water (as hydra, aquatic, MV 18'')	04-15
Leviathan*	16-17
Men, barbarian (raider)	18-29
Men, buccaneer	30-39
Men, merchant	40-64
Men, pirate	65-74
Merman	75-86
Shark	87-00

* Indicates monster described in this volume. All others are from **MONSTER MANUAL.**

NONHUMANS' DEITIES

There is a whole host of creatures which have been created for the game of **ADVANCED DUNGEONS AND DRAGONS** that have either been spawned from the minds and myths of past man or created entirely from the minds of the game masters. Such a wide diversity of creatures and sub-cultures requires an equally wide diversity of deities and lesser beings of power. The nonhuman races occupy different places in every Dungeon Master's individual world. Therefore, it would be extremely difficult to create complete pantheons of nonhuman gods that would be appropriate to every campaign. This section seeks only to outline some major beings important to the races created in the **AD&D** family. A complete pantheon of all dwarven gods, demigods and heroes can be easily imagined, but its complete notation is too awesome a task for a work of this limited size (as would be the complete notation of the deities of any of the nonhuman races). Let this section serve as a springboard for the DM. It presents a start for any extensive pantheon that the referee feels he or she may need.

As humanoid shamans (and witch doctors) increase in level, they also increase to a degree in hit dice and combat ability. For each level of ability above the 1st, the shaman adds 1-4 hit points (1d4) to his or her total. For every two levels of shaman ability, the creature fights as if one hit dice better on the **ATTACK MATRIX FOR MONSTERS**.

Witch doctors' clerical (shaman) and magic-user levels are not added together, but are paired, like multi-classed characters. They gain 2-5 hit points for each level above 1st/1st as long as they advance in tandem, but only the normal 1-4 hit points per level when their shaman abilities surpass their maximum magic-user abilities. The levels of experience of witch doctors' magic-user abilities are not detailed in this volume, but may be found in the **DUNGEON MASTERS GUIDE**.

Examples: A 4th level gnoll shaman would have the following hit dice: 2d8 (his normal amount) + 3d4 (his shaman bonus). He would fight as a 4 hit dice monster. A 5th level goblin shaman would have 4d4 plus 1-7 hit points, and would fight as a 3-1 (or "2-3+") hit dice monster. A 3/3 orc witch doctor would have 1d8 plus 2d4 + 2 hit points, and would fight as a 2 hit dice monster.

NOTE: The following beings from the **MONSTER MANUAL** and **FIEND FOLIO** should be treated as lesser gods, though they very rarely have human worshipers:

MONSTER MANUAL

Demon:
Demogorgon
Juiblex
Orcus
Yeenoghu

Devil:
Asmodeus
Baalzebul
Dispater
Geryon

Dragon:
Bahamut
Tiamat

FIEND FOLIO

Demon:
Lolth (detailed in this volume)

Elemental Princes of Evil

Slaad:
Ssendam
Ygorl

BUGBEARS

HRUGGEK

Lesser god

ARMOR CLASS: 0
MOVE: 12''
HIT POINTS: 221
NO. OF ATTACKS: 1 or 2
DAMAGE/ATTACK: 3-30 (+11) or 2-16/2-16
SPECIAL ATTACKS: Nil
SPECIAL DEFENSES: +2 or better weapon to hit
MAGIC RESISTANCE: 25%
SIZE: L (12' tall)
ALIGNMENT: Chaotic evil
WORSHIPER'S ALIGN: Chaotic evil (bugbears)
SYMBOL: Morningstar
PLANE: Pandemonium
CLERIC/DRUID: 15th level cleric
FIGHTER: As 16+ HD monster
MAGIC-USER/ILLUSIONIST: Nil
THIEF/ASSASSIN: Nil
MONK/BARD: Nil
PSIONIC ABILITY: Nil
S: 23 (+5, +11)   I: 17   W: 8   C: 24   CH: 7 (23 to bugbears)

Bugbears have a simple pantheon of six deities, including gods of earth, death, fertility, hunting and fear. Hruggek, the god of battle, is the most powerful and important, though he doesn't rule the others.

Hruggek appears as a huge, powerful bugbear with great fangs and clawed hands and feet. These clawed hands can each strike for 2-16 points of damage. He wields a ten-foot +3 morningstar that does 3-30 points of damage when it hits.

Hruggek lives in a great cave in Pandemonium which is decorated with the severed heads of his conquered opponents. Bugbear shamans worship Hruggek by offering him the blood of their enemies. The shamans' status is dependent upon how many opponents they have defeated. Bugbear shamans can rise to the 5th level in clerical ability.

CENTAURS

SKERRIT "The Forester"

Lesser god

ARMOR CLASS: *Variable (at least 2)*
MOVE: *Variable*
HIT POINTS: *290*
NO. OF ATTACKS: *Variable*
DAMAGE/ATTACK: *Variable*
SPECIAL ATTACKS: *See below*
SPECIAL DEFENSES: *−4 to be hit in forests*
MAGIC RESISTANCE: *35%*
SIZE: *Variable*
ALIGNMENT: *Neutral (tends to chaotic good)*
WORSHIPER'S ALIGN: *Neutral-chaotic good (centaurs and satyrs)*
SYMBOL: *Oak growing from acorn*
PLANE: *Happy Hunting Grounds*
CLERIC/DRUID: *14th level in each*
FIGHTER: *As 16+ HD monster*
MAGIC-USER/ILLUSIONIST: *10th level illusionist*
THIEF/ASSASSIN: *Nil*
MONK/BARD: *9th level bard*
PSIONIC ABILITY: *V*
S: *25 (+7, +14)* I: *19* W: *17* D: *23* C: *24* CH: *21*

Skerrit represents the great guiding hand of the forces of nature that keep everything in balance. He maintains the forest so that all of its denizens can fulfill their proper roles; he provides prey for the hunters and food for the hunted. Skerrit can appear in the form of any creature of the forest, and sometimes his spirit seems to temporarily possess various plants and animals to enable them to carry out his will.

Centaurs often portray Skerrit as the most perfect example of one of their own race, and in this form he wields a bow and a +3 spear that strikes for 2-20 points of damage (plus strength bonus). As a centaur, Skerrit is armor class 2 and moves at a rate of 21″. When in the forest, all opponents are −4 to hit him, as the branches from the trees move to block blows, leaves fly in the attackers' faces, etc.

Centaurs worship Skerrit through dances and mock hunts on every night of the full moon. Centaur shamans may advance up to the 3rd level. Many satyrs also worship Skerrit, though they have no clerical members.

DWARVES

MORADIN "The Soul Forger"

Greater god

ARMOR CLASS: *−9*
MOVE: *12″*
HIT POINTS: *400*
NO. OF ATTACKS: *2*
DAMAGE/ATTACK: *4-40 (+14)*
SPECIAL ATTACKS: *Nil*
SPECIAL DEFENSES: *Forged weapons cannot harm him*
MAGIC RESISTANCE: *60%*
SIZE: *L (20′)*
ALIGNMENT: *Lawful good*
WORSHIPER'S ALIGN: *Lawful good (dwarves)*
SYMBOL: *Hammer and anvil*
PLANE: *Seven Heavens*
CLERIC/DRUID: *15th level cleric/14th level druid*
FIGHTER: *20th level fighter*
MAGIC-USER/ILLUSIONIST: *19th level magic-user*
THIEF/ASSASSIN: *Nil*
MONK/BARD: *Nil*
PSIONIC ABILITY: *VI*
S: *25 (+7, +14)* I: *23* W: *20* D: *21* C: *25* CH: *19 (25 to dwarves)*

Moradin is the head of a fairly large pantheon of dwarven deities. (The exact members of this pantheon vary from clan to clan.) It is said that Moradin created the race of dwarves from iron and mithral, forging them in the fires at the center of the world. The dwarves' souls entered their bodies when Moradin blew on his creations to cool them.

Moradin's symbol and weapon is a huge glowing hammer. It is a +5 weapon and strikes for 4-40 points of damage. It cannot be used by any save the god himself, as it disappears from others' hands and returns to its owner. He wears magical armor and shield of his own making, which gives him armor class −9. This equipment cannot be removed from his body by any save Moradin.

The center of a shrine to Moradin is always the great ever-burning hearth and forge. Sacrifices, be they of common or precious metal, are melted down at the forge and reformed into shapes useable by the clergy of Moradin. Non-player character dwarven clerics can rise as high as the 7th level, though this usually takes hundreds of years.

Other dwarven gods include Clanggedin (god of battle), Dumathoin (god of secrets under mountains), and Abbathor (evil god of greed).

ELVES

CORELLON LARETHIAN

Greater god

ARMOR CLASS: *−4*
MOVE: *15″/18″*
HIT POINTS: *350*
NO. OF ATTACKS: *2*
DAMAGE/ATTACK: *2-20 (longbow) or 3-30 (+9; sword)*
SPECIAL ATTACKS: *Bow never misses*
SPECIAL DEFENSES: *+3 or better weapon to hit*
MAGIC RESISTANCE: *95%*
SIZE: *M (7′)*
ALIGNMENT: *Chaotic good*
WORSHIPER'S ALIGN: *Chaotic good (elves)*
SYMBOL: *Quarter moon*
PLANE: *Olympus*
CLERIC/DRUID: *13th level in each*
FIGHTER: *20th level ranger*
MAGIC-USER/ILLUSIONIST: *20th level in each*
THIEF/ASSASSIN: *Nil*
MONK/BARD: *15th level bard*
PSIONIC ABILITY: *I*
S: *21 (+4, +9)* I: *25* W: *25* D: *25* C: *21* CH: *25*

Corellon Larethian represents the highest ideals of elvenkind: "he" is skilled in all the arts and crafts, and is the patron of music, poetry, and magic. Corellon is alternately male or female, both or neither. The god is also mighty in battle, and is said to have personally banished such demons as Lolth from the sunlit Upperworld. Elven lore states that the race of elves sprang from the drops of blood Corellon shed in this epic battle.

Corellon Larethian uses a magical bow; arrows fired from it never miss their target and do 2-20 points of damage. "He" also has a +5 magic sword made from a star that strikes for 3-30 points of damage, and always detects which of the god's opponents are the most dangerous. Any other being who picks up this sword will be burned for 10-100 points of damage.

Corellon's clerics always wear a blue quarter-moon talisman; non-player character elven clerics can attain the 7th level. The elves build no shrines, but always use natural geological formations or amphitheaters for places of worship. Other elven deities include Rillifane Rallathil (god of nature), Labelas Enoreth (god of longevity), and Hanali Celanil (goddess of romantic love).

ELVES, Aquatic

DEEP SASHELAS

Lesser god

ARMOR CLASS: –3
MOVE: 12''//24''
HIT POINTS: 300
NO. OF ATTACKS: 1.
DAMAGE/ATTACK: 3-30
SPECIAL ATTACKS: Double damage
    under water
SPECIAL DEFENSES: 100% magic
    resistance under water
MAGIC RESISTANCE: Standard (out
    of water)
SIZE: M (7')
ALIGNMENT: Chaotic good
WORSHIPER'S ALIGN: Chaotic good
    (aquatic elves) and sailors
SYMBOL: Dolphin
PLANE: Olympus
CLERIC/DRUID: 19th level cleric
FIGHTER: 15th level fighter
MAGIC-USER/ILLUSIONIST: 12th level
    in each
THIEF/ASSASSIN: Nil
MONK/BARD: 10th level bard
PSIONIC ABILITY: III
S: 25 (+7, +14) I: 20 W: 18 D: 21 C: 21 CH: 23

Sashelas is the "Knowledgeable One", the being who always knows where food or the enemy can be found. He is master of the dolphins and 20 of their strongest always follow him in the sea. Mortal sailors sacrifice to the god for their safety and aquatic elven clerics take these offerings and trade with other mortals for the gain of the entire race. Clerics of Sashelas time their religious ceremonies to coincide with especially high or low tides. The sea elves, like their friends the dolphins, are mortal enemies of sharks. Clerics will often conduct ritual shark hunts. They, like their cousins, can advance to the 7th level of clerical ability.

ELVES, Drow

LOLTH *(demon queen of spiders)*

Lesser goddess

ARMOR CLASS: –10 (–2)
MOVE: 1'' *9'' (15'')
HIT POINTS: 66
NO. OF ATTACKS: 1 and 1 (1)
DAMAGE/ATTACK: 4-16 and webs
    (by weapon type)
SPECIAL ATTACKS: Poison
SPECIAL DEFENSES: See below
MAGIC RESISTANCE: 70%
SIZE: L (M)
ALIGNMENT: Chaotic evil
WORSHIPER'S ALIGN: Chaotic evil
    (Drow)
SYMBOL: Spider
PLANE: Abyss
CLERIC/DRUID: See below
FIGHTER: As 16+ HD monster
MAGIC-USER/ILLUSIONIST: See
    below
THIEF/ASSASSIN: Nil
MONK/BARD: Nil
PSIONIC ABILITY: See below
S: 21 (+4, +9) I: 21 W: 16 D: 21 C: 21 CH: 3 (23)

The dark elves worship demon lords from the Abyss. The best known example is the worship of the Demon Queen Lolth. Drow sacrifice both blood (of others) and riches to her. (For particulars, see ADVANCED D&D DUNGEON MODULES D3, **THE VAULT OF THE DROW**, and Q1, **QUEEN OF THE DEMONWEB PITS**.) Female Drow with wisdoms of 18 can progress as high as the 14th level of clerical ability.

The demoness Lolth is a very powerful and feared demon Lord. She usually takes the form of a giant black widow spider when she is on the Prime Material Plane, and sometimes assumes this form on her own plane as well, but she also enjoys appearing as an exquisitely beautiful female dark elf (the statistics for this form are given in parenthesis). Little is known about her aims, and only the fact that the Drow worship of Lolth causes her to assume form on the earth permits compilation of any substantial information whatsoever.

Lolth enjoys the company of spiders of all sorts — giant species while in her arachnid shape, those of normal, large and even huge species while in her humanoid form. She is able to converse with all kinds of spiders, and they understand and obey her unquestioningly.

Although the Queen of Spiders has but 66 hit points, her high armor class prevents most damage, and she is able to *heal* herself at will, up to thrice/day. As Lolth enjoys roving about in one form or another, she will seldom be encountered in her lair no matter what the plane, unless worshipers have invoked her to some special shrine or temple.

In the form of a giant spider, Lolth is able to cast web strands 30' long from her abdomenal spinnerets which are equal to a *web* spell with the addition of 1-4 points of damage per round accruing to webbed victims due to a poisonous excretion upon the strands; and during the same melee round she is able to deliver a vicious biting attack for 4-16 hit points of damage plus death if the victim fails to make his, her, or its saving throw vs. poison at –4. In her humanoid form, Lolth will use weapons common to Drow.

As a giant spider, the demoness can use any one of the following powers, one per melee round, at will: *comprehend languages, confusion* (creature looked at only), *darkness* (10' radius), *dispel magic*; once per day *gate* in a type I (45%), type II (35%), or type III (20%) demon (with 66% chance of success), *summon* 9-16 large (20%), 7-12 huge (30%), 2-8 giant (40%) or 1-4 phase (10%) spiders, *teleport* with no error, *tongues, true seeing*; twice per day use *phase door, read magic,* and *shape change*. In her humanoid shape, Lolth is a 16th level cleric/14th level magic-user with commensurate abilities. However, in spider form she is unable to wear armor of any sort, and her psionic powers are lost (see below).

Lolth is not affected by weapons which are not magical, silver does her no harm (unless magicked to at least +1), and cold, electrical and gas attack forms cause only one-half damage. Acid, *magic missiles* (if her magic resistance fails her, of course), and poison affect the demoness normally. Lolth is especially susceptible to holy water, taking 6 points of damage from a splash and 6-21 points (3d6+3) from a direct hit.

The visual range of the demoness extends into the infrared and ultraviolet spectrums to a normal distance of 120'. Lolth has limited *telepathic* communication ability as do demons in general.

Lolth's psionic disciplines are the minor devotions of *body equilibrium, clairvoyance, domination,* and the major sciences of *dimension walking, mind bar, molecular rearrangement,* and *probability travel*. These disciplines (as well as her magical powers) are performed at 16th level of ability (experience).

ELVES, Wood

RILLIFANE RALLATHIL "The Leaflord"

Lesser god

ARMOR CLASS: −2
MOVE: 12"
HIT POINTS: 317
NO. OF ATTACKS: 2
DAMAGE/ATTACK: *See below*
SPECIAL ATTACKS: *See below*
SPECIAL DEFENSES: *+2 or better*
weapon to hit
MAGIC RESISTANCE: 75%
SIZE: *See below*
ALIGNMENT: *Chaotic good*
WORSHIPER'S ALIGN: *Chaotic good*
(wood elves)
SYMBOL: *Oak*
PLANE: *Olympus*
CLERIC/DRUID: *14th level in each*
FIGHTER: *15th level ranger*
MAGIC-USER/ILLUSIONIST: *12th level*
in each
THIEF/ASSASSIN: *Nil*
MONK/BARD: *10th level in each*
PSIONIC ABILITY: *I*
S: 19 (+3, +7)   I: 23   W: 19   D: 25   C: 21   CH: 24

Rillifane is often likened by his clerics to a giant ethereal oak tree so huge that its roots mingle with the roots of every other plant in the world. On a more mundane level, Rillifane can appear on the Prime Material Plane as a green-skinned elf clad in bark armor and carrying a magic bow. Arrows shot from this bow by Rillifane always slay their target if they hit (no saving throw).

Rillifane is primarily concerned that all creatures have the opportunity to act out their roles in nature without abusing them. Rillifane's clerics are deadly enemies of those who hunt for sport and those who harm trees maliciously or unnecessarily.

While the majority of the wood elves worship Rillifane, many of those more neutral in alignment prefer to honor Skerrit the Forester (see **CENTAURS, Skerrit**). There is no friction between the two cults. Non-player character clerics of both can work up to the 7th level.

ETTINS

see, **GIANTS, Hill**

GIANTS, Fire

The deity of the fire giants is **Surtur** (q.v.). Fire giants can rise up to the 7th level as shamans. As a talisman, fire giant shamans often carry a severed head (usually human) that has been cured and dipped in molten steel.

GIANTS, Frost

Thrym (q.v.) is the patron of the frost giants, whose shamans, like those of other giants, can attain the 7th level. Frost giant shamans often placate Thrym by freezing their still-living sacrifices in new ice.

GIANTS, Hill

GROLANTOR

Lesser god

ARMOR CLASS: 0
MOVE: 21"
HIT POINTS: 259
NO. OF ATTACKS: 2
DAMAGE/ATTACK: 4-40 (+14)
SPECIAL ATTACKS: *Nil*
SPECIAL DEFENSES: *+2 or better*
weapon to hit
MAGIC RESISTANCE: 45%
SIZE: *L (25' tall)*
ALIGNMENT: *Chaotic evil*
WORSHIPER'S ALIGN: *Chaotic evil*
(hill giants)
SYMBOL: *Wooden club*
PLANE: *Tarterus*
CLERIC/DRUID: *10th level cleric*
FIGHTER: *As 16+ HD monster*
MAGIC-USER/ILLUSIONIST: *Nil*
THIEF/ASSASSIN: *Nil*
MONK/BARD: *Nil*
PSIONIC ABILITY: *VI*
S: 25 (+7, +14)   I: 14   W: 10   D: 19   C: 20   CH: 16

Grolantor appears to be a huge and powerful hill giant. He wields a huge club named Dwarfcrusher that hits for 4-40 points of damage, and he usually wears several belts of woven dwarfbeards.

Grolantor's creed is persecution of all inferior races (i.e. all those smaller than hill giants). Hill giant shamans will refuse to admit that other giants are actually larger than they, preferring to think of them as equals. Hill giant shamans range up to the 7th level of clerical ability.

Ettins also worship Grolantor, though in a slightly different (two-headed) aspect. However, this does not necessarily make them friendly toward hill giants. Despite (or perhaps because of) their two heads, ettins are less wise than giants, and cannot become greater than 3rd level shamans.

GIANTS, Stone

SKORAEUS STONEBONES "King of the Rock"

Lesser god

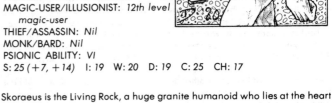

ARMOR CLASS: 0
MOVE: 15"
HIT POINTS: 380
NO. OF ATTACKS: 2
DAMAGE/ATTACK: 6-60
SPECIAL ATTACKS: *Earthquake*
SPECIAL DEFENSES: *Regeneration,*
+2 or better weapon to hit
MAGIC RESISTANCE: 50%
SIZE: *L (30' tall)*
ALIGNMENT: *Neutral*
WORSHIPER'S ALIGN: *Neutral (stone*
giants)
SYMBOL: *Stalactite*
PLANE: *Prime Material Plane*
CLERIC/DRUID: *15th level cleric*
FIGHTER: *As 16+ HD monster*
MAGIC-USER/ILLUSIONIST: *12th level*
magic-user
THIEF/ASSASSIN: *Nil*
MONK/BARD: *Nil*
PSIONIC ABILITY: *VI*
S: 25 (+7, +14)   I: 19   W: 20   D: 19   C: 25   CH: 17

Skoraeus is the Living Rock, a huge granite humanoid who lies at the heart of the world. He knows everything that happens in areas touching rock by listening to the vibrations that are carried to him.

Stonebones will never venture above ground, and he cannot even be *gated* there. While touching raw stone, he regenerates 5 hit points per round. He can strike with his fists for 6-60 points of damage each. Skoraeus can cast one *earthquake* spell per round, at the 30th level of ability. He can also instantly *summon* 2-20 stone giants to his aid.

Stone giant shamans cultivate an attitude of indifference and aloofness. It is their belief that the doings of lesser mortals should have little influence upon the affairs of stone giants. They regard both law and chaos with suspicion, and are inclined to repulse the overtures of either. Stone giant shamans can attain the 7th level of clerical ability.

GNOLLS

Gnolls worship the Demon Prince Yeenoghu (see **MONSTER MANUAL**, *DEMON, Yeenoghu*). Gnoll shamans compel worship of Yeenoghu through fear of the god's wrath should he be slighted. Yeenoghu's symbol is his triple flail, and all of his shamans wield similar (though non-magical) weapons. Gnoll shamans can advance up to the 5th level of clerical ability.

GNOMES

GARL GLITTERGOLD

Greater god

ARMOR CLASS: –2
MOVE: 12"
HIT POINTS: 350
NO. OF ATTACKS: 3/2
DAMAGE/ATTACK: 3-30 (+8)
SPECIAL ATTACKS: See below
SPECIAL DEFENSES: +3 or better
   weapon to hit
MAGIC RESISTANCE: 25%
SIZE: S (4' tall)
ALIGNMENT: Lawful good
WORSHIPER'S ALIGN: Lawful good
   (gnomes)
SYMBOL: Gold nugget
PLANE: Twin Paradises
CLERIC/DRUID: 15th level cleric
FIGHTER: 10th level fighter
MAGIC-USER/ILLUSIONIST: 16th level
   illusionist
THIEF/ASSASSIN: 20th level thief
MONK/BARD: 8th level bard
PSIONIC ABILITY: Nil
S: 20 (+3, +8) I: 23 W: 22 D: 24 C: 22 CH: 24

Garl appears as a handsome golden-skinned gnome with ever-changing gemstones for eyes. His mischievous exploits form the basis of an entire cycle of stories which are told and retold around the gnomish hearths in the hills.

However, there is another side to Garl than that of the witty adventurer who collapsed the Kobold King's cavern. When his people are threatened, Garl is a grim and determined war leader who out-thinks as well as out-fights his opponents. He wields *Arumdina*, an intelligent +5 mithral-steel battle axe that cuts stone as easily as it does enemies. *Arumdina* strikes for 3-30 points of damage and can *heal* Garl completely once per day.

The gnomes have five or six other deities besides Garl Glittergold, but he is their leader, and none are as popular as he. Garl's clerics require gold (or other precious metals, if no gold is available) for sacrifices to the deity. Gnome non-player character clerics can advance to the 7th level.

GOBLINS

MAGLUBIYET

Greater god

ARMOR CLASS: –2
MOVE: 12"
HIT POINTS: 350
NO. OF ATTACKS: 2
DAMAGE/ATTACK: 2-20
SPECIAL ATTACKS: Nil
SPECIAL DEFENSES: +3 or better
   weapon to hit
MAGIC RESISTANCE: 50%
SIZE: L (11' tall)
ALIGNMENT: Lawful evil
WORSHIPER'S ALIGN: Lawful evil
   (goblins and hobgoblins)
SYMBOL: Bloody axe
PLANE: Nine Hells
CLERIC/DRUID: 10th level cleric
FIGHTER: As 16+ HD monster
MAGIC-USER/ILLUSIONIST: 6th level
   illusionist
THIEF/ASSASSIN: 10th level assassin
MONK/BARD: Nil
PSIONIC ABILITY: VI
S: 20 (+3, +8) I: 19 W: 17 D: 20 C: 22 CH: –2

Both goblins and hobgoblins worship Maglubiyet, the Mighty One, Lord of the Depths and Darkness. Maglubiyet appears as a huge black goblin-type with red flames for eyes, sharp fangs and clawed hands. Maglubiyet is a war god and a great general. He commands mighty armies of goblin spirits in Hell, where they eternally war against Gruumsh's orcish spirit army. (Goblin and hobgoblin shamans claim that Maglubiyet always wins these battles, but there is no permanent death in Hell, so the destroyed orcish spirits always re-form.)

Goblins and hobgoblins both have other evil deities as well, but Maglubiyet rules them all with an iron hand. The Mighty One requires sacrifices of creatures with souls, and these ceremonies usually take place on nights of a new moon. It is possible for goblin and hobgoblin shamans to rise as high as 7th level clerics.

HALFLINGS

YONDALLA

Greater goddess

ARMOR CLASS: 2
MOVE: 12"
HIT POINTS: 350
NO. OF ATTACKS: 3/2
DAMAGE/ATTACK: By weapon type
SPECIAL ATTACKS: Withering
SPECIAL DEFENSES: +3 or better
   weapon to hit
MAGIC RESISTANCE: 75%
SIZE: M (4½' tall)
ALIGNMENT: Lawful good
WORSHIPER'S ALIGN: Lawful good
   (halflings)
SYMBOL: Shield
PLANE: Seven Heavens
CLERIC/DRUID: 12th level in each
FIGHTER: 10th level fighter
MAGIC-USER/ILLUSIONIST: 25th level
   illusionist
THIEF/ASSASSIN: 15th level thief
MONK/BARD: Nil
PSIONIC ABILITY: Nil
S: 19 (+3, +7) I: 25 W: 25 D: 25 C: 23 CH: 22

Yondalla has two aspects: the Provider and the Protector. As the Provider, she is a goddess of fertility and growing things, of birth and youth. She can make barren things fertile and increase the growing rate of plants and animals to any speed she chooses. What she can give, she can also take away: with a wave of her hand she can affect creatures as if three charges had been expended from a *staff of withering*, i.e. inflict 2-5 hit points damage, age them 10 years, and wither and shrivel a limb or member so that it becomes useless. She can do this once per round, and there is no saving throw vs. this ability.

As the Protector, Yondalla wards off evil influences and intrusions (thus her shield symbol), and gives halflings the strength and determination to defend themselves. In this aspect, Yondalla most often uses her illusionist powers to protect her worshipers.

Halflings set aside one day per week for worship of Yondalla (called "safeday"), a day which is most spent in rest and play. Non-player character halfling clerics may rise to the 5th level of ability.

HOBGOBLINS

See **GOBLINS**

IXITXACHITL

These creatures worship Demogorgon, a Demon Lord from the Abyss (see **MONSTER MANUAL**, DEMON, Demogorgon). They have been known to progress as high as the 8th level in clerical ability.

KOBOLDS

KURTULMAK

Lesser god

ARMOR CLASS: 0
MOVE: 12"
HIT POINTS: 219
NO. OF ATTACKS: 2
DAMAGE/ATTACK: 2-24/1-6
SPECIAL ATTACKS: Poison
SPECIAL DEFENSES: Fear aura, +2 or better weapon to hit
MAGIC RESISTANCE: 55%
SIZE: M (5½' tall)
ALIGNMENT: Lawful evil
WORSHIPER'S ALIGN: Lawful evil (kobolds)
SYMBOL: Skull (gnomish)
PLANE: Nine Hells
CLERIC/DRUID: 10th level cleric
FIGHTER: As 16+ HD monster
MAGIC-USER/ILLUSIONIST: Nil
THIEF/ASSASSIN: 12th level assassin
MONK/BARD: Nil
PSIONIC ABILITY: VI
S: 22 (+4, +10) I: 19 W: 9 D: 19 C: 19 CH: 19

Kurtulmak appears as a giant kobold (5½' tall) with scales of steel and a tail with a poisonous stinger. He hates all life but kobolds, and is said to have taught the first kobolds the important arts of mining, ambushing and looting.

Kurtulmak can smell gnomes up to a mile away, the scent of which drives him into a killing frenzy. He exudes a *fear* aura, and all enemies who come within 10' of him must save vs. spells or flee in panic (gnomes save at −4). He wields a +4 spear that strikes for 2-24 points of damage. He can also attack with his tail, which stings for 1-6 points plus poison (save or die).

Kobold shamans always wear orange robes with a white death's-head sigil on the chest. They can rise up to the 5th level of clerical ability.

KUO-TOA

BLIBDOOLPOOLP "Sea Mother"

Lesser goddess

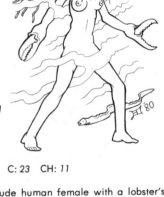

ARMOR CLASS: 1
MOVE: 12"/ /48"
HIT POINTS: 310
NO. OF ATTACKS: 2
DAMAGE/ATTACK: 4-24/4-24
SPECIAL ATTACKS: Insanity
SPECIAL DEFENSES: +2 or better weapon to hit
MAGIC RESISTANCE: 55%
SIZE: L (20' tall)
ALIGNMENT: Neutral evil (chaotic tendencies)
WORSHIPER'S ALIGN: Neutral evil (Kuo-Toa)
SYMBOL: Lobster head or black pearl
PLANE: Elemental Plane of Water
CLERIC/DRUID: 15th level cleric
FIGHTER: 15th level fighter
MAGIC-USER/ILLUSIONIST: 20th level magic-user
THIEF/ASSASSIN: 15th level assassin
MONK/BARD: Nil
PSIONIC ABILITY: III
S: 21 (+4, +9) I: 20 W: 10 D: 21 C: 23 CH: 11

Blibdoolpoolp appears as a large nude human female with a lobster's head and clawed forearms. In general, she hates all humans, demihumans and humanoids for driving the Kuo-Toa into the underworld. Worshipers regularly sacrifice lobsters to her. If a favor is desired, she must be given great quantities of gems, preferably pearls. There is a 1% chance per every 1,000 gp worth of gems sacrificed that the Sea Mother will look upon her worshiper's request with favor. (If pearls are contributed, this chance is 1% per 500 gp value.)

Each of Blibdoolpoolp's claws can snap for 4-24 points of damage. Any creature hit by both claws will be drawn to the Sea Mother's face to peer into her eyes. At close range, her gaze causes insanity in creatures who fail to save vs. spells at −4. In addition, the Sea Mother can summon up to 3-30 giant lobsters (treat as giant crayfish) and 1-10 16 HD water elementals to her aid per day.

On the most important ceremonial occasions, the clerics of Blibdoolpoolp sacrifice captured humans to her by drowning. Kuo-Toan clerics can attain 12th level maximum. For more information about the worship of the Sea Mother, see ADVANCED D&D DUNGEON MODULE D2, **SHRINE OF THE KUO-TOA**.

LIZARD MEN

SEMUANYA

Lesser god

ARMOR CLASS: −4
MOVE: 12″//24″
HIT POINTS: 211
NO. OF ATTACKS: 1
DAMAGE/ATTACK: 2-20 (+11)
SPECIAL ATTACKS: See below
SPECIAL DEFENSES: Regeneration,
  +2 or better weapon to hit
MAGIC RESISTANCE: 78%
SIZE: L (12′ tall)
ALIGNMENT: Neutral
WORSHIPER'S ALIGN: Neutral
SYMBOL: Egg
PLANE: Concordant Opposition
CLERIC/DRUID: 13th level in each
FIGHTER: As 16+ HD monster
MAGIC-USER/ILLUSIONIST: 15th level
  magic-user
THIEF/ASSASSIN: Nil
MONK/BARD: Nil
PSIONIC ABILITY: II
S: 23 (+5, +11) I: 20 W: 19 D: 20 C: 22 CH: 7 (25
  toward lizard men)

Semuanya is the unemotional and amoral reptilian ideal. Neither good nor evil, neither chaotic nor lawful, Semuanya merely exists and existance is its purpose. Live long, reproduce, ensure the safety of yourself and the race; this is the entire creed of Semuanya. Nothing else is of real importance, unless it bears directly on survival and propagation.

Semuanya appears as a normal lizard man, but it is strong and quick of mind and body. It never speaks unless talk is necessary. In battle, it wields a large club lined with razor-sharp shells that strikes for 2-20 points of damage. Semuanya can command all lizards, and can summon 3-18 minotaur lizards at will. It regenerates 5 points per round.

Lizard man shamans emulate Semuanya's taciturnity, and usually counsel avoidance of humans, humanoids and demi-humans. They are often the leaders of lizard man tribes. Lizard man shamans can attain the 7th level.

LOCATHAH and MERMEN

EADRO

Lesser god

ARMOR CLASS: 0 or −6 (amorphous
  form)
MOVE: 12″//24″
HIT POINTS: 227
NO. OF ATTACKS: 1 or 8
DAMAGE/ATTACK: By weapon type
  or 1-10
SPECIAL ATTACKS: Nil
SPECIAL DEFENSES: +2 or better
  weapon to hit
MAGIC RESISTANCE: 72%
SIZE: M (7′ tall)
ALIGNMENT: Neutral
WORSHIPER'S ALIGN: Neutral
  (locathah & mermen)
SYMBOL: Spiral design
PLANE: Concordant Opposition
CLERIC/DRUID: 20th level cleric
FIGHTER: 15th level fighter
MAGIC-USER/ILLUSIONIST: Nil
THIEF/ASSASSIN: Nil
MONK/BARD: Nil
PSIONIC ABILITY: II
S: 21 (+4, +9) I: 22 W: 18 D: 22 C: 21 CH: 19

Both locathah and mermen worship Eadro, who appears as a being of

living water, able to take any shape it pleases. Usually Eadro takes the shape of a locathah or merman, though in battle the god often becomes an amorphous blob that can lash out with 8 water-whips, each inflicting 1-10 points of damage. Eadro can summon 2-8 16 HD water elementals at will.

The god's worshipers believe that Eadro bathes their gills in the Water of Life before dropping them into the Current of Existence. Between lives on the Prime Material Plane, Eadro watches over their spirits in the ocean on the plane of Concordant Opposition, where they take the form of tiny fish. The god's symbol is a spiral, which indicates growth through unity.

Locathah have shamans of up to the 3rd level, while mermen clerics can reach the 5th level. Though they worship the same deity, locathah and mermen are not always allies, as they often must compete for the same sea-space.

OGRES

VAPRAK *"The Destroyer"*

Demigod

ARMOR CLASS: 0
MOVE: 15″
HIT POINTS: 198
NO. OF ATTACKS: 3
DAMAGE/ATTACK: 2-20/2-20/1-12
SPECIAL ATTACKS: Nil
SPECIAL DEFENSES: Regeneration,
  +1 or better weapon to hit
MAGIC RESISTANCE: 50%
SIZE: L (15′ tall)
ALIGNMENT: Chaotic evil
WORSHIPER'S ALIGN: Chaotic evil
  (ogres and trolls)
SYMBOL: Taloned hand
PLANE: Abyss
CLERIC/DRUID: 10th level cleric
FIGHTER: As 16+ HD monster
MAGIC-USER/ILLUSIONIST: Nil
THIEF/ASSASSIN: Nil
MONK/BARD: Nil
PSIONIC ABILITY: VI
S: 25 (+7, +14) I: 18 W: 12 D: 17 C: 19 CH: −1

Ogres and trolls worship Vaprak the Destroyer. This deity appears as an exceedingly horrid mottled brown and green humanoid. Vaprak has great strength, and he prefers to tear his prey apart with his claws rather than use weapons. It is said that this vicious being is always hungry, and in times of great troubles he walks the Prime Material Plane, robbing, killing and eating whatever he finds in his path. Vaprak regenerates 7 hit points per melee round.

Ogres and trolls revere Vaprak for his uncompromising ferocity and ability to destroy whatever lies in his path or causes him trouble. Vaprak sometimes (2% chance) rewards his worshipers by granting them berserk rage in battle, if they pray for it (+2 to hit and damage, but −2 from armor class). Ogres and trolls can be shamans of up to the 3rd level.

ORCS

GRUUMSH

Greater god

ARMOR CLASS: −1
MOVE: 12''
HIT POINTS: 350
NO. OF ATTACKS: 1
DAMAGE/ATTACK: 3-30 (+10)
SPECIAL ATTACKS: Paralysis
SPECIAL DEFENSES: +3 or better
    weapon to hit
MAGIC RESISTANCE: 75%
SIZE: L (10' tall)
ALIGNMENT: Lawful evil
WORSHIPER'S ALIGN: Lawful evil
    (orcs)
SYMBOL: Unwinking eye
PLANE: Nine Hells
CLERIC/DRUID: 15th level cleric
    using only destructive spells
FIGHTER: As 16+ HD monster
MAGIC-USER/ILLUSIONIST: 6th level
    magic-user
THIEF/ASSASSIN: 8th level assassin
MONK/BARD: Nil
PSIONIC ABILITY: V
S: 22 (+4, +10) I: 19 W: 18 D: 23 C: 24 CH: 8 (25 to orcs)

The orcs have many gods, but their leader is Gruumsh. His name is never spoken by non-shaman orcs, who refer to him as He-Who-Watches or He-Who-Never-Sleeps. Gruumsh's symbol is a great unwinking eye, which represents the belief that Gruumsh watches each and every orc and judges him fit or unfit. Gruumsh himself has but one large eye in the center of his forehead. He appears as a huge orcish humanoid wearing gleaming black plate mail, holding a flaming torch in one hand and a great iron spear in the other. This spear is a +5 weapon that strikes for 3-30 points of damage plus *paralysis* (save at −4).

The orcs say that Gruumsh commands a mighty army of spirit-orcs in Hell, and these war continuously with a similar army of spirit-goblins controlled by Maglubiyet. The orcs always defeat the goblins, but the goblin spirits always re-form to start the battle again.

To become a shaman of Gruumsh, an orc must pluck out his own left eye. The proper worship of Gruumsh requires blood in large quantities, preferably blood from a human or demi-human race (elves are best of all). Orcish shamans range up to the 5th level of ability.

SAHUAGIN

SEKOLAH

Lesser god

ARMOR CLASS: 0
MOVE: 36''
HIT POINTS: 329
NO. OF ATTACKS: 2
DAMAGE/ATTACK: 6-60
SPECIAL ATTACKS: Swallow whole
SPECIAL DEFENSES: +2 or better
    weapon to hit
MAGIC RESISTANCE: 47%
SIZE: L (35' long)
ALIGNMENT: Lawful evil
WORSHIPER'S ALIGN: Lawful evil
    (sahuagin)
SYMBOL: Shark
PLANE: Nine Hells
CLERIC/DRUID: 15th level cleric
FIGHTER: As 16+ HD monster
MAGIC-USER/ILLUSIONIST: Nil
THIEF/ASSASSIN: Nil
MONK/BARD: Nil
PSIONIC ABILITY: I
S: 25 I: 18 W: 18 D: 19 C: 25 CH: 16

Sekolah always appears in the form of a giant white shark. Sahuagin lore says that Sekolah swims in the deepest parts of the seas of the Nine Hells, where he hunts only the largest and fiercest of prey. He can bite for 6-60 points of damage, swallowing man-sized creatures whole on a "to hit" roll of 16 or better.

When the tides are right, the sahuagin sacrifice their weak, crippled and aged to Sekolah by feeding them to the 1-3 holy sharks which always accompany sahuagin clerics. Sahuagin clerics can advance up to the 5th level of ability.

SATYRS

See **CENTAURS.**

TROGLODYTES

LAOGZED

Demigod

ARMOR CLASS: 0
MOVE: 15''
HIT POINTS: 187
NO. OF ATTACKS: 1
DAMAGE/ATTACK: 6-60
SPECIAL ATTACKS: Stinking cloud
SPECIAL DEFENSES: Poison
MAGIC RESISTANCE: 29%
SIZE: L (10' tall)
ALIGNMENT: Chaotic evil
WORSHIPER'S ALIGN: Chaotic evil
    (troglodytes)
SYMBOL: Image of the god
PLANE: Abyss
CLERIC/DRUID: 15th level cleric
    using only harmful spells
FIGHTER: As 16+ HD monster
MAGIC-USER/ILLUSIONIST: Nil
THIEF/ASSASSIN: Nil
MONK/BARD: Nil
PSIONIC ABILITY: Nil
S: 21 (+4, +9) I: 18 W: 17 D: 19 C: 19 CH: −2

Troglodytes worship the disgusting Laogzed, a vile being whose appearance suggests both toad and lizard. Laogzed's oozing skin is covered with loose patches of dead flesh. The liquid on his skin is an acidic poison; any creature touching it takes 3-18 points of damage and must save vs. poison at −4. Weapons or other objects touching it must save vs. acid or be destroyed. Laogzed can exhale a *stinking cloud* at will. His huge mouth is lined with many rows of needle-sharp teeth; he bites for 6-60 points of damage.

The most important rites in the worship of Laogzed are always held far below ground at Midwinter. At this time, troglodytes gather together for the ritual of the Shedding of Skins, where the trogs (who grow throughout their lives) remove their old, dull skins, and then sacrifice these husks to Laogzed. Troglodyte shamans can work up to the 3rd level of clerical ability.

NORSE MYTHOS

The Norse people created a race of gods that were as grim and savage as the people themselves. Their legends were of mighty battles against foes that were sometimes more powerful than themselves. We have grouped most of the gods, their enemies, and their helpers here for your use.

The vast majority of gods that we list are the Aesir, who come from Odin, Vili, and Ve's line. These beings all dwell above the Prime Material Plane and visit it often for their own needs. A second group of gods called the Vanir are beings of the air. They are to be allies of the Aesir in the final battle of Ragnarok, but are quite separate from the Aesir in that they don't deal with the lives of men, and they derive their spiritual powers from elsewhere.

Ragnarok is to be the last epic battle where the forces of good (represented by Odin and his kind) are to fight the forces of evil (represented by Loki and the giants of Jotunheim). In this battle, evil will triumph: they will destroy all the mightiest of the gods, and they themselves will be destroyed to the last evil creature, leaving only a few of the gentlest of good beings to foster an even mightier race of Norse gods.

Because of their very warlike nature, the majority of these gods and goddesses cannot cure beings with clerical cure spells. Only those noted in the text can do so. The clerical leader of a group will always sacrifice an enemy (if available) or a steer (if not) before any given voyage of conquest or special battle of importance. In any human sacrifice, the victim is simultaneously hanged and thrust through the heart with a spear, and the remains are burned on a pyre of oak.

Norse temples are always rectangular halls with the main supports being carved oaken images of humans. These areas (where the images of the gods are stored) are not worship halls, but places where the gods' forms were carved and protected from the elements. For worship, these images are taken out every lunar month, and given sacrifices in the form of gold and silver articles (which had to be both useful and pleasing to the eye).

Almost the only way to offend the gods is to have dealings with giantkind in any way or show some act of cowardice in battle. Many acts that would be called blasphemous in other religions (such as swearing and breaking an oath to a god, taking a god's name in vain, or defacing an image of god) can all be forgiven by success in the next battle.

LOCATION

Most of the Aesir live in an area of the plane of Gladsheim known as Asgard, which is connected to the Prime Material Plane by Bifrost, the Rainbow Bridge. (Bifrost is kept well hidden, and few mortals have ever pierced the veil of illusion which hides it.) Asgard includes Odin's court of Valhalla, the various holds of the gods, and large expanses of wilderness and sea. It is adjacent to the blighted land of Jotunheim, the giants' home, an anomalous blot of evil upon the plane of Gladsheim.

DWARVES

The Dwarves were thought of as Troll-like beings in Norse mythology, and are called such in legends. Dwarves will be found living underground in their traditional caves trying to stay far away from all other forms of intelligent life. They aid the gods for the power that such aid can bring them in the form of returned favors. There are two principal races of dwarves: Modsogner and Durin. The Modsogner are able to produce magic items of a non-violent nature and rival all beings in this art. The Durin can create magical weapons of tremendous power and often do so for giants and gods alike.

EINHERIAR

These are all the honored heroes that have been brought from the Prime Material Plane to Asgard upon their death. They are always of the 4th level and above, and there are hundreds of 8th and higher level fighters!

They fight constantly on a practice field that raises them from the dead at the end of the day. There is no telling the exact number of this group, but the Valkyries have been picking the best warriors for thousands of years. They will be the army led by the Norse gods to Ragnarok.

GIANTS AND JOTUNHEIM

While the **Monster Manual** deals with giants in a very comprehensive manner, just as there are many unusual people, there are many very unusual giants. Norse giants are magically gifted races, and the most powerful have clerical or illusionist powers, as well as magical weapons.

All of these giants are found in Jotunheim, which is directly attached to the planes of Gladsheim. The giants of this land are crafty and ruthless when it comes to war, but weak-willed and naive when it comes to everyday dealings with giants of other types, gods, and men. They are known to sometimes invite the gods to fun and games and will sometimes trade with them.

Many of the giants on the Prime Material Plane are descended from or have contact with those of Jotunheim. This is particularly true in the case of the frost and fire giants, who regard Thrym and Surtur as their leaders and deities.

ODIN "ALL FATHER" (supreme ruler of the gods)

Greater god

ARMOR CLASS: −6
MOVE: 15''
HIT POINTS: 400
NO. OF ATTACKS: 2
DAMAGE/ATTACK: By weapon type
SPECIAL ATTACKS: See below
SPECIAL DEFENSES: +3 or better
  weapon to hit; also see below
MAGIC RESISTANCE: 85%
SIZE: M (6½')
ALIGNMENT: Neutral good
WORSHIPER'S ALIGN: Good and
  neutral beings
SYMBOL: Watching blue eye
PLANE: Gladsheim (Valhalla)
CLERIC/DRUID: 30th level cleric
  (Special)/14th level druid
FIGHTER: 18th level ranger
MAGIC-USER/ILLUSIONIST: 30th level
  magic-user
THIEF/ASSASSIN: Nil
MONK/BARD: 15th level bard
PSIONIC ABILITY: I
S: 25 (+7, +14) I: 25 W: 25 D: 25 C: 25 CH: 25

While Odin is supreme among the gods, he has limitations that are dictated by those that worship him. He cannot raise the dead, and healing anyone forces him to sleep for 1-10 days. On the other hand, he has great power in the form of personal attributes. His telepathy has a range of 300 miles, he *shape changes* at will, and he inspires berserker rages in all beings he chooses within 30 yards of his person. Allies within 20 yards of him gain 4 levels of fighting ability for a number of turns equal to the original number of levels each of the individual beings had. If Odin becomes angry, he can paralyze any non-divine creature he transfixes with his gaze (one being per round, save vs. paralysis at −4 applicable).

Odin's spear is called *Gungnir*; it is a +5 weapon, and in battle it points at the strongest member of any enemy force (for Odin's personal attention). Furthermore, all adversaries within 20 yards when Odin holds it aloft are stricken with fear (as the *fear symbol*). Those who Odin allows to touch Gungnir (usually in battle) will be blessed with a double effect *prayer* for the duration of the battle (but this takes one hit point away from the god per touch). All enemies that dare touch Gungnir fare much worse: touchers of a different alignment from Odin will be polymorphed into normal ants (no save); beings of the same alignment will suffer loss of 50% of their original hit points. (NOTE: This works only when Odin is not fighting with this weapon.)

Odin's Bow is a +3 composite recurved bow and it can fire a total of 10 +3 arrows per melee round!

Odin's Rune Wand is golden and etched with Norse Runes of Power on its surface. It is an artifact and as such cannot be detected by magical detection spells of any type. Every time this wand is used, the particular Rune that represents the power called upon will shine. The wand's powers are:

1.) as a *rod of rulership*
2.) summons 1-4 elementals of the All Father's choice once per week
3.) stores 12 spells of Odin's choice
4.) drains 6 energy levels and 100 hit points everytime it is grabbed by any other being in the universe
5.) causes instantaneous death to any mortal touching it

Odin wears a +5 corselet of mail and a +5 helm in battle.

His ring *Draupnir* is an item of great power. It produces a non-magical twin to itself worth 30,000 gold pieces every night, if Odin desires. Odin often gives these away to his faithful servants, the Einheriar, or those that please him greatly.

Odin has a pair of ravens, a pair of wolves, and a magical horse that will be dealt with later in this section.

His halls and lodgings are numerous. Among them are Valhalla (Odin's council hall and the hall of many of the other gods), Gladshelf, and his palace Valaskialf, where Hlidskialf, his magical "all-seeing throne" is located (treat as unlimited duration *crystal ball with clairaudience*).

He occasionally walks among men in the guise of an old man riding a mangy horse. This is to find out how his cult is doing on earth.

His curing power is rarely used, and never on non-gods. It forces him to go into a temporary coma from which nothing can wake him. During these times, great mischief is often done by Loki and others, making Odin very reluctant to perform such healings.

Freke and Gere *(Odin's wolves)*

FREQUENCY: *Unique*
NO. APPEARING: *2*
ARMOR CLASS: *4*
MOVE: *24"*
HIT DICE/POINTS: *75 hp each*
% IN LAIR: *Nil*
TREASURE TYPE: *Nil*
NO. OF ATTACKS: *1*
DAMAGE/ATTACK: *2-20*
SPECIAL ATTACKS: *See below*
SPECIAL DEFENSES: *Nil*
MAGIC RESISTANCE: *50%*
INTELLIGENCE: *Very*
ALIGNMENT: *Neutral*
SIZE: *L (10' at the shoulder)*
PSIONIC ABILITY: *Nil*
    Attack/Defense Modes: *Nil*
LEVEL/X.P. VALUE: *IX/8875*

These creatures are giant black wolves with greying muzzles. They are able to travel about the planes for Odin and tell him what is happening in the various worlds. They are able to teleport at will through the planes, and they can see any hidden object and sense all things magical. Their bite does 2-20 points of damage and they use it in the service of Odin as punishers whenever a human aids the giants against the gods. They attack as 16 hit dice monsters.

Hugin and Munin *(Odin's ravens)* "Thought & Memory"

FREQUENCY: *Unique*
NO. APPEARING: *2*
ARMOR CLASS: *2*
MOVE: *1"/48"*
HIT DICE/POINTS: *30 hp each*
% IN LAIR: *Nil*
TREASURE TYPE: *Nil*
NO. OF ATTACKS: *1*
DAMAGE/ATTACK: *1-8*
SPECIAL ATTACKS: *Nil*
SPECIAL DEFENSES: *Immune to magi-*
    cal control
MAGIC RESISTANCE: *75%*
INTELLIGENCE: *Very*
ALIGNMENT: *Neutral*
SIZE: *S (3')*
PSIONIC ABILITY: *Nil*
    Attack/Defense Modes: *Nil*
LEVEL/X.P. VALUE: *VI/815*

These ravens are used for aerial reconnaissance and are able to carry verbal messages from Odin to those he wishes to communicate with. They are immune to magical control of any type and have the ability to teleport from plane to plane. They attack as 7 hit dice monsters, doing 1-8 points of damage with shrewd strikes from their beaks.

They are Odin's spies, and he is able to see and hear through them. When the other gods are away from home, these creatures may be used to warn them of impending attacks, which Odin may become aware of by using his "all-seeing throne".

Sleipner *(Odin's eight-legged steed)*

FREQUENCY: *Unique*
NO. APPEARING: *1*
ARMOR CLASS: *−1*
MOVE: *24"*
HIT DICE/POINTS: *200 hp*
% IN LAIR: *Nil*
TREASURE TYPE: *Nil*
NO. OF ATTACKS: *3*
DAMAGE/ATTACK: *2-20/2-20/1-10*
SPECIAL ATTACKS: *Nil*
SPECIAL DEFENSES: *Nil*
MAGIC RESISTANCE: *25%*
INTELLIGENCE: *Very*
ALIGNMENT: *Lawful neutral*
SIZE: *L (12' at the shoulder)*
PSIONIC ABILITY: *Nil*
    Attack/Defense Modes: *Nil*
LEVEL/X.P. VALUE: *X/20,600*

This animal usually won't let anyone but Odin ride it, though it will at times take beings in extreme need on one-ride trips to safety at Odin's order. Odin was known to honor some exceptionally fine heroes in death by letting a Valkyrie pick that hero up on Sleipner.

In battle, the creature moves so fast and with such agility that only one being can attack its rider per round. It also teleports at will through all the planes and can be ridden in any medium (air, earth, water, and the like).

Sleipner is gray in color, with its shank section showing white on each of its eight legs. The creature can pull amost any weight, but will only obey one master at a time. It fights as a 16+ hit dice monster, biting for 1-10 points and kicking with its fore-hooves for 2-20 points each.

AEGIR (god of storms and the sea)

Lesser god

ARMOR CLASS: −5
MOVE: 42″
HIT POINTS: 387
NO. OF ATTACKS: 2
DAMAGE/ATTACK: 4-40 (+11)
SPECIAL ATTACKS: Nil
SPECIAL DEFENSES: See below
MAGIC RESISTANCE: 50%
SIZE: M (7′)
ALIGNMENT: Chaotic neutral
WORSHIPER'S ALIGN: Chaotic
  neutral
SYMBOL: Rough ocean waves
PLANE: Gladsheim
CLERIC/DRUID: 15th level cleric
FIGHTER: 15th level ranger
MAGIC-USER/ILLUSIONIST: 10th level
  in each
THIEF/ASSASSIN: Nil
MONK/BARD: 5th level bard
PSIONIC ABILITY: V
S: 23 (+5, +11) I: 23 W: 18 D: 23 C: 24 CH: 9

Aegir is neither Aesir nor Vanir, and is actually related to the Giants.

This god usually appears as a human with a long gray beard, and delights in overturning ships and dragging them down to his realm under the water if they have not sacrificed to him. He uses a club in the shape of a maiden which does 4-40 points per strike. All those that meet him in battle under the water are *slowed* (no saving throw). When in the sea, the god is 60 feet tall, and in this form will fight any of the Aesir and the Vanir who dare to enter his realm without his permission. He has a great castle underwater where he lives with Ran, his wife.

Aegir will calm storms as often as create them, especially if it will aid those who are his friends. He is friendly and sociable with the Aesir, but they keep a close watch on Aegir because of his unpredictable nature.

BALDER (god of beauty, "charisma")

Greater god

ARMOR CLASS: −4
MOVE: 18″
HIT POINTS: 388
NO. OF ATTACKS: 3/2
DAMAGE/ATTACK: 3-30 (+10)
SPECIAL ATTACKS: See below
SPECIAL DEFENSES: See below
MAGIC RESISTANCE: 75%
SIZE: M (6′)
ALIGNMENT: Neutral good
WORSHIPER'S ALIGN: Neutral good
SYMBOL: Gem-encrusted silver
  chalice
PLANE: Gladsheim
CLERIC/DRUID: 12th level in each
FIGHTER: 10th level ranger
MAGIC-USER/ILLUSIONIST: Nil
THIEF/ASSASSIN: Nil
MONK/BARD: 20th level bard
PSIONIC ABILITY: VI
S: 22 (+4, +10) I: 24 W: 24 D: 24 C: 25 CH: 25

This god is able to grant 2 points of charisma to any being he wishes (once in their life). Those mortal females that look upon this god must save or become immediately "enchanted" with his beauty. Those enchanted must roll another magical saving throw; if they fail, they will follow his faith with slavish devotion for the rest of their lives. The god may ask those females with 15 or greater charismas to serve him personally in his holdings on a 1% chance. He cannot be harmed by any weapon without mistletoe in it. He lives in Gladsheim in his hall of Breidablik.

He fights with a +3 two-handed sword which does 3-30 points of damage. No female of any species can attack him, even if controlled by someone else.

BRAGI (god of poetry, eloquence, and song)

Lesser god

ARMOR CLASS: −4
MOVE: 18″
HIT POINTS: 370
NO. OF ATTACKS: 3/2
DAMAGE/ATTACK: 2-20 (+11)
SPECIAL ATTACKS: See below
SPECIAL DEFENSES: See below
MAGIC RESISTANCE: 75% (when
  singing, totally immune)
SIZE: M (6′)
ALIGNMENT: Neutral good
WORSHIPER'S ALIGN: Neutral good
  and all bard types
SYMBOL: Harp
PLANE: Elysium
CLERIC/DRUID: 10th level in each
FIGHTER: 7th level ranger
MAGIC-USER/ILLUSIONIST: 15th level
  illusionist
THIEF/ASSASSIN: Nil
MONK/BARD: 23rd level bard
PSIONIC ABILITY: V
S: 23 (+5, +11) I: 24 W: 24 D: 25 C: 25 CH: 24

All beings with violence on their minds that come within 30 yards of Bragi while he is singing will be overcome by the god's song or verse (no save). Beings so affected will lose all of their former intentions and join this god for song and revelry until he is satisfied that they have learned their lesson, whereupon he will set them free. Bragi cannot have violence on his mind at this time either and this power will not stop the enemies of the gods from fighting after the song is over. This power will work for up to 5 hours at a time with any given creature.

Any human hearing his *Harp of Calm* will cease fighting or quarreling for 7 days (unless attacked in that time). This harp has all the powers of all magical bard instruments plus the ability to stop any creature from attacking for a short period of time, plus the ability to uncharm anything.

There is a 5% chance that every bard of this religion, at the time of their first performance in front of a crowd of more than 50 beings, will be granted a "great legend" by the god, in the form of knowledge of the nearest lost treasure in the area.

The god strikes with a +2 sword for 2-20 points of damage.

FENRIS WOLF

FREQUENCY: Unique
NO. APPEARING: 1
ARMOR CLASS: −4
MOVE: 24″/12″
HIT DICE/POINTS: 400 hp
% IN LAIR: Nil
TREASURE TYPE: Nil
NO. OF ATTACKS: 1
DAMAGE/ATTACK: 9-90
SPECIAL ATTACKS: Nil
SPECIAL DEFENSES: +4 or better
  weapon to hit
MAGIC RESISTANCE: 99%
INTELLIGENCE: Average
ALIGNMENT: Chaotic evil
SIZE: L (50′ at the shoulder)
PSIONIC ABILITY: Nil
  Attack/Defense Modes: Nil
LEVEL/X.P. VALUE: X/33,200

This wolfish monster lived in Asgard due to a technicality that allowed the offspring of the gods (in this case Loki's) to remain unharmed by other gods. But this dangerous creature could not remain free. The dwarves made the only chain that could bind it, forging it from thoughts and concepts. This silken, golden thread stopped the creature from roaming, as it was unbreakable until the time of Ragnarok.

The wolf's bite does 9-90 points of damage, and if the total amount of damage is more than half of the victim's hit points, he or she will be swallowed whole. In form, the creature looks like a giant timber wolf.

FJALAR (dwarven hero of the Durin race)

ARMOR CLASS: –3
MOVE: 12''
HIT POINTS: 99
NO. OF ATTACKS: 2
DAMAGE/ATTACK: 2-20/2-20
SPECIAL ATTACKS: Nil
SPECIAL DEFENSES: See below
MAGIC RESISTANCE: Standard
SIZE: S (4')
ALIGNMENT: Neutral
CLERIC/DRUID: 5th level cleric
FIGHTER: 10th level fighter
MAGIC-USER/ILLUSIONIST: Nil
THIEF/ASSASSIN: 10th level thief
MONK/BARD: Nil
PSIONIC ABILITY: Nil
　　Attack/Defense Modes: Nil
S: 19 (+3, +7) I: 15 W: 15 D: 18 C: 18 CH: 12

Fjalar often defends the dwarves against the fire giants or their allies. He uses two magical iron gauntlets in combat that let him punch for 2-20 points each with a +3 on "to hit" ability. His knowledge of magical weaponry is so great that he cannot be hit by weapons of +2 or better quality, because he is able to influence the magical properties of the weapon to make it shun his skin.

Fjalar is the battle leader of his people, and he is often called on by his race to bring vegeance down on their enemies.

FORSETI (god of justice) "Peacemaker"

Greater god

ARMOR CLASS: –4
MOVE: 18''
HIT POINTS: 389
NO. OF ATTACKS: 3/2
DAMAGE/ATTACK: 1-10 (+12)
SPECIAL ATTACKS: See below
SPECIAL DEFENSES: See below
MAGIC RESISTANCE: 85%
SIZE: M (6')
ALIGNMENT: Lawful good
WORSHIPER'S ALIGN: Lawful good
SYMBOL: The head of a bearded
　　man
PLANE: Gladsheim
CLERIC/DRUID: 10th level druid
FIGHTER: 15th level ranger
MAGIC-USER/ILLUSIONIST: 10th level
　　in each
THIEF/ASSASSIN: Nil
MONK/BARD: Nil
PSIONIC ABILITY: II
S: 24 (+6, +12) I: 25 W: 24 D: 22 C: 25 CH: 23

This god's hall is Glitner, which is said to be made out of gold and silver. He is the son of Balder and has never been known to lie. His sword does 1-10 points of damage and always hits a being that has lied in the last 7 days or is chaotic.

All evil beings suffer a –1 on their chance to hit this god, and he attacks all evil beings at a +2 bonus, both "to hit" and damage. A +3 or better weapon is needed to hit him.

Forseti is called on time and time again to decide matters in which Odin cannot be impartial. With his ability to detect lies, he is often needed to ascertain the truth of certain stories the gods hear.

FOSSERGRIM (enchanted being)

FREQUENCY: Very rare
NO. APPEARING: 1
ARMOR CLASS: 0
MOVE: 9''//36''
HIT DICE/POINTS: 5 HD
% IN LAIR: 80%
TREASURE TYPE: D
NO. OF ATTACKS: 2
DAMAGE/ATTACK: By weapon type
SPECIAL ATTACKS: See below
SPECIAL DEFENSES: Regeneration,
　　also see below
MAGIC RESISTANCE: 100% in splash-
　　ing water, otherwise standard
INTELLIGENCE: Very
ALIGNMENT: Neutral
SIZE: M (6')
PSIONIC ABILITY: Nil
　　Attack/Defense Modes: Nil
LEVEL/X.P. VALUE: V/320 + 5 per
　　hp

These beings live in waterfalls. They appear to be normal men in chain-mail and will act as such until attacked, or someone tries to force them away from their waterfalls. They cannot live more than a mile from the falls they have made their home. They are said to mate with maidens who come to bathe in such places, and their offspring are always male and will always find a waterfall to live in upon reaching maturity.

In battle, they cannot miss any being that stands in the water. In splashing water they regenerate 5 points per melee round.

FREY (god of sunshine & the elves)

Greater god

ARMOR CLASS: –5
MOVE: 18''
HIT POINTS: 388
NO. OF ATTACKS: 3/2
DAMAGE/ATTACK: 2-20 (+12) or
　　special
SPECIAL ATTACKS: See below
SPECIAL DEFENSES: +3 or better
　　weapon to hit
MAGIC RESISTANCE: 75%
SIZE: M (6')
ALIGNMENT: Neutral good
WORSHIPER'S ALIGN: Neutral good
SYMBOL: Ice-blue two-handed
　　sword
PLANE: Gladsheim
CLERIC/DRUID: 13th level in each
FIGHTER: 15th level ranger
MAGIC-USER/ILLUSIONIST: 20th level
　　magic-user
THIEF/ASSASSIN: Nil
MONK/BARD: 15th level bard
PSIONIC ABILITY: II
S: 24 (+6, +12) I: 24 W: 23 D: 24 C: 25 CH: 23

·D· '80

Frey is not an Aesir, but a Vanir, the son of Njord and Skadi. He is the god of Fairyland and has at his command all the elves of that land. He is also a weather deity and controls all manner of storms and calms.

Frey's ship *Skidbladnir*, a gift from the dwarves, can hold all the gods and their mounts, and travels at a rate of 60''. When not in use, it folds to fit the god's pocket as a 1 inch cube. It sails according to the verbal direction of Frey.

Frey owns a magical boar and horse (details follow, below).

The god lives and rules in Alfheim (fairyland) and when not there, is served by a special mortal called Skirnir.

Frey's +4 two-handed sword does 2-20 points of damage per hit on all creatures but giants; it does 10-100 points to fire giants, and 5-50 to all others.

Blodug-Hofi (Frey's horse)

FREQUENCY: *Unique*
NO. APPEARING: *1*
ARMOR CLASS: *3*
MOVE: *24"/18"*
HIT DICE/POINTS: *50 hp*
% IN LAIR: *Nil*
TREASURE TYPE: *Nil*
NO. OF ATTACKS: *3*
DAMAGE/ATTACK: *1-10/1-10/1-6*
SPECIAL ATTACKS: *See below*
SPECIAL DEFENSES: *Resistant to fire*
MAGIC RESISTANCE: *75%*
INTELLIGENCE: *Very*
ALIGNMENT: *Neutral*
SIZE: *L (9' at the shoulder)*
PSIONIC ABILITY: *Nil*
    Attack/Defense Modes: *Nil*
LEVEL/X.P. VALUE: *VIII/4,500*

This horse teleports at will, and glows with the light of day in any battle. This light kills all undead types with the touch of a light beam for those within 200 yards.

Blodug-Hofi has a burnished coat of light brown and a pale white mane and tail. It fights along with Frey in battle, and if its master is down it stays near to defend him, which it will do unto death. It fights as an 11 hit dice monster, biting for 1-6 points and kicking with each of its fore-hooves for 1-10 points each. Its coat is fire resistant, giving it +4 on saves vs. fire attacks, and subtracting 1 point per die of damage taken.

Gullin-Bursti (golden bristles — Frey's golden boar)

FREQUENCY: *Unique*
NO. APPEARING: *1*
ARMOR CLASS: *-4*
MOVE: *18"/32"*
HIT DICE/POINTS: *100 hp*
% IN LAIR: *80%*
TREASURE TYPE: *Nil*
NO. OF ATTACKS: *2*
DAMAGE/ATTACK: *2-20/2-20*
SPECIAL ATTACKS: *Nil*
SPECIAL DEFENSES: *+2 or better
    weapon to hit; regeneration*
MAGIC RESISTANCE: *75%*
INTELLIGENCE: *Low*
ALIGNMENT: *Neutral*
SIZE: *L (10' at the shoulder)*
PSIONIC ABILITY: *Nil*
    Attack/Defense Modes: *Nil*
LEVEL/X.P. VALUE: *X/22,300*

This creature appears to be a giant rust-colored boar with head bristles of pure gold. Frey uses Gullin-Bursti to pull his war chariot into battle. The boar was a gift of the dwarven race, and with a god on it it can teleport where the god wills. It was much like Thor's goats in that it could be eaten during the day, and if its bones were not broken, it would regenerate at night from the bones and skin. It normally regenerates 1 hit point per round. The creature attacks as a 16+ hit dice monster.

Skirnir (Frey's shield-man)

ARMOR CLASS: *-3*
MOVE: *12"*
HIT POINTS: *99*
NO. OF ATTACKS: *3/2*
DAMAGE/ATTACK: *By weapon type*
SPECIAL ATTACKS: *Nil*
SPECIAL DEFENSES: *See below*
MAGIC RESISTANCE: *Standard*
SIZE: *M (6')*
ALIGNMENT: *Neutral good*
CLERIC/DRUID: *Nil*
FIGHTER: *9th level ranger*
MAGIC-USER/ILLUSIONIST: *Nil*
THIEF/ASSASSIN: *Nil*
MONK/BARD: *5th level bard*
PSIONIC ABILITY: *VI*
S: *17 (+1, +1)* I: *14* W: *18* D: *18* C: *18* CH: *18*

This fighter is loyal to the god Frey and is always at his side in battle. A split second before he is struck by a blow or affected by a spell that would end his life, he is automatically teleported to Alfheim, whether he wants to go or not.

Skirnir wears +4 chainmail and wields a +3 two-handed sword.

FREYA (goddess of love and fertility)

Greater goddess

ARMOR CLASS: *-3*
MOVE: *18"/48"*
HIT POINTS: *339*
NO. OF ATTACKS: *1*
DAMAGE/ATTACK: *By weapon type*
SPECIAL ATTACKS: *See below*
SPECIAL DEFENSES: *+3 or better
    weapon to hit, also see below*
MAGIC RESISTANCE: *80%*
SIZE: *M (6')*
ALIGNMENT: *Neutral good*
WORSHIPER'S ALIGN: *Neutral good
    and all lovers*
SYMBOL: *Falcon*
PLANE: *Gladsheim*
CLERIC/DRUID: *15th level cleric/10th
    level druid*
FIGHTER: *7th level ranger*
MAGIC-USER/ILLUSIONIST: *15th level
    illusionist*
THIEF/ASSASSIN: *Nil*
MONK/BARD: *12th level bard*
PSIONIC ABILITY: *VI*
S: *24 (+6, +12)* I: *24* W: *24* D: *24* C: *25* CH: *20*

Freya commands all fire spells as a 30th level spell caster, and is able to remove any curse with a touch of her hand. She often travels in falcon guise, but she can *shape change* into any bird form. When traveling in human form, she rides in a chariot pulled by 2 gigantic cats (AC 5, HD 5, hp 30, D 1-8/1-8/1-12) which moves at a rate of 18".

Freya uses a +3 *frost brand* in battle. No avian or fire attack can hurt her.

Freya possesses the necklace Brisingamen, a piece of jewelry of fantastic value (1 million gold pieces) that glows when a lie is told in its presence. She also has a cloak of falcon feathers that allows her to fly in falcon form at 48".

This goddess is the leader of the Valkyries, and sometimes accompanies them to choose the slain at the greatest battles.

Freya is actually a Vanir, and the twin sister of Frey.

FRIGGA (goddess of the atmosphere) "Wife of Odin"

Greater goddess

ARMOR CLASS: −4
MOVE: 15"
HIT POINTS: 366
NO. OF ATTACKS: *As per shape*
DAMAGE/ATTACK: *As per shape*
SPECIAL ATTACKS: *See below*
SPECIAL DEFENSES: +3 *or better*
    weapon to hit, also as per shape
MAGIC RESISTANCE: 75%
SIZE: M (6')
ALIGNMENT: *Lawful neutral*
WORSHIPER'S ALIGN: *Lawful neutral*
SYMBOL: *Large cat*
PLANE: *Gladsheim*
CLERIC/DRUID: *15th level cleric*
FIGHTER: *7th level ranger*
MAGIC-USER/ILLUSIONIST: *18th level*
    magic-user
THIEF/ASSASSIN: *Nil*
MONK/BARD: *10th level bard*
PSIONIC ABILITY: *II*
S: 20 (+3, +8) I: 23 W: 20 D: 24 C: 25 CH: 25

Frigga is able to control all forms of weather and is able to view any area that has a breeze blowing through it. She has a magical necklace of black opals that will charm anyone or anything she wishes within sight of it (magic saving throw applicable). The charmed being will then be able to do nothing but flatter the goddess.

There is a 1% chance (once a month) that the goddess will personally deliver one worshiper who calls out her name from mortal danger.

In battle, the goddess *shape changes* into creatures and fights with their powers. She starts out with dragon forms and goes to avian forms towards the end of any given battle.

Her handmaidens are Valkyries; the names of some of them are Fulla, Vara, Lofn, Vor, Gna, Eira, Hlin, Syn, Vjofn, and Snotra.

In her role as Odin's wife, she is often worshiped by housewives and those seeking marriage. She spins flax into gold for Odin's clothes.

GARM (guardian of Hel-gate)

FREQUENCY: *Unique*
NO. APPEARING: *1*
ARMOR CLASS: −1
MOVE: 18"
HIT DICE/POINTS: 200 hp
% IN LAIR: 95%
TREASURE TYPE: H, U
NO. OF ATTACKS: 1
DAMAGE/ATTACK: 6-60
SPECIAL ATTACKS: *Fear*
SPECIAL DEFENSES: +2 *or better*
    weapon needed to hit
MAGIC RESISTANCE: 80%
INTELLIGENCE: *Average*
ALIGNMENT: *Lawful evil*
SIZE: L (12' at the shoulder)
PSIONIC ABILITY: *Nil*
    Attack/Defense Modes: *Nil*
LEVEL/X.P. VALUE: X/26,200

This beast is responsible for guarding the gateway to the land of the dead, so that beings do not enter or leave. It looks like a giant dire wolf with a disproportionately large head. Over the centuries it has fought and killed several heroes and gods who were trying to retrieve a loved one. Its treasure consists of the goods of those who unsuccessfully attempted to pass.

The sight of this monster is so terrible that beings of the 6th level or less will automatically flee in terror, and those of higher level must save vs. a *fear* spell at −4.

Garm obeys the laws of Hel, and is allowed to travel on all planes when Hel is out collecting dead and the way to her domain is magically closed. When it travels, it takes a pack of 20 dire wolves along for company.

Garm attacks as a 16+ hit dice monster, biting with its huge jaws for 6-60 points of damage.

HEIMDALL (the bright god) "Guardian of the Bifrost Bridge"

Greater god

ARMOR CLASS: −5
MOVE: 15"
HIT POINTS: 390
NO. OF ATTACKS: 2
DAMAGE/ATTACK: 3-30 (+14) *plus*
    see below
SPECIAL ATTACKS: *Surprise*
SPECIAL DEFENSES: *Never surprised*
MAGIC RESISTANCE: 80%
SIZE: M (7')
ALIGNMENT: *Lawful good*
WORSHIPER'S ALIGN: *Lawful good*
    and magic-users
SYMBOL: *His horn*
PLANE: *Gladsheim*
CLERIC/DRUID: *12th level in each*
FIGHTER: *17th level ranger*
MAGIC-USER/ILLUSIONIST: *Nil*
THIEF/ASSASSIN: *Nil*
MONK/BARD: *8th level bard*
PSIONIC ABILITY: *III*
S: 25 (+7, +14) I: 23 W: 24 D: 25 C: 25 CH: 23

This god's main function is to guard Bifrost, the rainbow bridge. Heimdall always attacks with surprise and is gifted with exceptional senses (eyesight, hearing, touch). His eyesight acts as an unlimited range and duration *clairvoyance spell*. He never travels about without his sword Hofud ("head"). This sword is a *vorpal weapon*, and is also a *sword of frost giant slaying*. It inflicts 3-30 points of damage at a strike, plus Heimdall's strength bonus of 14 points.

Heimdall wears a +3 white armor into battle that has the same effect as a *gem of brightness*. His horn, called Gjaller, is the alarm system for Asgard. Heimdall will blow a blast upon it to announce the coming of the frost giants, and the gods and their hosts will issue out to fight the last battle (Ragnarok). This horn is also sounded in a different way to proclaim a visitor.

Heimdall is the sworn enemy of Loki, who mocks him and his steadfast guardianship.

HEL (goddess of death)

Greater goddess

ARMOR CLASS: −5
MOVE: *Infinite*
HIT POINTS: 350
NO. OF ATTACKS: 3/2
DAMAGE/ATTACK: 5-50 (+8)
SPECIAL ATTACKS: *See below*
SPECIAL DEFENSES: *See below*
MAGIC RESISTANCE: 95%
SIZE: M (6½')
ALIGNMENT: *Neutral evil*
WORSHIPER'S ALIGN: *All alignments*
SYMBOL: *Her face*
PLANE: *Hades*
CLERIC/DRUID: *20th level cleric/10th
   level druid*
FIGHTER: *12th level ranger*
MAGIC-USER/ILLUSIONIST: *15th level
   in each*
THIEF/ASSASSIN: *15th level assassin*
MONK/BARD: *10th level bard*
PSIONIC ABILITY: *I*
S: 20 (+3, +8)   I: 24   W: 25   D: 24   C: 25   CH: 25

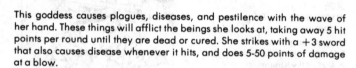

This goddess causes plagues, diseases, and pestilence with the wave of her hand. These things will afflict the beings she looks at, taking away 5 hit points per round until they are dead or cured. She strikes with a +3 sword that also causes disease whenever it hits, and does 5-50 points of damage at a blow.

Within a 90 yard radius of her body is an aura of withering that subtracts 20 hit points from all those not making their magical saving throws. She is also totally impervious to all physical weaponry.

The goddess of death lives in a dismal palace in the area of Hades known as Niflheim. She appears as a gaunt woman, whose body is completely white on the left side and jet black on the right. The left half of her face is totally blank. She rides a white, spectral three-legged horse.

IDUN (goddess of spring and eternal youth)

Lesser goddess

ARMOR CLASS: −3
MOVE: 12"/18"
HIT POINTS: 329
NO. OF ATTACKS: 3/2
DAMAGE/ATTACK: *By weapon type*
SPECIAL ATTACKS: *Nil*
SPECIAL DEFENSES: +2 or better
   weapon to hit
MAGIC RESISTANCE: 25%
SIZE: M (6')
ALIGNMENT: *Chaotic good*
WORSHIPER'S ALIGN: *Chaotic good
   and all farmers*
SYMBOL: *Apples in a wicker chest*
PLANE: *Gladsheim*
CLERIC/DRUID: *15th level cleric/14th
   level druid*
FIGHTER: *7th level ranger*
MAGIC-USER/ILLUSIONIST: *Nil*
THIEF/ASSASSIN: *Nil*
MONK/BARD: *13th level bard*
PSIONIC ABILITY: *V*
S: 20 (+3, +8)   I: 22   W: 23   D: 24   C: 24   CH: 24

This goddess protects the "Apples of Youth" which the gods eat to remain immortal. These apples are able to return 10 years of youth and restore up to 50 lost hit points per bite. These apples are carried in a 1 foot by 1 foot wicker chest which always appears full of apples but can hold any amount of them put in it. Idun is the wife of Bragi.

JORMUNGANDR (Midgard Serpent)

FREQUENCY: *Unique*
NO. APPEARING: 1
ARMOR CLASS: −3
MOVE: *See below*
HIT DICE/POINTS: *Head: 300 points;
   Body: infinite*
% IN LAIR: *Nil*
TREASURE TYPE: *Nil*
NO. OF ATTACKS: 1
DAMAGE/ATTACK: 5-50
SPECIAL ATTACKS: *Constriction,
   poison*
SPECIAL DEFENSES: *Regeneration*
MAGIC RESISTANCE: 99%
INTELLIGENCE: *Very*
ALIGNMENT: *Chaotic evil*
SIZE: L (25,000 miles long)
PSIONIC ABILITY: *Nil*
   Attack/Defense Modes: *Nil*
LEVEL/X.P. VALUE: X/55,000

Jormungandr was the offspring of Loki and the giantess Angur-boda, and was the brother of the Fenris Wolf and Hel. By custom Odin could not slay divine progeny, but he feared that the monster would cause trouble and threw him into the sea when he was young. Jormungandr grew unchecked, until at last he circled the earth and could bite his own tail. It is the writhing of this great serpent that causes the tempests. Thor has tried many times to slay him, but the Norns have foretold that he will not succeed until the day of Ragnarok, when he will drown in a sea of venom from the dying serpent.

Since the Midgard Serpent circles the world, he can shift his body and locate his head anywhere he desires in one melee round. The head is the only vulnerable spot on this monster, since he regenerates all damage in the melee round after it is inflicted; this means that 300 or more points of damage must be delivered to its head in one round in order to kill it. If Jormungandr is slain, all beings within 50 feet of the head must save vs. poison at −5 or die, as the creature spews forth its venom. Attacks on the body of the serpent can be made, but they will prove fruitless as the body (like the head) will regenerate all lost hit points in the next melee round, even if totally severed.

Jormungandr bites once per round for 5-50 points of damage, and anyone thus bitten must save versus poison at −5 or die within two melee rounds from the extremely potent venom. The serpent can also make one constriction attack per round (near its head or anywhere along its body length), doing 10-100 points. It attacks as a 16+ HD monster.

LOKI (god of mischief, strife and fire)

Greater god

ARMOR CLASS: −4
MOVE: 12"/12"
HIT POINTS: 300
NO. OF ATTACKS: 3/2
DAMAGE/ATTACK: *By weapon type*
SPECIAL ATTACKS: *See below*
SPECIAL DEFENSES: *Immune to fire
   and magical control, +3 or
   better weapon to hit*
MAGIC RESISTANCE: 75%
SIZE: M (6')
ALIGNMENT: *Chaotic evil*
WORSHIPER'S ALIGN: *Chaotic evil*
SYMBOL: *Flame*
PLANE: *Pandemonium or Gladsheim*
CLERIC/DRUID: *12th level in each*
FIGHTER: *12th level ranger*
MAGIC-USER/ILLUSIONIST: *11th level
   magic-user/20th level illusionist*
THIEF/ASSASSIN: *15th level assassin*
MONK/BARD: *5th level in each*
PSIONIC ABILITY: *IV*
S: 24 (+6, +12)   I: 25   W: 19   D: 24   C: 24   CH: 24

While this god moves among the others in Asgard, he is known to be the one most likely to betray them to the giants. Depending upon his current status with the other gods, he makes his home in Gladsheim or Pandemonium. He is tolerated because he is blood brother to Odin and has acted in the far past to save the Asgardians from certain death and destruction. While the god can *shape change* at will, he usually relies on his power to force beings to do what he desires via his *suggestion* power. Looking at the god for 3 melee rounds or more negates all saving throws against that *suggestion*, and this applies to all beings. (Magic resistance is still effective.) He wears a pair of boots that combine the powers of *water walking*, *flying*, *travelling*, and *speed*.

Though Loki cannot be magically controlled, illusions will work on him, but only when cast by beings of greater than the 20th level.

The god's colors are red and black and he wears them at all times, even when in the guise of something else.

MAGNI (god of strength)

Lesser god

ARMOR CLASS: -4
MOVE: 18''
HIT POINTS: 325
NO. OF ATTACKS: 2
DAMAGE/ATTACK: 8-80
SPECIAL ATTACKS: Nil
SPECIAL DEFENSES: +2 or better
(edged) weapon to hit
MAGIC RESISTANCE: 70%
SIZE: M (7')
ALIGNMENT: Chaotic good
WORSHIPER'S ALIGN: Chaotic good
SYMBOL: Mountain
PLANE: Gladsheim
CLERIC/DRUID: Nil
FIGHTER: 15th level fighter
MAGIC-USER/ILLUSIONIST: Nil
THIEF/ASSASSIN: Nil
MONK/BARD: 5th level bard
PSIONIC ABILITY: VI
S: 25 (special) I: 20 W: 20 D: 24 C: 25 CH: 22

Thor's son, this god transcends the normal definition of strength in the **AD&D** sense, in that his was supposed to be almost limitless.

He can bend anything he can grip, put his fist through anything, lift nearly anything (judge's option), even things that are supposed to be unliftable like his father's hammer. Any material object thrown at him, he can catch and throw back at the caster (hitting 90% of the time), and with his +3 hammer he does 8-80 points of damage per strike.

This god is so tough and hardy that blunt weapons of any type cannot harm him.

MODI (god of courage and berserk rage)

Lesser god

ARMOR CLASS: -4
MOVE: 21''
HIT POINTS: 379
NO. OF ATTACKS: 2 (or 4)
DAMAGE/ATTACK: 25 or 50
SPECIAL ATTACKS: Vorpal blade
SPECIAL DEFENSES: +2 or better
weapon to hit
MAGIC RESISTANCE: 95%
SIZE: M (7')
ALIGNMENT: Chaotic good
WORSHIPER'S ALIGN: Chaotic good
SYMBOL: Sword and hammer
crossed
PLANE: Gladsheim
CLERIC/DRUID: Nil
FIGHTER: 15th level fighter
MAGIC-USER/ILLUSIONIST: Nil
THIEF/ASSASSIN: Nil
MONK/BARD: 9th level bard
PSIONIC ABILITY: IV
S: 24 (+6, +12) I: 23 W: 22 D: 24 C: 25 CH: 25

Using a *vorpal blade* that strikes for 25 points of damage per hit (plus its decapitating power), Thor's son Modi is always in the forefront of any battle, and his presence inspires his followers with such courage that they do an extra 4 points of damage per hit (affecting all those in a 90 yard radius). He is immune to all forms of magical control or illusions. In battle, the god is able to "know" when the best time comes to retreat and regroup his forces for best effect.

After the god has sustained more than half of his hit points in damage, he will go into a berserker rage which allows him to double all his powers in combat, so that he hits 4 times per round for 50 points per hit.

NORNS (the fates)

ARMOR CLASS: 0
MOVE: 12''/21''
HIT POINTS: 299 each
NO. OF ATTACKS: 1
DAMAGE/ATTACK: 1-10 plus special
(see below)
SPECIAL ATTACKS: See below
SPECIAL DEFENSES: See below
MAGIC RESISTANCE: 80%
SIZE: M (5')
ALIGNMENT: Neutral
WORSHIPER'S ALIGN: None
SYMBOL: Lightning bolt
PLANE: Concordant Opposition
CLERIC/DRUID: 12th level in each
FIGHTER: 5th level ranger
MAGIC-USER/ILLUSIONIST: 15th level
in each
THIEF/ASSASSIN: 10th level thief
MONK/BARD: 8th level in each
PSIONIC ABILITY: I
S: 23 (+5, +11) I: 22 W: 25 D: 23 C: 25 CH: 9

The Norns, called Urd, Verdandi, and Skuld, represent the past, present, and future, but they are only willing to tell of these things as long as they deal with themselves or answer questions of slight import. They travel about the Prime Material Plane in the form of swans, and in this shape they deal out fate in the form of prophecy. At the birth of every mortal male, they know what the babe's fate will be and may tell if presented with expensive gifts of gold and silver (1% of the time). They tend the tree of life, called Yggdrasil, and often advise the gods on special situations.

They fight with daggers, when forced into this situation, and their weapons do 1-10 points of damage, plus the magical bonus of subtracting one point from every ability score a being has (intelligence, wisdom, etc.), no saving throw allowed. They are immune to all nonmagical attacks, i.e., they can only be hurt by magic or magical weapons.

The Norns are not normal goddesses, and do not have worshipers as such. They weave the web of fate impartially.

SIF (goddess of excellence and skill in battle)

Lesser goddess

ARMOR CLASS: −4
MOVE: 18''
HIT POINTS: 349
NO. OF ATTACKS: 2
DAMAGE/ATTACK: 3-30 (+11)
SPECIAL ATTACKS: Nil
SPECIAL DEFENSES: Immune to
  magical control, +2 or better
  weapon to hit
MAGIC RESISTANCE: 80%
SIZE: M (6')
ALIGNMENT: Chaotic good
WORSHIPER'S ALIGN: Chaotic good
SYMBOL: Sword upraised
PLANE: Gladsheim
CLERIC/DRUID: 12th level druid
FIGHTER: 12th level ranger
MAGIC-USER/ILLUSIONIST: Nil
THIEF/ASSASSIN: Nil
MONK/BARD: 12th level in each
PSIONIC ABILITY: VI
S: 23 (+5, +11) I: 24 W: 22 D: 25 C: 25 CH: 25

Thor's wife Sif has beautiful golden hair (a gift from the dwarves) and is dressed in white and silver most of the time. She uses a +3 sword in battle which does 3-30 points of damage (plus her strength bonus).

She is the patron of young warriors, and there is a 1% chance that a 1st level fighter devoted to her may receive a *bless* spell if he or she prays to Sif before a battle.

SURTUR (lord of the fire giants)

Lesser god

ARMOR CLASS: −2
MOVE: 15''
HIT POINTS: 380
NO. OF ATTACKS: 2
DAMAGE/ATTACK: 6-60
SPECIAL ATTACKS: See below
SPECIAL DEFENSES: Immune to fire,
  +3 or better weapon to hit
MAGIC RESISTANCE: 60%
SIZE: L (20')
ALIGNMENT: Lawful evil
WORSHIPER'S ALIGN: Lawful evil
  (fire giants)
SYMBOL: Flaming sword
PLANE: Gladsheim (Jotunheim)
CLERIC/DRUID: 15th level cleric
FIGHTER: 20th level fighter
MAGIC-USER/ILLUSIONIST: 5th level
  magic-user
THIEF/ASSASSIN: Nil
MONK/BARD: Nil
PSIONIC ABILITY: Nil
S: 25 (+7, +14) I: 19 W: 14 D: 12 C: 25 CH: 20

Most fire giants regard Surtur as their leader and their deity. Deep in Jotunheim, Surtur waits for the day when he can lead the fire giants to the great battle of Ragnarok.

Surtur looks like an immense fire giant, with crackling flames for hair and eyebrows. He wears heavy iron armor which is hot to the touch (1-10 points of damage to any who contact it with exposed flesh), and wields a 15-foot flaming iron sword. He strikes with this twice per round, inflicting 6-60 points of damage on a hit. Surtur is immune to fire attacks of any kind.

THOR (god of thunder)

Greater god

ARMOR CLASS: −4
MOVE: 18''
HIT POINTS: 399
NO. OF ATTACKS: 2 (3)
DAMAGE/ATTACK: 10-100 (+16)
SPECIAL ATTACKS: See below
SPECIAL DEFENSES: +3 or better
  weapon to hit; and see below
MAGIC RESISTANCE: 80%
SIZE: M (7')
ALIGNMENT: Chaotic good
WORSHIPER'S ALIGN: All
  alignments, especially warriors,
  beings needing certain weather,
  or ones wanting fair play
SYMBOL: Hammer
PLANE: Gladsheim
CLERIC/DRUID: 10th level druid
FIGHTER: 20th level fighter
MAGIC-USER/ILLUSIONIST: Nil
THIEF/ASSASSIN: Nil
MONK/BARD: 3rd level bard
PSIONIC ABILITY: VI
S: 25 (Special: +7, +16) I: 20 W: 20 D: 25 C: 25 CH: 24

Thor appears as a large red-haired and red-bearded man dressed in black and yellow +3 chainmail. He rides through the sky on his golden chariot, which is pulled by his two magical goats, Tanngrisner and Tanngjost. Thor is a particular friend to mankind among the Norse gods, and will often alert his worshipers to incursions of evil. The god often fights on Gladsheim against giant types, and his name is enough to make giants check morale. When within 90 yards of him, the servants and allies of Thor gain a benefit of +2 on all dice throws.

Thor's normal strength is 25, but he has a magical girdle and a magical glove which enable him to exceed even this limit. *Meginjarder*, his girdle, gives him the strength to wield his mighty hammer (described below), and enable him to break any barrier or object. His magical glove, *Jarn Grieper*, gives him the ability to strike three times per melee round and to handle his hammer even while red-hot.

Mjolnir, Thor's +5 magic hammer, has the following abilities:

It does 10-100 points of damage.

It can be thrown up to 200 yards, and it never misses when thrown. It returns to Thor's hand automatically. (If Thor throws Mjolnir, that is his only attack in that round.)

It can cast *lightning bolts* at any target within sight, up to a total of 100 dice of *lightning bolts* per day. This base 100 dice can be broken up into lightning bolts of any size Thor desires, i.e., 25 4 dice bolts, or 10 3 dice bolts and 1 70 dice bolt, etc.

It is so heavy that only beings with a strength of 25 can even lift it, and it requires more than a 25 strength to wield it as a weapon.

When Thor throws Mjolnir, it trails a lightning bolt behind it, and when it hits, there is a large clap of thunder which affects all beings within 30' as a *power word, stun* (save vs. magic negates).

If any other being uses a *lightning* spell within 200'' of Thor, it will automatically turn and strike the caster, whether the Thunderer wills it or not.

All of Thor's clerics rely on hammers for their weapons.

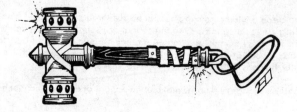

Tanngrisner & Tanngjost (Thor's goats)

FREQUENCY: Unique
NO. APPEARING: 2
ARMOR CLASS: 0
MOVE: 24''/24''
HIT DICE/POINTS: 100
% IN LAIR: Nil
TREASURE TYPE: Nil
NO. OF ATTACKS: 3
DAMAGE/ATTACK: 3-24
SPECIAL ATTACKS: Nil
SPECIAL DEFENSES: See below
MAGIC RESISTANCE: 25%
INTELLIGENCE: Low
ALIGNMENT: Neutral
SIZE: L (9' at the shoulder)
PSIONIC ABILITY: Nil
    Attack/Defense Modes: Nil
LEVEL/X.P. VALUE: X/14,100

These two enchanted animals are used to pull Thor's chariot through the air and on the land.

The creatures are often eaten by Thor and his friends, as they magically regenerate from the bones and skin with the light of the morning sun.

They appear as giant goats. Tanngrisner is white and Tanngjost is black. They attack by butting with their large horns. They add +6 to damage inflicted when they charge, and they attack as 16+ hit dice monsters.

THRYM (lord of the frost giants)

Lesser god

ARMOR CLASS: –2
MOVE: 15''
HIT POINTS: 300
NO. OF ATTACKS: 2
DAMAGE/ATTACK: 4-40 (+14)
SPECIAL ATTACKS: Nil
SPECIAL DEFENSES: +3 or better
    weapon to hit, immune to cold
    attacks
MAGIC RESISTANCE: 60%
SIZE: L (21')
ALIGNMENT: Chaotic evil
WORSHIPER'S ALIGN: Chaotic evil
    (frost giants)
SYMBOL: White double-bladed
    axe
PLANE: Gladsheim (Jotunheim)
CLERIC/DRUID: 10th level cleric
FIGHTER: 20th level fighter
MAGIC-USER/ILLUSIONIST: 3rd level
    illusionist
THIEF/ASSASSIN: Nil
MONK/BARD: Nil
PSIONIC ABILITY: Nil
S: 25 (+7, +14) I: 16 W: 12 D: 21 C: 25 CH: 20

JEFF DEE 1980

Thrym is both leader and deity of the frost giants. Like Surtur, he waits for the day when he can lead the frost giants against the Aesir in the last battle. Thrym wields a huge +3 doublebladed axe which inflicts 4-40 points of damage on a hit. He wears a coat of white fur over his suit of chainmail. Otherwise, he appears much like an oversized frost giant.

Thrym has ten brothers who are in most ways like normal frost giants (AC 4, MV 12'', #AT 1, D 4-24). However, each has 100 hit points and attacks as a 16+ hit dice monster.

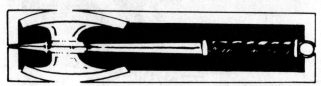

TYR (god of war and law)

Greater god

ARMOR CLASS: –5
MOVE: 18''
HIT POINTS: 380
NO. OF ATTACKS: 3
DAMAGE/ATTACK: 2-20 (+12)
SPECIAL ATTACKS: Nil
SPECIAL DEFENSES: +3 or better
    weapon to hit, and see below
MAGIC RESISTANCE: 25%
SIZE: M (6½')
ALIGNMENT: Lawful good
WORSHIPER'S ALIGN: All warriors
SYMBOL: Sword
PLANE: Gladsheim
CLERIC/DRUID: 13th level druid
FIGHTER: 25th level paladin
MAGIC-USER/ILLUSIONIST: 10th level
    illusionist
THIEF/ASSASSIN: 15th level thief
MONK/BARD: 10th level in each
PSIONIC ABILITY: I
S: 24 (+6, +12) I: 20 W: 20 D: 25 C: 25 CH: 24

Tyr appears as a powerful-looking bearded man who has lost his right hand. It was the losing of this hand that firmly established Tyr as the god of law and trust. When the dwarves finally forged a cord that could bind the Fenris Wolf, the great monster would only consent to having the cord put upon it if one of the Aesir would place his hand in the Wolf's mouth. Tyr, knowing what was planned, placed his right hand in Fenris' mouth without hesitation. When Fenris found that he was bound, he bit off Tyr's hand, but he could not escape. By honoring this contract, Tyr became the god of law.

In his aspect of war god, Tyr watches over the Valkyries and makes sure that only the most valiant mortal warriors are taken to Odin at Valhalla.

Tyr wields a +3 sword in his left hand that does 2-20 points of damage on a hit. He automatically senses the presence of any thief who comes within 100'' of him, and he can see invisible objects.

ULLER (god of hunting, archery and winter)

Lesser god

ARMOR CLASS: –3
MOVE: 24''
HIT POINTS: 390
NO. OF ATTACKS: 2
DAMAGE/ATTACK: 2-20 (+11)
SPECIAL ATTACKS: Longbow
SPECIAL DEFENSES: +2 or better
    weapon to hit; immune to fire,
    cold, lightning and elementals
MAGIC RESISTANCE: 50%
SIZE: M (7')
ALIGNMENT: Chaotic neutral
WORSHIPER'S ALIGN: Chaotic
    neutral
SYMBOL: Longbow
PLANE: Gladsheim
CLERIC/DRUID: 13th level druid
FIGHTER: 18th level ranger
MAGIC-USER/ILLUSIONIST: 12th level
    illusionist
THIEF/ASSASSIN: 12th level assassin
MONK/BARD: 12th level bard
PSIONIC ABILITY: I
S: 23 (+5, +11) I: 24 W: 24 D: 25 C: 25 CH: 25

Uller was once a great god, but his power has waned with the ascension of Odin. As the greatest hunter of the Aesir, Uller spends a great deal of time in the wilderness areas of Asgard, and is thus immune to the effects of the elements. He cannot be harmed by fire, cold, lightning, or any of the various elementals.

Though Uller is in many ways an outsider, the other Aesir have a high regard for his capabilities, and he has been known to temporarily rule in Odin's place when Odin was elsewhere.

Uller is the patron of archers, and a mighty bowman. He uses a +5 long bow; he can shoot it at any target that he can see, with no range penalties, and he never misses targets less than 200'' away. He also wields a +4 two-handed sword that strikes for 2-20 points of damage (plus strength bonus).

Uller is also the god of winter, and sometimes gives aid to those less able to survive it than he.

VALKYRIES *"Choosers of the Slain"*

ARMOR CLASS: –2
MOVE: 15''
HIT POINTS: 100
NO. OF ATTACKS: 2
DAMAGE/ATTACK: *By weapon type*
SPECIAL ATTACKS: *Nil*
SPECIAL DEFENSES: *Nil*
MAGIC RESISTANCE: 25%
SIZE: *M (5½')*
ALIGNMENT: *Chaotic neutral*
CLERIC/DRUID: *Nil*
FIGHTER: *15th level fighter*
MAGIC-USER/ILLUSIONIST: *Nil*
THIEF/ASSASSIN: *Nil*
MONK/BARD: *8th level bard*
PSIONIC ABILITY: *Nil*
  Attack/Defense Modes: *Nil*
S: 19 (+3, +7) I: 17 W: 17 D: 18 C: 19 CH: 19

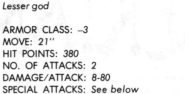

These warrior maidens ride pegasi of maximum hit points. These mounts are the offspring of Sleipner. It is the Valkyries' duty to bring the souls of the best and most valiant slain warriors from battlefields to Valhalla, the hall of Odin. They act as serving maids in Odin's hall and as handmaidens to Frigga. When they ride forth to choose the slain, their armor gives off a pearly, flickering light that is said to cause the Aurora Borealis. They travel ethereally, and are only visible to warriors in mortal danger.

VIDAR *(god of strength and silence)*

Lesser god

ARMOR CLASS: –3
MOVE: 21''
HIT POINTS: 380
NO. OF ATTACKS: 2
DAMAGE/ATTACK: 8-80
SPECIAL ATTACKS: *See below*
SPECIAL DEFENSES: *Silence, +2 or*
    better weapon to hit
MAGIC RESISTANCE: 95%
SIZE: *L (20')*
ALIGNMENT: *Chaotic good*
WORSHIPER'S ALIGN: *Chaotic good*
SYMBOL: *Iron shoe*
PLANE: *Gladsheim*
CLERIC/DRUID: *10th level druid*
FIGHTER: *18th level ranger*
MAGIC-USER/ILLUSIONIST: *Nil*
THIEF/ASSASSIN: *Nil*
MONK/BARD: *Nil*
PSIONIC ABILITY: *VI*
S: 25 (+7, +14) I: 20 W: 19 D: 25 C: 25 CH: 22

Vidar, a son of Odin, is a stoic bastion of strength for the Aesir in times of need. He speaks only when he must, and then he uses as few words as possible. Though not a sociable god, his hate of evil is strong, and when the Aesir don't need him, he combats it in his own way.

Though not a greater god, Vidar's strength and constitution are renowned, and he is a fearsome opponent to enemies such as giants. On his right foot he wears a magical iron shoe, with which he can strike twice per round for 8-80 points of damage. Any object or person that Vidar steps on with this shoe (successful "to hit" roll required) will be pinned until the god chooses to let them go. No creature can fight or cast spells when under Vidar's shoe.

At will, Vidar can make a 24'' radius around himself completely *silent*. This effect cannot be countered by *dispel magic, spell turning,* or anything else.

SUMERIAN · MYTHOS.

This culture was among man's first attempts at civilization, and it is one of man's first recorded religions. Because of this, the gods are unusually close to their worshipers and every worshiper is a *servant* of his or her god. We constantly see a willingness to help that is soon lost to all other mythoi.

Every city has its patron deity; all the people belong to that temple and none other. All officials of the city are clerics of the temple and the high priest is always the king or queen of that city-state. The temples have a stepped pyramid shape in the manner of the Aztec temples.

Sacrifices and gifts to the deities are all made as items that will dress up altars and the temple surroundings; the richer and more valuable the better. The clerics themselves make items to be directly sacrificed to the gods by burning at the same time that human lives are sacrificed to the gods (primarily condemned criminals).

Each temple has an image of its god on a raised platform in an inner shrine closed off to the public. Before the image is a table used as an altar that has all the gifts of the year placed upon it. There is a central courtyard beyond the main entrance for public worship. The building will have side chapels and storerooms of several types. The main entrance to the temple is set at right angles to the inner temple. The more important temples are raised up on artificial hills (or ziggurats) of red brick.

Clerics serve the best meat and drink to the gods on special tables beside altars. This food is burnt every night for the gods' use. The seventh, fifteenth, and twenty-fifth days of the month are holy days. A sacrifice is always held on the night of the new moon.

There are three degrees of punishment for clerical sins. Committing the first major transgression results in an acute severe gastro-intestinal disease (as per **DMG**) for the offending cleric. The second transgression results in a punishment of 15 troubles, each worse than the last (though none are automatically fatal). Thus, a cleric might be stung by a bee, then sprain an ankle, then suffer food poisoning, etc. If these warnings are not enough, the third transgression results in the death of the offending one. Any transgression can be erased in the sight of the deity by a sacrifice sufficient in proportion to the nature of the offense. These sacrifices must be important and/or expensive.

Clerics of this pantheon must shave all hair from their bodies and wear kilts and robes of white with colorful borders. The shape and color of the border indicates the cleric's patron deity. Female clerics wear rounded conical hats to cover their baldness.

Note: The geographical area of the Sumerian mythos is almost exactly the same as the Babylonian. Though separated by time, they share similar cultures and ideas. (This overlap is in much the same manner as that of the Greek and Roman mythoi.) While we could have listed these groups together, we thought that there was enough diversity between these two sections to warrant separation. In some cases, this diversity has been deliberately increased in order to prevent overlap.

ENLIL (air & war god) "ruler of the pantheon"

Greater god

ARMOR CLASS: −2
MOVE: 12"/36"
HIT POINTS: 400
NO. OF ATTACKS: 2
DAMAGE/ATTACK: 50 points
SPECIAL ATTACKS: See below
SPECIAL DEFENSES: See below
MAGIC RESISTANCE: 50%
SIZE: M (6½')
ALIGNMENT: Neutral good
WORSHIPER'S ALIGN: All good
   alignments
SYMBOL: Pickaxe
PLANE: Elysium
CLERIC/DRUID: 20th level cleric
FIGHTER: 19th level ranger
MAGIC-USER/ILLUSIONIST: 15th level
   magic-user
THIEF/ASSASSIN: Nil
MONK/BARD: 12th level bard
PSIONIC ABILITY: Nil
S: 25 (+7, +14) I: 25 W: 25 D: 23 C: 25 CH: 24

Enlil always appears as a tall man with a heavy dark beard and curly hair. At will, the god can *shape change*, and can *ESP* at any distance. Enlil can raise electrical storms, and from them direct lightning bolts at targets up to a mile distant, doing 40 points of damage per strike (save vs. spells for half damage). Unlike the other deities of this pantheon, Enlil has the power to raise the dead. Enlil takes no damage from lightning or electrical attacks.

In battle, the god wears a war helm that is not affected by *anything*. When Enlil is wearing it, he feels no shock or harm from objects hitting the helm. In any given melee, when attacked by only one weapon, that weapon is forced to hit the helm (no saving throw). In other words, if Enlil were fighting Thor, who uses *Mjolnir*, the hammer would be forced to hit the helm every time, no matter what Thor wanted, and Enlil would feel nothing. If attacked by two or more weapons, Enlil chooses which shall strike his helm. The god wields a stone axe in battle that does 50 points of damage per strike, but no damage if it hits metal. (Enlil's percentage chance of not hitting metal (if in combat with a metallically-armored opponent) is equal to the base armor class of the opponent times ten. For example, Enlil would have only a 30% chance of striking an unarmored portion of a person in plate mail, if he "hits".) Enlil's axe does disenchant any magic item that it comes in contact with (no save). It cannot be broken, will *teleport* to the god's hand if taken more than 100 feet from the body of the god, and has a 25% chance of negating any spell tossed at the god before the spell reaches him. (In addition, Enlil has 50% magic resistance, and a saving throw, if applicable.)

ENKI *(god of the rivers & oceans)*

Greater god

ARMOR CLASS: −2
MOVE: 12''/24''
HIT POINTS: 388
NO. OF ATTACKS: 3/2
DAMAGE/ATTACK: 35 points
SPECIAL ATTACKS: See below
SPECIAL DEFENSES: See below
MAGIC RESISTANCE: 50%
SIZE: M (6')
ALIGNMENT: Lawful neutral
WORSHIPER'S ALIGN: Lawful neutral
SYMBOL: Ibex (mountain goat)
PLANE: Nirvana
CLERIC/DRUID: 20th level cleric
FIGHTER: 13th level paladin
MAGIC-USER/ILLUSIONIST: 13th level
    in each
THIEF/ASSASSIN: Nil
MONK/BARD: 10th level bard
PSIONIC ABILITY: Nil
S: 23 (+5, +11) I: 25 W: 24 D: 23 C: 25 CH: 23

This god is always green in color in any of his human manifestations. At will, he *shape changes*. Enki is aware of and can *summon* any being that has died in the water to do his bidding. (One being of any species can be summoned per day. The summoned being instantly appears and does the bidding of the god; that particular being cannot be summoned ever again.) Enki moves like a blink dog, and is immune to all forms of heat. He can only teleport to areas where there is water in quantities of more than 50 gallons.

The god is known for his great hatred of demons, and he will slay any person in his presence that has ever dealt with these monsters in a friendly manner. In battle, he fights the strongest enemy facing his group first. He uses a small jade green mace that has several powers: it strikes for 35 points of damage on a successful hit; it is ethereal when not held by the god; it negates any spell below the 6th level cast at the god; and it will never cause harm to a lawful neutral being it strikes. His armor, helm, and shield are made out of water, and automatically absorb the first two hits made against the god in any given melee round.

Enki is also the patron of jewelers, goldsmiths, and stonecutters. Naturally, because of Enki's interest in this area, only the finest jewels, gold items, and carvings can be given to the god's temples in homage.

INANNA *(war goddess/goddess of love)*

Greater goddess

ARMOR CLASS: −2
MOVE: 12''/24''
HIT POINTS: 391
NO. OF ATTACKS: 2
DAMAGE/ATTACK: 25 points
SPECIAL ATTACKS: See below
SPECIAL DEFENSES: See below
MAGIC RESISTANCE: 66%
SIZE: M (6')
ALIGNMENT: Lawful evil
WORSHIPER'S ALIGN: Warriors and
    lovers
SYMBOL: A shepherd's staff
PLANE: Nine Hells
CLERIC/DRUID: 10th level in each
FIGHTER: 20th level ranger
MAGIC-USER/ILLUSIONIST: 12th level
    in each
THIEF/ASSASSIN: 15th level thief
MONK/BARD: 10th level bard
PSIONIC ABILITY: II
S: 20 (+3, +8) I: 21 W: 19 D: 25 C: 24 CH: 25

This goddess usually appears in the form of a beautiful woman, and will on rare occasions pick exceptionally brave warriors in battle and aid them.

This aid takes the form of that warrior never being hit, always making his or her saving throw, and never missing an attempted hit. This lasts for the duration of the melee.

At will, the goddess can *shape change*, *animate* statutes of herself in her temples, and can *summon* from the dead any being she has killed in a past battle to aid any given side (only on a one time basis per being).

She uses a small double bladed brass axe in battle that has the following abilities: it strikes for 25 points of damage per hit, causes any armor it strikes to turn to dust (no saving throw), and the user is never surprised. Her breast plates negate any damage caused by heat, cold, fang, or claw to her body.

The goddess is a fickle being and requires the sacrificing of the best in magical or high quality weapons on her altars.

In battle, she drives a chariot pulled by seven lions to which she has given the gift of flight (MV 30''). They are otherwise normal beasts which are under her complete control.

KI *(goddess of nature)*

Greater goddess

ARMOR CLASS: −2
MOVE: 15''/36''//36''
HIT POINTS: 380
NO. OF ATTACKS: 0
DAMAGE/ATTACK: Nil
SPECIAL ATTACKS: See below
SPECIAL DEFENSES: See below
MAGIC RESISTANCE: 90%
SIZE: M (5')
ALIGNMENT: Neutral
WORSHIPER'S ALIGN: Neutral
SYMBOL: Iris
PLANE: Prime Material Plane
CLERIC/DRUID: 30th level cleric/14th
    level druid
FIGHTER: 10th level paladin
MAGIC-USER/ILLUSIONIST: 20th level
    in each
THIEF/ASSASSIN: Nil
MONK/BARD: 20th level bard
PSIONIC ABILITY: I
S: 25 I: 23 W: 25 D: 23 C: 25 CH: 25

Ki appears as an elfin woman of great beauty. The goddess cannot be touched by anything material cast through the air at her. At will, she can *shape change* (into non-monster forms only). She can give the "luck of the gods" to those she favors. This luck takes the form of the recipient always making his or her saving throw and only suffering half damage from any attack; this lasts for a 24 hour period.

Any non-monster animal of any species is hers to *summon* instantly, in any number up to 100. No species can be summoned more than once per week. Thus, she can *summon* 100 tigers, 100 lions, 100 condors, etc., in any given week and they will instantly come to her call. She can only *summon* one type of creature at a time. She also has the power to instantly know where any given thing is on the surface of the earth.

When forced to do combat, she will take only half damage from any attack and will always make her saving throw on all things.

Ki's clerics are druids; her Great Druid may receive communications directly from the goddess.

NANNA-SIN (moon god)

Lesser god

ARMOR CLASS: −2
MOVE: 12″/24″
HIT POINTS: 339
NO. OF ATTACKS: 2
DAMAGE/ATTACK: 30 points
SPECIAL ATTACKS: Nil
SPECIAL DEFENSES: See below
MAGIC RESISTANCE: 75%
SIZE: M (6′)
ALIGNMENT: Chaotic good
WORSHIPER'S ALIGN: Chaotic good
SYMBOL: Jet black axe over the
   moon
PLANE: Elysium
CLERIC/DRUID: 13th level in each
FIGHTER: 16th level fighter
MAGIC-USER/ILLUSIONIST: 15th level
   in each
THIEF/ASSASSIN: Nil
MONK/BARD: 15th level bard
PSIONIC ABILITY: Nil
S: 25 (+7, +14) I: 24 W: 25 D: 19 C: 23 CH: 25

This human-appearing god is always bathed in a blue glow that acts as a rod of beguiling to all who come within 10 feet of it. At will, Nanna-Sin can negate any of the following: heat, cold, electricity, light, and darkness.

He uses a +3 jet black axe in battle which strikes for 30 points of damage per hit; it also acts as a sword of sharpness.

NIN-HURSAG (goddess of the earth)

Lesser goddess

ARMOR CLASS: −2
MOVE: 9″/12″
HIT POINTS: 355
NO. OF ATTACKS: 3/2
DAMAGE/ATTACK: 2-20
SPECIAL ATTACKS: Gravity control,
   withering
SPECIAL DEFENSES: See below
MAGIC RESISTANCE: 50%
SIZE: M (6′)
ALIGNMENT: Neutral
WORSHIPER'S ALIGN: Neutral
SYMBOL: Blue-white diamond
PLANE: Elysium
CLERIC/DRUID: 13th level druid
FIGHTER: 11th level fighter
MAGIC-USER/ILLUSIONIST: 30th level
   magic-user
THIEF/ASSASSIN: Nil
MONK/BARD: Nil
PSIONIC ABILITY: Nil
S: 23 (+5, +11) I: 23 W: 23 D: 23 C: 23 CH: 23

This deity always appears as a dark-skinned female. She is mistress of gravity and magnetism and has complete control over these forces. She can give the gift of flight to those she especially favors. She also has the power to wither those she hates. This withering takes the form of a special 9th level spell that works like three charges from a staff of withering. It requires the same components as a wish spell.

UTU (sun god)

Greater god

ARMOR CLASS: −2
MOVE: Infinite
HIT POINTS: 377
NO. OF ATTACKS: 3/2
DAMAGE/ATTACK: 50 points
SPECIAL ATTACKS: Light rays, poly-
   morphing
SPECIAL DEFENSES: Heat aura,
   regeneration
MAGIC RESISTANCE: 90%
SIZE: M (6′)
ALIGNMENT: Chaotic good
WORSHIPER'S ALIGN: Chaotic good
SYMBOL: Radiant sun disc
PLANE: Nirvana
CLERIC/DRUID: 15th level cleric/14th
   level druid
FIGHTER: 13th level ranger
MAGIC-USER/ILLUSIONIST: 15th level
   in each
THIEF/ASSASSIN: Nil
MONK/BARD: 5th level bard
PSIONIC ABILITY: VI
S: 24 (+6, +12) I: 20 W: 22 D: 22 C: 24 CH: 25

This deity, always in human form, is constantly bathed in a dazzling 10′ radius yellow glow. The glow causes all enemies to suffer a −2 on all strikes at the god, and all undead wither to dust at a touch of his glow. He can cast two light rays per round at anything in sight, each of which does 20 points of damage when they hit (save vs. spells for half damage). He regenerates all lost hit points when touched by heat of any degree above 100° F, and he is able to polymorph living matter into dirt, with a −3 on the being's saving throw.

In battle, the god throws bits of the sun he has pulled away. These sun-bits can be thrown up to 2 miles away from the god, and they strike for 50 points of heat damage when they hit. His aura also causes anything striking his body to melt unless the thing is indestructible.

CLOUD CHARIOTS

All of the gods and goddesses have cloud chariots at their personal command. These devices appear to be clouds that give off a dazzling radiance. When a god steps on them, they become platforms of transportation for the gods and also a means to impress worshipers and non-believers alike.

A cloud chariot travels at a rate of 24″, and can teleport itself to any place where there are clouds in the sky. It is unaffected by any material force and is never destroyed. The gods will always appear to their clerics on such devices to prove that they are gods. These devices are capable of carrying anything the controlling deity wishes.

APPENDICES

APPENDIX 1: THE KNOWN PLANES OF EXISTENCE

There exists an infinite number of parallel universes and planes of existence in the fantastic "multiverse" of **ADVANCED DUNGEONS & DRAGONS**. All of these "worlds" co-exist, but how "real" each is depends entirely upon the development of each campaign referee. The charts and explanations which follow show only the various planes tied to that of normal existence. The parallel universes are not shown, and their existence might or might not be actual.

THE INNER PLANES

The Prime Material Plane

The *Prime Material Plane* (or *Physical Plane*) is at the "center" of the *Inner Planes*. It houses the universe and all of its parallels. It is the plane of Terra, and your campaign, in all likelihood. The *Prime Material* is bounded or permeated by all of the *Inner Planes* and the *Astral Plane*. The *Prime Material Plane* is made up of the four elements plus positive and negative energy.

The Positive Material Plane

This is a place of energy and light, the place which is the source of much that is vital and active, the power supply for good. Any creature from the *Prime Material* that tried to enter the *Positive Material Plane* (e.g. from the *Ethereal Plane*) would probably be instantly consumed by the powerful energies there.

The Negative Material Plane

This is a place of anti-matter and negative force, the source of power for undead, the energy area from which evil grows. No one is certain what types of creature may exist on the *Negative* (or *Positive*) *Material Plane*. Any creature from the *Prime Material Plane* would probably be completely drained of all life and energy.

The Elemental Planes

The planes of *Air, Earth, Fire* and *Water* "surround" the *Prime Material Plane*. Fig. 1 shows one way of visualizing their relationship to each other and the other *Inner Planes*. The *Elemental Planes* are represented by the band that surrounds the *Prime Material Plane(s)*. Don't be fooled by the apparent sizes of the planes represented in Fig. 1. There are an infinite number of parallel *Prime Material Planes*, and each and every one of these are bounded by the *Elemental Planes*, so the *Elemental Planes* are themselves infinite, in effect. Fig. 2 shows one way of visualizing the *Elemental Planes'* relationship to each other. It is possible to actually physically move from one *Elemental Plane* to another by moving through the *Para-Elemental Planes*.

The *Elemental Planes* are the homes of many different kinds of elemental creatures, and some of them have the ability to travel to the *Prime Material Plane*. There is probably more traffic between the *Prime Material* and the *Elemental* planes than between any others. This is usually either direct travel (through *gates* or *summoning*) or by way of the *Ethereal Plane*. There are also *nexial points* in distant, out-of-the-way places on the *Prime Material Plane* that lead directly to the *Elemental Planes*. These *nexial points* would most likely be found in the deepest ocean (to the *Plane of Water*), high in the atmosphere (to the *Plane of Air*), far underground (to the *Plane of Earth*), or in an active volcano (to the *Plane of Fire*). Temporary *nexial points* may also be established occasionally, such as an opening to the *Elemental Plane of Fire* in the middle of a raging forest fire.

The Para-Elemental Planes

Where the *Elemental Planes* meet are the lesser *Para-elemental Planes*. These are:

The *Plane of Ice*, where *Air* and *Water* meet.
The *Plane of Dust*, at the conjunction of *Air* and *Fire*.
The *Plane of Heat*, where *Fire* and *Earth* converge (lava).
The *Plane of Vapor*, at the meeting of *Earth* and *Water*.

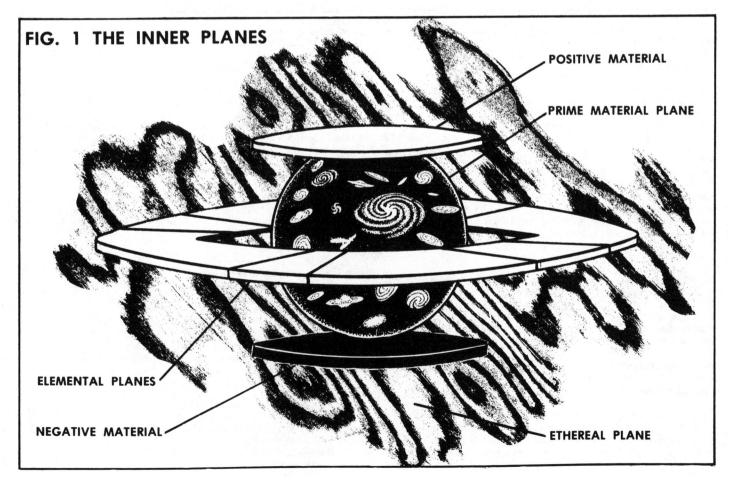

FIG. 1 THE INNER PLANES

POSITIVE MATERIAL

PRIME MATERIAL PLANE

ELEMENTAL PLANES

NEGATIVE MATERIAL

ETHEREAL PLANE

FIG. 2 THE ELEMENTAL PLANES

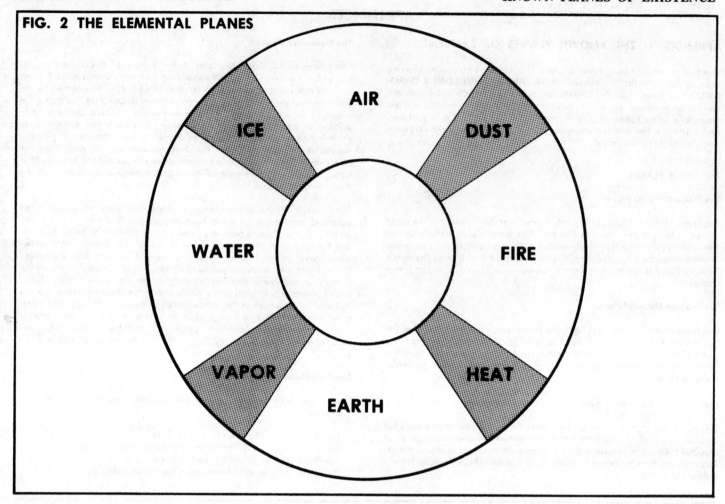

These planes are home to many para-elementals, and they can be reached in the same manners the *Elemental Planes* can be reached.

The Ethereal Plane

The *Ethereal Plane* surrounds, touches and permeates all of the *Inner Planes* and the endless parallel worlds of the universe without being a part of them. The *Ethereal Plane* is basically insubstantial, and few "real" creatures actually live there (though there are rumors of floating islands of solid ether, populated by exiles, which drift about the *Ethereal Plane*). To creatures on the *Ethereal Plane*, objects on the *Prime Material Plane* (or any of the *Inner Planes*) appear as incorporeal phantoms. Ethereal creatures may pass through these phantoms with no difficulty, although a person being "passed through" might experience a chill down the spine. Ethereal beings or things are "real" to each other, however. Note that the *Ethereal Plane* does not extend to the *Outer Planes*, so it is not possible for creatures on those planes to "go ethereal". Ethereal travel and combat are explained later.

The Plane of Shadow

The *Plane of Shadow* co-exists with the *Prime Material Plane*, and is a result of the interaction of that plane and the *Positive* and *Negative Material Planes*. The *Negative* plane provides the darkness, and the *Positive* plane the light; these meet at the *Prime Material Plane*, which casts the shadow. Thus the *Plane of Shadow* is a place of distorted and mutable shadow-creatures, of white, black and all shades of gray.

THE OUTER PLANES

The Astral Plane

This plane radiates from the *Prime Material* to a non-space where endless vortices spiral to the parallel *Prime Material Planes*, and to the *Outer Planes* as well. This plane can be used to travel to distant worlds, to parallel planes, or to the *Outer Planes* themselves. Note that the *Astral Plane* touches only the upper layer of each of the *Outer Planes*, and of the

Inner Planes it touches only the *Prime Material*, see Fig. 3. Astral travel and combat are explained later.

The Outer Planes of Alignment

These planes are the homes of the deities and the source of alignment (religious/philosophical/ethical ideals). There is an exact correspondence between alignment and the *Outer Planes*. Figure 4 and Figure 5 can be used to visualize this more clearly. Note that the alignment positions on the Character Alignment Graph match up exactly with the *Outer Planes* of identical alignment. There are nine basic alignments, and nine planes which correspond to those alignments. There are also eight other planes between the nine which represent "borderline" alignments.

As Fig. 4 shows, alignment is a matter of degree rather than absolute definition. Thus, a lawful evil character who tended towards neutral evil would probably end up in *Gehenna* rather than *Hades* or the *Nine Hells*. The seventeen *Outer Planes* are as follows:

The *Seven Heavens* of absolute lawful good.
The *Twin Paradises* of lawful/neutral good.
The layers of *Elysium* of neutral good.
The *Happy Hunting Grounds* of chaotic/neutral good.
The layers of *Olympus* of absolute chaotic good.
The layers of *Gladsheim* (Asgard, Vanaheim, etc.) of neutral/good chaotics.
The layers of *Limbo* of neutral (absolute) chaos.
The layers of *Pandemonium* of neutral/evil chaotics.
The 666 layers of the *Abyss* of absolute chaotic evil.
The layers of *Tarterus* of neutral/chaotic evil.
Hades' "Three Glooms" of neutral (absolute) evil.
The furnaces of *Gehenna* of neutral/lawful evil.
The *Nine Hells* of absolute lawful evil.
The nether layers of *Acheron* of neutral/evil law.
Nirvana of neutral (absolute) law.
The layers of *Arcadia* of neutral/good law.
The plane of *Concordant Opposition* of true neutrals.

FIG. 3 THE OUTER PLANES

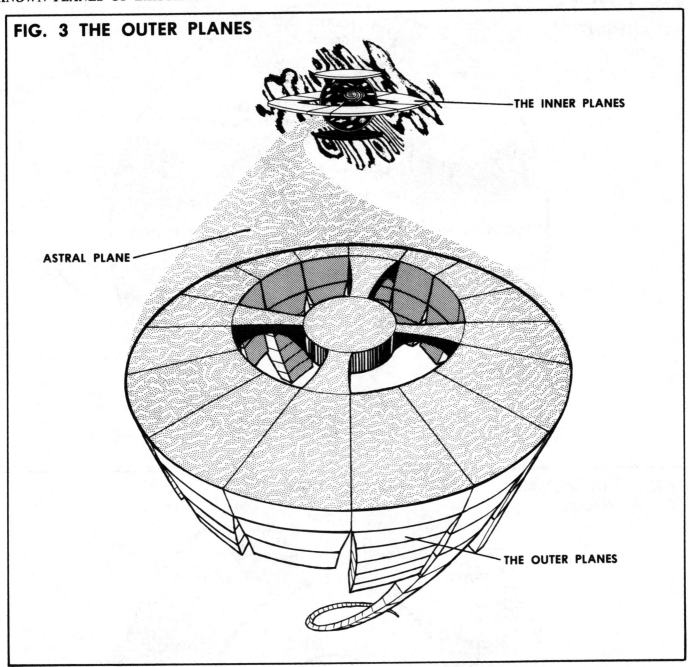

THE INNER PLANES

ASTRAL PLANE

THE OUTER PLANES

As can be seen from Fig. 3, the seventeen *Outer Planes* contact each other at their topmost layers. It is possible to move directly from the upper layer of one *Outer Plane* to an *adjacent* one (though it is not necessarily advisable or safe). Thus a being could go from the topmost layer of the *Abyss* to *Pandemonium* or *Tarterus*, and it is likewise possible to move from *Hades* to *Tarterus*, *Gehenna*, or the plane of *Concordant Opposition*.

ETHEREAL TRAVEL AND COMBAT

A character can achieve the ethereal state (move to the *Ethereal Plane*) by various means which include magic spells, magic items, magical ointment (*oil of etherealness*) or psionic discipline. It is possible to move to or about any of the *Inner Planes* which the *Ethereal Plane* permeates, and it is possible to move from plane to plane ethereally. To move on the *Ethereal Plane*, an entity has but to will movement for it to happen. If concentration upon movement lapses, progress immediately halts. Ethereal travel is tireless and rapid. Creatures in ethereal state need neither food, drink, rest nor sleep. Ethereal creatures may move from plane to plane by moving from the shadow of one plane to the shadow of another. This may be accomplished by concentrating upon moving to the desired destination. This gets easier with practice, as the being marks out a mental "trail" through

the ether. The first time a journey between two points is made, the DM should check for encounters three times. On the second journey, he or she should check twice, and on all subsequent journeys between the two known points, only one check need be made.

All movement and travel in the *Ethereal Plane* is subject to certain hazards. Some monsters are able to function partially in this plane, while some roam the plane freely. The worst hazard, however, is the *Ether Cyclone*. All these dangers are detailed below.

Ethereal Encounters

Encounters occur on a 1 in 20; if the party is following an unfamiliar "path", check three times total: at the beginning, midpoint, and at the end of the journey. If an encounter is indicated, consult the **Ethereal Encounter Table** (below) and roll percentile dice. Read to the right on the table to find the creature (and number) encountered. Evasion is possible only if the adventurers are able to move more quickly than the monster encountered. This will occur if the party is both following a familiar "path" and the least-intelligent member of the party has a higher intelligence score than the most-intelligent pursuer (due to the fact that ethereal travel is a function of mental concentration).

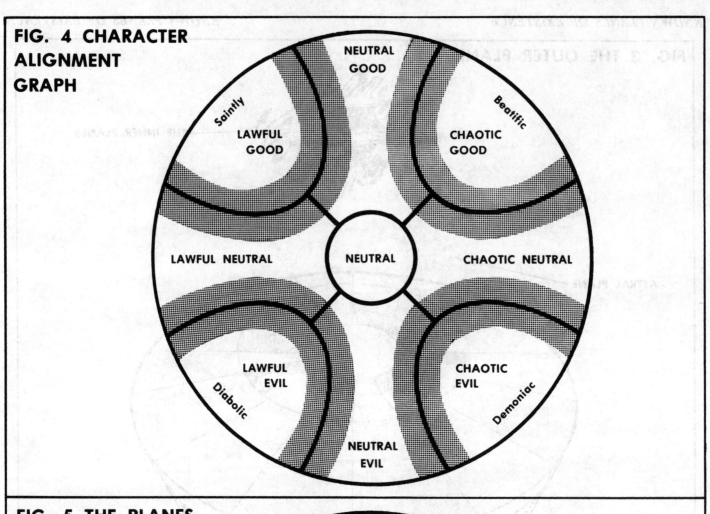

FIG. 4 CHARACTER ALIGNMENT GRAPH

NEUTRAL GOOD

Saintly

LAWFUL GOOD

Beatific

CHAOTIC GOOD

LAWFUL NEUTRAL

NEUTRAL

CHAOTIC NEUTRAL

LAWFUL EVIL

Diabolic

CHAOTIC EVIL

Demoniac

NEUTRAL EVIL

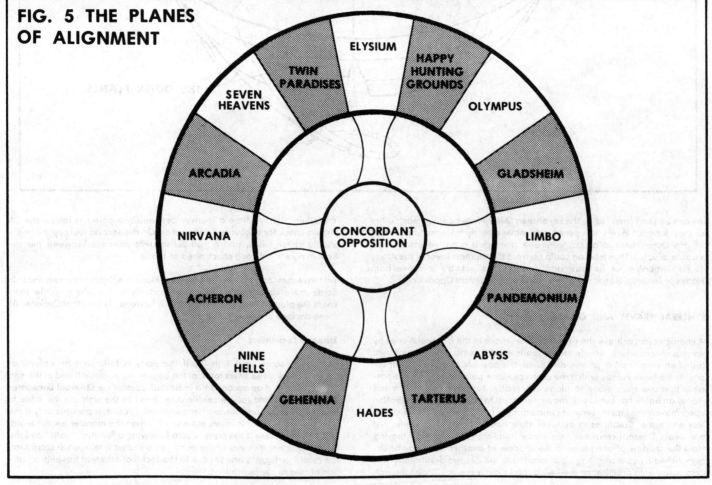

FIG. 5 THE PLANES OF ALIGNMENT

ELYSIUM

TWIN PARADISES

HAPPY HUNTING GROUNDS

SEVEN HEAVENS

OLYMPUS

ARCADIA

GLADSHEIM

NIRVANA

CONCORDANT OPPOSITION

LIMBO

ACHERON

PANDEMONIUM

NINE HELLS

ABYSS

GEHENNA

TARTERUS

HADES

Ethereal Encounter Table

Dice Score	Creature Encountered	Numbers
01-04	Aerial servant	1
05-08	Basilisk*	1-2
09-11	Cockatrice*	1-4
12-16	Couatl	1-4
17-23	Djinni	1-6
24	Dragon, chromatic	1
25	Dragon, platinum	1
26-27	Efreeti	1-3
28-32	Elemental, air	1
33-34	Elemental, earth	1
35-36	Elemental, fire	1
37	Elemental, water	1
38-42	Ghost	1
43-44	Gorgon*	1-2
45-46	Groaning spirit	1-2
47-51	Human traveller — see **Character Subtable****	
52-53	Intellect devourer	1-2
54-56	Invisible stalker	1-3
57-61	Ki-rin	1
62-68	Lammasu	2-8
69-70	Medusa*	1-2
71-72	Nightmare	1-4
73-74	Salamander	2-5
75-77	Shedu	1
78-81	Spider, phase	1-6
82-88	Thought eater	1-3
89	Titan, elder	1
90-92	Titan, lesser	1
93-94	Titan, major	1
95-97	Wind walker	2-5
98-00	Xorn	3-6

* These creatures' perceptions extend into the *Astral* and *Ethereal Planes* (as do their magical attack forms), but they do not actually travel therein. Their possible appearance applies only to situations in which the encountering party is near to the *Prime Material Plane*, and could therefore possibly be affected by the creatures' attack forms.

** The **Character Subtable** used for **DUNGEON RANDOM MONSTER ENCOUNTERS** in the **DUNGEON MASTERS GUIDE** is used, with the following modifications: Party size will be only 1-6. No limits to the number of characters of one class apply. There will always be 1 cleric; if there are 2 or more in the party, there will also be a minimum of 1 magic-user. Character level will be:

CLERIC	9th - 18th
Druid	7th - 14th
FIGHTER	8th - 15th
Paladin	7th - 16th
Ranger	7th - 16th
MAGIC-USER	11th - 20th
Illusionist	10th - 17th
THIEF	9th - 16th
Assassin	10th - 15th
MONK	8th - 17th
BARD†	11th - 18th

† 7th or 8th level fighter ability, 6th to 9th level (d4 +5) thief ability.

The Ether Cyclone

The twisting vortex of the *Ether Cyclone* is caused by fluctuations of the *Inner Planes*, and as such is only encountered on ethereal journeys between planes. There is a non-cumulative 5% chance per plane crossed that a party will encounter the *Ether Cyclone*. The effects of being caught in the *Cyclone* are detailed below:

Dice Score	Effect Of Cyclone
1-10	Blows so as to move party in random direction at 120' per round, and if travelling is involved, party is slowed so as to incur 1 additional encounter check.
11-15	Blows to a plane different than that which the party is near or desires to travel to; the usual encounter checks must be made.
16-18	Blows so as to cause party to be lost for 5-60 days, and when no longer lost the party will arrive at a different plane as determined by random means.
19-20	Storm cyclone causes party to be lost for 10-120 days, and unless saving throw versus spells is made, the party is blown to the *Astral Plane*. If a save is successful, then party will still arrive at a randomly determined plane touched by the ether.

Ethereal Combat

Though the *Inner Planes* are mere phantoms to creatures on the *Ethereal Plane*, such creatures will certainly be "real" to each other, and normal melee or spell casting is possible between ethereal beings. It is also possible to combat creatures who exist or function partially on the *Ethereal Plane*. Thus, those creatures whose attack forms extend to the ethereal can be attacked by ethereal creatures. It is only in these instances that spells can be cast from the *Ethereal* to the *Prime Material Plane*, and then they will only affect the creature with ethereal connections. Ethereal combat damage is actual damage.

ASTRAL TRAVEL AND COMBAT

Astral travel is possible by various means including magic spells and psionic discipline. The *Astral Plane* touches only the endless *Prime Material Plane* and the 17 "first layers" of the *Outer Planes*. The *Astral Plane* does not touch any of the *Inner Planes* other than the *Prime Material Plane*. It is possible to move about, in, or to any of the *Prime Material* universes or to the first layers of the *Outer Planes* by means of astral travel (see the clerical *astral spell* for pertinent details). As with ethereal travel, movement through the *Astral Plane* is speedy, and while there the individual needs no food, drink, rest or even sleep.

Beings in an astral state move from place to place simply by concentrating upon moving to the desired destination. As with ethereal travel, this gets easier with practice, as the astral traveller "learns the way". The DM should check for encounters three times on the first journey between two points, twice on the second journey, and only once on any subsequent journeys.

Astral Encounters

Encounters in the *Astral Plane* occur on a 1 in 20 chance; check one, two or three times per journey, depending on the party's familiarity with the route followed. Use the table below to determine creature(s) encountered. Evasion is handled as described under **Ethereal Encounters** (q.v.).

Astral Encounter Table

Dice Score	Creature Encountered	Numbers
01-04	Aerial servant	1
05-10	Basilisk*	1-2
11-13	Cockatrice*	1-4
14-16	Demon, major	1
17-22	Demon, minor	1-3
23	Demon, prince	1
24	Devil, arch-	1
25-28	Devil, greater-	1
29-37	Devil, lesser-	1-3
38	Dragon, chromatic	1
39	Dragon, platinum	1
40-41	Gorgon*	1-2
42-46	Human traveller — see **Character Subtable****	
47-49	Intellect devourer	1-2
50-55	Invisible stalker	1-3
56-61	Ki-rin	1
62-63	Medusa*	1-2
64-71	Night hag	1-4
72-74	Nightmare	1-4
75-79	Rakshasa	1-3
80-91	Shedu	2-5
92	Titan, elder	1
93-97	Titan, lesser	1
98-00	Titan, major	1

*See beneath **Ethereal Encounter Table**.

See beneath **Ethereal Encounter Table.

The Psychic Wind

Perhaps the most dangerous thing that can happen to an astral traveller is getting caught in the *psychic wind*. No one knows how or why the wind blows, but all fear its effects. The chance of a delayed or disrupted journey is a non-cumulative 5% per plane crossed (including alternate worlds of the *Prime Material*) or solar system travelled to (if journeying across the *Prime Material*). The effects of the *psychic wind* are shown below:

Dice Score	Effect Of Wind
1-12	Slows travel only, incur 1 additional check for random encounter.
13-16	Blows off course, and party is lost for 2-20 days' time, then must return to starting place.
17-19	Blows off course so that party arrives at a different destination as determined by random method.
20	Storm blows, and unless a saving throw versus magic is made, the silver cord is broken, and the party is killed. If a save is successful, the party is lost for 4-40 days and must return to the starting place thereafter.

Note: If *astral projection* does not involve a silver cord attachment, then the party concerned is both lost and arrives at a different destination when struck by a *psychic storm wind*.

Astral Combat

As on the *Ethereal Plane*, astral beings are "real" to each other, and can cast spells and melee normally. The major impediment to these activities is that astral travellers employing an *astral spell* or the psionic *astral projection* discipline do not carry their possessions with them into the *Astral Plane* (except for certain magic items that have a multi-planar existence, e.g. an *amulet of the planes*). Beings travelling astrally by these modes will therefore have to rely on their natural weaponry or spells without material components in any astral melee. Most creatures can do no more than destroy the astral body, causing the *silver cord* to return to the material body and preventing further astral travel for a period of time. Very powerful beings (gods, demigods, etc.) might be able to snap the silver cord, thus killing the astral and material bodies simultaneously.

PLANAR TRAVEL

The purpose of this section is to sum up all of the information that has been stated or implied about planar travel. First, travel among the *Inner Planes*: this is usually done by means of the *Ethereal Plane*, as it permeates all of the *Inner Planes*. (It is not possible for creatures on the *Outer Planes* to "go ethereal".) As with all planar travel, it is also possible to pass directly from one plane to another by means of "gates", thereby avoiding ethereal travel. A gate may be formed by a magic spell (such as a *gate* spell, or *conjure elemental*, which forms a direct opening between the planes) a magic item (e.g. an *amulet of the planes*, a *well of many worlds*, a *cubic gate*, or any of the various elemental-summoning devices), or divine intervention. There are also direct *nexial points* connecting the *Prime Material* and *Elemental Planes*.

Travel to and from the *Outer Planes* is usually by means of gates or via the *Astral Plane*. (Note that the *Astral Plane* can only be entered from the *Prime Material Plane* or one of the "first layers" of the 17 *Outer Planes*.) If a being is gated to one of the *Outer Planes*, he comes complete with body and possessions, leaving no part of himself behind. However, if a being astrally projects and travels the *Astral Plane* to one of the *Outer Planes*, he leaves his material body behind on the *Prime Material Plane*, connected to his essence by a *silver cord*. If his material body is destroyed or the silver cord is snapped while he is in the *Astral Plane*, the being is permanently and irrevocably killed. If he moves to one of the *Outer Planes* from the *Astral Plane*, a body forms around him, but it is devoid of possessions. Both bodies are now connected by the silver cord, and if either body is destroyed, the being will continue on in the remaining body (returning instantly to the *Prime Material* if the *Outer Plane* body is killed). If the silver cord is snapped on the *Astral Plane*, the unoccupied body dies.

Random Determination of Planes

If for some reason it becomes necessary to choose a plane of existence at random, the following tables may be used:

Inner Planes

Die Roll	Plane
1-2	Prime Material Plane
3	Prime Material Plane (alternate world)
4	Positive Material Plane
5	Negative Material Plane
6-7	Elemental Plane of Air
8-9	Elemental Plane of Earth
10-11	Elemental Plane of Fire
12-13	Elemental Plane of Water
14	Para-Elemental Plane of Dust
15	Para-Elemental Plane of Heat
16	Para-Elemental Plane of Ice
17	Para-Elemental Plane of Vapor
18-19	Ethereal Plane
20	Plane of Shadow

Outer Planes

Die Roll	Plane
1-3	Astral Plane
4	Seven Heavens
5	Twin Paradises
6	Elysium
7	Happy Hunting Grounds
8	Olympus
9	Gladsheim
10	Limbo
11	Pandemonium
12	Abyss
13	Tarterus
14	Hades
15	Gehenna
16	Nine Hells
17	Acheron
18	Nirvana
19	Arcadia
20	Concordant Opposition

APPENDIX 2: TEMPLE TRAPPINGS

The listing below gives a representative sample of typical items that might be found in a temple of some of the deities listed in this work. Any worshipers or servitors of the temple should be keyed by the DM. The DM should choose from the list to stock the temple, using random selection only to fill in details or in spur-of-the-moment situations. Note that some of the items below will not be applicable to certain religions (e.g., no flame pits for living sacrifices in a lawful good temple).

01-05	altar	51-52	incense burners
06-07	bells	53-54	lectern/dais
08-09	braziers	55-56	mosaics
10-11	candlesticks	57-61	offertory
12	chalice	62-63	paintings
13	chimes	64	pedal organ
14	choir area	65-68	pews
15-16	cassocks	69	prayer wheels
17-18	cloth, altar	70-74	pulpit
19-22	columns	75-79	robes
23-24	crypts/floor marker stones	80	sacrifice
25	flame pit	81-82	sanctuary
26-27	font/immersion chamber	83	scrolls
28-29	gong	84-86	shrine
30-35	holy/unholy books and tomes	87	stained glass
36-40	holy/unholy inscriptions	88-91	statue
41-45	holy/unholy symbols	92-95	tapestry
46	holy/unholy treasure	96	throne
47-48	holy/unholy weapons (non-magical)	97-98	vestry
49-50	idol/icon	99-00	vestments

APPENDIX 3: CLERICAL QUICK-REFERENCE CHARTS

This listing has been provided for quick reference when specific information about a cleric's religion is needed. Deities are arranged alphabetically within their pantheon, except that the most important deity is listed first. The information presented here is to be used as guidelines only — all clerics of one deity will not necessarily dress identically, for example. Rank within the temple is often differentiated by variations in color, lining or stripes, etc. Special sacrifices and holy days may be ordained at any time, at the pleasure of the temple (or its deity).

SPHERE OF CONTROL: This refers to the item, condition, or element over which the deity exerts some measure of control (e.g. Air, Rain, The Hunt, Affairs of the Heart, etc.).

ANIMAL: The animal or animals listed here are the ones most commonly associated with or sacred to that deity. Clerics of this deity will often protect this type of animal. Some deities are not associated with an animal, however.

CLERICS: This describes whether the clerics of this deity can be male (M), female (F), or non-human (N-H).

RAIMENT: This is the prescribed form of adornment for a cleric of this deity. This may include: robes, headdresses, hairstyles, tattoos, makeup, physical disfigurations (e.g. a notched ear, misshapen head, etc.), ornaments or jewelry, footwear, etc.

COLOR(S): This lists the colors, if any, associated with the deity or its clerics. Items using these colors might include ceremonial robes, altar drapings, candles, holy banners, etc.

HOLY DAYS: This listing gives the highest holy days associated with a deity and its worshipers. Sacrifices, rituals, and prayers on these days are more likely to be heard and acknowledged by the deity. Note that acknowledgement is *not* the same thing as granting a prayer or request!

SACRIFICE/PROPITIATION: Listed here are both the frequency and form of sacrifices expected of the worshipers of this deity. In addition, tithings and actual sacrifices should be made by a dutiful worshiper when grateful (returning from an adventure alive, for example), repentant, begging a favor (removal of famine from the area, etc.), and so on. Actual items of sacrifice may include: animals, monsters, humans (or non-humans), food or crops, items of wealth (jewelry, fine linens, rare woods, etc.), items of power (magic), incenses and perfumes, services, etc. The way these items are offered to the deity may vary greatly, but include: libation, cremation, vivisection, burial, immersion in holy water, casting into a pit, et al.

PLACE OF WORSHIP: This gives the most common locale or construction, whether natural or man-made, in which clerics of the deity gather (with or without a congregation) to worship that deity.

DEITY	SPHERE OF CONTROL	ANIMAL	CLERICS M	F	N-H	RAIMENT HEAD	BODY	COLOR(S)	HOLY DAYS	SACRIFICE/PROPITIATION FREQUENCY	FORM	PLACE OF WORSHIP
AMERICAN INDIAN MYTHOS												
Raven	nature; creation	raven	X	X		bare	loincloth	black	n/a	varies	offerings	fireside
Coyote	knowledge	coyote	X	X		feather	rawhide vest	brown	n/a	varies	offerings	fireside
Hastseltsi	racing	hawk or horse	X	X		feather	deerskin vest	maroon	n/a	varies	offerings	mountainside
Hastsezini	fire	snake	X	X		bare	snake fang ornaments	jade green	n/a	varies	self inflicted wounds	tribal center
Heng	thunder; weather	eagle	X	X		feather	amber studs	amber	solstices	varies	offerings	tribal center
Hotoru	wind; weather	falcon	X	X		fur cap	fur tunic	gray	spring equinox	varies	berry juices	fireside
Shakak	winter	wolf	X	X		fur cap	fur tunic	white	winter solstice	varies (in winter)	offerings	in the wild
Snake-Man	reptiles	snake	X	X	X	bare	loincloth	emerald	n/a	varies	crafted item	fireside
Tobadzistsini	war	ant	X	X		bare	war harness	blood red	n/a	varies	war trophy	tribal center
BABYLONIAN MYTHOS												
Anu	sky	dragon	X	X		brass skullcap	kilt	azure	full moon	monthly	gems	temple
Anshar	darkness	raven	X	X		bald	kilt	deep gray	winter solstice	annually	precious metals	temple

DEITY	SPHERE OF CONTROL	ANIMAL	CLERICS M	F	N-H	RAIMENT HEAD	BODY	COLOR(S)	HOLY DAYS	SACRIFICE FREQUENCY	SACRIFICE/PROPITIATION FORM	PLACE OF WORSHIP
Druaga	devils	devil	X	X		bald	breech cloth	yellow	full moon	monthly	humans	temple
Girru	fire	phoenix	X	X		bald	leather armor	scarlet	equinox	semiannually	precious metals	temple
Ishtar	love; war	lion	X	X		pointed helm	bronze mail	sapphire	new moon	monthly	weapons	temple, battlefield
Marduk	cities; weather	any bird	X	X	X	bald	gold badge	gold	quarter moon	monthly	jewelry	temple
Nergal	underworld	earth grub	X	X		bald	black robes	black	new moon	monthly	good creatures	temple
Ramman	storms	seagull	X	X		bald	kilt	amber	full moon	monthly	precious liquids	temple
CELTIC MYTHOS												
Dagda	authority; rulership	n/a	X			knit cap	kilt	earth	new moon	monthly	spilt wine	grove
Arawn	death	n/a		X		helm	kilt	black	n/a	at death	valuables	grave
Brigit	fire; poetry	n/a	X	X		helm	kilt	vermilion	n/a	in battle	verse	battlefield
Diancecht	healing	n/a	X	X		bare	kilt	hazel	new moon	monthly	burnt herbs	forest temple
Dunatis	mountains	n/a	X			leather cap	boots	roan	n/a	varies	precious metals	mountains
Goibhnie	metalworking	n/a	X	X	X	bare	kilt	iron	n/a	varies	weapons	forge, temple
Lugh	generality	n/a	X	X		bare	kilt	off-white	n/a	varies	spilt wine	anywhere
Manannan Mac Lir	sea	n/a	X	X		helm	kilt	emerald	n/a	varies	gold	shipboard, coast
Morrigan	war	n/a	X	X		helm	armor	carmine	n/a	in battle	enemy casualties	battlefield
Nuada	war	n/a	X	X		helm	armor	silver	n/a	in battle	silver	battlefield
Oghma	knowledge	n/a	X	X		bare	kilt	gray	n/a	varies	extension of knowledge	anywhere
Silvanus	nature	n/a	X	X		bare	kilt	sapphire	equinox	varies	tree planting	forest
CENTRAL AMERICAN MYTHOS												
Quetzalcoatl	air	snake	X	X		feathered helm	feathered cloak	lemon yellow	new moon	monthly	gold	temple
Camaxtli	fate	lizard	X	X		jeweled helm	feathered kilt	gold	full moon	monthly	precious metals	temple
Camazotz	bats; evil	bat	X	X	X	leather helm	leather armor	saffron	quarter moon	varies	insects	caves
Chalchiuhtlicue	life; love; water	fish	X	X		shell helm	feathered cloak	jade green	n/a	varies	jade	temple
Huhueteotl	fire	phoenix	X	X		leather helm	leather armor	cherry red	n/a	waning moon	humans, precious metals	active volcanoes
Huitzilopochtli	war	eagle	X			feathered helm	metal armor	scarlet	n/a	varies	human heart	battlefield
Itzamna	healing	any bird	X	X		feathered helm	feathered cloak	yellow	equinox	spring	burnt herbs, squirrels	gardens, fields

DEITY	SPHERE OF CONTROL	ANIMAL	CLERICS M	F	N-H	RAIMENT HEAD	BODY	COLOR(S)	HOLY DAYS	SACRIFICE/OBLATION FREQUENCY	OBLATION FORM	PLACE OF WORSHIP
Mictlantecuhtli	death	dog	X	X		feathered helm	leather armor	maroon	n/a	new moon	human hearts	temple
Tezcatlipoca	sun	jaguar	X	X		jeweled helm	feathered kilt	orange	spring equinox	annually	human hearts	temple
Tlaloc	rain	deer	X	X		leather helm	feathered cloak	ash gray	spring equinox	annually	human babies	temple
Tlazolteotl	vice	ocelot	X	X	X	feathered helm	expensive kilt	orange	n/a	varies	gems	temple
Xochipilli	gambling; chance	monkey	X	X		jeweled helm	feathered vest	copper	n/a	varies	flowers	anywhere
CHINESE MYTHOS												
Shang-Ti	leadership	sparrow	X	X		bald	tattered robes	gold	first day of spring	annually	gems	temple
Chao Kung Ming	war	tiger	X			helm	splint mail	blood red	n/a	before war	ritual weapons	temple
Chih-Chiang Fyu-Ya	archery	elephant	X			pointed cap	leather vest	green	spring equinox	annually	golden arrows	temple
Chih Sung-Tzu	rain	seagull	X	X		war helm	gray robe	blue	spring equinox	annually	spilt wine	fields, temple
Chung Kuel	truth	fox	X	X		bald	rich robes	white	new moon	monthly	crafted items	temple
Fei Lien & Feng Po	wind	eagle	X	X		bare	splint mail	pale blue	spring equinox	annually	spilt wine	temple
Huan-Ti	war	pegasus	X			war helm	red splint mail	red	full moon	monthly	war prizes	temple
Kuan Yin	mercy	nightingale	X	X		bare	green satin	pale green	full moon	monthly	requests	temple, home
Lei Kung	foul weather	raven	X			bare	black leather	deep gray	fall equinox	annually	gold	temple
Lu Yueh	epidemics	carrion bird	X			pointed cap	padded tunic	muddy yellow	full moon	monthly	gems	temple
No Cha	thieving	mockingbird	X	X		pocketed hat	pocketed tunic	silver	new moon	monthly	stolen items	temple
Shan Hai Ching	sea	whale	X	X		green cap	tunic	sea green	fall equinox	before ocean voyages	precious objects	temple, ship
Tou Mu	space	n/a	X			face-covering helm	black splint mail	midnight blue	winter solstice	annually	burnt offerings	temple
Wen Chung	thunderstorms	n/a	X			bald	silver belt	steel	rainy season	annually	silver coins	temple
Yen-Wang-Yeh	dead	winterhawk	X	X		bald	black tunic	inky black	equinox	semiannually	burnt offerings	temple
EGYPTIAN MYTHOS												
Ra	sun	hawk	X	X		gold helm	kilt	gold	equinox, solstice	often	valuables	temple
Anhur	war	lion	X			helm	leather	blood red	equinox	in battle; semiannually	enemies	temple
Anubis	guards dead	jackal	X	X		bare	onyx jewelry	black	full moon	monthly	valuables	temple
Apshai	insects	scarab	X	X	X	bare	yellow kilt	yellow	spring equinox	annually	animal	temple
Bast	felines	cat	X	X	X	cat helm	gray kilt	tan	full moon	monthly	snakes	temple, home
Bes	luck	fox	X	X		silvered helm	leather vest, kilt	orange	new moon	monthly	valuables	temple

Deity	Domain	Animal			Helm	Garb	Color	Holy Day	Frequency	Offering	Temple
Geb	earth	goose	X	X	n/a	ring mail	brown	half moon	monthly	precious stones	temple
Horus	vengeance	falcon	X	X	helm	war harness	bright blue	solstice	semiannually	precious fluids	temple, home
Isis	magic	gull	X	X	bare	scarlet kilt	crimson	full moon	monthly	valuables	temple
Nephthys	protection; wealth	raven	X	X	bare	black tunic	charcoal	new moon	monthly	valuables	temple
Osiris	nature; the dead	dog	X	X	bare	green tunic	bright green	equinox	semiannually	offerings	temple
Ptah	universe	dragon	X	X	black helm	jade ornaments	black, silver	new moon	monthly	precious stones	temple
Seker	light	sparrowhawk	X		feathered helm	white tunic	white	summer solstice	annually	jewelry	temple
Set	evil	serpent	X	X	black helm	leather tunic	emerald, black	full moon	monthly	valuables	temple
Shu	sky	ostrich	X	X	bare	blue vest	light blue	equinox	semiannually	gems	temple
Tefnut	storms; water	carp	X	X	scaled helm	leather vest	rusty red	spring equinox	annually	animal	temple
Thoth	knowledge	ibis	X	X	bare	cotton tunic	purple	equinox	semiannually	offerings	temple
FINNISH MYTHOS											
Ahto	water	turtle	X	X	shell helm	green cloak	sea green	spring equinox	annually	precious jewelry	special hall
Hiisi	evil	wolf	X	X	bare	leather cloak	maroon	n/a	n/a	n/a	n/a
Ilmatar	motherhood	dove	X		bare	white shift	white	full moon	monthly	crafted items	special hall
Kiputytto	sickness	worm	X	X	silver helm	black shift	gray	fall equinox	annually	gold cups	special hall
Loviatar	pain	fly	X		white fur cap	ivory cloak	ivory	winter solstice	annually	burnt offering	special hall
Mielikki	nature	elk	X	X	bare	green tunic	forest green	spring equinox	annually	burnt herbs	forest glens
Surma	death	fox	X	X	pointed fur cap	red boots	crimson	n/a	n/a	n/a	n/a
Tuonetar	underworld	spider	X	X	feathered helm	brown shift	charcoal black	n/a	n/a	n/a	n/a
Tuoni	underworld	snake	X	X	leather helm	leather vest	purple	n/a	n/a	n/a	n/a
Ukko	sky; air	eagle	X	X	war helm	chain mail	gold	full moon	monthly	silver armbands	special hall
Untamo	sleep; dreams	wood duck	X	X	bare	blue tunic	pale blue	new moon	monthly	precious liquids	special hall
GREEK MYTHOS											
Zeus	air	eagle	X	X	bare	tunic	white	red sunrise	full moon	cow	temple, grove
Aphrodite	love; beauty	dove		X	bare	tunic	ivory	spring	every 10 days	artistic creation	temple
Apollo	sun; music; archery	falcon	X		laurel wreath	tunic	gold	every 10 days in summer	new moon	valuables	temple, cave
Ares	war	wolf	X	X	helm	breastplate	crimson	wartime	before battles	ox	battlefield
Artemis	hunt; moon	deer	X	X	bare	deerskin	moss green	equinox	full moon	deer	glen

DEITY	SPHERE OF CONTROL	ANIMAL	CLERICS M	CLERICS F	CLERICS N-H	RAIMENT HEAD	RAIMENT BODY	COLOR(S)	HOLY DAYS	SACRIFICE/PROPITIATION FREQUENCY	SACRIFICE/PROPITIATION FORM	PLACE OF WORSHIP
Athena	wisdom; combat	owl	X	X		helm	armor or tunic	gray	n/a	new moon	cow	temple
Demeter	agriculture	cow	X	X		bare	tunic	green	spring equinox	annually	seeds	field, temple
Dionysus	wine	dolphin	X	X		bare	tunic	purple	spring equinox	annually	spilt wine	anywhere
Hades	underworld	nightmare	X	X	X	helm	armor	black	n/a	at death	valuables	grave
Hecate	magic	hell hound	X	X		bare	tunic	blue-white	fall equinox	monthly at full moon	ox	mountain glen
Hephaestus	blacksmiths	bull	X		X	bare	leather apron	bronze	n/a	varies	gold, gems	forge
Hera	marriage; intrigue	peacock	X	X		bare	tunic	iridescent blue	full moon	monthly	hair	temple
Hermes	thieves; liars; gamblers	fox	X	X		winged cap	tunic	silver	n/a	seldom	bird feathers	temple, open plain
Nike	victory	pegasus	X	X		olive wreath	tunic	red	spring thaw	victory	ox	temple
Pan	nature	satyr	X		X	wreath	fur	olive	spring equinox	annually	fowl	glen
Poseidon	sea; earthquakes	horse	X	X	X	bare	tunic	blue-green	n/a	varies	fish	temple
Prometheus	creation	man	X	X		bare	tunic	amber	equinox	never	n/a	home
Tyche	good fortune	bluebird	X	X		bare	tunic	blue	n/a	varies	spilt wine	anywhere

INDIAN MYTHOS

DEITY	SPHERE OF CONTROL	ANIMAL	CLERICS M	CLERICS F	CLERICS N-H	RAIMENT HEAD	RAIMENT BODY	COLOR(S)	HOLY DAYS	SACRIFICE/PROPITIATION FREQUENCY	SACRIFICE/PROPITIATION FORM	PLACE OF WORSHIP
Indra	air; storms; rain	elephant	X			bald	multicolored robes	rainbow	n/a	monthly	valuables	temple
Agni	fire; lightning	tiger	X	X		bald	orange robes	orange-red	n/a	monthly	burnt butter	temple
Kali	evil	snake	X	X	X	bald	black robes	black	n/a	often	human blood	temple, underground
Karttikeya	war	peacock	X			bald	blue leather armor	blue	before battle	before battle	weapons	temple, battlefield
Lakshmi	fortune	cobra	X	X		bald	gold robes	gold	n/a	monthly	lotus	temple
Ratri	night; thieves	monkey	X	X	X	bald	dark gray robes	dark gray	new moon	monthly	stolen items	temple
Rudra	storms; the dead	jackal	X	X		bald, black hood	red robes	red, black	n/a	at death	valuables	temple, grave
Surya	sun	pegasus	X	X		bald	red robes	red	summer solstice	annually	gold, horses	temple
Tvashtri	artifice; science	mongoose	X	X	X	bald	green robes	green	n/a	monthly	crafted items	temple, workshop
Ushas	dawn	songbirds		X		bald, red hood	gold robes	red, gold	n/a	monthly, at dawn	precious stones	temple
Varuna	order; oaths	dog	X	X		bald	white robes	white	full moon	monthly	valuables	temple
Vishnu	mercy; light	bird	X	X	X	bald	silver chain mail	silver	new moon	monthly	beautiful offerings	temple
Yama	death	water buffalo	X			bald	red robes with copper tracery	red, copper	n/a	at death	tales of dead one's deeds, valuables	temple, grave or pyre

DEITY	SPHERE OF CONTROL	ANIMAL	CLERICS M	F	N-H	RAIMENT HEAD	BODY	COLOR(S)	HOLY DAYS	SACRIFICE/PROPITIATION FREQUENCY	SACRIFICE/PROPITIATION FORM	PLACE OF WORSHIP
JAPANESE MYTHOS												
Amaterasu Omikami	sun	goldfish	X	X		bare	green vestments	gold	solstice	semiannually	handicrafts	temple
Ama-Tsu-Mara	blacksmiths	badger	X	X		leather cap	leather vest	black	equinox	semiannually	metalwork	hearth
Daikoku	wealth; luck	swan	X	X		blue cap	gray robes	yellow	solstice	semiannually	precious metals	temple
Ebisu	luck; work	bee	X	X		bare	brown robes	light green	spring equinox	annually	precious fluids	temple
Hachiman	war	bear	X			helm	splint mail	emerald green	fall equinox	annually	weapons	temple
Kishijoten	fate	dove	X	X		bare	white vestments	white	solstice	semiannually	written wishes	temple
Oh-Kuni-Nushi	heroism	tiger	X	X		bare	war vestments	scarlet	n/a	n/a	used weapons	temple
Raiden	weather	goose	X	X		red cap	crimson vestments	amber	solstice	semiannually	gems	temple
Susanowo	storms; seas	whale	X	X		bare	hide tunic	sea green	full moon	monthly	jade	temple
Tsukiyomi	moon	nightingale	X	X		bare	dark blue vestments	light blue	new moon	monthly	ivory	temple
NEHWON MYTHOS												
Aarth	knowledge	cheetah	X	X		bald	white kilt	tan	new year's day	annually	jewelry	temple
Death	death	raven	X	X	X	black helm	plate mail	black	n/a	n/a	n/a	n/a
Gods of Lankhmar	Lankhmar	n/a	X	X		skull cap	cloth wrappings	dark yellow	year's end	n/a	n/a	temple
Gods of Trouble	evil fate	n/a	X	X		n/a	n/a	amber	n/a	n/a	n/a	n/a
Hate	harm; hate	n/a	X	X		turban	cotton uniform	gray	fall equinox	annually	mental draining	underground temple
Issek of the Jug	suffering	n/a	X	X		bald	breechcloth	red	new year's day	annually	gold	outdoor temple
Kos	doom	polar bear	X	X		fur cap	fur tunic	white	spring equinox	annually	burnt offering	temple
Earth God	earth	n/a	X	X		felt cap	light tunic	red with black web	midsummer's day	monthly	human	temple
Rat God	underground areas	rat	X		X	bald	gray tunic	gray	spring equinox	annually	human	temple
Red God	fire	red-tailed hawk	X	X		pointed helm	red studded leather	bronze	summer solstice	annually	valuables	temple
Spider God	fear	spider	X	X		bald	black kilt	lime green	summer solstice	frequently	human	temple
Tyaa	evil birds	bird of Tyaa		X		tiara	cotton shift	silver	spring equinox	monthly	precious items	temple
Votishal	stealth	fox	X		X	leather cap	leather tunic	gold	new year's day	monthly	precious items	temple

CLERICAL QUICK REFERENCE CHART

NONHUMANS' DEITIES

DEITY	SPHERE OF CONTROL	ANIMAL	CLERICS M	CLERICS F	CLERICS N-H	RAIMENT HEAD	RAIMENT BODY	COLOR(S)	HOLY DAYS	SACRIFICE/PROPITIATION FREQUENCY	SACRIFICE/PROPITIATION FORM	PLACE OF WORSHIP
Blibdoolpoolp	Kuo-toa	lobster			X	shell helm	nets	pearl	new moon	monthly	gems, pearls, humans, lobsters	underwater shrines
Corellon Larethian	elves	n/a			X	silver circlet	gossamer robes	azure	quarter moon	monthly	beautiful objects	natural geological formations
Deep Sashelas	aquatic elves	dolphin			X	bare	shell mail	sea green	highest & lowest tides	varies	precious natural objects	undersea coral temples
Demogorgon	ixitxachitl	n/a			X	bare	n/a	reptile green	n/a	n/a	n/a	n/a
Eadro	locathah; mermen	jellyfish			X	bare	n/a	sand	n/a	n/a	n/a	dens
Garl Glittergold	gnomes	n/a			X	war helm	gold belt	gold	new moon	monthly	gold	cave halls
Grolantor	hill giants	dire wolf			X	skulls	horn armor	dark brown	n/a	n/a	n/a	n/a
Gruumsh	orcs	giant rat			X	war helm	black plate mail	dark red	new moon	monthly	blood	lairs
Hruggek	bugbears	n/a			X	skulls	bare	black	full moon	monthly	blood	cave halls
Kurtulmak	kobolds	rook			X	iron helm	scale mail	orange	crescent moon	monthly	enemies	cave temples
Laogzed	troglodytes	toad			X	bare	bone belt	topaz	midwinter's day	annually	burnt humans	natural caverns
Lolth	Drow	arachnids			X	Drow helm	Drow tunic	red & black	full moon	monthly	enemies & riches	underground marble temples
Maglubiyet	goblins	n/a			X	conical hat	scale mail	gray-green	new moon	monthly	hearts	cave temples
Moradin	dwarves	n/a			X	silvered helm	chain mail	earthy	crescent moon	monthly	melted metals	forges & hearths
Rillifane Rallathil	wood elves	forest birds			X	laurel wreath	tree bark armor	dark green	equinox	semiannually	carved items	tree platforms
Sekolah	sahuagin	shark			X	bare	n/a	gray-white	highest & lowest tides	varies	enemies	natural caverns
Semuanya	lizard men	alligator			X	bare	hide kilt	blue-green	full moon	monthly	hunting prizes	stone shrines
Skerrit	centaurs	n/a			X	bare	leafy vest	tan	full moon	monthly	ritual hunt, dances	large groves
Skoraeus Stonebones	stone giants	cave bear			X	bare	skins	stone gray	n/a	n/a	n/a	n/a
Surtur	fire giants	hell hound			X	war helm	iron plate mail	fiery red	midsummer's day	n/a	n/a	n/a
Thrym	frost giants	white dragon			X	horned helm	white fur	snowy white	midwinter's day	n/a	n/a	n/a
Vaprak	ogres	n/a			X	war helm	plate mail	blood red	n/a	n/a	n/a	dens
Yeenoghu	gnolls	n/a			X	skulls	long tunic	muddy yellow	quarter moon	monthly	blood	cave temples
Yondalla	halflings	dove			X	bare	saffron cloak	yellow-green	5th day of the week	weekly	food offering	homes

DEITY	SPHERE OF CONTROL	ANIMAL	CLERICS M	CLERICS F	CLERICS N-H	RAIMENT HEAD	RAIMENT BODY	COLOR(S)	HOLY DAYS	SACRIFICE/PROPITIATION FREQUENCY	SACRIFICE/PROPITIATION FORM	PLACE OF WORSHIP
NORSE MYTHOS												
Odin	authority; rulership	wolves, ravens	X			war helm	ring mail	sapphire	equinox	semiannually	burnt offering	temple hall
Aegir	storms; the sea	gull	X	X		felt cap	green cloak	emerald	half moon	monthly	burnt offering	temple hall
Balder	charisma	horse	X	X		silver helm	ring mail	silver	full moon	monthly	crafted items	meadows
Bragi	poetry; song	lark	X	X		pointed cap	costly tunic	crimson	equinox	semiannually	crafted items	meadows
Forseti	justice	owl	X	X		bare	ring mail	ivory	n/a	n/a	n/a	n/a
Frey	elves	unicorn	X	X	X	ornate helm	leather vest	bright green	n/a	n/a	n/a	n/a
Freya	love	falcon	X	X		ornate cap	yellow cloak	yellow	full moon	monthly	crafted items	temple hall
Frigga	weather	cat		X		bare	costly gown	sky blue	new moon	monthly	burnt offering	temple hall
Heimdall	gates; open paths	eagle	X			war helm	white plate mail	white	midyear's day	annually	burnt offering	temple hall
Hel	death	wolf	X			bare	black leather	black & white	midwinter's day	annually	human	temple hall
Idun	spring; youth	sparrow hawk	X	X		bare	costly robe	apple green	spring equinox	annually	crafted items	forest meadows
Loki	strife; fire	monsters	X			war helm	leather vest	red & black	midwinter's day	annually	burnt offering	temple hall
Magni	strength	ox	X			horned helm	ring mail	purple	full moon	monthly	precious metals	temple hall
Modi	courage	bear	X			war helm	ring mail	ruby red	before battle	varies	burnt offering	temple hall
Sif	battle skills	blue jay	X	X		war helm	chain mail	silver & white	full moon	monthly	weapons	temple hall
Surtur — see Nonhumans' Deities												
Thor	thunder	goat	X	X		war helm	ring mail	black & gold	new moon	monthly	burnt animals	temple hall
Thrym — see Nonhumans' Deities												
Tyr	war; law	war horse	X	X		war helm	black cloak	gray	new moon	monthly	crafted items	temple hall
Uller	hunting skills	hound	X	X		leather cap	leather	forest green	equinox	semiannually	burnt offering	forest meadows
Vidar	strength	horse	X			bare	leather vest	orange	summer solstice	annually	burnt offering	temple hall
SUMERIAN MYTHOS												
Enlil	air; war	raven	X	X		bare	kilt	red, white	full moon	monthly	gems	temple
Enki	rivers; oceans	ibex	X	X	X	bare	kilt	sea green	quarter moon	monthly	precious metals	temple
Inanna	love; war	cat	X	X		conical hat	kilt	lime	full moon	monthly	artworks	temple
Ki	nature	tiger	X	X	X	conical hat	kilt	forest green	equinox	semiannually	burnt rams	temple
Nanna-Sin	moon	owl	X			bare	kilt	silver, blue	full moon	monthly	gems	temple
Nin-Hursag	earth	mole	X	X		bare	kilt	dust	spring equinox	annually	weapons	temple
Utu	sun	falcon	X			bare	kilt	orange	eclipses	annually	weapons	temple

APPENDIX 4: FURTHER REFERENCE

The books listed below constitute some of the references used in compiling this work. They, as well as numerous other works, contain much more detailed accounts of the gods and their divine characteristics than can be included herein. Further research is recommended to the DM who wishes to augment the given information.

Aldington, R. et al. (translators). *New Larousse Encyclopedia of Mythology.* New York: Putnam, 1968.

Budge, E. A. Wallis. *The Egyptian Book of the Dead.* New York: Dover, 1967. Paperback.

Bullfinch, Thomas. *The Age of Fable.* New York: Cromwell, 1970.

Christie, Anthony. *Chinese Mythology.* England: Paul Hamlyn, 1968.

Davidson, H. R. Ellis. *Gods and Myths of Northern Europe.* New York: Penguin Books Ltd., 1964. Paperback.

Frazer, Sir James G. *The Golden Bough.* New York: University Books, 1961.

Gantz, Jeffrey (trans.). *The Mabinogion.* Middlesex, England: Penguin Books Ltd., 1977.

Hackin, J. et al. *Asiatic Mythology.* New York: Crescent, (no date).

Hamilton, Edith. *Mythology.* Boston: Little, Brown & Co., 1942.

Hodge, Frederick Webb. *Handbook of American Indians.* New York: Rowan & Littlefield, 1965 (2 volumes).

Kramer, Samuel N. (ed.). *Mythologies of the Ancient World.* New York: Doubleday, 1961.

Leach, Maria & Fried, Jerome (eds.). *Funk & Wagnall's Standard Dictionary of Folklore, Mythology, and Legend.* New York: Funk & Wagnall, 1972.

Malory, Sir Thomas. *Le Morte d'Arthur* (2 volumes). England: Penguin Books, 1978. Paperback.

Nicholson, Irene. *Mexican and Central American Mythology.* England: Paul Hamlyn, 1967.

Schwab, Gustav. *Gods and Heroes.* New York: Pantheon, 1946.

Squire, Charles. *Celtic Myth and Legend.* Hollywood: Newcastle Press, 1975. Paperback.

Tripp, Edward. *Meridian Handbook of Classical Mythology.* New York: Crowell, 1970.

Stormbringer, White Wolf and Elric!; Chaosium, Inc., P.O. Box 6302, Albany, CA 94706.

INDEX OF PROPER NAMES

A boldfaced number indicates that the term is a separate entry in this book.